Yes, the fourth volume of Beet is already out. Once we land in the Black Horizon, loads of new Vandels who work for Grineed will make their appearance! These Vandels, including Grineed, have a strange human-like nature, and that seems to contribute to their underground popularity. Vandels have abilities much beyond those of humans, and I suppose that's why their wishes and desires are also much stronger. I'd like to continue coming up with Vandels who have unique personalities. By the way, I'm told my face looks very much like Frausky's when I'm stroking my beloved cat.
— Riku Sanjo

Author Riku Sanjo and artist Koji Inada were both born in Tokyo in 1964. Sanjo began his career writing a radio-controlled car manga for the comic **Bonbon**. Inada debuted with **Kussotare Daze!!** in **Weekly Shonen Jump**. Sanjo and Inada first worked together on the highly successful **Dragon Quest–Dai's Big Adventure**. **Beet the Vandel Buster**, their latest collaboration, debuted in **Monthly Shonen Jump** in 2002 and was an immediate hit, inspiring an action-packed video game and an animated series on Japanese TV.

BEET THE VANDEL BUSTER
VOL. 4
The SHONEN JUMP Graphic Novel Edition

STORY BY RIKU SANJO
ART BY KOJI INADA

English Adaptation/Shaenon K. Garrity
Translation/Naomi Kokubo
Touch-Up & Lettering/Mark McMurray
Design/Andrea Rice
Editor/Pancha Diaz

Managing Editor/Elizabeth Kawasaki
Director of Production/Noboru Watanabe
Editorial Director/Alvin Lu
Executive Vice President & Editor in Chief/Hyoe Narita
Sr. Director of Acquisitions/Rika Inouye
Vice President of Sales & Marketing/Liza Coppola
Vice President of Strategic Development/Yumi Hoashi
Publisher/Seiji Horibuchi

Published by VIZ, LLC
P.O. Box 77064
San Francisco, CA 94107

SHONEN JUMP Graphic Novel Edition
10 9 8 7 6 5 4 3 2 1
First printing, March 2005

THE WORLD'S
MOST POPULAR MANGA

www.viz.com

www.shonenjump.com

SHONEN JUMP GRAPHIC NOVEL

Beet™ The Vandel Buster

Volume 4

Story by **Riku Sanjo**
Art by **Koji Inada**

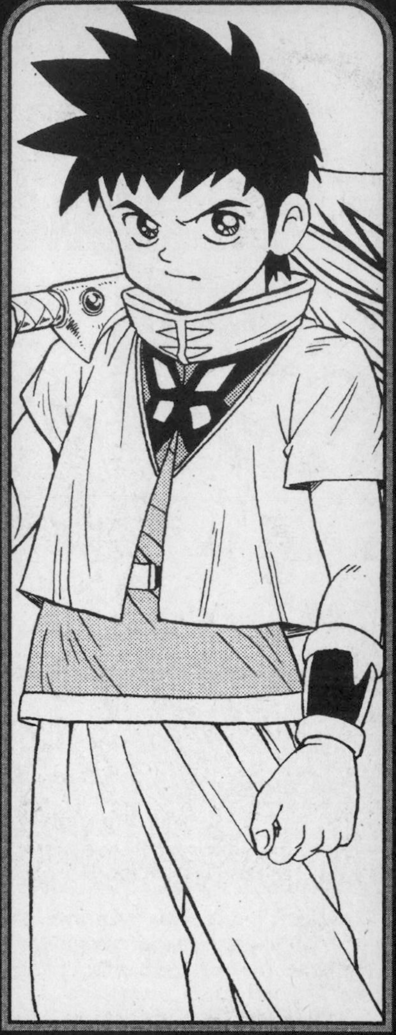

BEET

The hero of this story.
Believing in justice, he sets out on a journey to save the world. He received five Saiga weapons from the Zenon Warriors.

POALA

Beet's childhood friend.
She has an unyielding spirit. Poala joins Beet in his journey as the second of the Beet Warriors. She is skilled at attacking enemies using her Divine Attack.

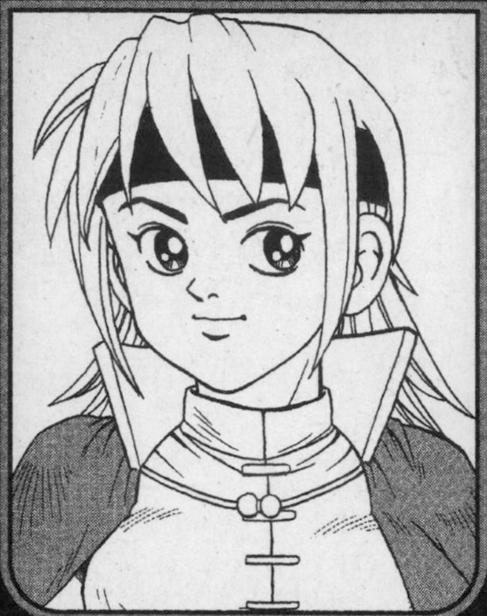

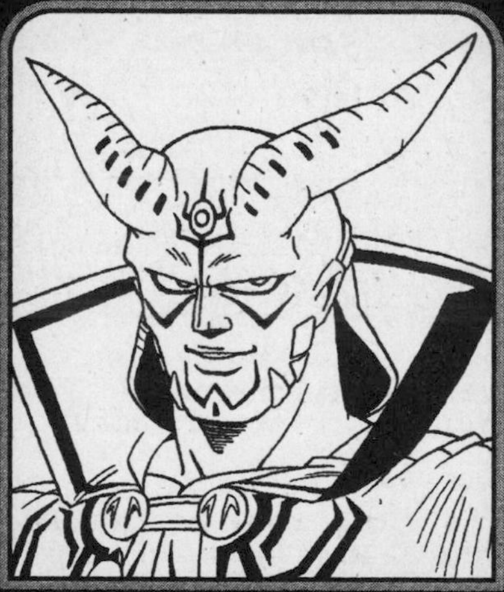

BELTORZE

Known as the "King of Tragedy," he is a five-star Vandel, feared by humans. He always wants to fight against the strongest human warriors.

STORY

CHARACTERS

SHAGIE
The world's busiest Vandel. Shagie is in charge of the evaluation and supervision of all Vandels. He is also the Chief of the Dark House of Sorcery.

GRINEED
He is a Vandel who believes in being emotionless and cool at all times. Despite this, he is capable of immense brutality.

ZENON
Beet's older brother. No one has seen him since the Zenon Warriors' violent battle against Beltorze.

"Vandels"... In this story, that's what we call evil creatures with magical powers. One day they appeared on the surface of the Earth, releasing monsters and destroying the peace and order of nations. People called this seemingly endless era "The Dark Age."

Beet, a young boy who believes in justice, binds himself with a contract to become a Vandel Buster, and conquer Vandels for a living. However, Beet stumbles into the middle of a battle between Beltorze and the Zenon Warriors, where he suffers a fatal injury. He miraculously survives by receiving the Saiga of the Zenon Warriors.

Three years later, Beet sets out on a journey with his friend Poala to carry on the Zenon Warriors' mission. At the port city of Ledeux, he fights a death match with Beltorze, his archenemy. Thanks to his expert handling of his Saiga, Beet wins the battle. However, he learns that he defeated only a phantom double of Beltorze, and that the real Beltorze is still alive. Beet and Poala set out toward the Black Horizon, an area controlled by Grineed, hoping to find a third warrior to join their team...

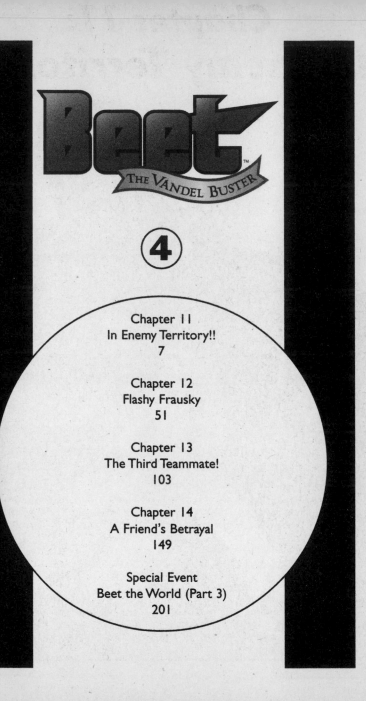

Beet
THE VANDEL BUSTER

4

Chapter 11
In Enemy Territory!!
7

Chapter 12
Flashy Frausky
51

Chapter 13
The Third Teammate!
103

Chapter 14
A Friend's Betrayal
149

Special Event
Beet the World (Part 3)
201

Chapter 11: In Enemy Territory!!

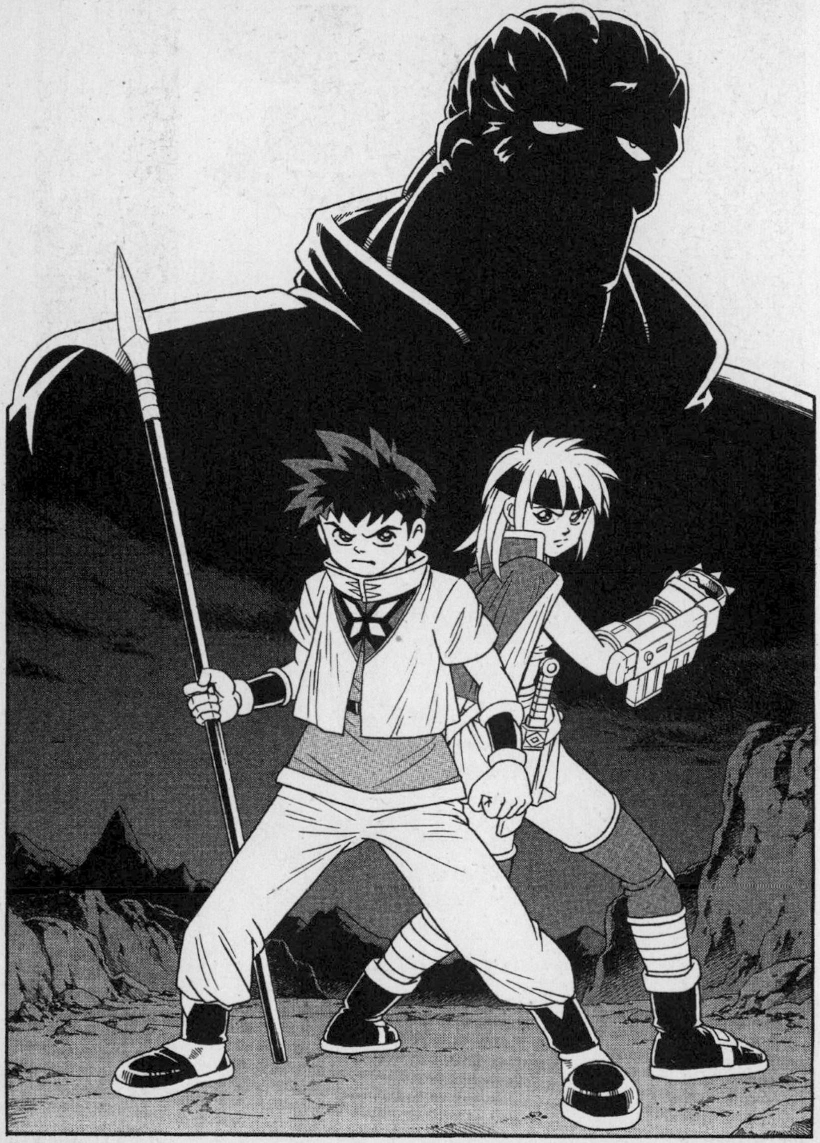

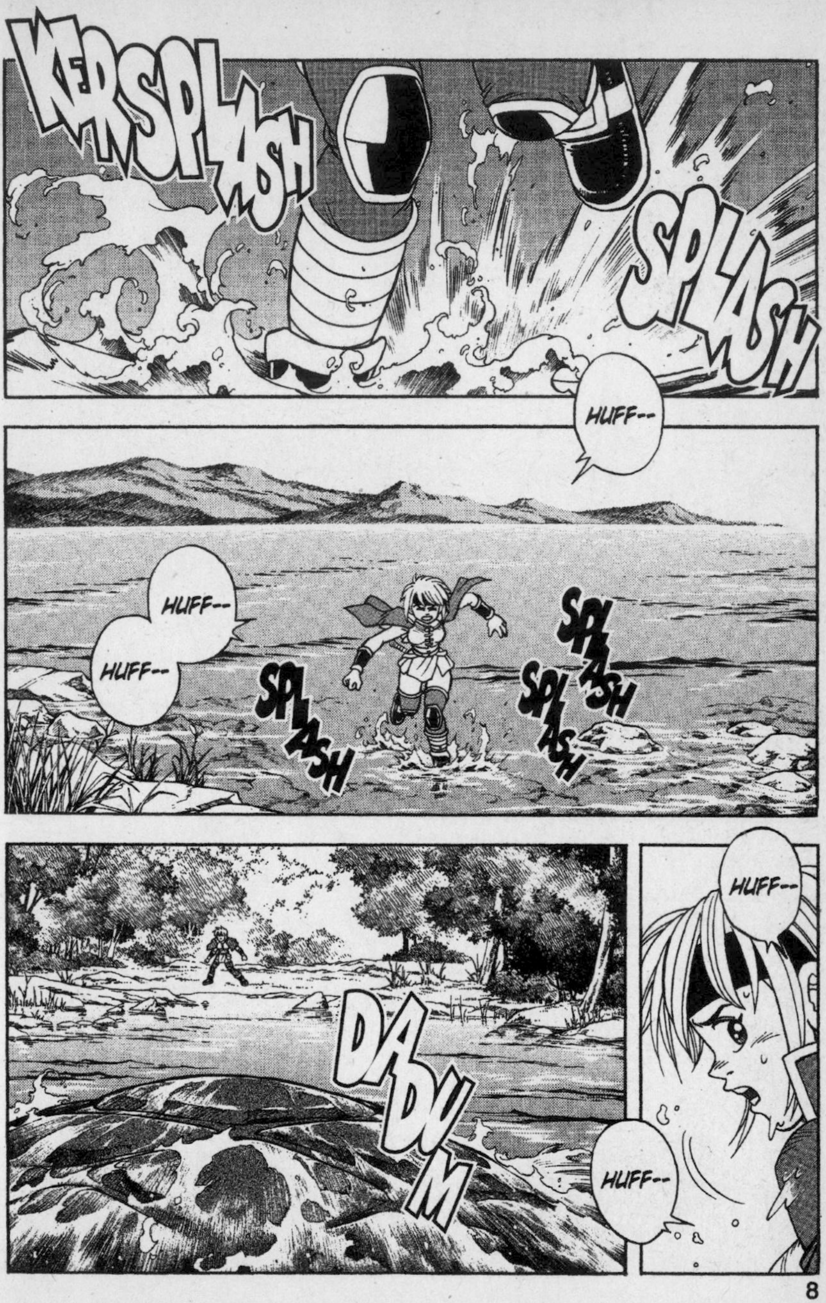
SPLASH
KERSPLASH
HUFF--
SPLASH
SPLASH
SPLASH
HUFF--
HUFF--
HUFF--
HUFF--
DADUM

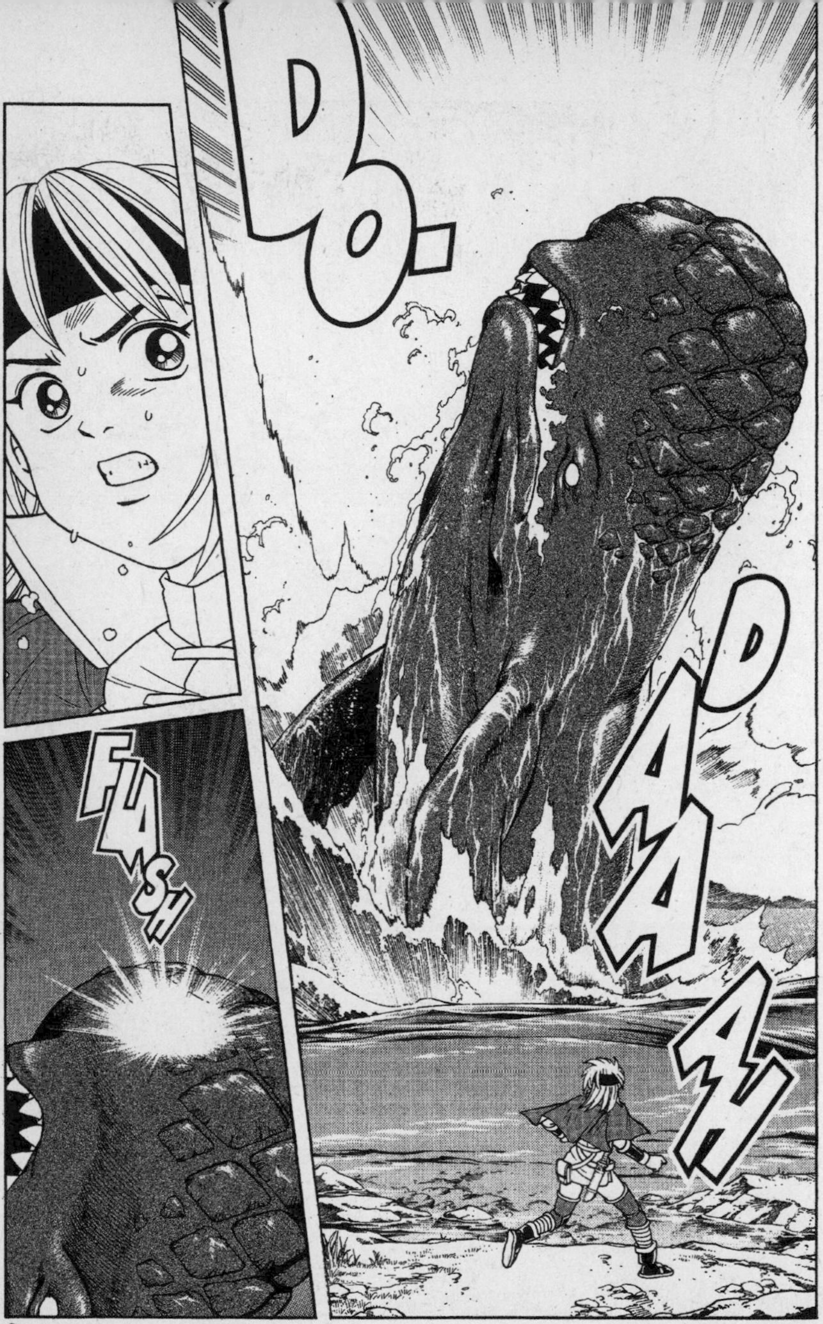
DO-
DAAAH
FLASH

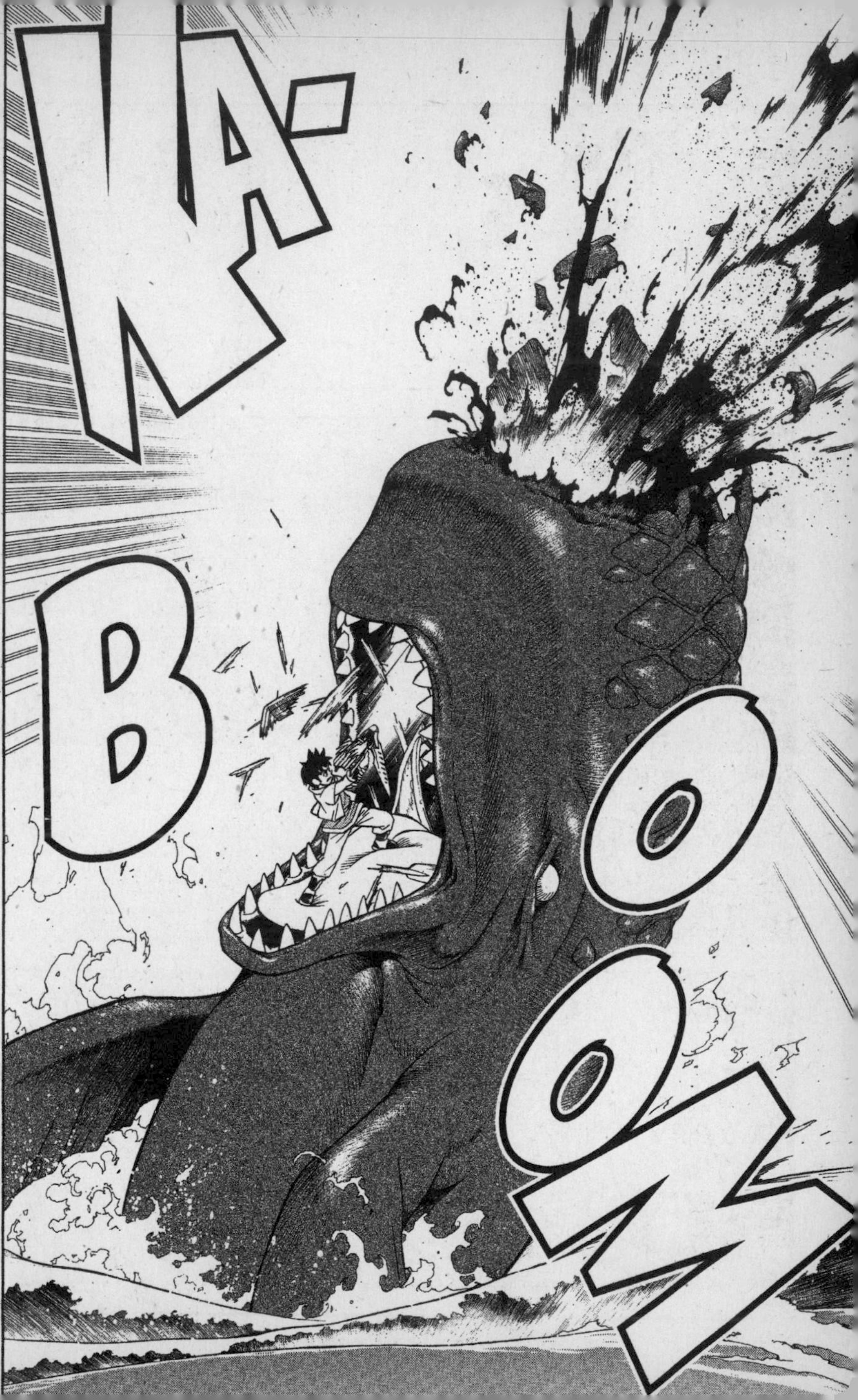
KA-BOOOM

READ THIS WAY

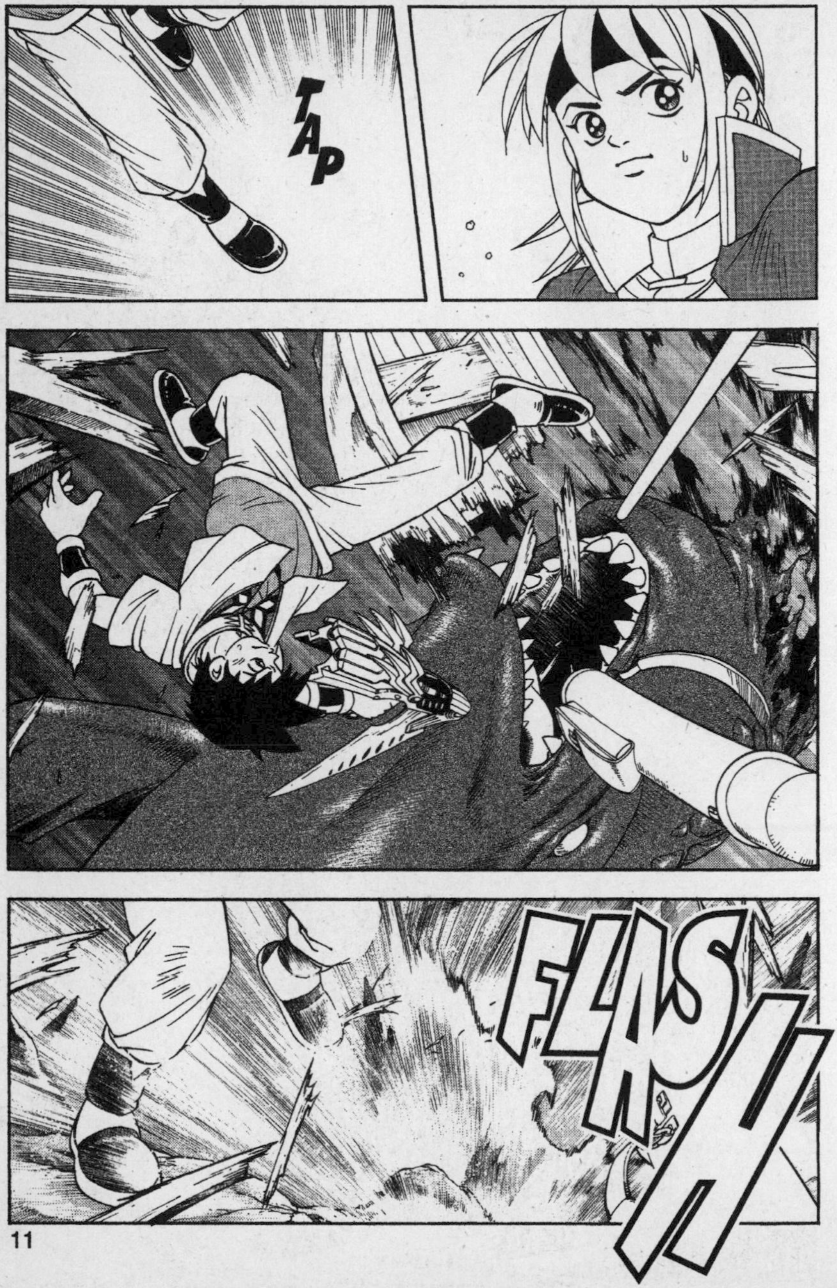
TAP
FLASH

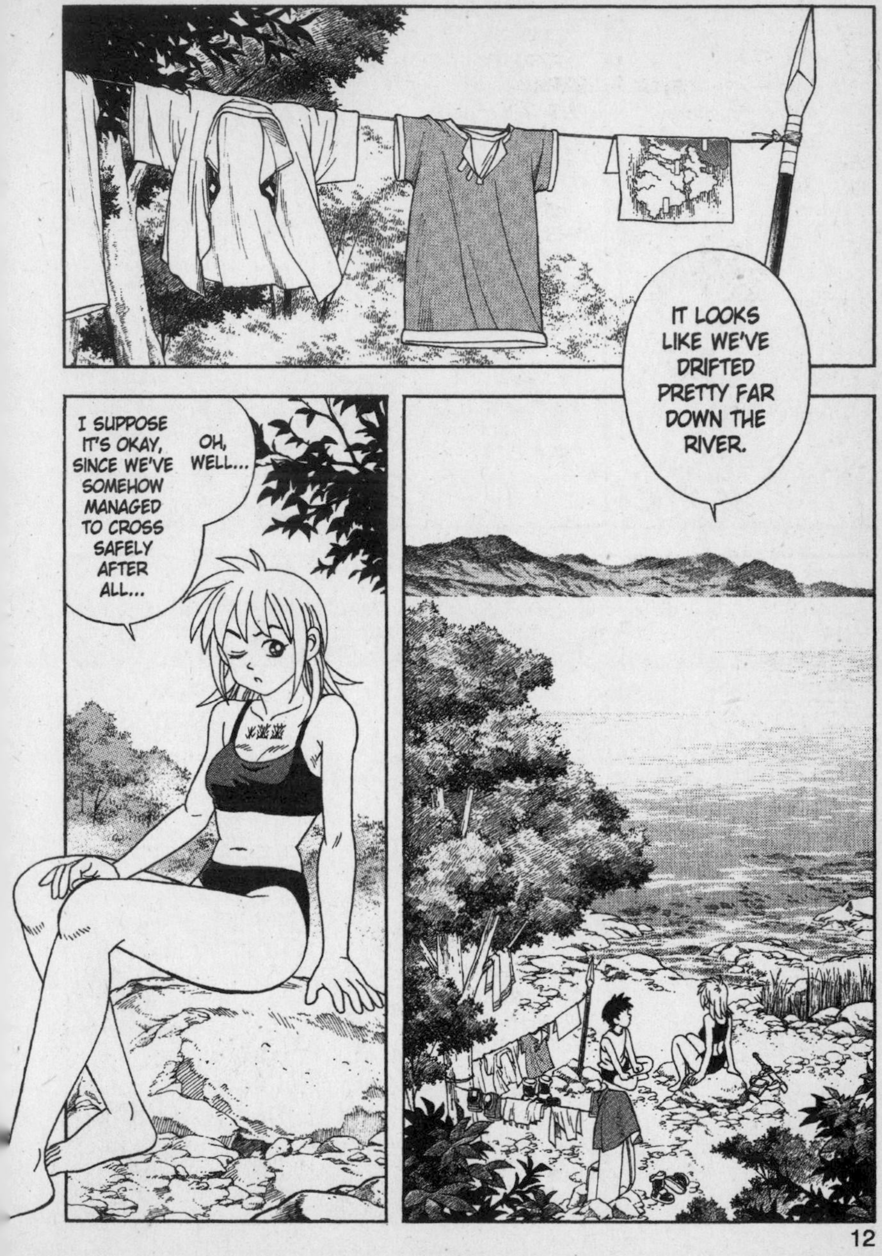
IT LOOKS LIKE WE'VE DRIFTED PRETTY FAR DOWN THE RIVER.
OH, WELL...
I SUPPOSE IT'S OKAY, SINCE WE'VE SOMEHOW MANAGED TO CROSS SAFELY AFTER ALL...

READ THIS WAY

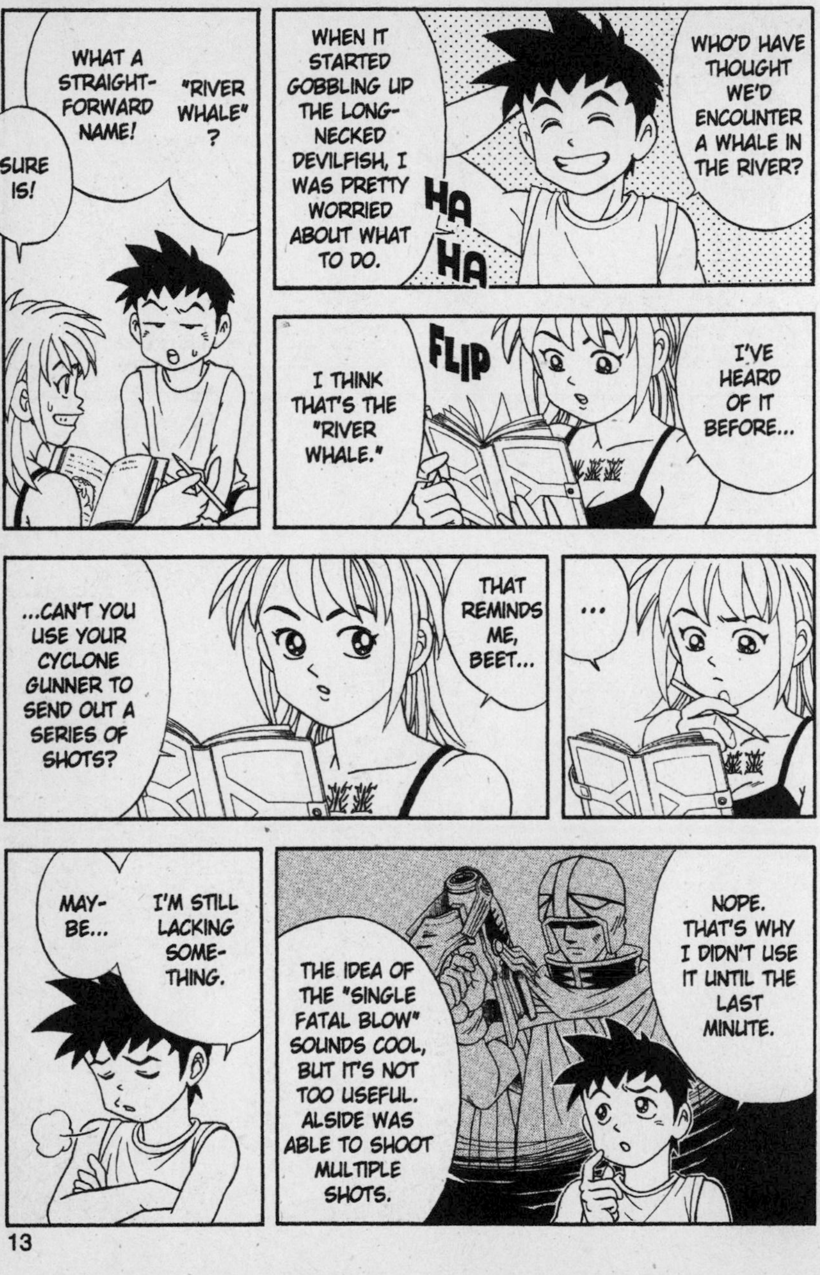
WHO'D HAVE THOUGHT WE'D ENCOUNTER A WHALE IN THE RIVER?
HA HA
WHEN IT STARTED GOBBLING UP THE LONG-NECKED DEVILFISH, I WAS PRETTY WORRIED ABOUT WHAT TO DO.
I'VE HEARD OF IT BEFORE...
FLIP
I THINK THAT'S THE "RIVER WHALE."
"RIVER WHALE"?
WHAT A STRAIGHT-FORWARD NAME!
SURE IS!
...
THAT REMINDS ME, BEET...
...CAN'T YOU USE YOUR CYCLONE GUNNER TO SEND OUT A SERIES OF SHOTS?
NOPE. THAT'S WHY I DIDN'T USE IT UNTIL THE LAST MINUTE.
THE IDEA OF THE "SINGLE FATAL BLOW" SOUNDS COOL, BUT IT'S NOT TOO USEFUL. ALSIDE WAS ABLE TO SHOOT MULTIPLE SHOTS.
I'M STILL LACKING SOME-THING.
MAY-BE...

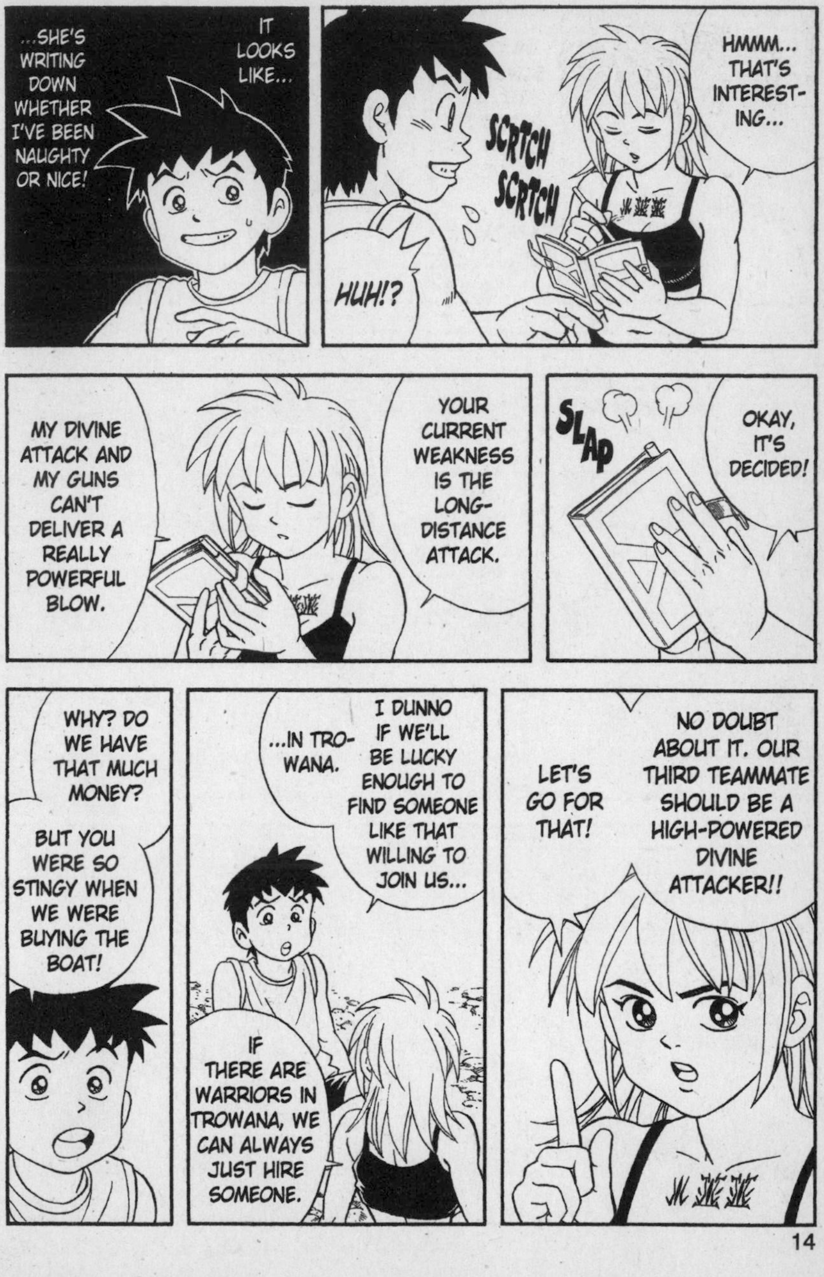
HMMM... THAT'S INTEREST-ING...
SCRTCH SCRTCH
HUH!?
IT LOOKS LIKE...
...SHE'S WRITING DOWN WHETHER I'VE BEEN NAUGHTY OR NICE!
SLAP
OKAY, IT'S DECIDED!
YOUR CURRENT WEAKNESS IS THE LONG-DISTANCE ATTACK.
MY DIVINE ATTACK AND MY GUNS CAN'T DELIVER A REALLY POWERFUL BLOW.
NO DOUBT ABOUT IT. OUR THIRD TEAMMATE SHOULD BE A HIGH-POWERED DIVINE ATTACKER!!
LET'S GO FOR THAT!
I DUNNO IF WE'LL BE LUCKY ENOUGH TO FIND SOMEONE LIKE THAT WILLING TO JOIN US...
...IN TRO-WANA.
IF THERE ARE WARRIORS IN TROWANA, WE CAN ALWAYS JUST HIRE SOMEONE.
WHY? DO WE HAVE THAT MUCH MONEY?
BUT YOU WERE SO STINGY WHEN WE WERE BUYING THE BOAT!

READ THIS WAY

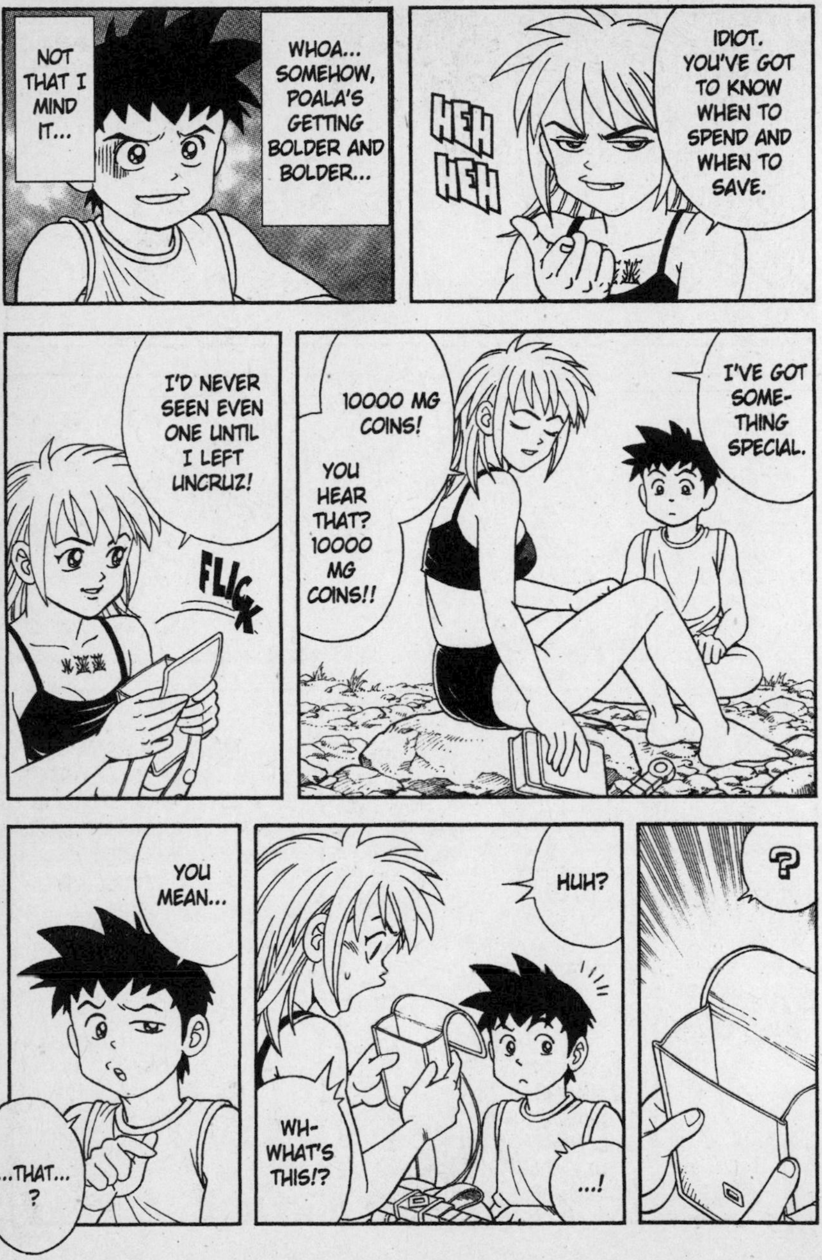
IDIOT. YOU'VE GOT TO KNOW WHEN TO SPEND AND WHEN TO SAVE.
HEH HEH
WHOA... SOMEHOW, POALA'S GETTING BOLDER AND BOLDER...
NOT THAT I MIND IT...
I'VE GOT SOME-THING SPECIAL.
10000 MG COINS!
YOU HEAR THAT? 10000 MG COINS!!
I'D NEVER SEEN EVEN ONE UNTIL I LEFT UNCRUZ!
FLICK
?
HUH?
WH-WHAT'S THIS!?
...!
YOU MEAN...
...THAT...?

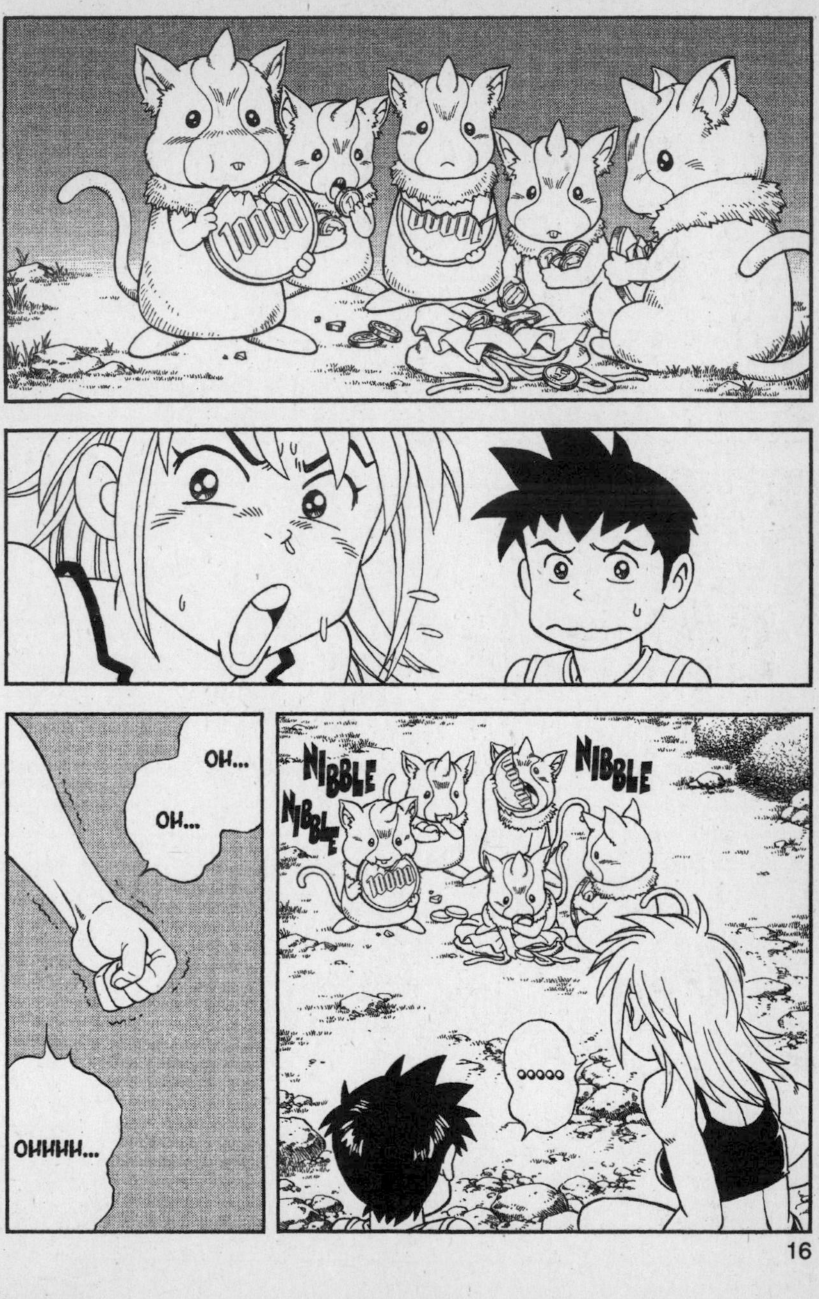
NIBBLE
NIBBLE
NIBBLE
.....
OH...
OH...
OHHHH...

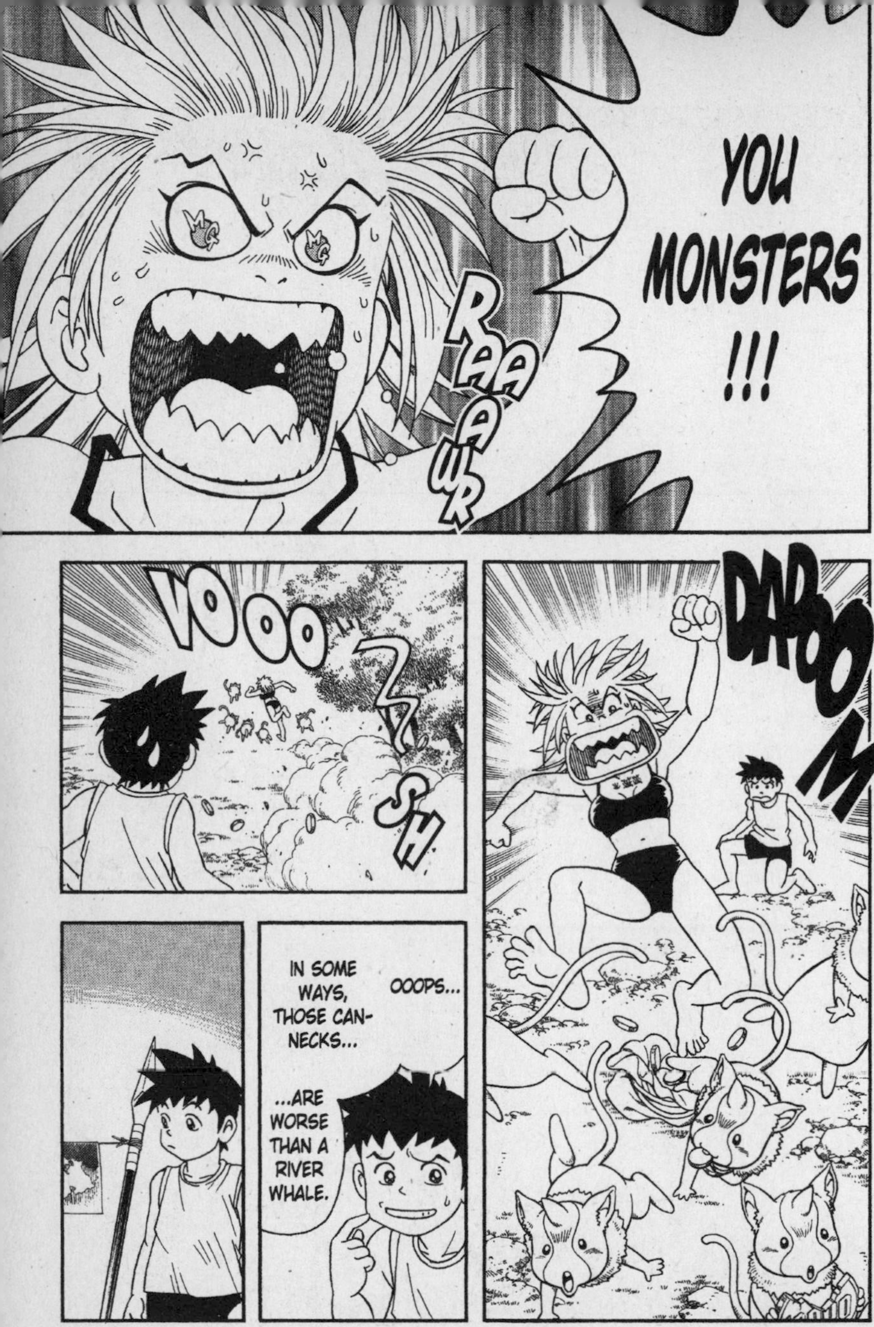
YOU MONSTERS !!!
RAAAUR
DABOOM
VOOOSH
OOOPS...
IN SOME WAYS, THOSE CAN-NECKS...
...ARE WORSE THAN A RIVER WHALE.

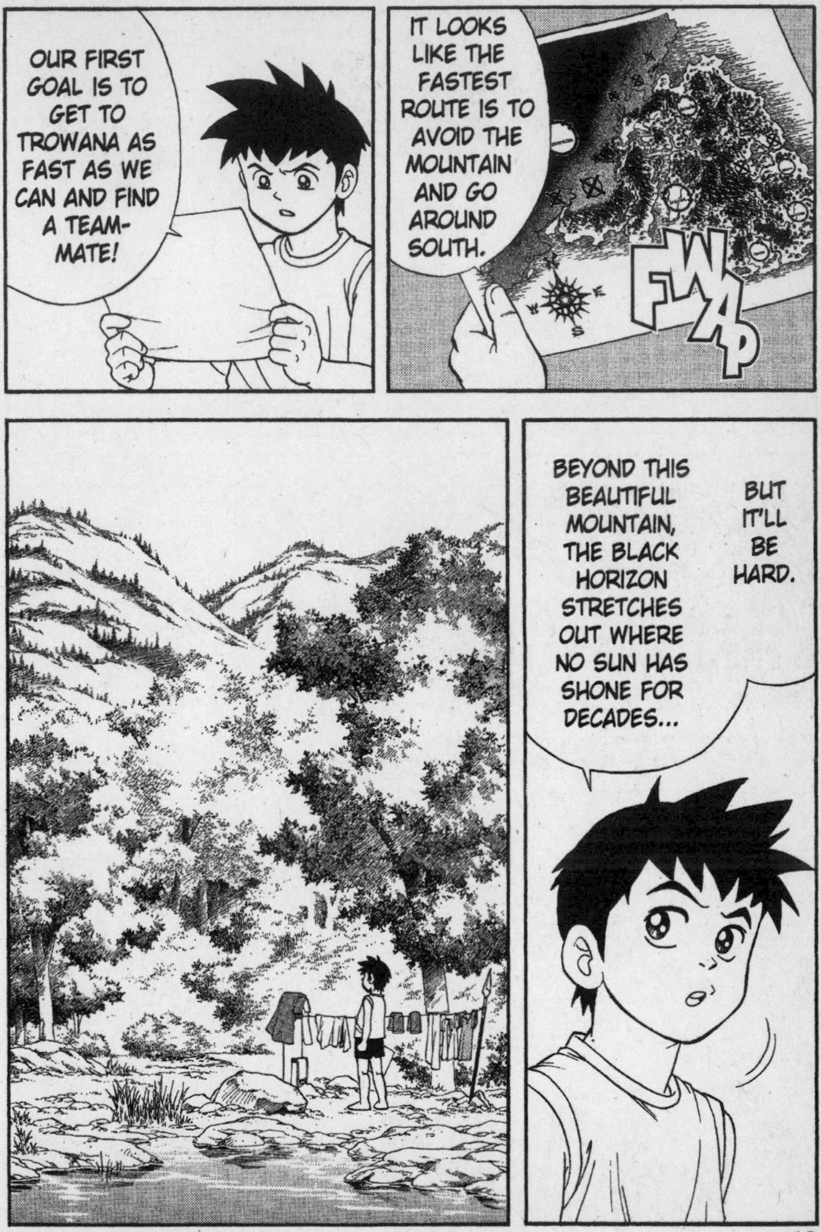
IT LOOKS LIKE THE FASTEST ROUTE IS TO AVOID THE MOUNTAIN AND GO AROUND SOUTH.
FWAP
OUR FIRST GOAL IS TO GET TO TROWANA AS FAST AS WE CAN AND FIND A TEAM-MATE!
BEYOND THIS BEAUTIFUL MOUNTAIN, THE BLACK HORIZON STRETCHES OUT WHERE NO SUN HAS SHONE FOR DECADES...
BUT IT'LL BE HARD.

READ THIS WAY

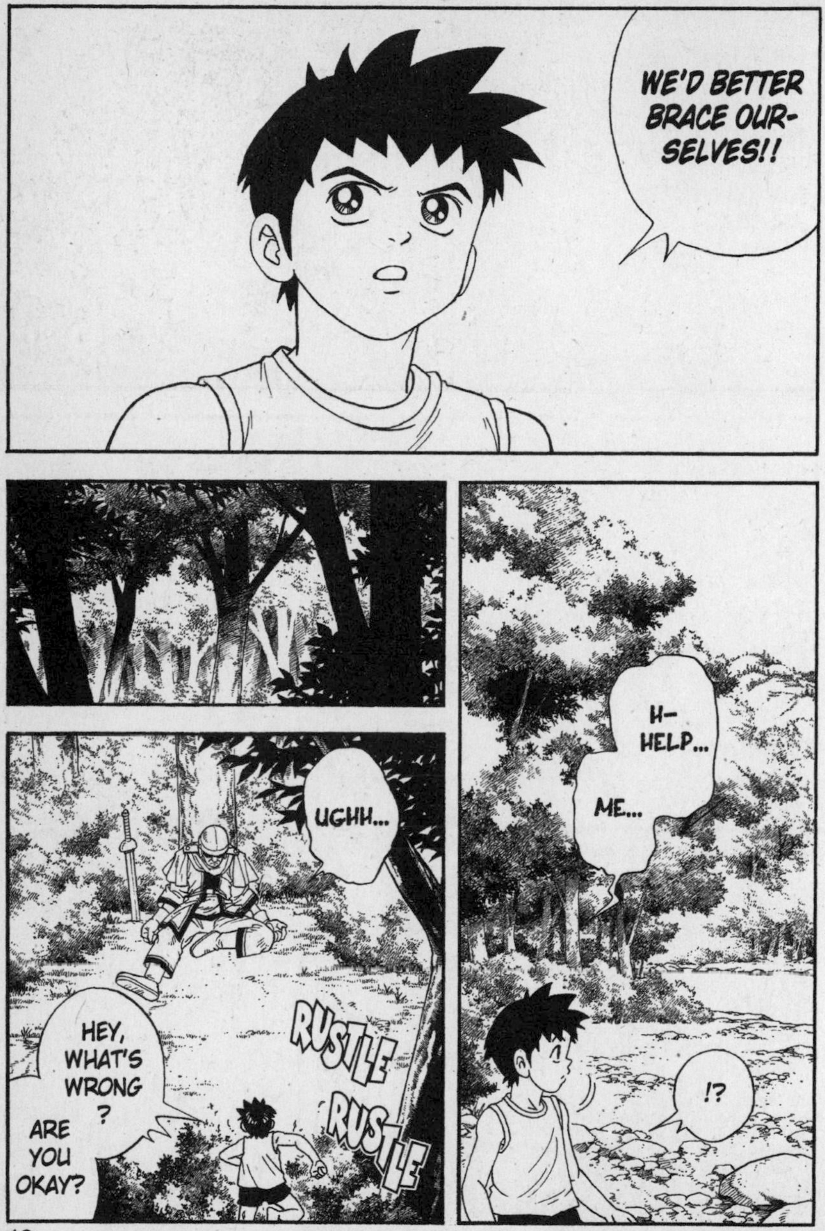
WE'D BETTER BRACE OUR-SELVES!!
H-HELP...
ME...
!?
UGHH...
RUSTLE
RUSTLE
HEY, WHAT'S WRONG?
ARE YOU OKAY?

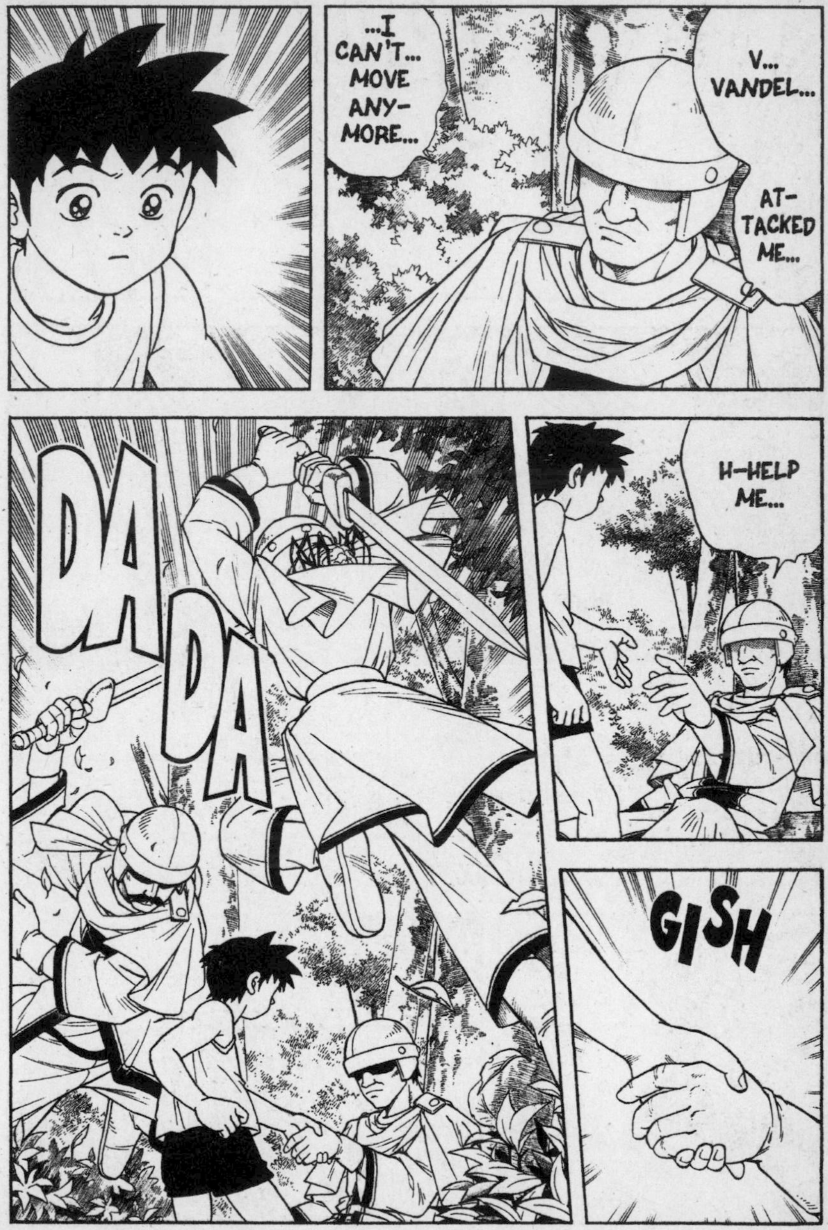
V... VANDEL...
AT-TACKED ME...
...I CAN'T... MOVE ANYMORE...
H-HELP ME...
GISH
DA DA DA

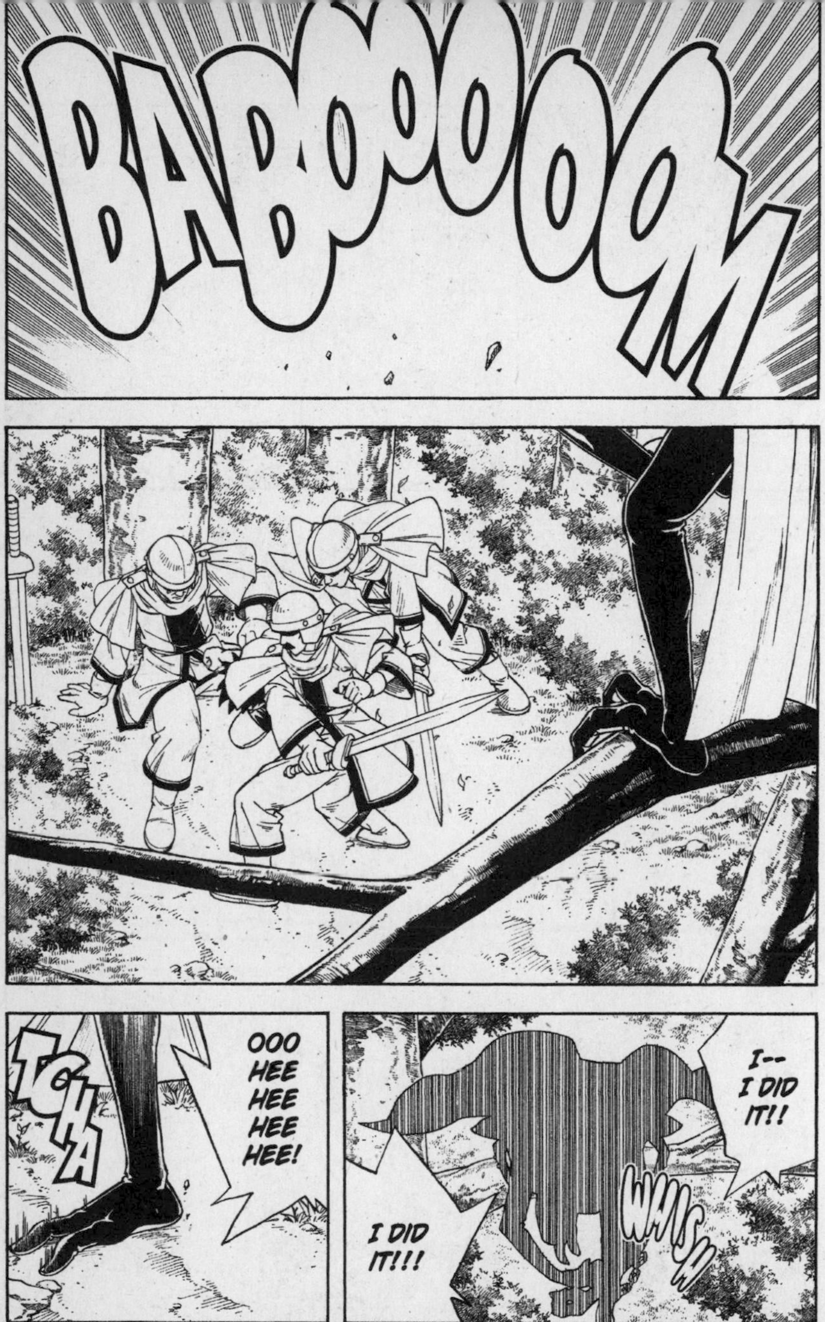
BABOOOOOM
I-- I DID IT!!
WHISH
I DID IT!!!
OOO HEE HEE HEE HEE!
TCHA

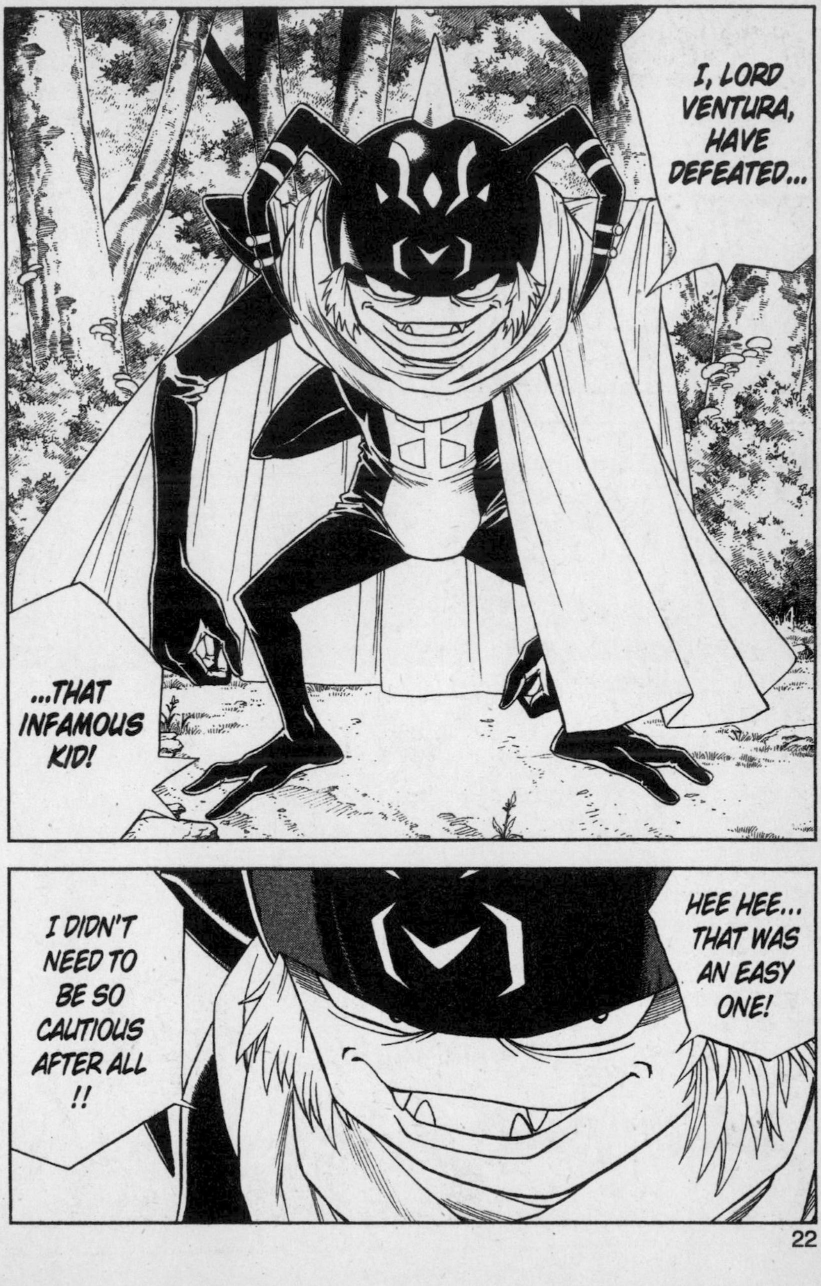
I, LORD VENTURA, HAVE DEFEATED...
...THAT INFAMOUS KID!
HEE HEE... THAT WAS AN EASY ONE!
I DIDN'T NEED TO BE SO CAUTIOUS AFTER ALL!!

READ THIS WAY

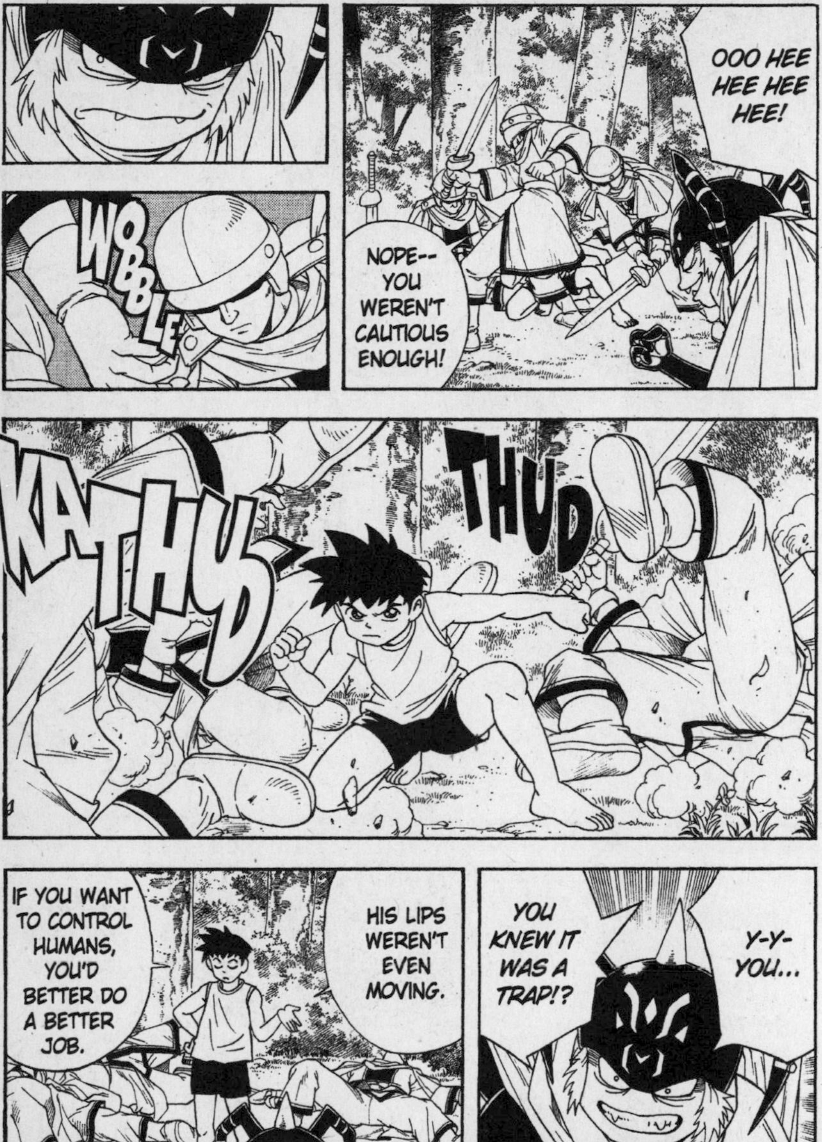

OOO HEE HEE HEE HEE!
NOPE-- YOU WEREN'T CAUTIOUS ENOUGH!
WOBBLE
THUD
KATHUD
Y-Y-YOU...
YOU KNEW IT WAS A TRAP!?
HIS LIPS WEREN'T EVEN MOVING.
IF YOU WANT TO CONTROL HUMANS, YOU'D BETTER DO A BETTER JOB.

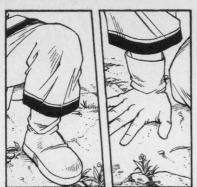

SNAP

H-HOW IMPERTI-NENT!

WAAAAH

WAAAA

BWOOSH

WHAT THE--!?

READ THIS WAY

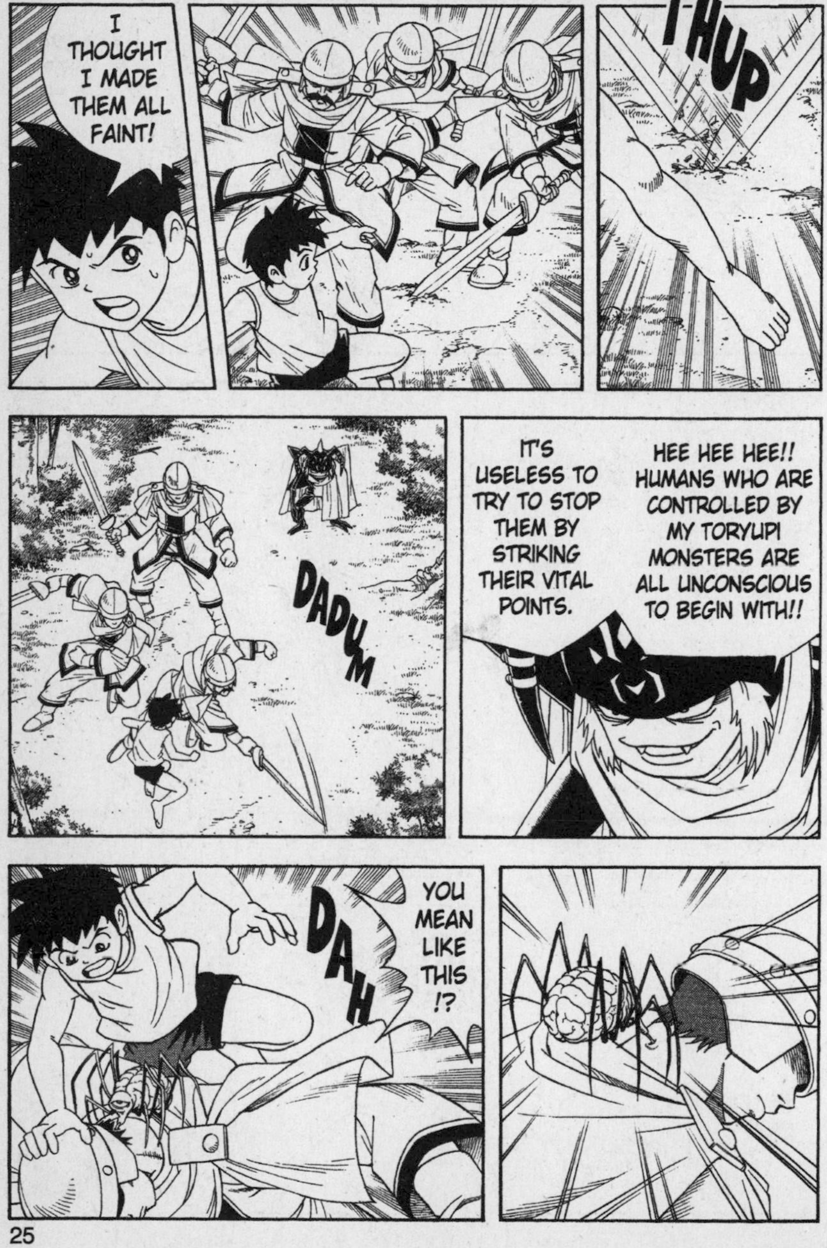
THUP
I THOUGHT I MADE THEM ALL FAINT!
HEE HEE HEE!! HUMANS WHO ARE CONTROLLED BY MY TORYUPI MONSTERS ARE ALL UNCONSCIOUS TO BEGIN WITH!!
IT'S USELESS TO TRY TO STOP THEM BY STRIKING THEIR VITAL POINTS.
DADUM
YOU MEAN LIKE THIS !?
DAH

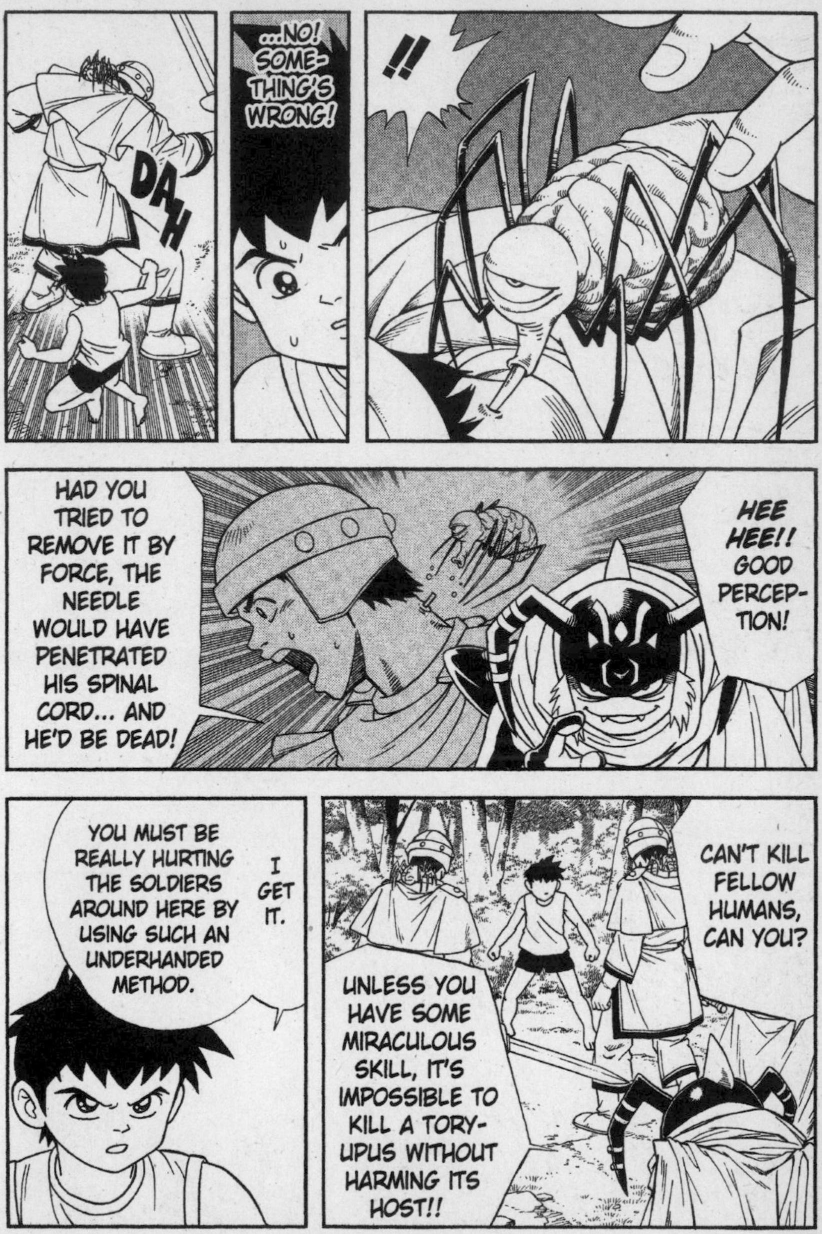
!!
...NO! SOMETHING'S WRONG!
DAH
HEE HEE!! GOOD PERCEPTION!
HAD YOU TRIED TO REMOVE IT BY FORCE, THE NEEDLE WOULD HAVE PENETRATED HIS SPINAL CORD... AND HE'D BE DEAD!
CAN'T KILL FELLOW HUMANS, CAN YOU?
UNLESS YOU HAVE SOME MIRACULOUS SKILL, IT'S IMPOSSIBLE TO KILL A TORYUPUS WITHOUT HARMING ITS HOST!!
I GET IT.
YOU MUST BE REALLY HURTING THE SOLDIERS AROUND HERE BY USING SUCH AN UNDERHANDED METHOD.

READ THIS WAY

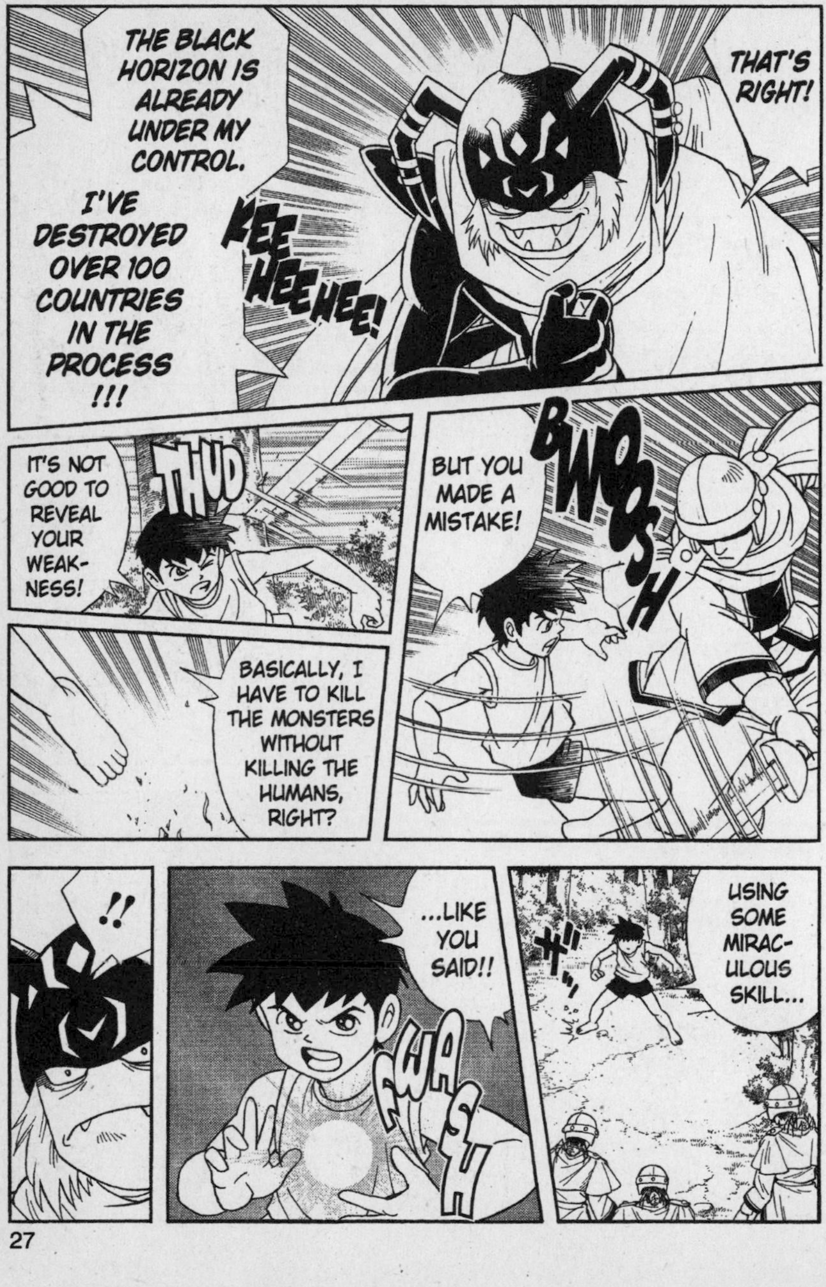

THAT'S RIGHT!
THE BLACK HORIZON IS ALREADY UNDER MY CONTROL.
KEE HEE HEE!
I'VE DESTROYED OVER 100 COUNTRIES IN THE PROCESS !!!
BWOOSH
BUT YOU MADE A MISTAKE!
THUD
IT'S NOT GOOD TO REVEAL YOUR WEAK-NESS!
BASICALLY, I HAVE TO KILL THE MONSTERS WITHOUT KILLING THE HUMANS, RIGHT?
USING SOME MIRAC-ULOUS SKILL...
ザッ
...LIKE YOU SAID!!
FWASH
!!

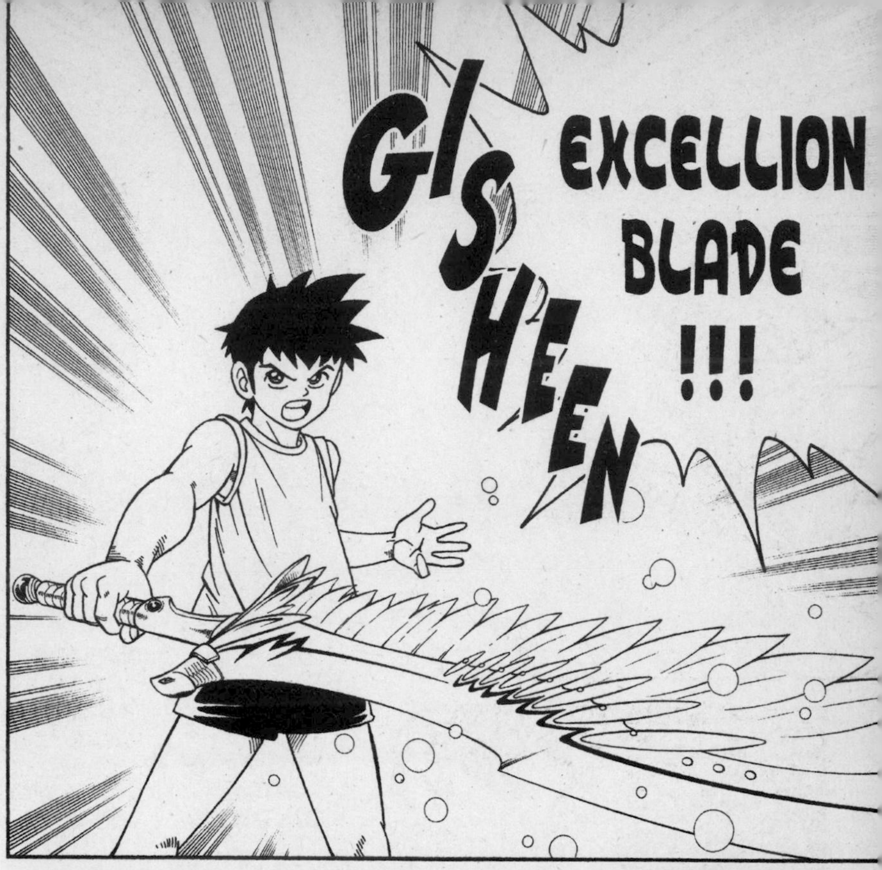
EXCELLION BLADE !!!
GISHEEN

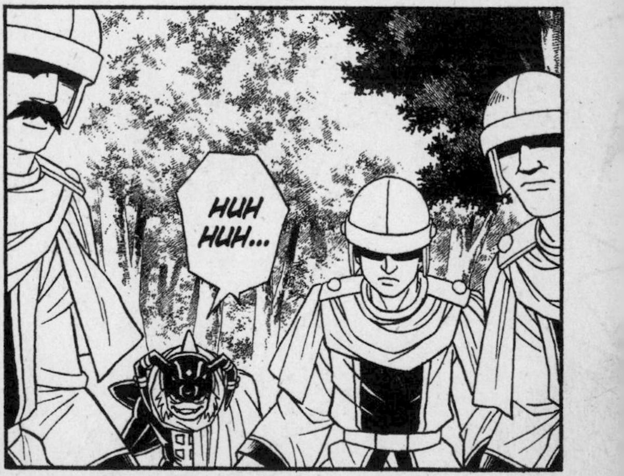
HUH HUH...

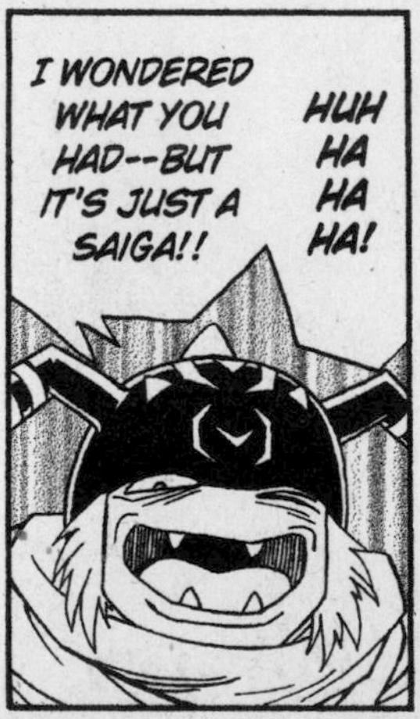
HUH HA HA HA!
I WONDERED WHAT YOU HAD--BUT IT'S JUST A SAIGA!!

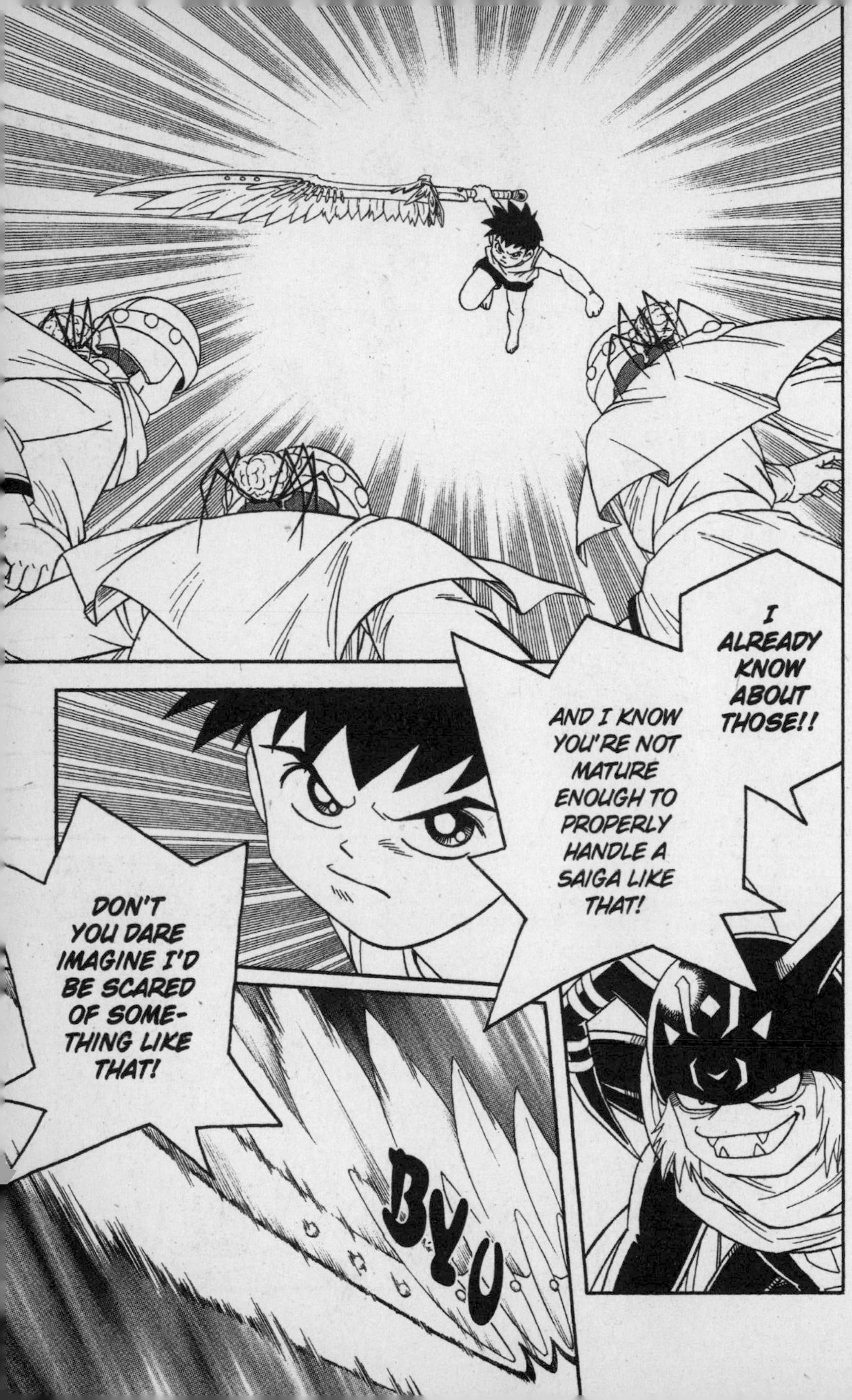
I ALREADY KNOW ABOUT THOSE!!
AND I KNOW YOU'RE NOT MATURE ENOUGH TO PROPERLY HANDLE A SAIGA LIKE THAT!
DON'T YOU DARE IMAGINE I'D BE SCARED OF SOME-THING LIKE THAT!
BYU

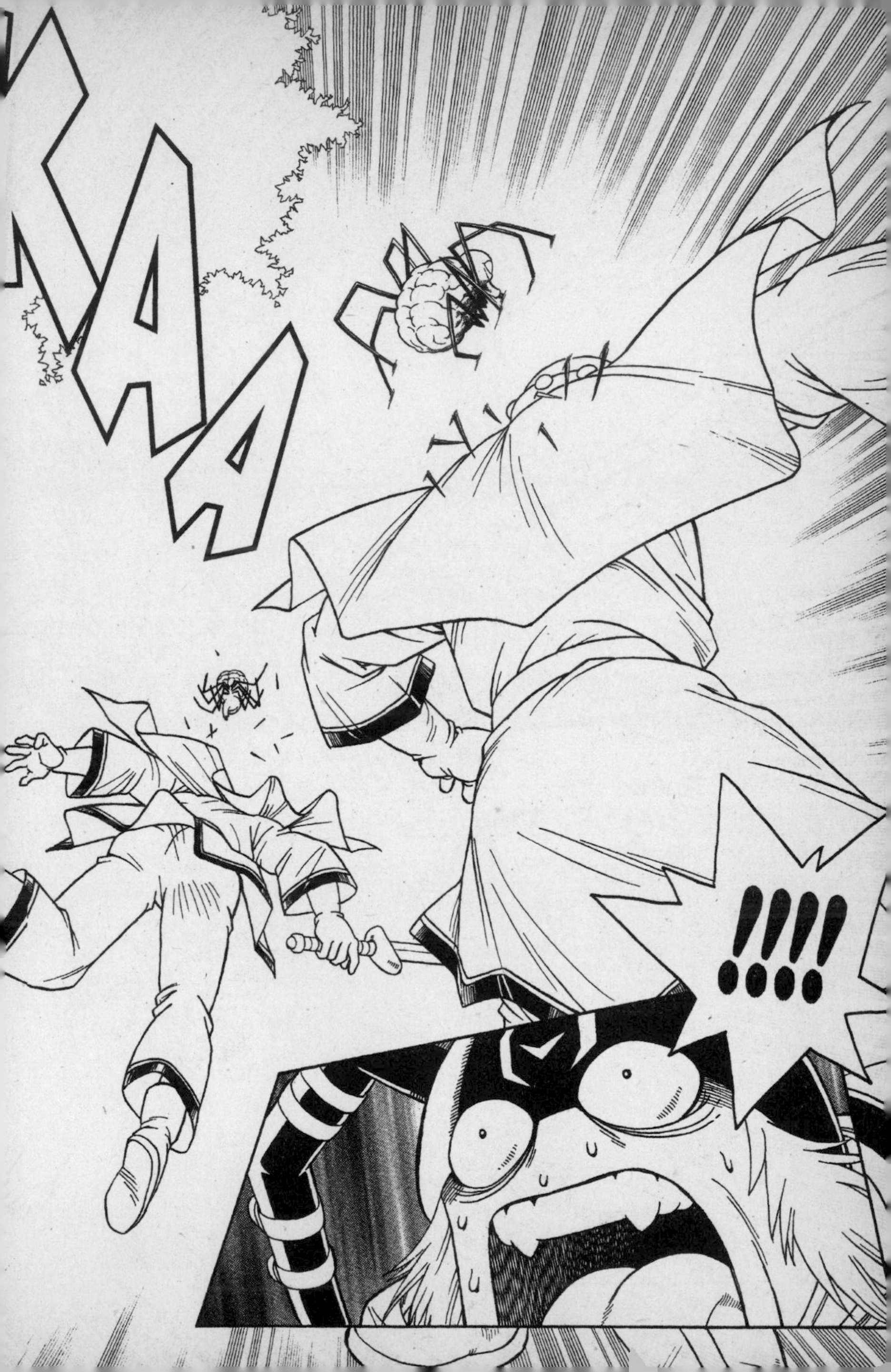
AA
!!!!

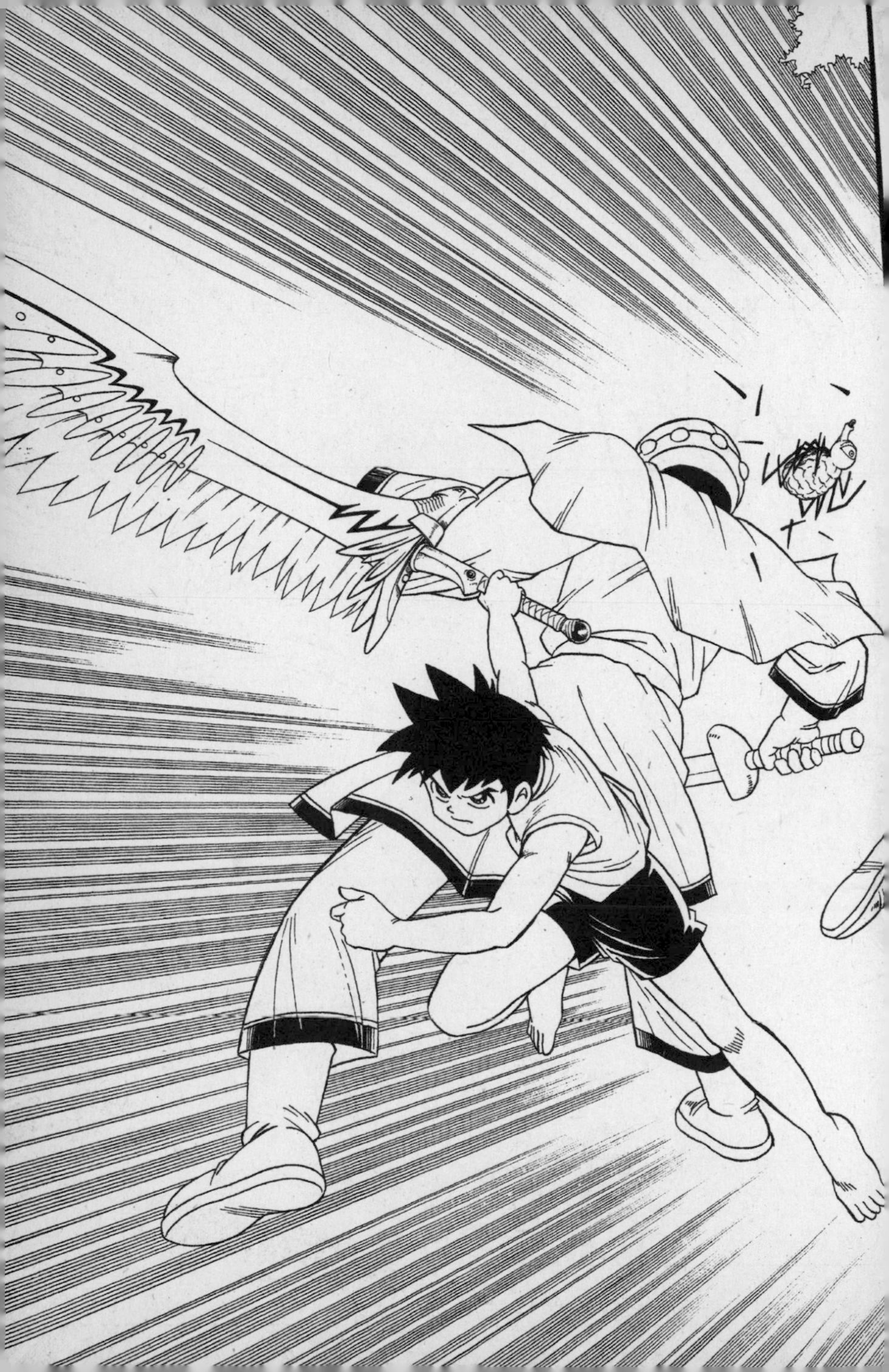

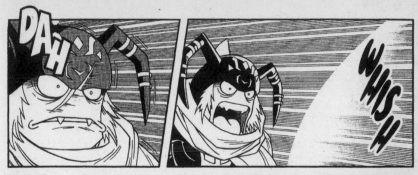

WHISH
DAH
SHF
THUD
TOO BAD, BUT EVEN MY IMPERFECT EXCELLION BLADE CAN SLICE THROUGH STEEL LIKE A HOT KNIFE THROUGH BUTTER!
I DIDN'T EVEN FIGURE OUT IT WAS IMPERFECT UNTIL I FOUGHT AGAINST BELTORZE.
IF MY OPPONENT IS JUST A REGULAR VANDEL...
...IT'S DEFI-NITELY...
...A LETHAL WEAPON!

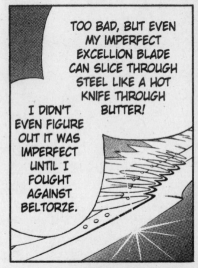

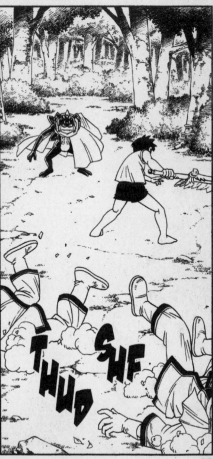

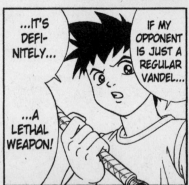

READ THIS WAY

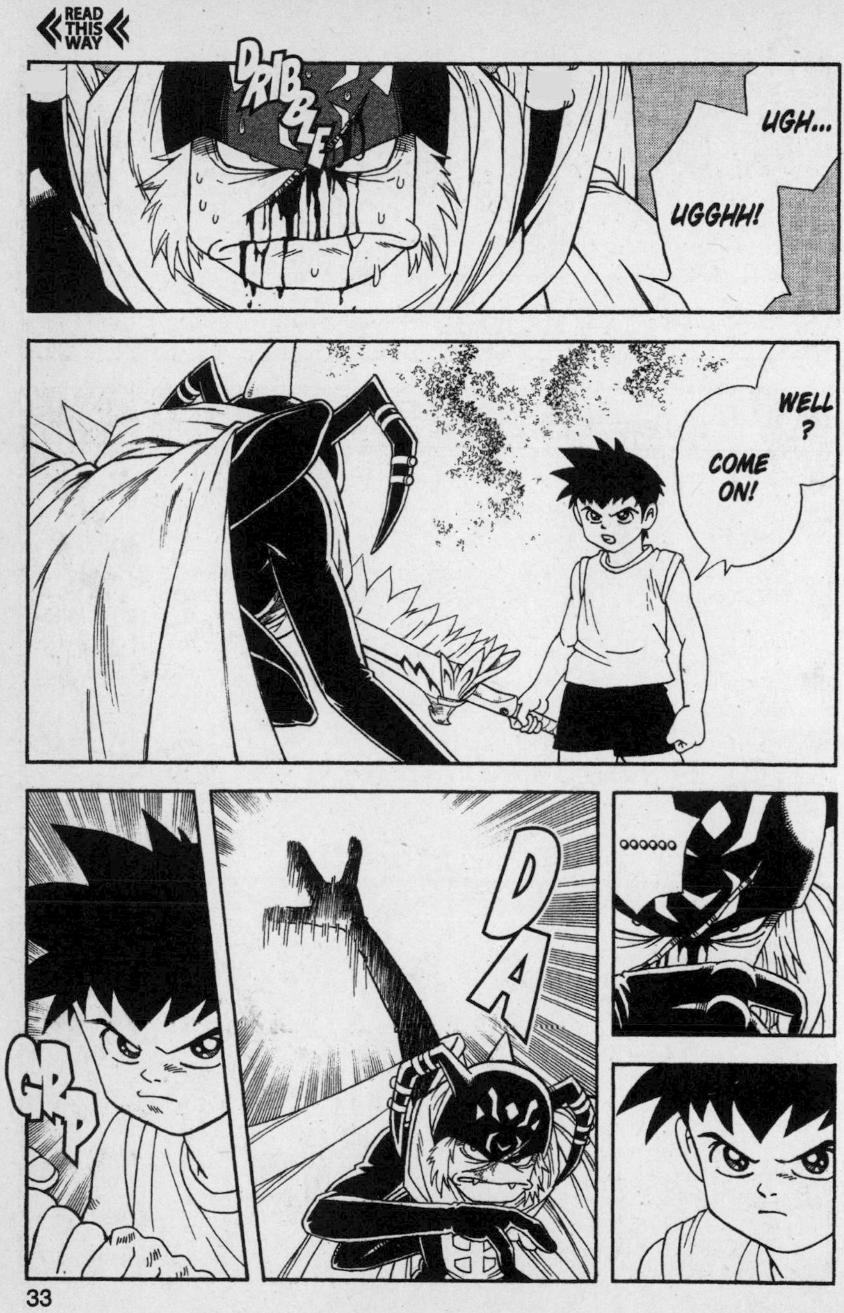
DRIBBLE
UGH...
UGGHH!
WELL? COME ON!
......
DA
GRP

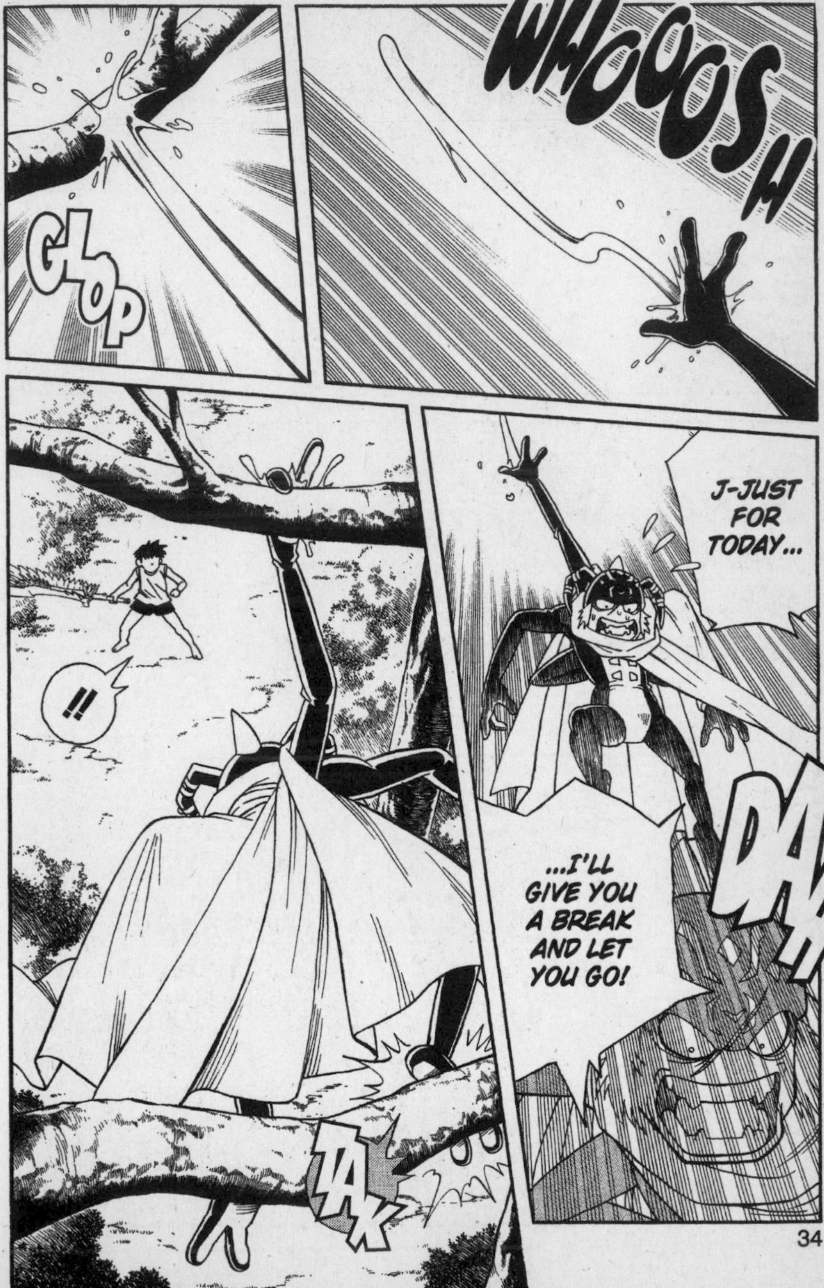
WHOOOSH
GLOP
J-JUST FOR TODAY...
...I'LL GIVE YOU A BREAK AND LET YOU GO!
DAH
!!
TAK

READ THIS WAY

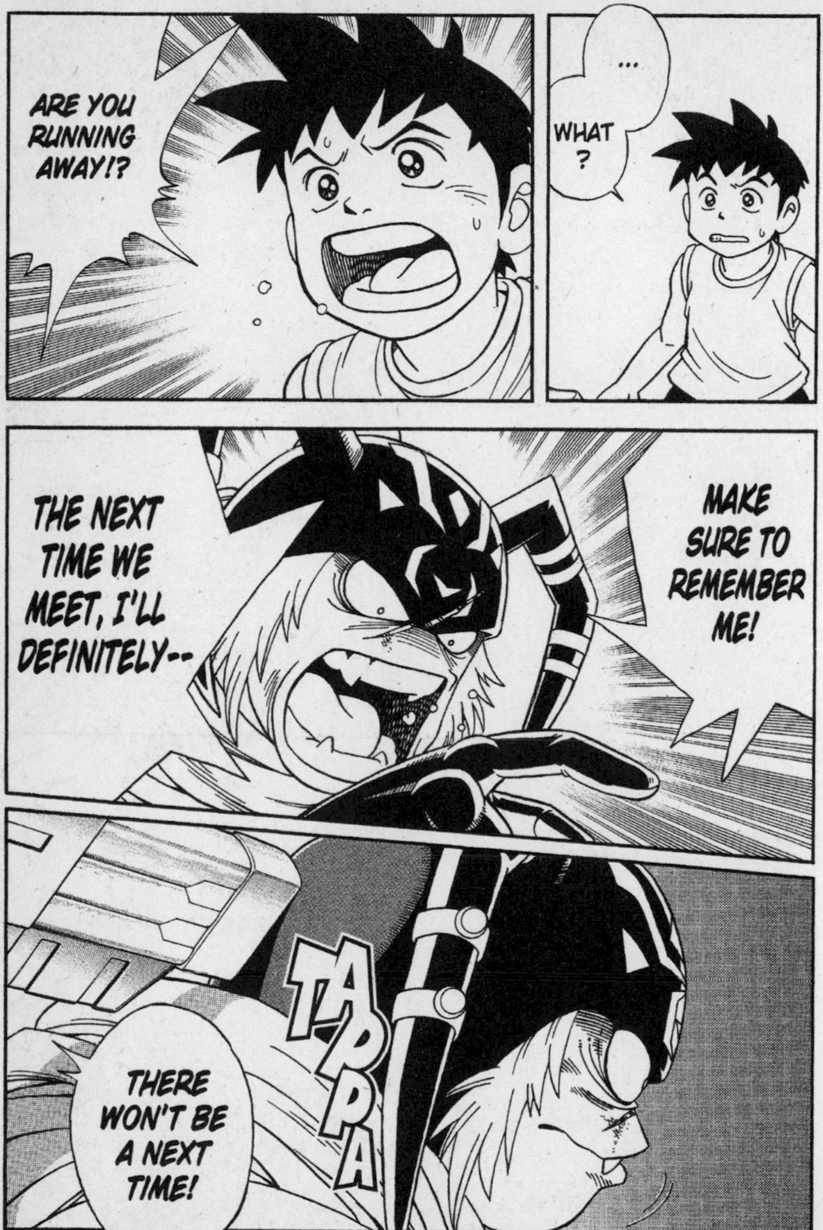

...
WHAT?
ARE YOU RUNNING AWAY!?
MAKE SURE TO REMEMBER ME!
THE NEXT TIME WE MEET, I'LL DEFINITELY--
TAPPA
THERE WON'T BE A NEXT TIME!

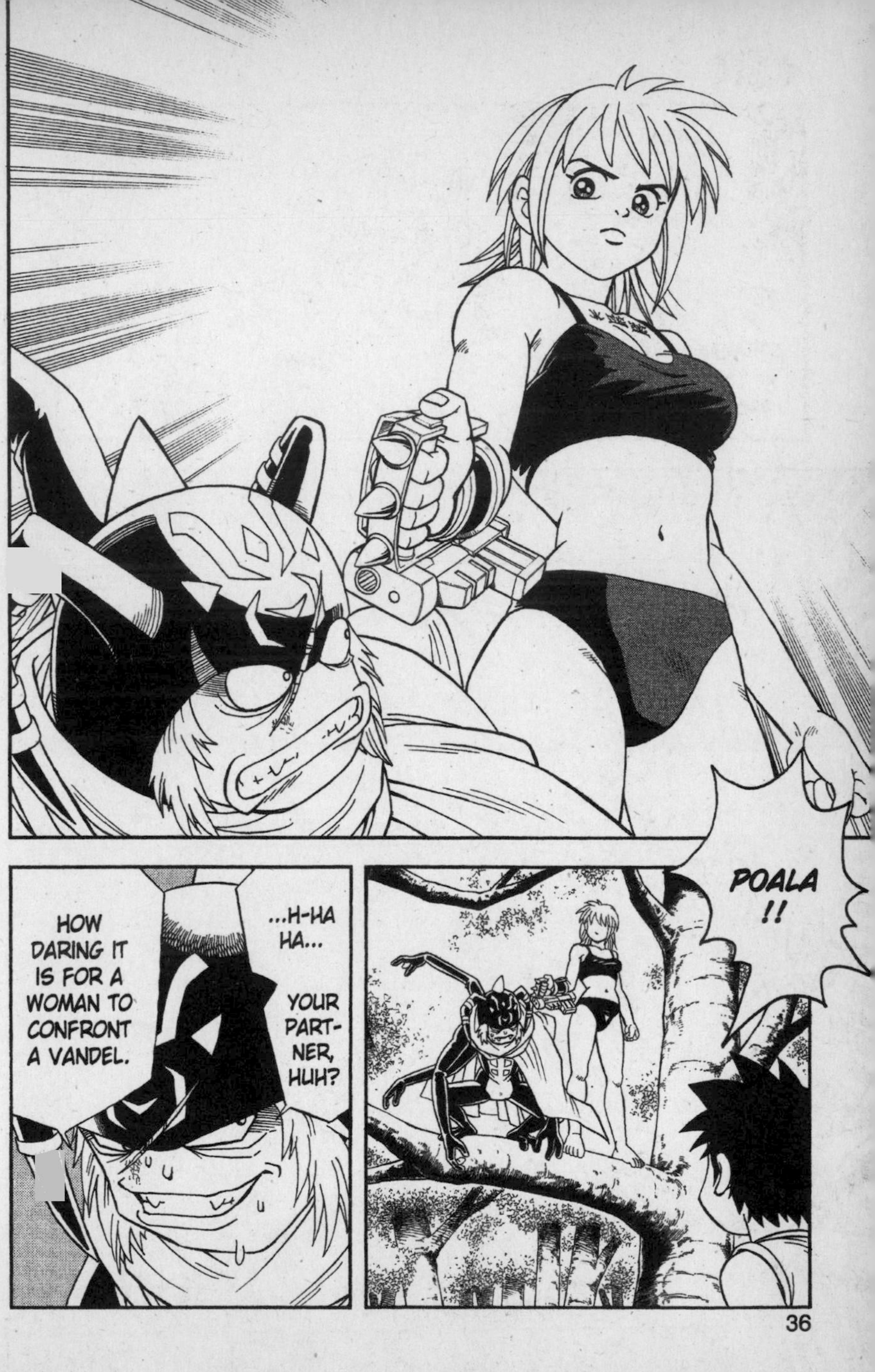
POALA !!
...H-HA HA...
YOUR PARTNER, HUH?
HOW DARING IT IS FOR A WOMAN TO CONFRONT A VANDEL.

READ THIS WAY

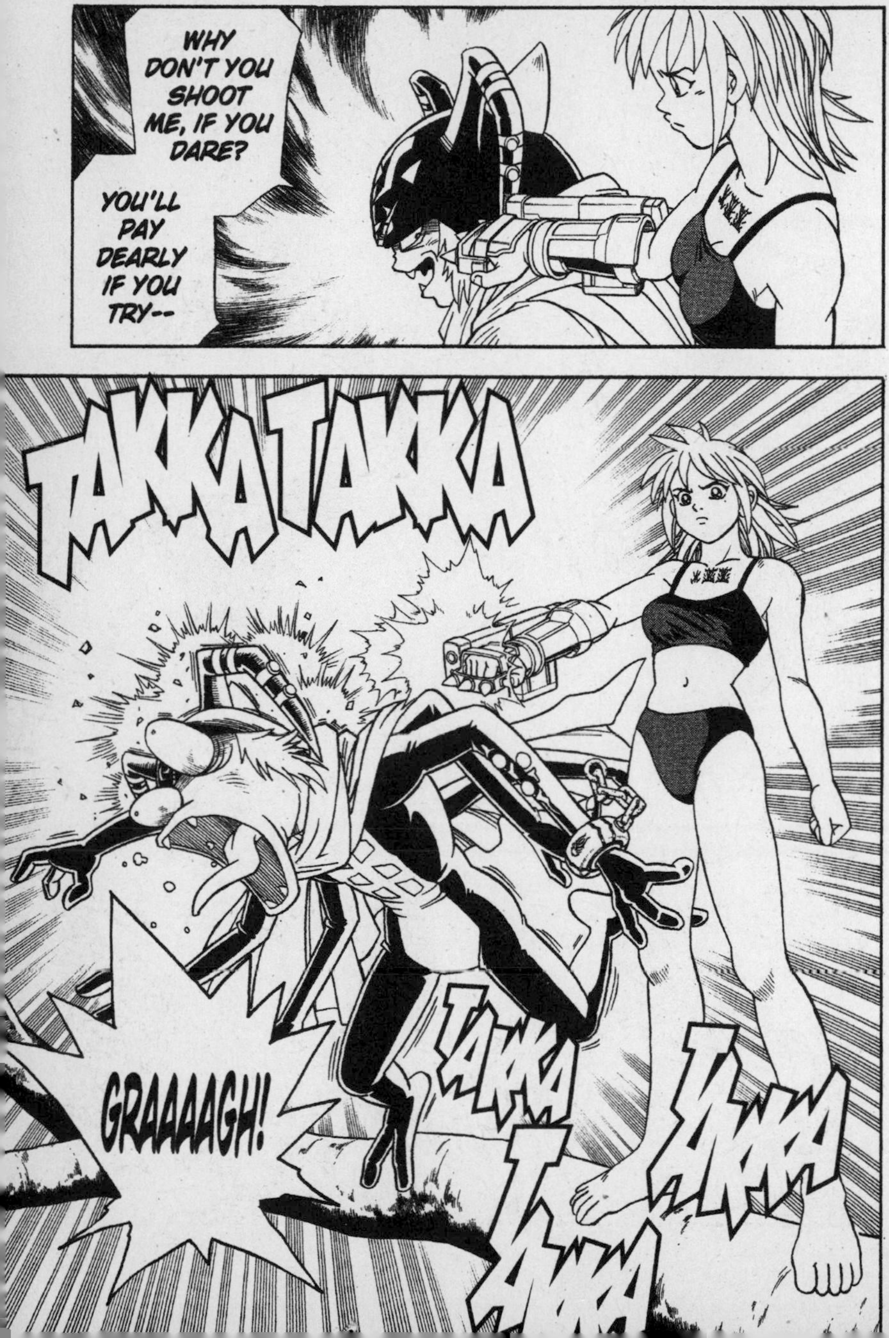
WHY DON'T YOU SHOOT ME, IF YOU DARE?
YOU'LL PAY DEARLY IF YOU TRY--
TAKKA TAKKA
TAKKA
TAKKA
TAKKA
GRAAAAGH!

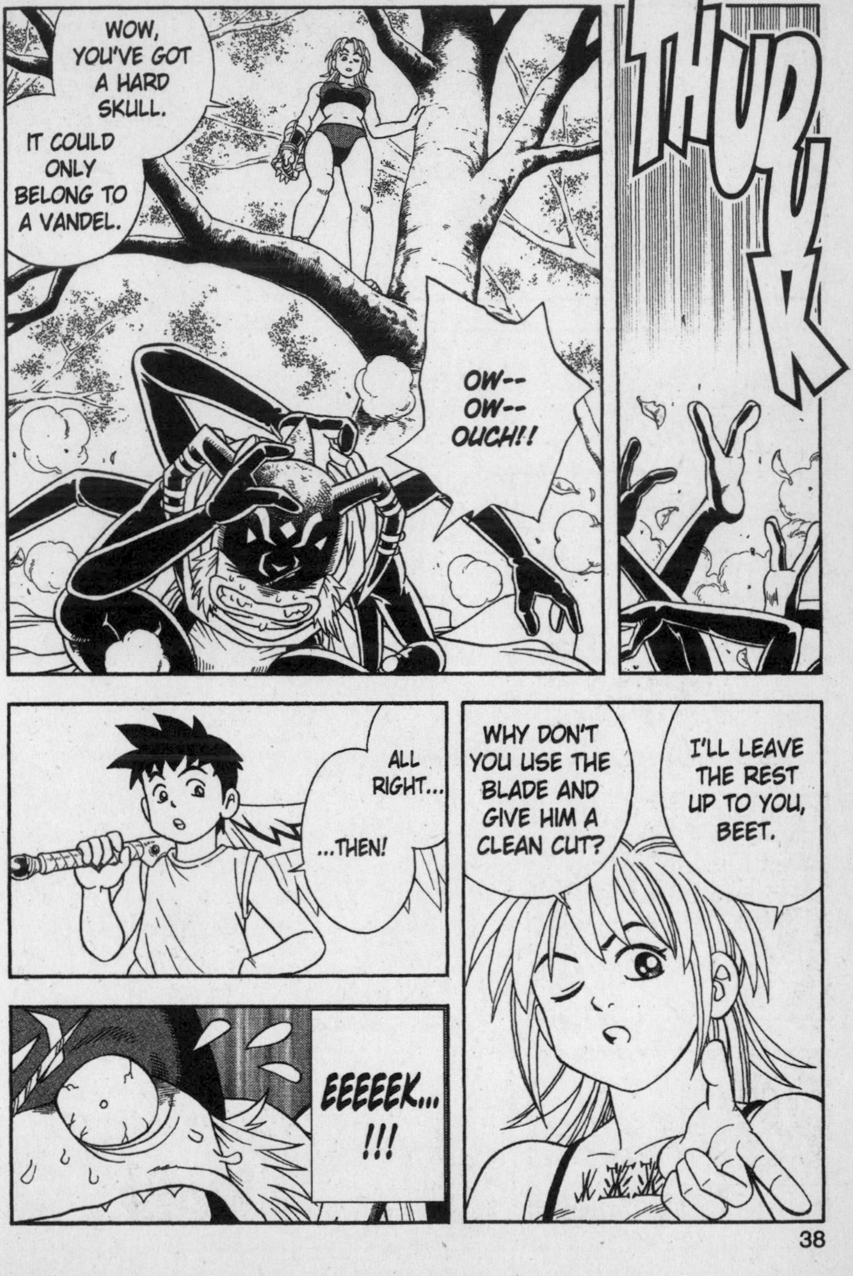
THUDK
WOW, YOU'VE GOT A HARD SKULL.
IT COULD ONLY BELONG TO A VANDEL.
OW-- OW-- OUCH!!
I'LL LEAVE THE REST UP TO YOU, BEET.
WHY DON'T YOU USE THE BLADE AND GIVE HIM A CLEAN CUT?
ALL RIGHT...
...THEN!
EEEEEK... !!!

READ THIS WAY

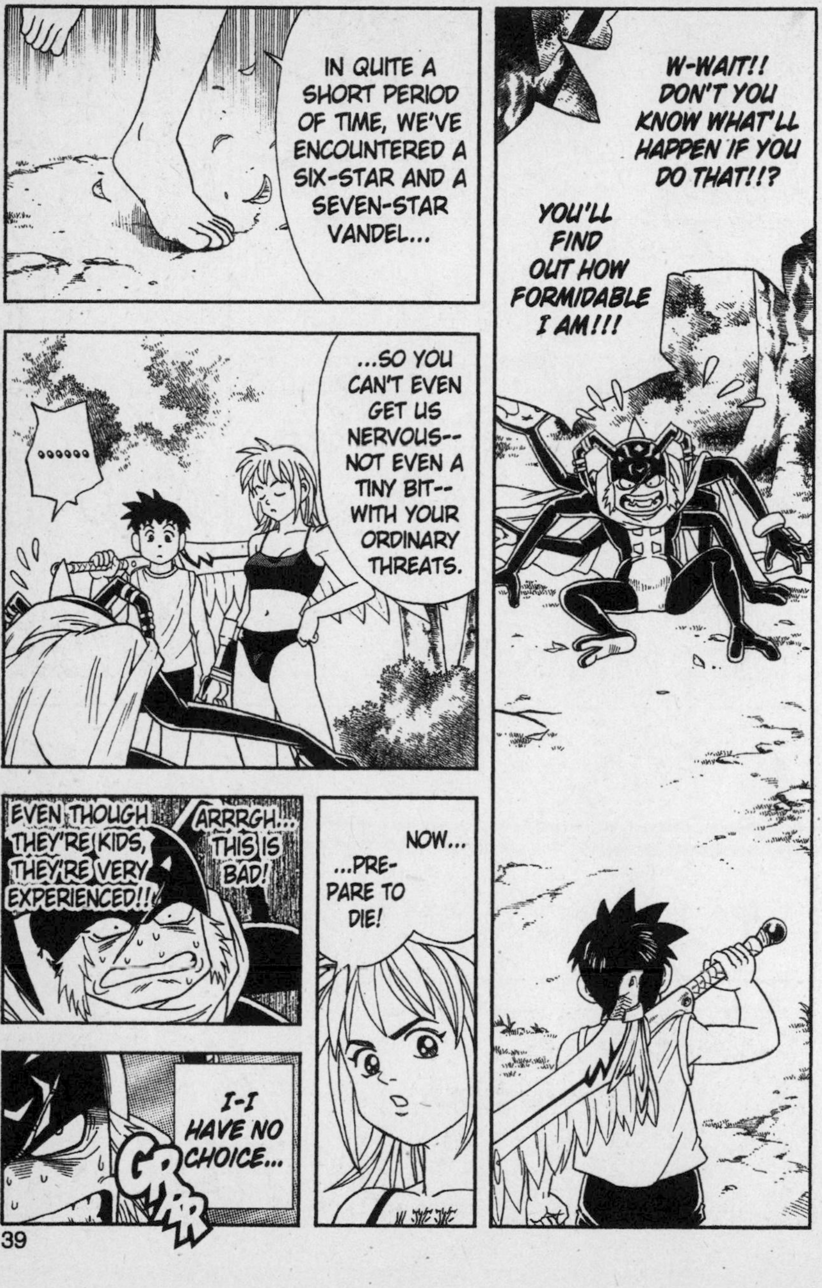

W-WAIT!! DON'T YOU KNOW WHAT'LL HAPPEN IF YOU DO THAT!!?
YOU'LL FIND OUT HOW FORMIDABLE I AM!!!
IN QUITE A SHORT PERIOD OF TIME, WE'VE ENCOUNTERED A SIX-STAR AND A SEVEN-STAR VANDEL...
...SO YOU CAN'T EVEN GET US NERVOUS--NOT EVEN A TINY BIT--WITH YOUR ORDINARY THREATS.
......
NOW...
...PRE-PARE TO DIE!
ARRRGH... THIS IS BAD!
EVEN THOUGH THEY'RE KIDS, THEY'RE VERY EXPERIENCED!!
I-I HAVE NO CHOICE...
GRRR

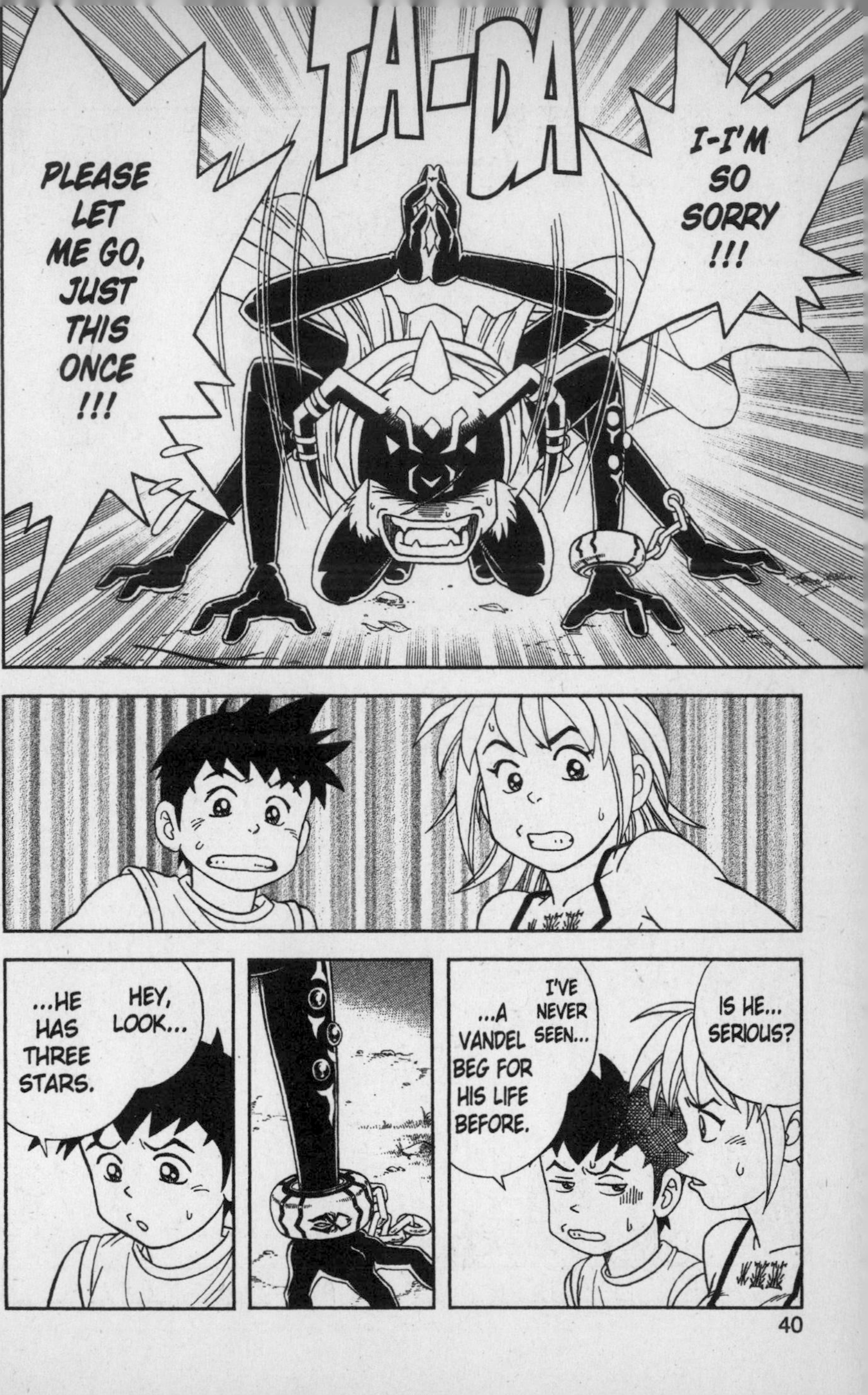
TA-DA
I-I'M SO SORRY!!!
PLEASE LET ME GO, JUST THIS ONCE!!!
IS HE... SERIOUS?
I'VE NEVER SEEN...
...A VANDEL BEG FOR HIS LIFE BEFORE.
HEY, LOOK...
...HE HAS THREE STARS.

READ THIS WAY

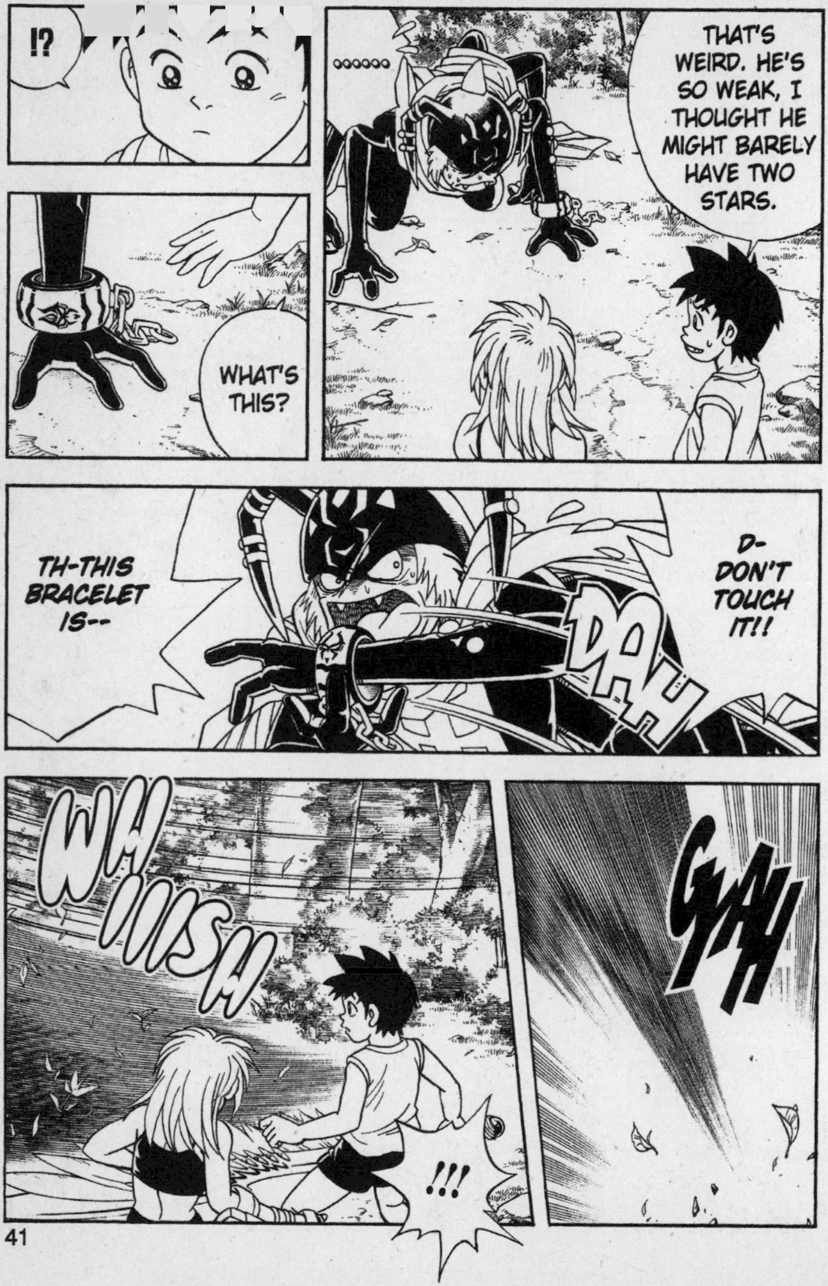

oooooo
THAT'S WEIRD. HE'S SO WEAK, I THOUGHT HE MIGHT BARELY HAVE TWO STARS.
!?
WHAT'S THIS?
D-DON'T TOUCH IT!!
DAH
TH-THIS BRACELET IS--
GYAH
WHIIISH
!!!

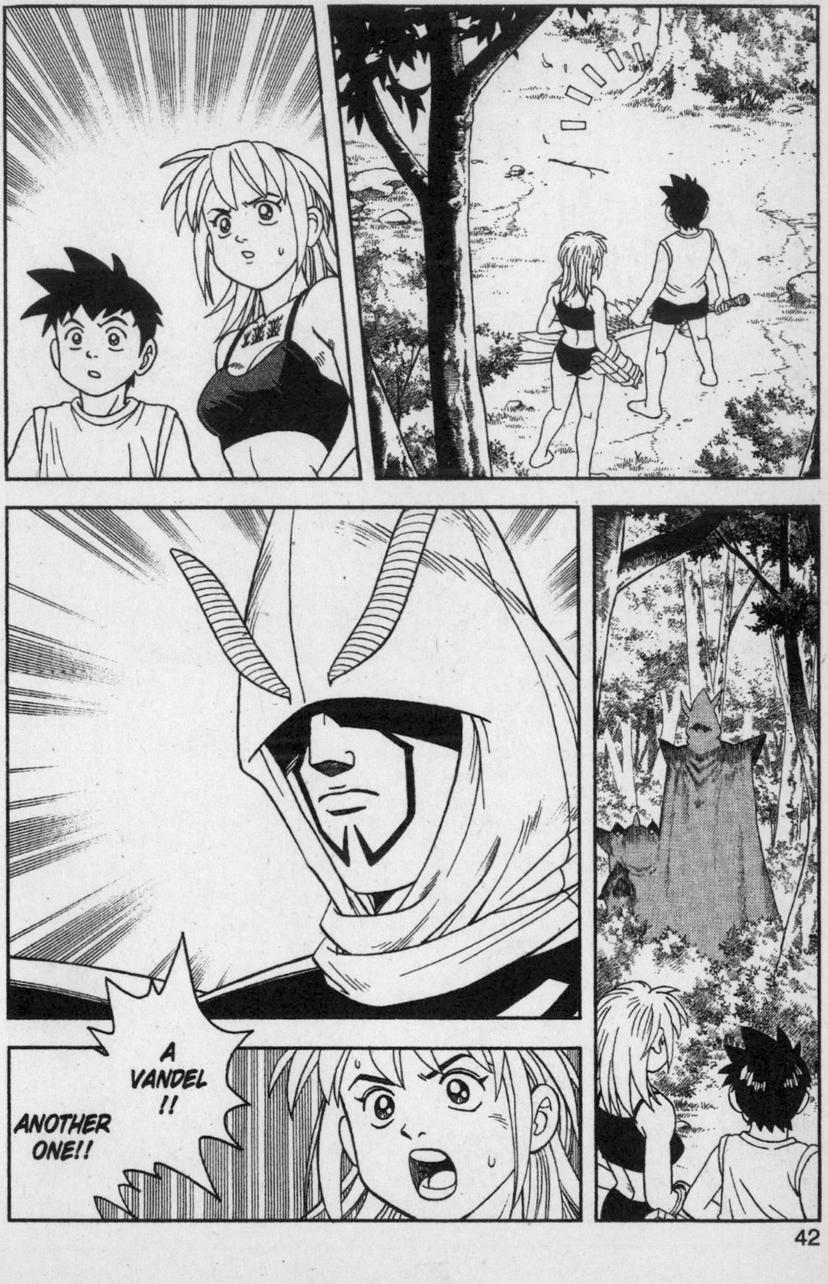
A VANDEL!!
ANOTHER ONE!!

READ THIS WAY

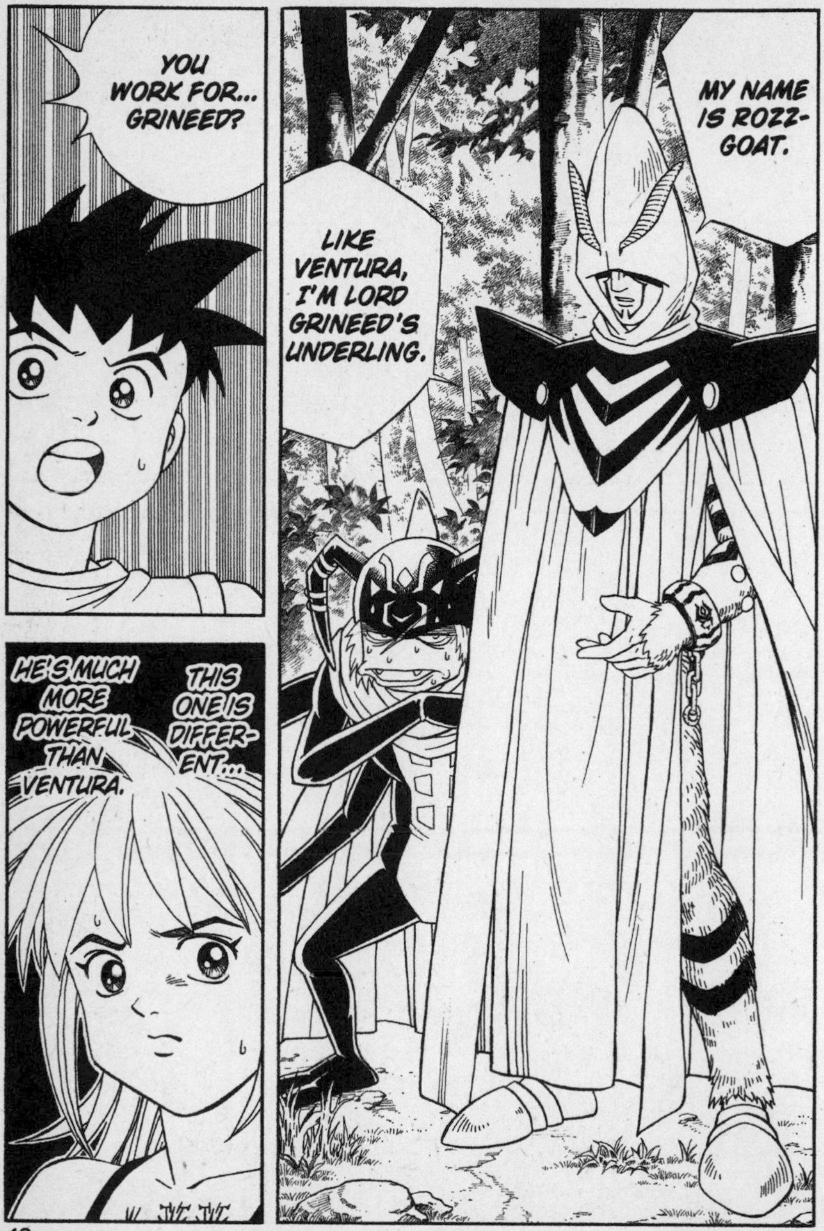
MY NAME IS ROZZ-GOAT.
LIKE VENTURA, I'M LORD GRINEED'S UNDERLING.
YOU WORK FOR... GRINEED?
THIS ONE IS DIFFER-ENT...
HE'S MUCH MORE POWERFUL THAN VENTURA.

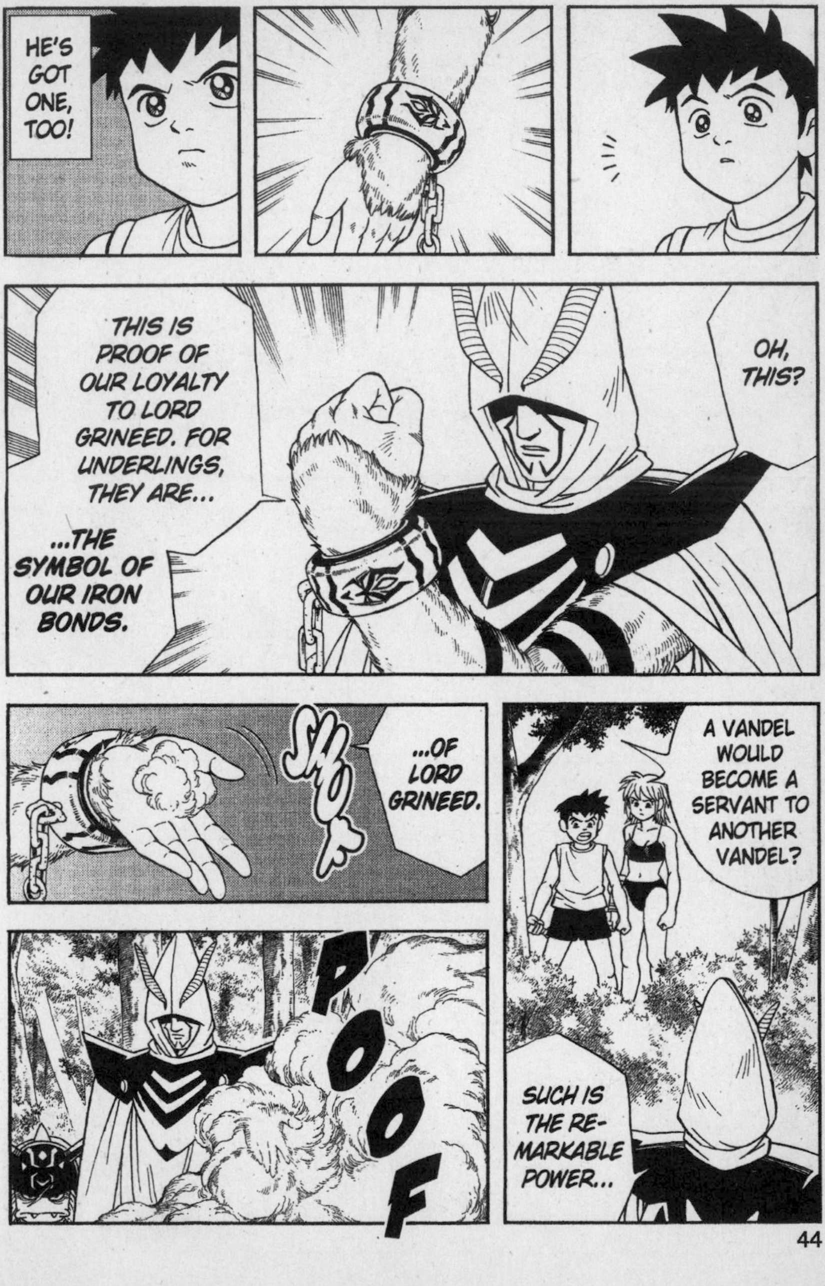
HE'S GOT ONE, TOO!
OH, THIS?
THIS IS PROOF OF OUR LOYALTY TO LORD GRINEED. FOR UNDERLINGS, THEY ARE...
...THE SYMBOL OF OUR IRON BONDS.
A VANDEL WOULD BECOME A SERVANT TO ANOTHER VANDEL?
SUCH IS THE RE-MARKABLE POWER...
...OF LORD GRINEED.
POOOF

READ THIS WAY

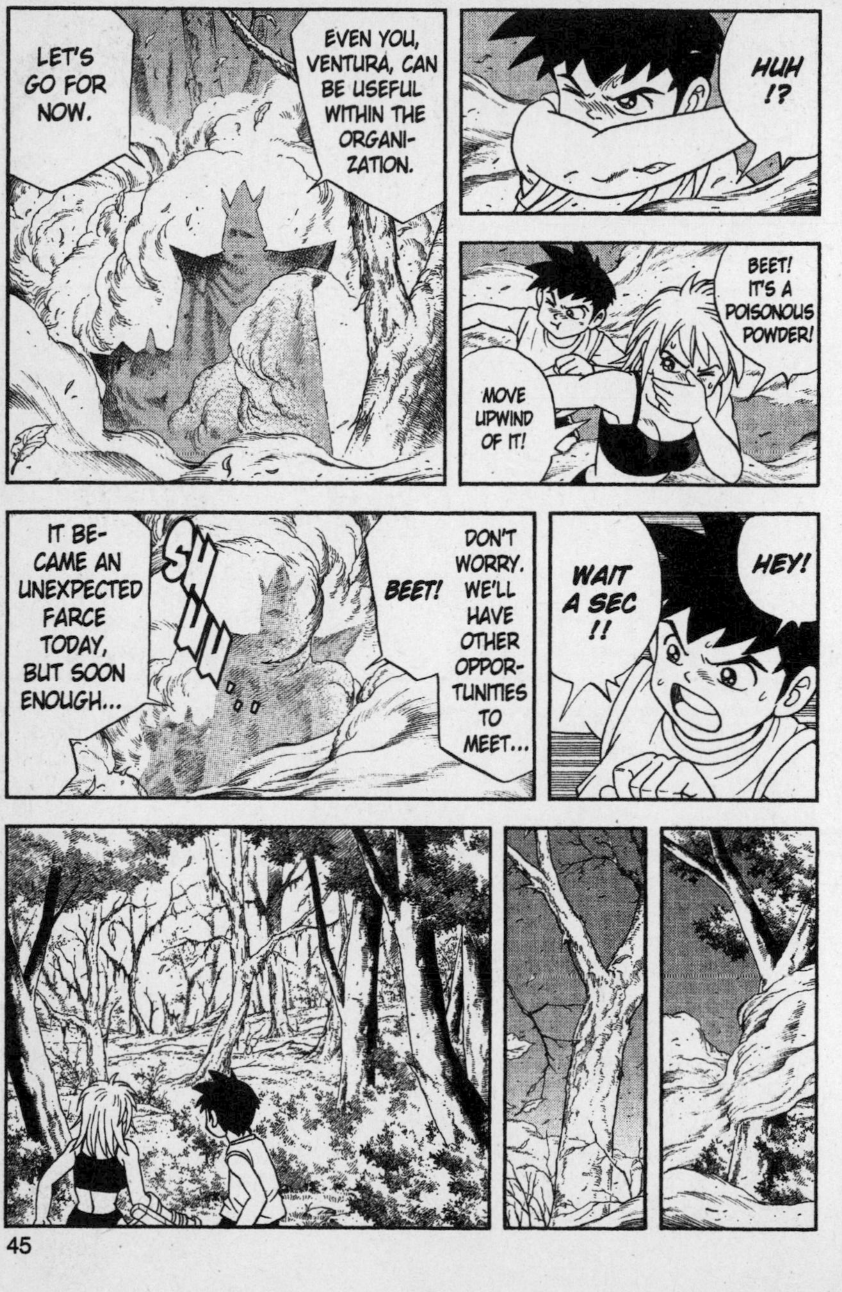
HUH!?
BEET! IT'S A POISONOUS POWDER!
MOVE UPWIND OF IT!
EVEN YOU, VENTURA, CAN BE USEFUL WITHIN THE ORGANI-ZATION.
LET'S GO FOR NOW.
HEY!
WAIT A SEC!!
DON'T WORRY. WE'LL HAVE OTHER OPPOR-TUNITIES TO MEET...
BEET!
SHUUU...
IT BE-CAME AN UNEXPECTED FARCE TODAY, BUT SOON ENOUGH...

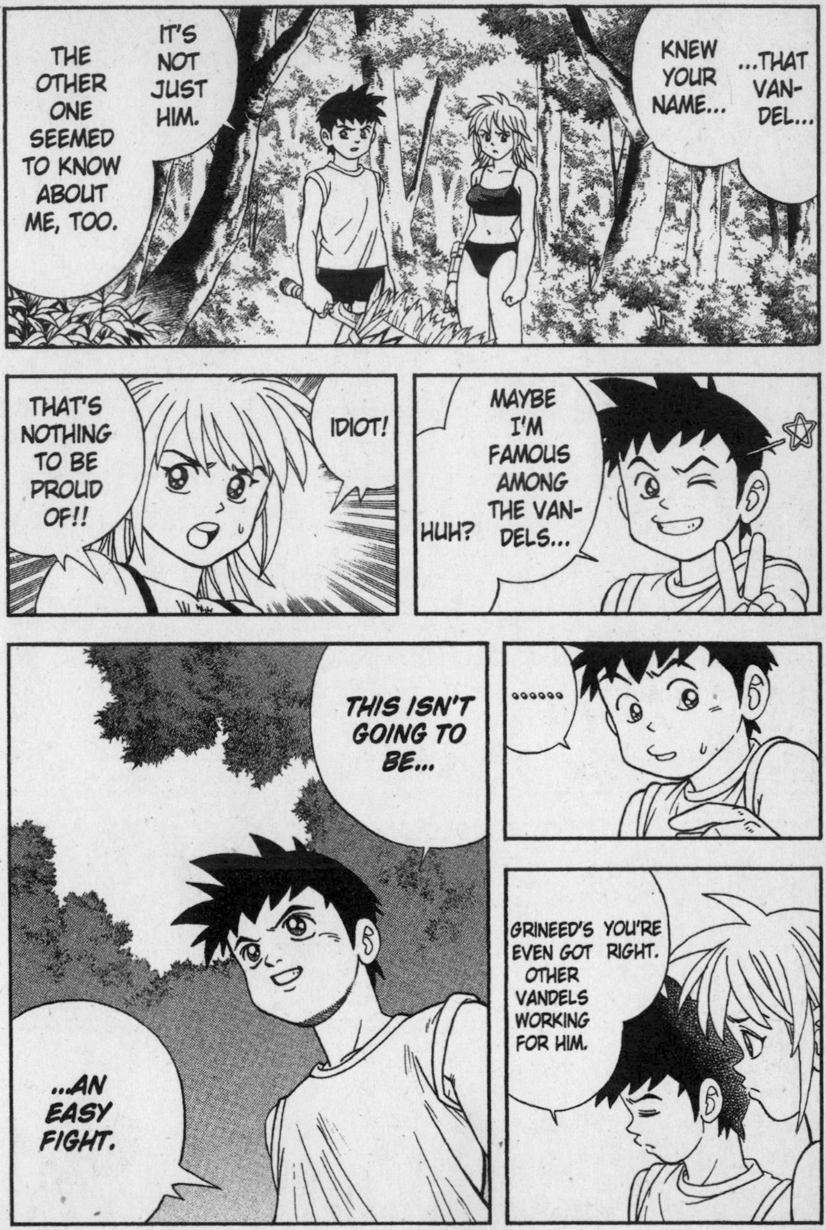
...THAT VANDEL... KNEW YOUR NAME...
IT'S NOT JUST HIM.
THE OTHER ONE SEEMED TO KNOW ABOUT ME, TOO.
MAYBE I'M FAMOUS AMONG THE VANDELS...
HUH?
IDIOT!
THAT'S NOTHING TO BE PROUD OF!!
......
YOU'RE RIGHT.
GRINEED'S EVEN GOT OTHER VANDELS WORKING FOR HIM.
THIS ISN'T GOING TO BE...
...AN EASY FIGHT.

READ THIS WAY

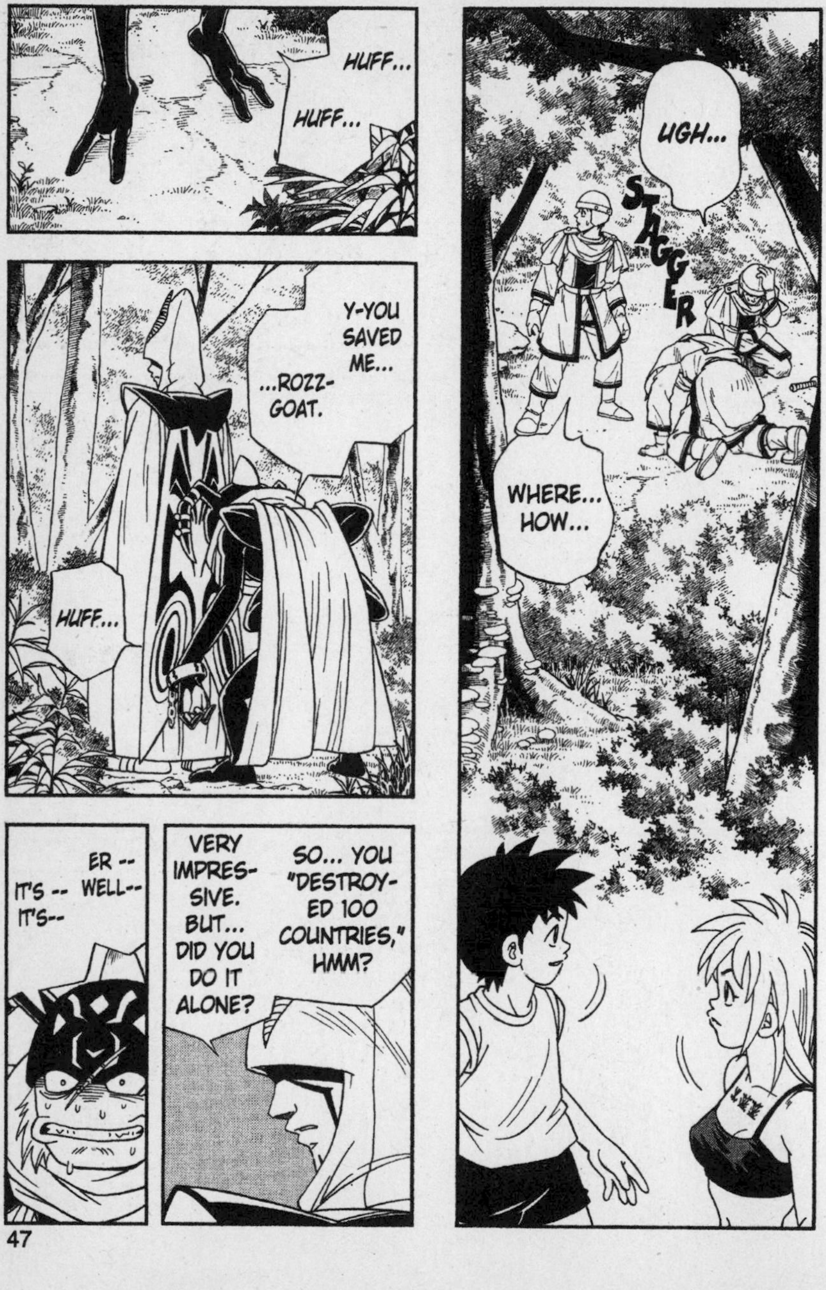

UGH...
STAGGER
WHERE... HOW...
HUFF...
HUFF...
Y-YOU SAVED ME...
...ROZZ-GOAT.
HUFF...
SO... YOU "DESTROYED 100 COUNTRIES," HMM?
VERY IMPRESSIVE. BUT... DID YOU DO IT ALONE?
ER -- WELL--
IT'S -- IT'S--

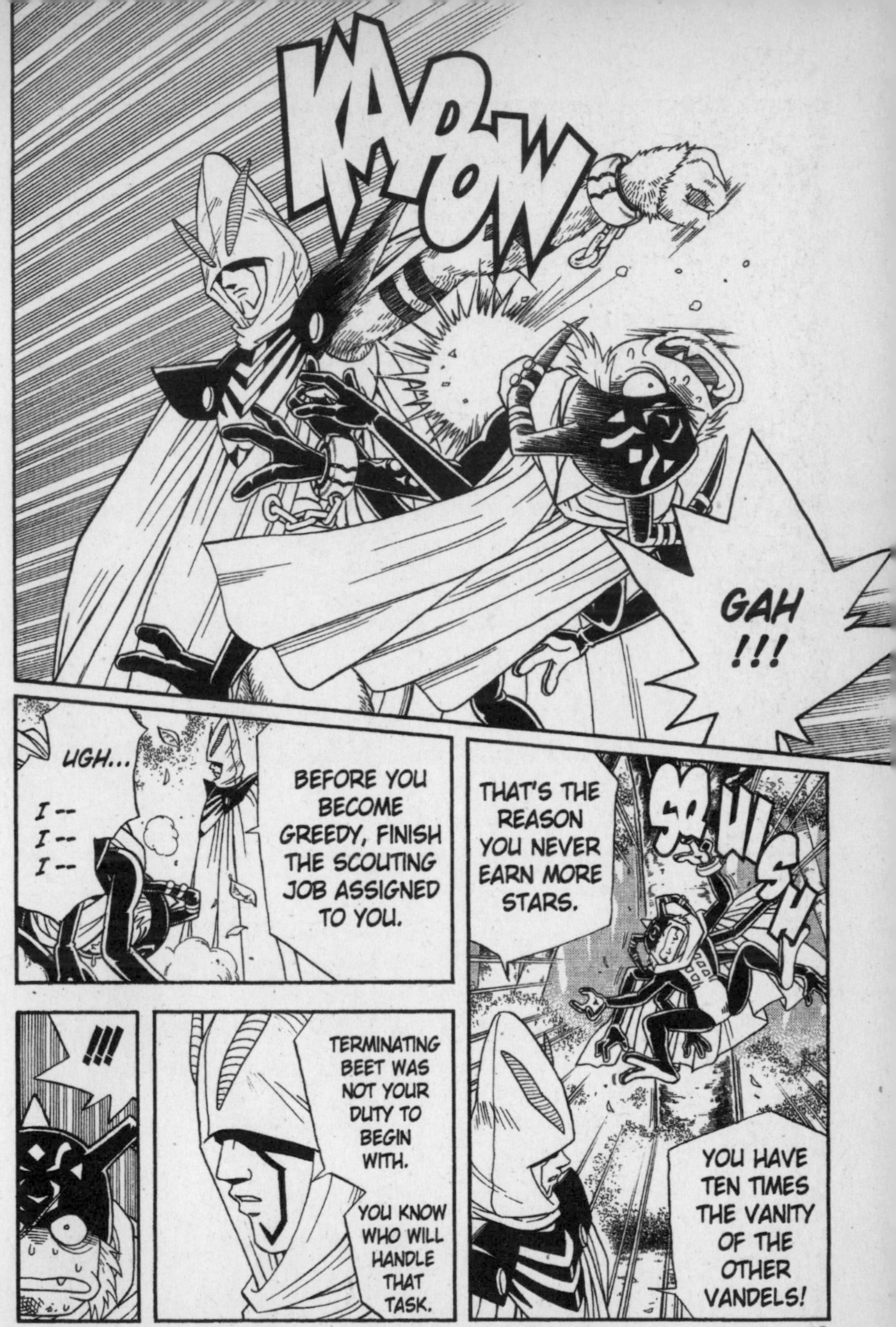
GAH !!!
SQUISH
THAT'S THE REASON YOU NEVER EARN MORE STARS.
YOU HAVE TEN TIMES THE VANITY OF THE OTHER VANDELS!
BEFORE YOU BECOME GREEDY, FINISH THE SCOUTING JOB ASSIGNED TO YOU.
UGH...
I --
I --
I --
TERMINATING BEET WAS NOT YOUR DUTY TO BEGIN WITH.
YOU KNOW WHO WILL HANDLE THAT TASK.
!!!

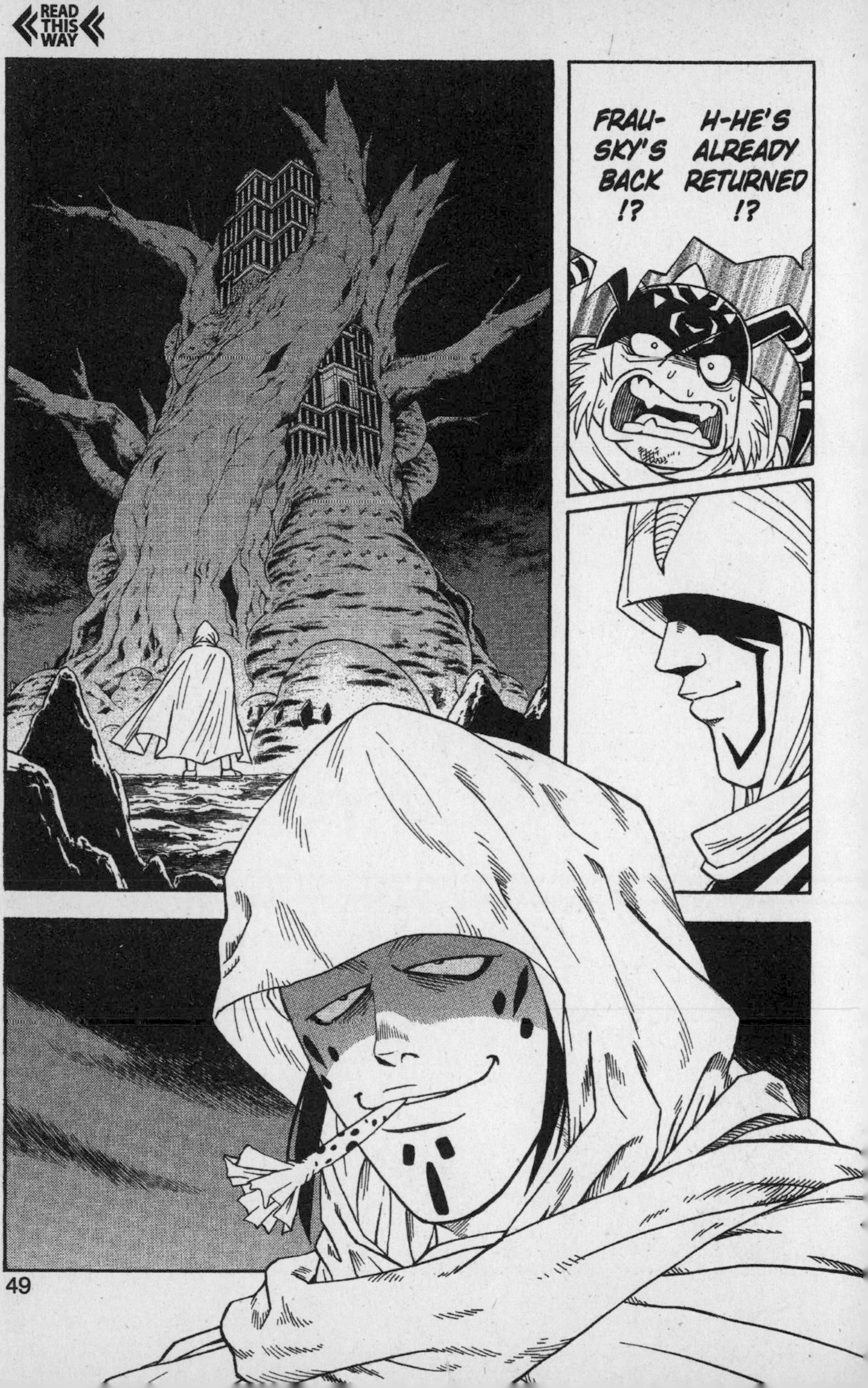
READ THIS WAY
H-HE'S ALREADY RETURNED !?
FRAU-SKY'S BACK !?

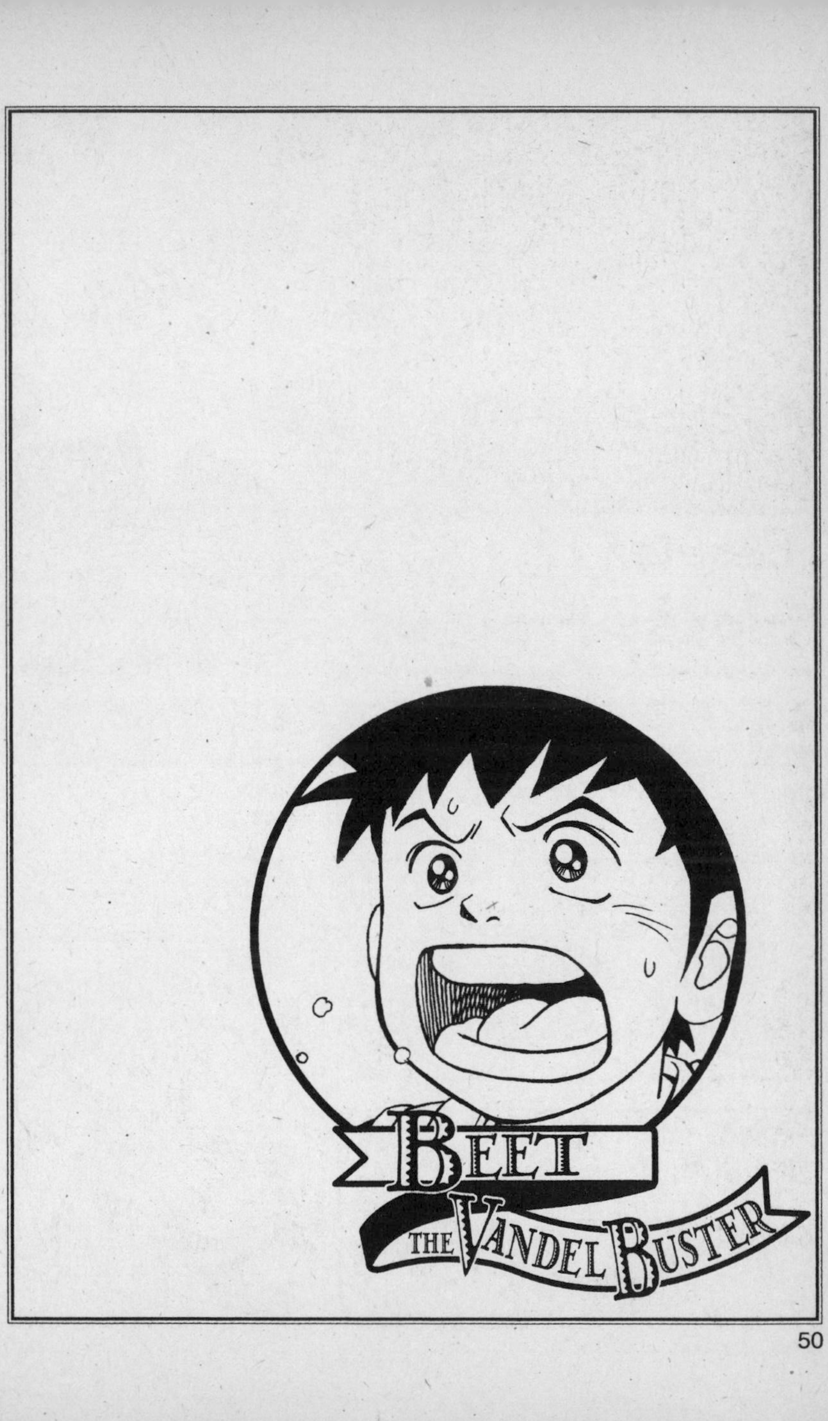
BEET
THE VANDEL BUSTER

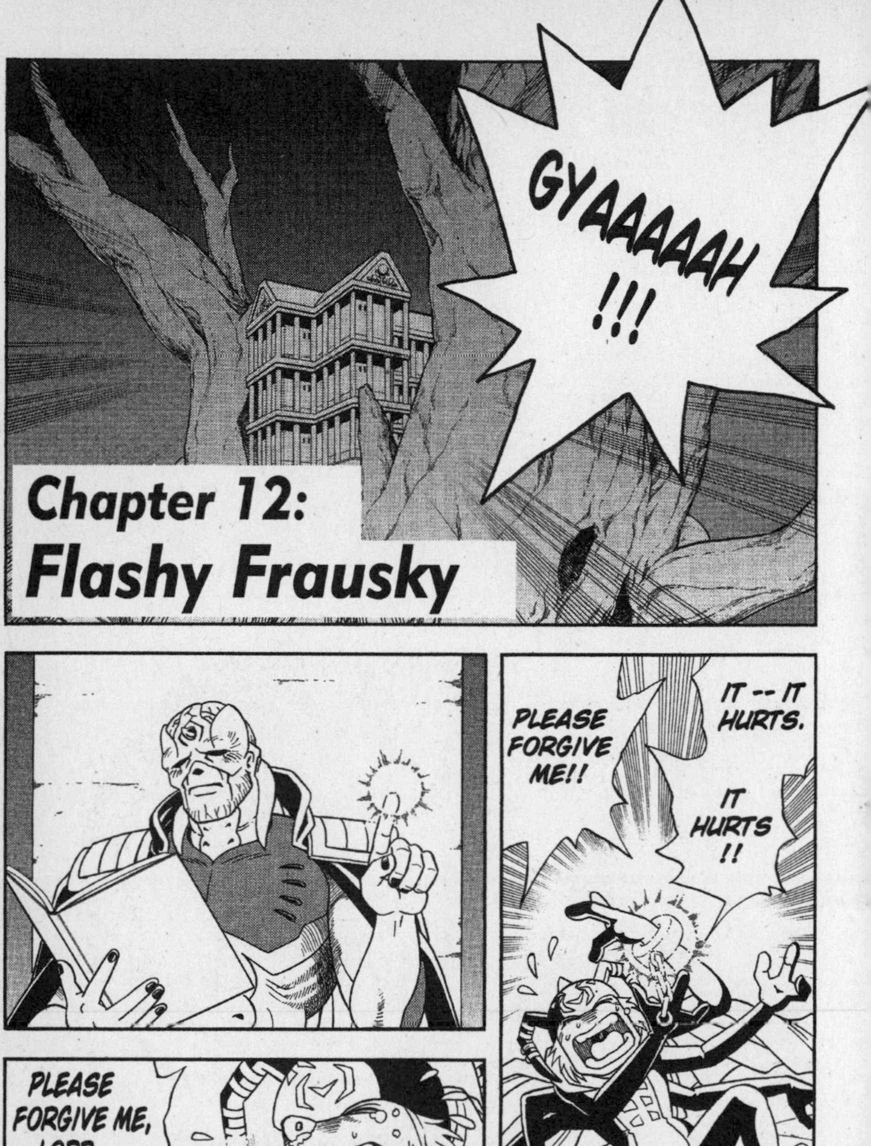
GYAAAAAH!!!
Chapter 12: Flashy Frausky
IT -- IT HURTS.
PLEASE FORGIVE ME!!
IT HURTS!!
PLEASE FORGIVE ME, LORD GRINEED!!

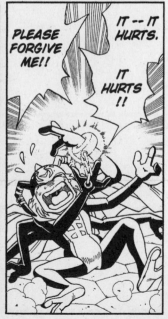

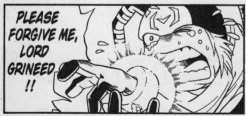

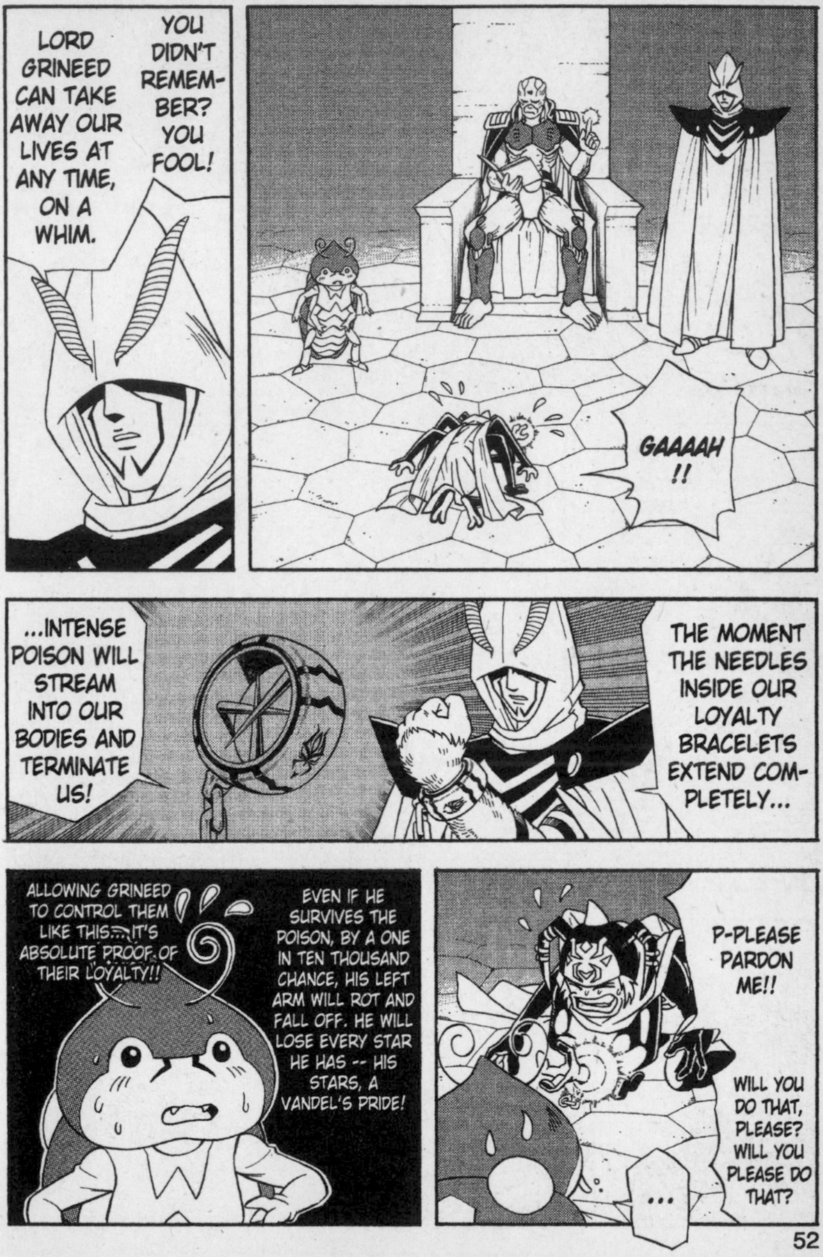
GAAAAH !!
YOU DIDN'T REMEMBER? YOU FOOL!
LORD GRINEED CAN TAKE AWAY OUR LIVES AT ANY TIME, ON A WHIM.
THE MOMENT THE NEEDLES INSIDE OUR LOYALTY BRACELETS EXTEND COMPLETELY...
...INTENSE POISON WILL STREAM INTO OUR BODIES AND TERMINATE US!
P-PLEASE PARDON ME!!
WILL YOU DO THAT, PLEASE? WILL YOU PLEASE DO THAT?
...
EVEN IF HE SURVIVES THE POISON, BY A ONE IN TEN THOUSAND CHANCE, HIS LEFT ARM WILL ROT AND FALL OFF. HE WILL LOSE EVERY STAR HE HAS -- HIS STARS, A VANDEL'S PRIDE!
ALLOWING GRINEED TO CONTROL THEM LIKE THIS... IT'S ABSOLUTE PROOF OF THEIR LOYALTY!!

READ THIS WAY

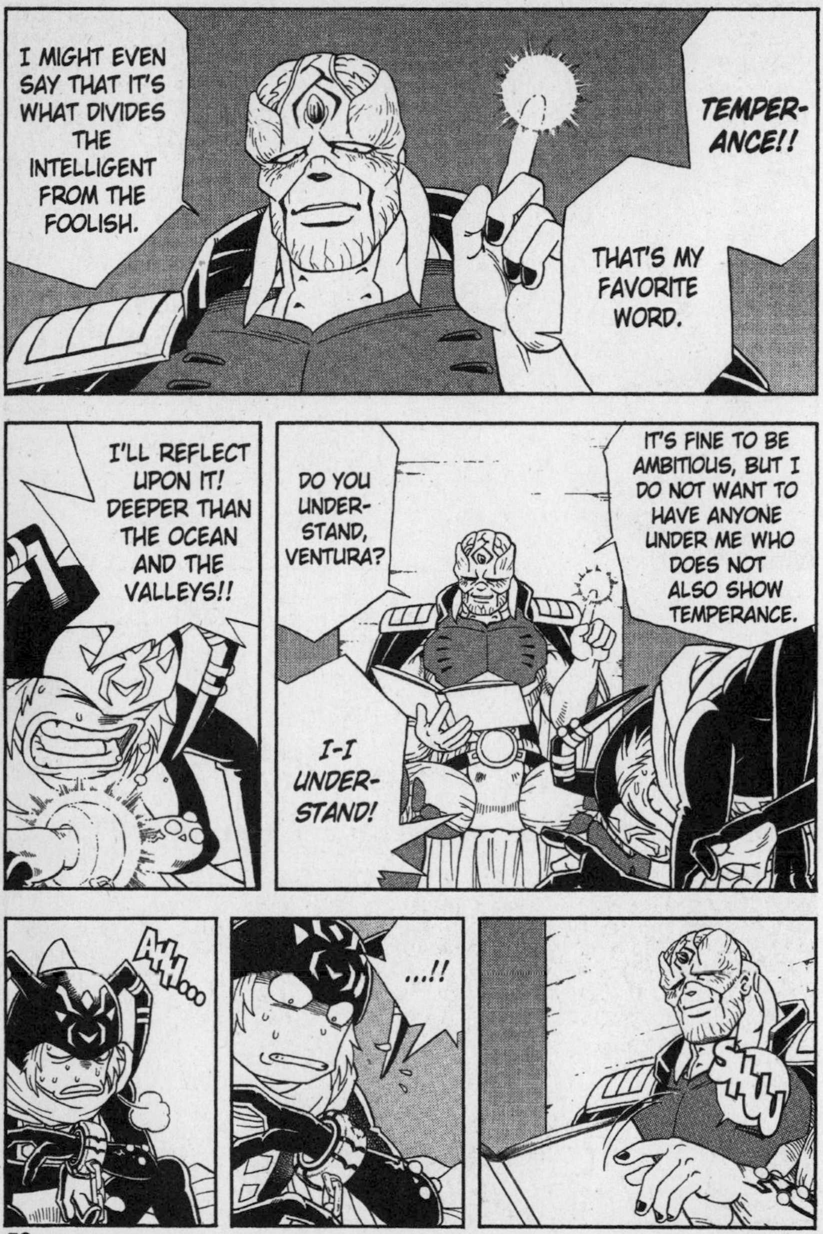
TEMPER-ANCE!!
THAT'S MY FAVORITE WORD.
I MIGHT EVEN SAY THAT IT'S WHAT DIVIDES THE INTELLIGENT FROM THE FOOLISH.
IT'S FINE TO BE AMBITIOUS, BUT I DO NOT WANT TO HAVE ANYONE UNDER ME WHO DOES NOT ALSO SHOW TEMPERANCE.
DO YOU UNDER-STAND, VENTURA?
I-I UNDER-STAND!
I'LL REFLECT UPON IT! DEEPER THAN THE OCEAN AND THE VALLEYS!!
SHUU
...!!
AHHooo

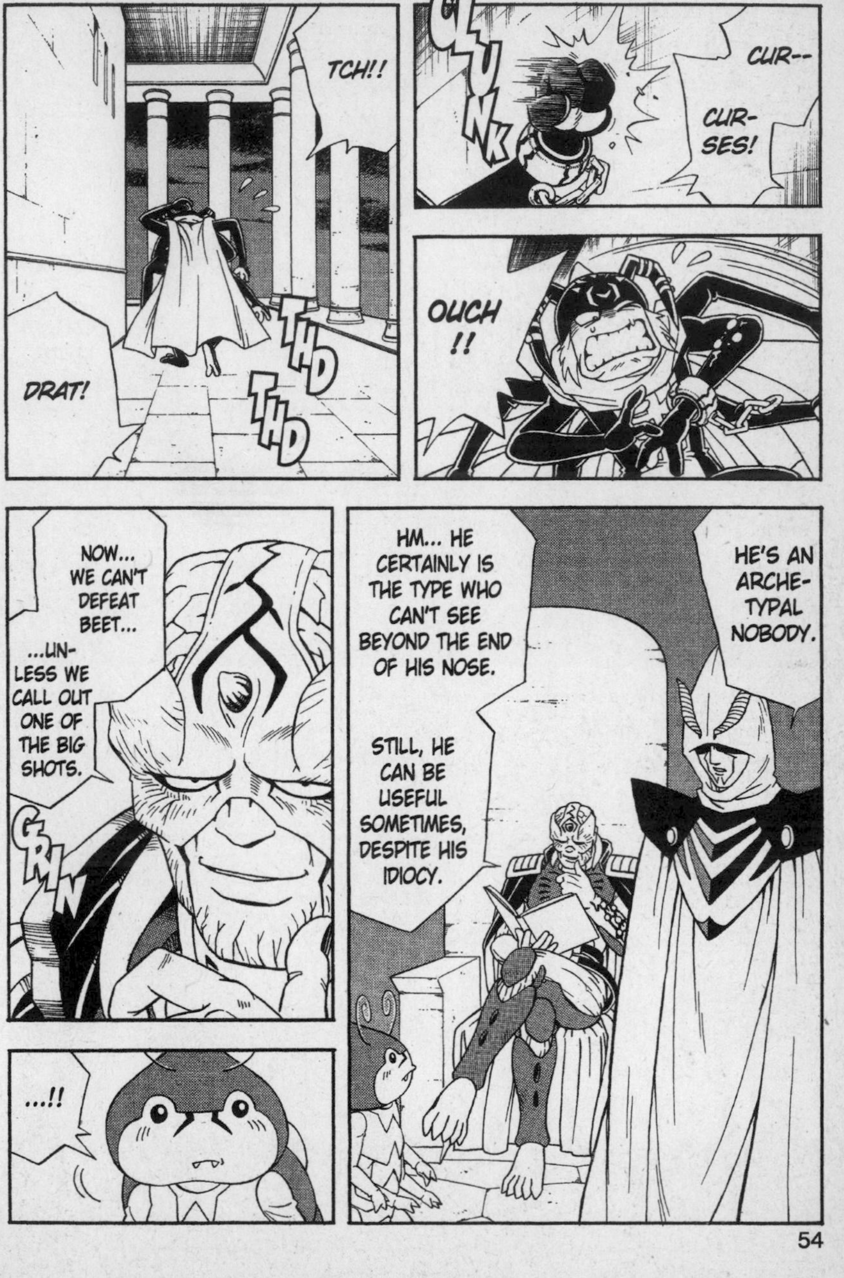
CLUNK
CUR--
CURSES!
OUCH!!
TCH!!
THD
THD
DRAT!
HE'S AN ARCHETYPAL NOBODY.
HM... HE CERTAINLY IS THE TYPE WHO CAN'T SEE BEYOND THE END OF HIS NOSE.
STILL, HE CAN BE USEFUL SOMETIMES, DESPITE HIS IDIOCY.
NOW... WE CAN'T DEFEAT BEET...
...UNLESS WE CALL OUT ONE OF THE BIG SHOTS.
GRIN
...!!

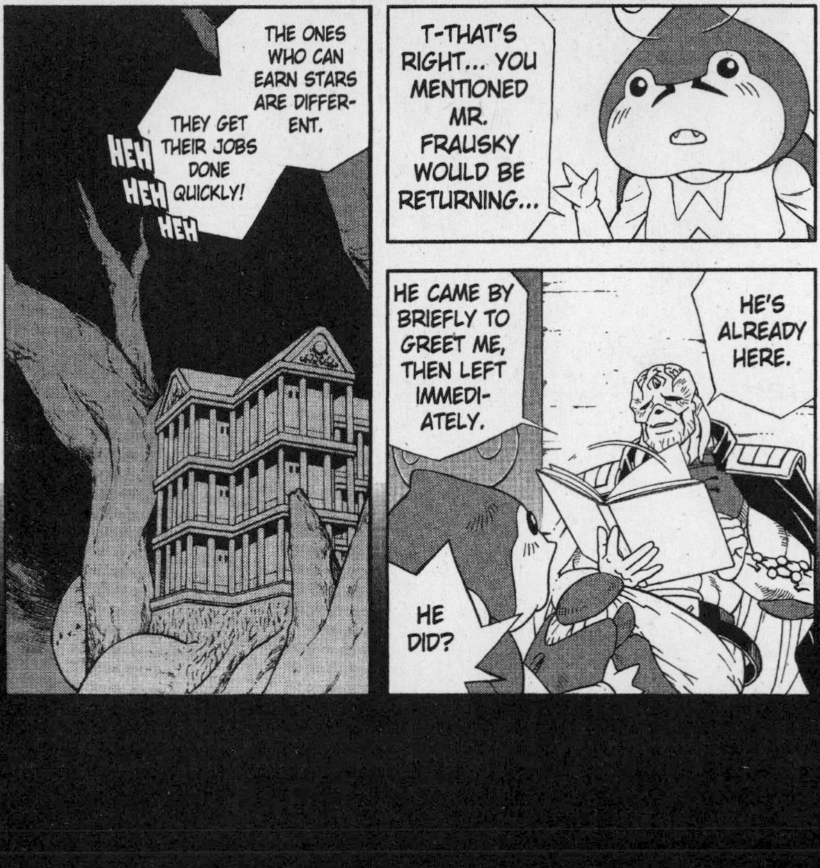
T-THAT'S RIGHT... YOU MENTIONED MR. FRAUSKY WOULD BE RETURNING...
HE'S ALREADY HERE.
HE CAME BY BRIEFLY TO GREET ME, THEN LEFT IMMEDIATELY.
HE DID?
THE ONES WHO CAN EARN STARS ARE DIFFERENT.
THEY GET THEIR JOBS DONE QUICKLY!
HEH HEH HEH

Chapter 12: Flashy Frausky!

DAKKA
DAKKA DAKDAK
BOOM
FWISH SCATTER
...
RUSTLE RUSTLE
WHAT THE HECK IS THIS PLACE?
IT'S LOADED WITH STRANGE BUGS!
TWITCH
SURE IS. IT FEELS LIKE...
...THERE'S NO END TO IT.
TWITCH PLIK

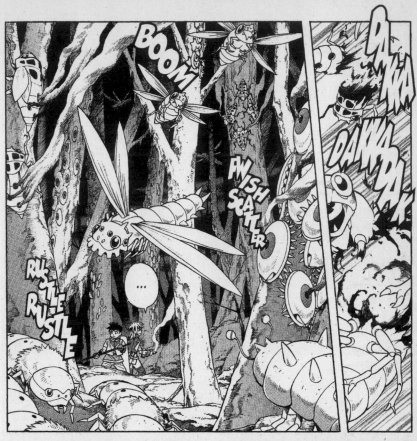

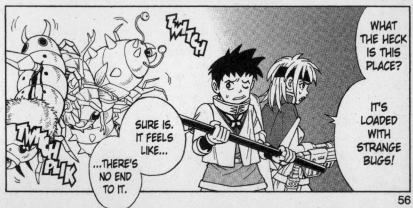

READ THIS WAY

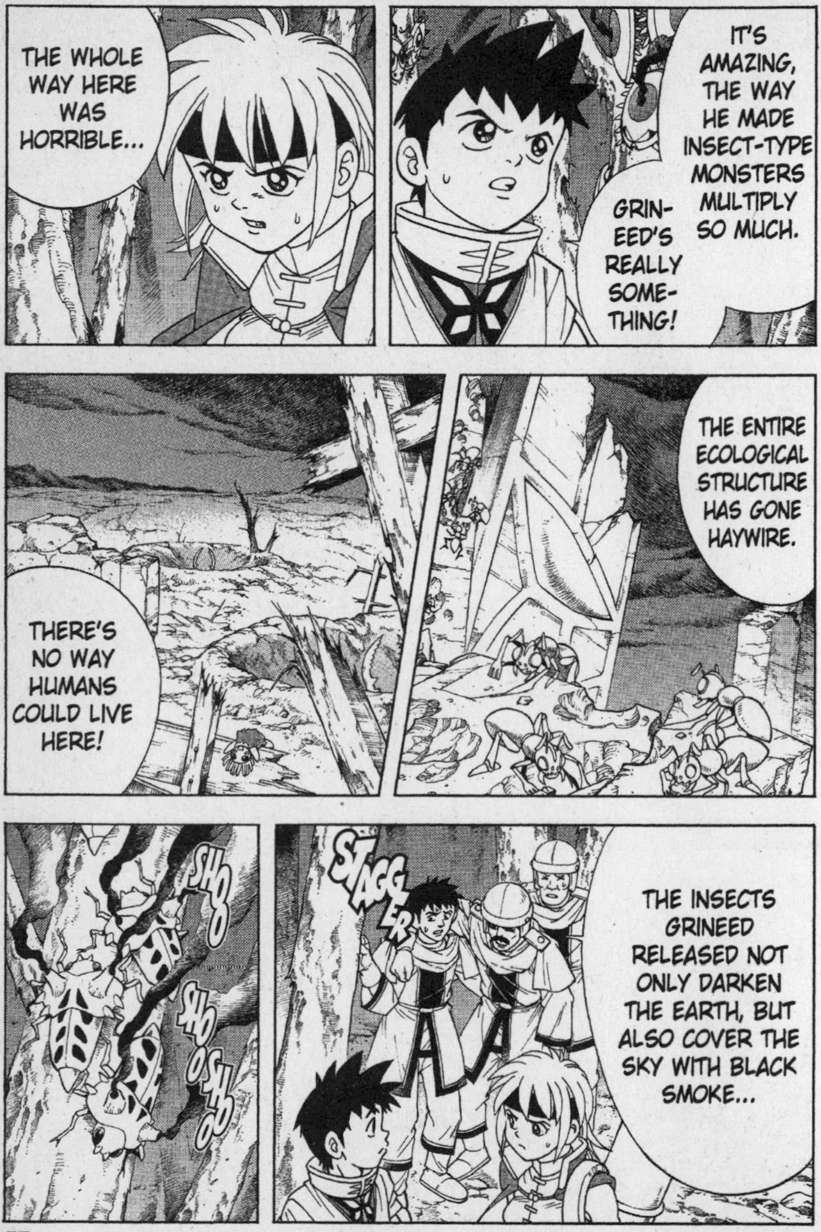
IT'S AMAZING, THE WAY HE MADE INSECT-TYPE MONSTERS MULTIPLY SO MUCH.
GRIN-EED'S REALLY SOME-THING!
THE WHOLE WAY HERE WAS HORRIBLE...
THE ENTIRE ECOLOGICAL STRUCTURE HAS GONE HAYWIRE.
THERE'S NO WAY HUMANS COULD LIVE HERE!
THE INSECTS GRINEED RELEASED NOT ONLY DARKEN THE EARTH, BUT ALSO COVER THE SKY WITH BLACK SMOKE...
STAGGER
SHOO
SHOO SHOO
SHOO

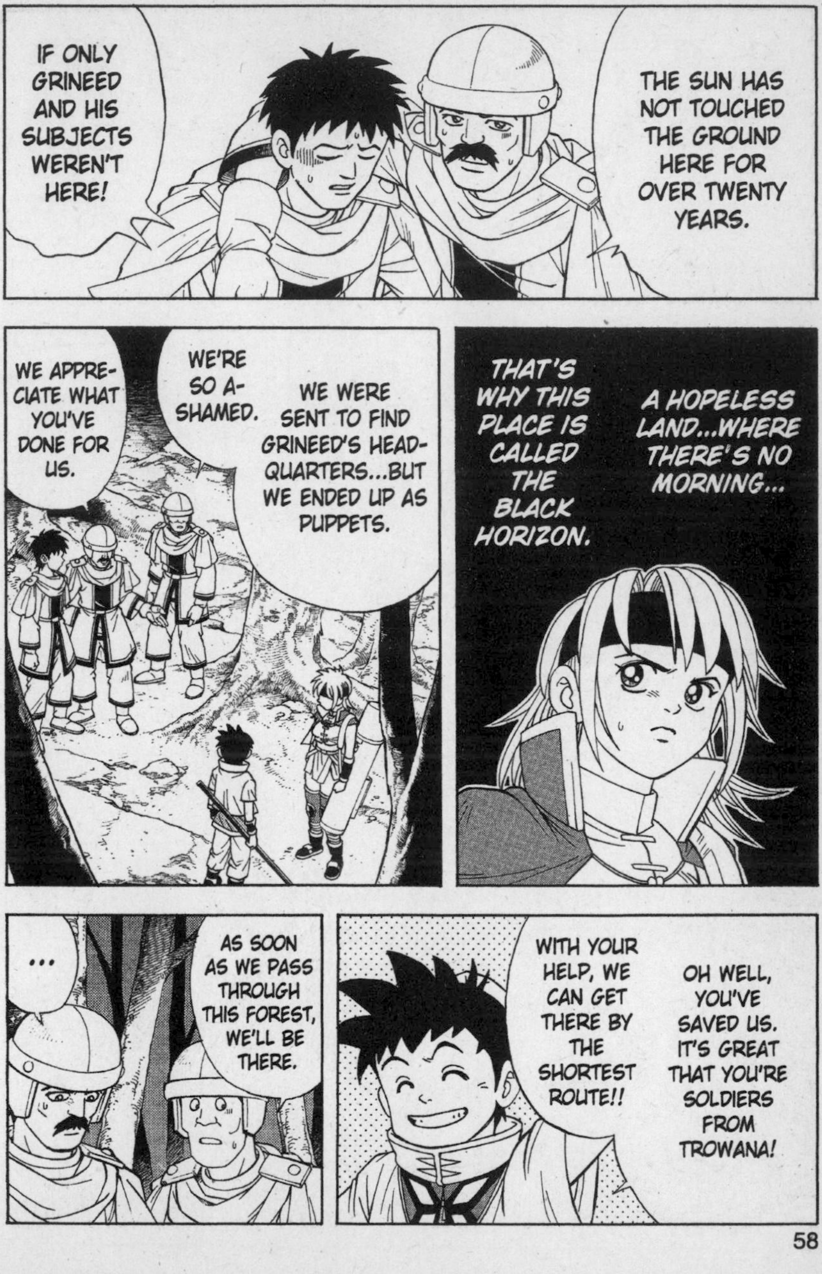
THE SUN HAS NOT TOUCHED THE GROUND HERE FOR OVER TWENTY YEARS.
IF ONLY GRINEED AND HIS SUBJECTS WEREN'T HERE!
A HOPELESS LAND...WHERE THERE'S NO MORNING...
THAT'S WHY THIS PLACE IS CALLED THE BLACK HORIZON.
WE WERE SENT TO FIND GRINEED'S HEAD-QUARTERS...BUT WE ENDED UP AS PUPPETS.
WE'RE SO A-SHAMED.
WE APPRE-CIATE WHAT YOU'VE DONE FOR US.
OH WELL, YOU'VE SAVED US. IT'S GREAT THAT YOU'RE SOLDIERS FROM TROWANA!
WITH YOUR HELP, WE CAN GET THERE BY THE SHORTEST ROUTE!!
AS SOON AS WE PASS THROUGH THIS FOREST, WE'LL BE THERE.
...

READ THIS WAY

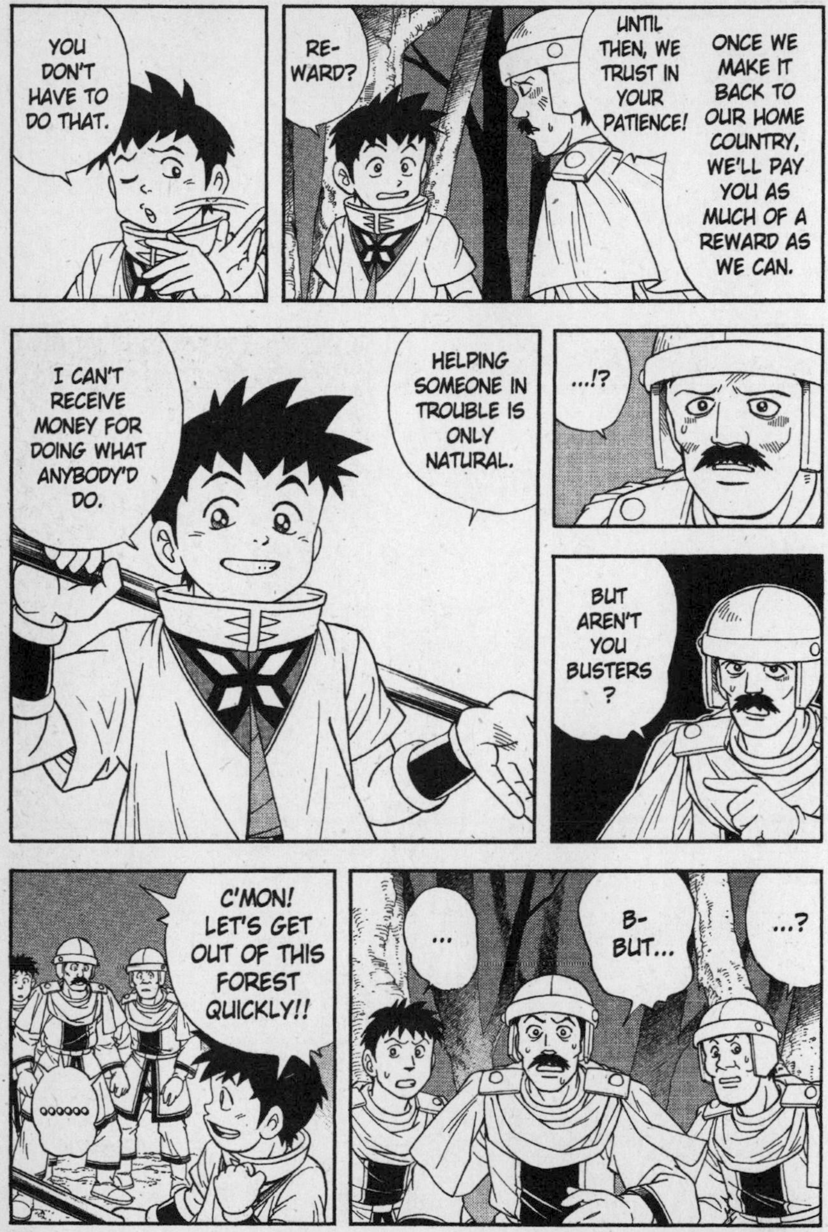
ONCE WE MAKE IT BACK TO OUR HOME COUNTRY, WE'LL PAY YOU AS MUCH OF A REWARD AS WE CAN.
UNTIL THEN, WE TRUST IN YOUR PATIENCE!
RE-WARD?
YOU DON'T HAVE TO DO THAT.
...!?
BUT AREN'T YOU BUSTERS?
HELPING SOMEONE IN TROUBLE IS ONLY NATURAL.
I CAN'T RECEIVE MONEY FOR DOING WHAT ANYBODY'D DO.
...?
B-BUT...
...
C'MON! LET'S GET OUT OF THIS FOREST QUICKLY!!
oooooo

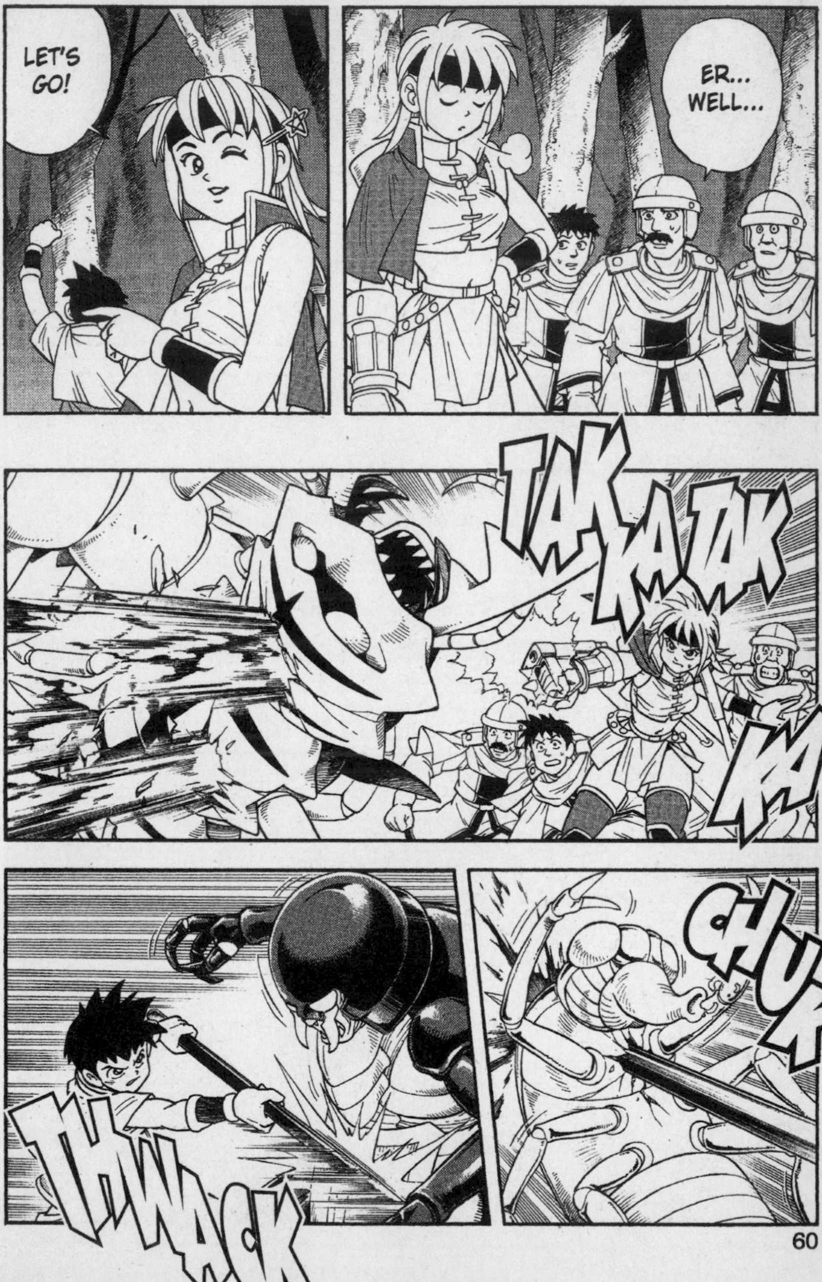
ER... WELL...
LET'S GO!
TAK KA TAK
KA
CHUK
THWACK

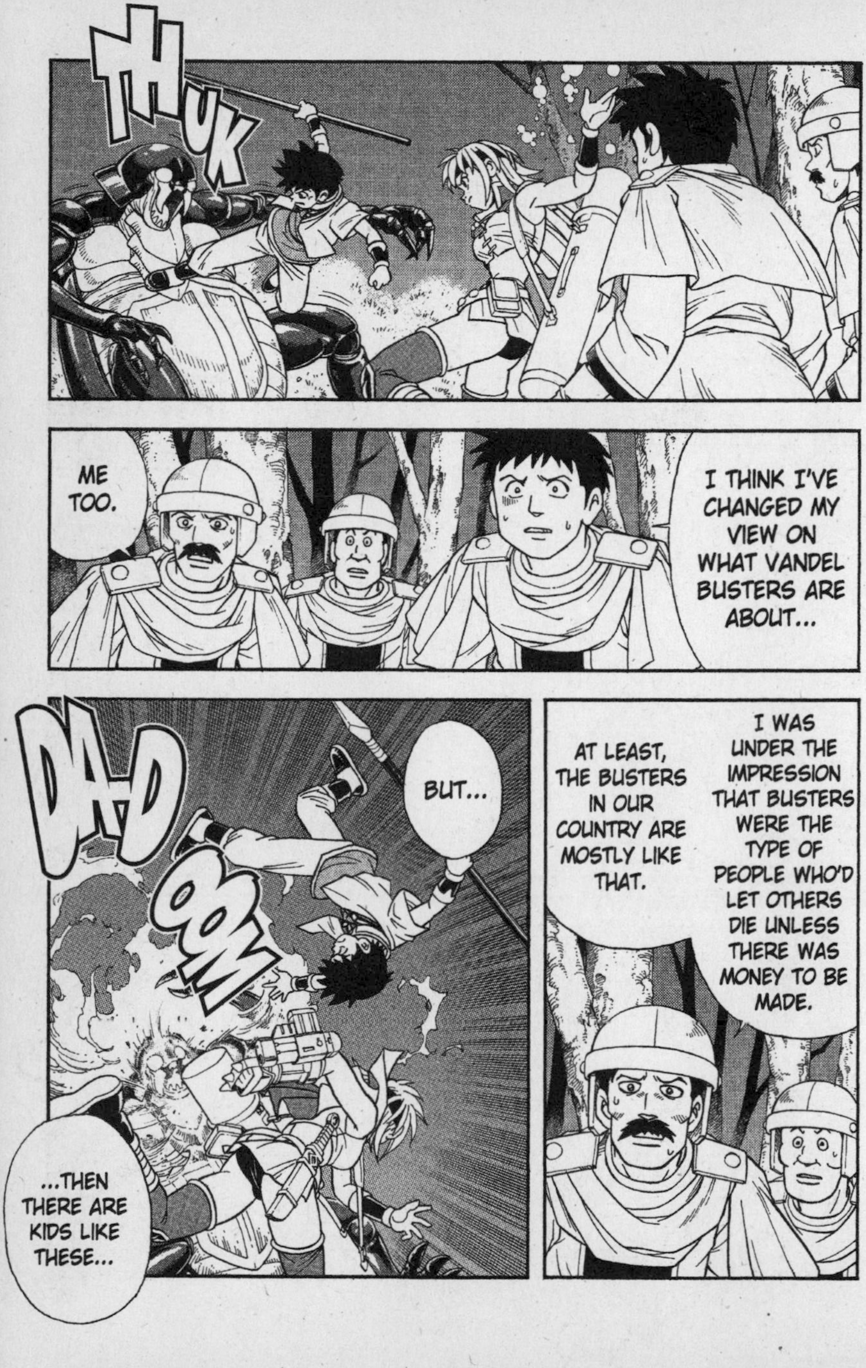
THUK
I THINK I'VE CHANGED MY VIEW ON WHAT VANDEL BUSTERS ARE ABOUT...
ME TOO.
I WAS UNDER THE IMPRESSION THAT BUSTERS WERE THE TYPE OF PEOPLE WHO'D LET OTHERS DIE UNLESS THERE WAS MONEY TO BE MADE.
AT LEAST, THE BUSTERS IN OUR COUNTRY ARE MOSTLY LIKE THAT.
BUT...
DA-D
OOM
...THEN THERE ARE KIDS LIKE THESE...

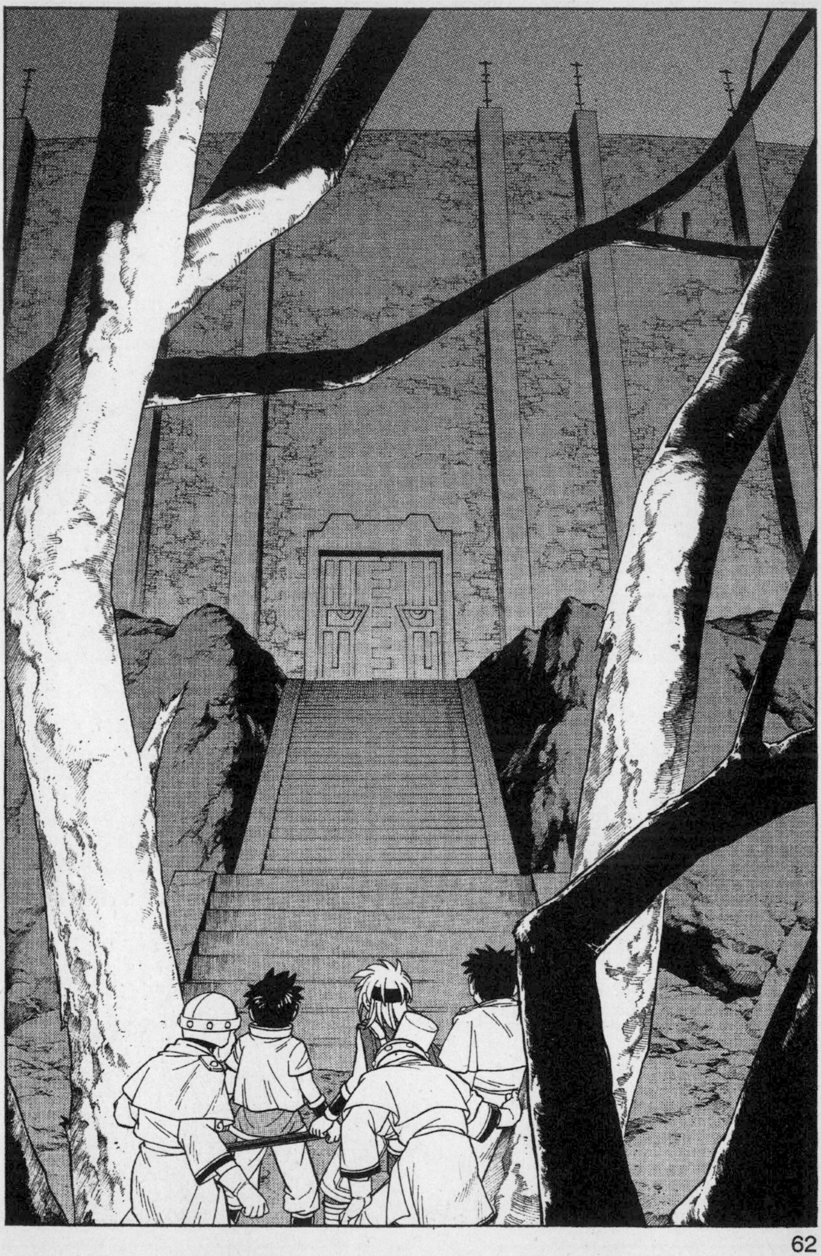

READ THIS WAY

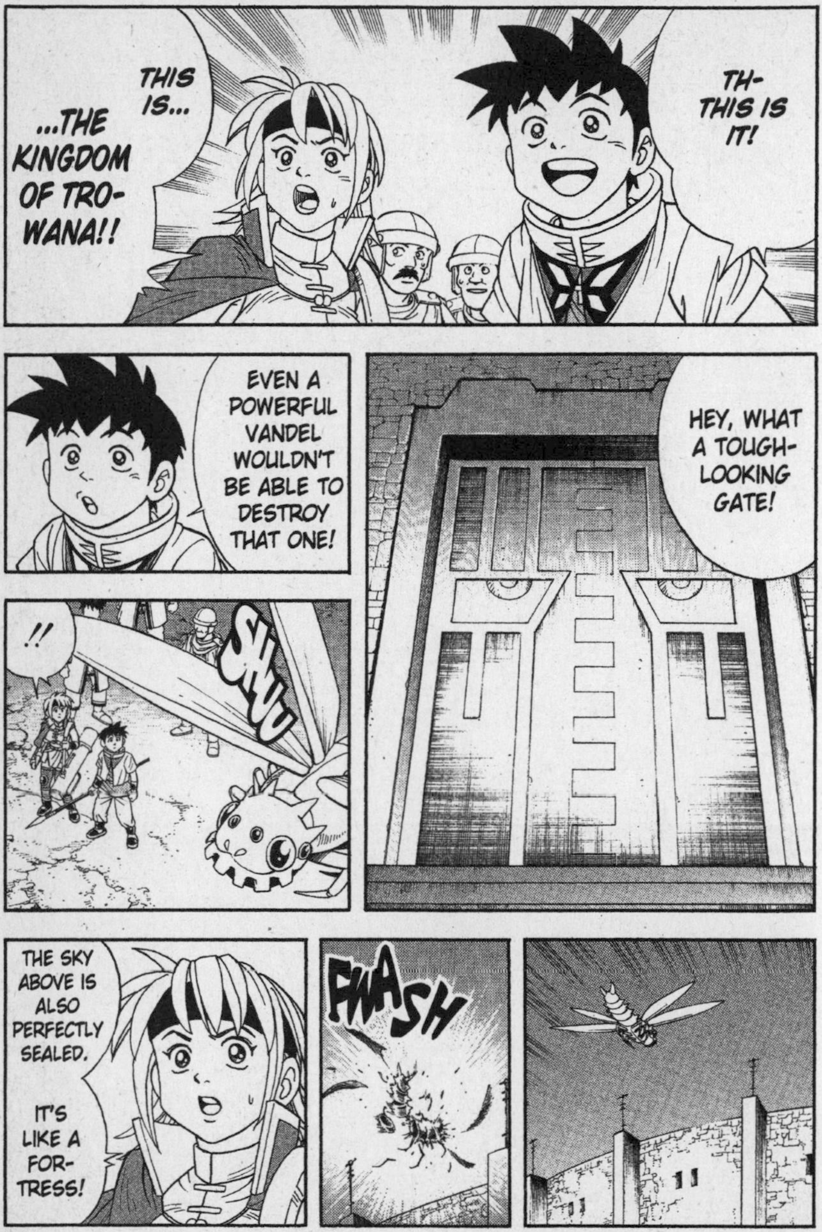
TH-THIS IS IT!
THIS IS...
...THE KINGDOM OF TRO-WANA!!
HEY, WHAT A TOUGH-LOOKING GATE!
EVEN A POWERFUL VANDEL WOULDN'T BE ABLE TO DESTROY THAT ONE!
!!
SHUU
FWASH
THE SKY ABOVE IS ALSO PERFECTLY SEALED.
IT'S LIKE A FOR-TRESS!

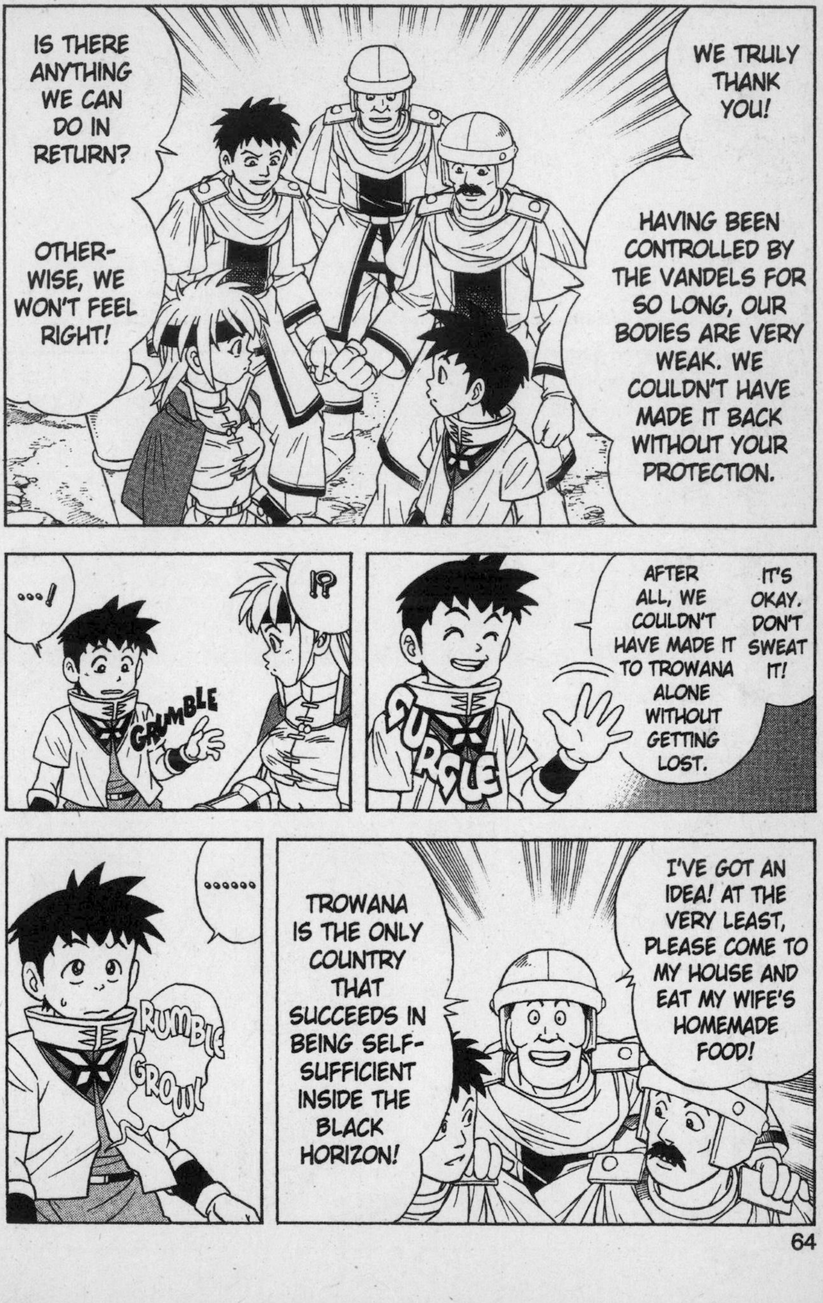
WE TRULY THANK YOU!
HAVING BEEN CONTROLLED BY THE VANDELS FOR SO LONG, OUR BODIES ARE VERY WEAK. WE COULDN'T HAVE MADE IT BACK WITHOUT YOUR PROTECTION.
IS THERE ANYTHING WE CAN DO IN RETURN?
OTHER-WISE, WE WON'T FEEL RIGHT!
IT'S OKAY. DON'T SWEAT IT!
AFTER ALL, WE COULDN'T HAVE MADE IT TO TROWANA ALONE WITHOUT GETTING LOST.
GURGLE
!?
...!
GRUMBLE
I'VE GOT AN IDEA! AT THE VERY LEAST, PLEASE COME TO MY HOUSE AND EAT MY WIFE'S HOMEMADE FOOD!
TROWANA IS THE ONLY COUNTRY THAT SUCCEEDS IN BEING SELF-SUFFICIENT INSIDE THE BLACK HORIZON!
......
RUMBLE
GROWL

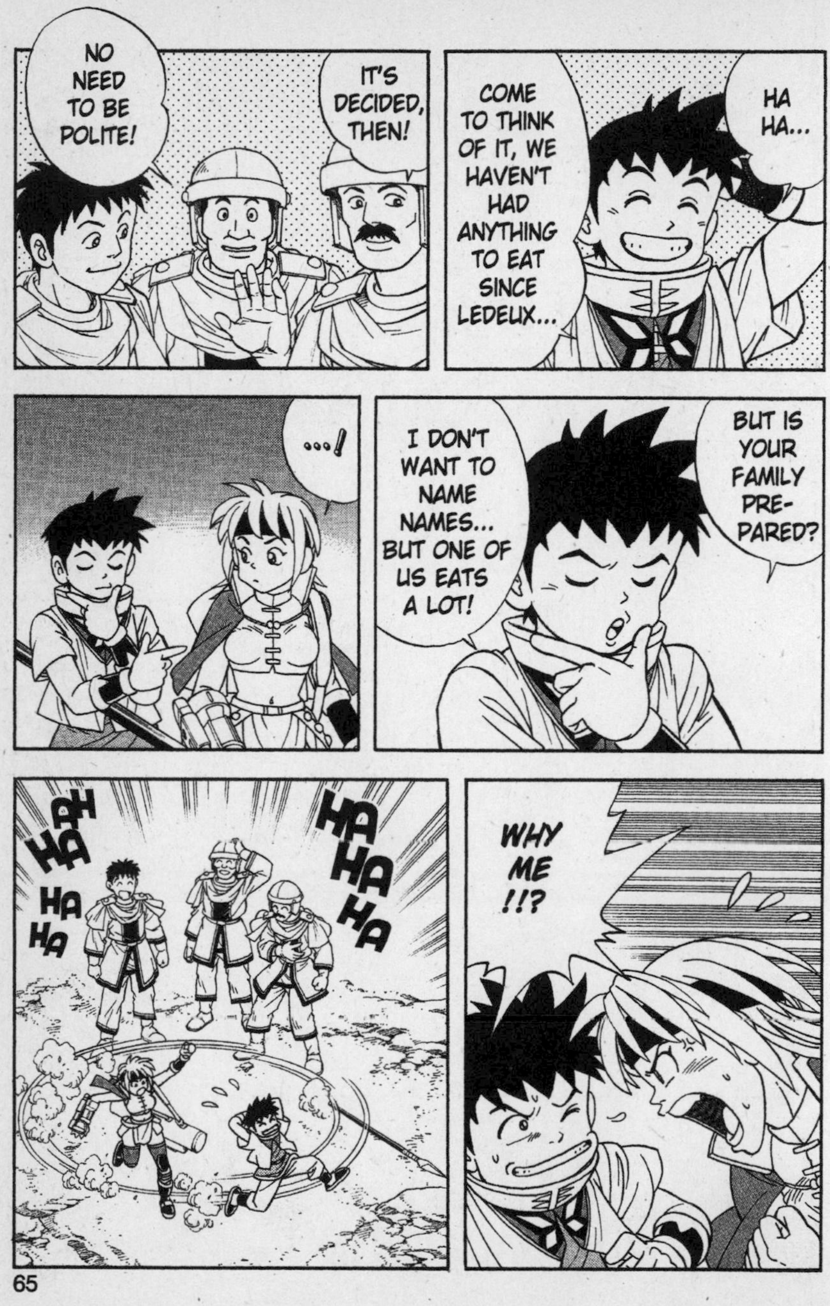
HA HA...
COME TO THINK OF IT, WE HAVEN'T HAD ANYTHING TO EAT SINCE LEDEUX...
IT'S DECIDED, THEN!
NO NEED TO BE POLITE!
BUT IS YOUR FAMILY PRE-PARED?
I DON'T WANT TO NAME NAMES... BUT ONE OF US EATS A LOT!
...!
WHY ME !!?
HA HA HA HA
HA HA
HA HA
HA HA

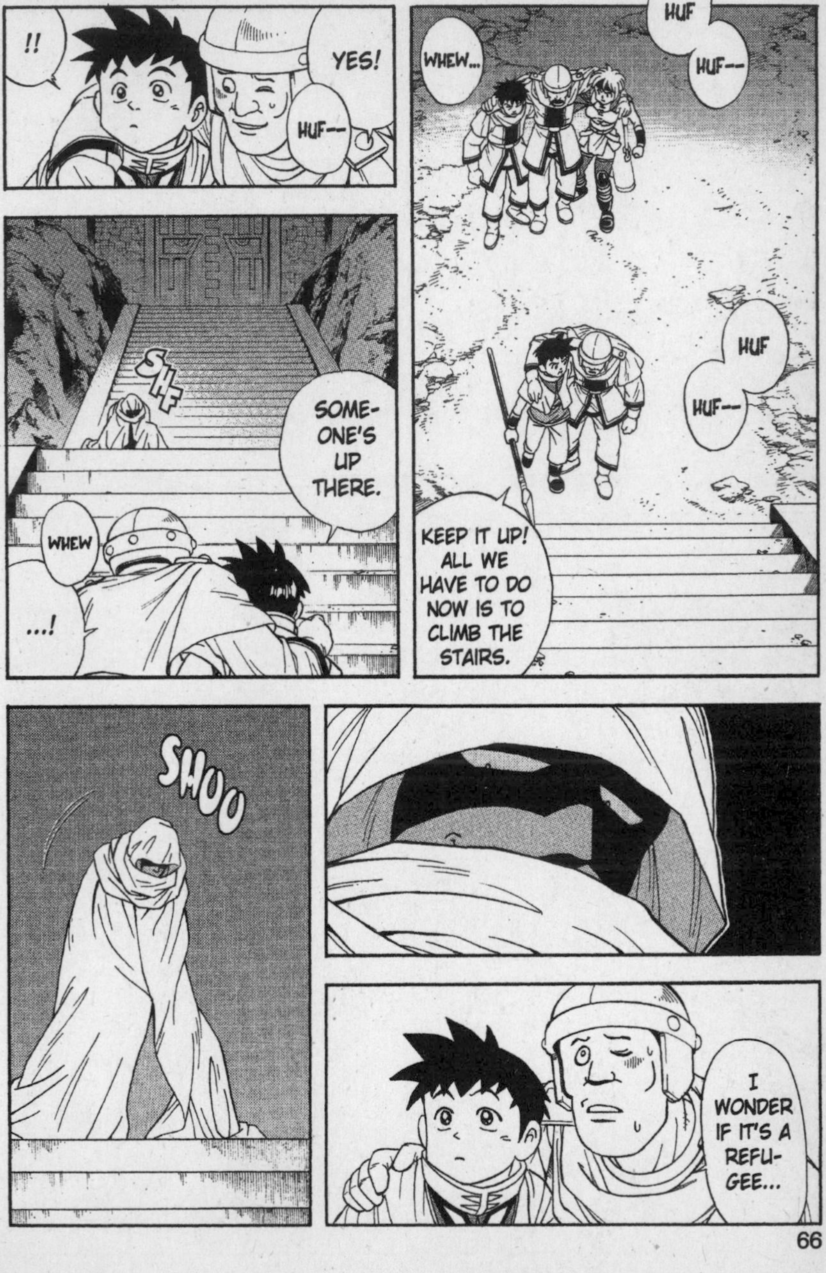
HUF
HUF--
WHEW...
HUF
HUF--
KEEP IT UP! ALL WE HAVE TO DO NOW IS TO CLIMB THE STAIRS.
YES!
HUF--
!!
SHF
SOME-ONE'S UP THERE.
WHEW
...!
I WONDER IF IT'S A REFU-GEE...
SHOO

READ THIS WAY

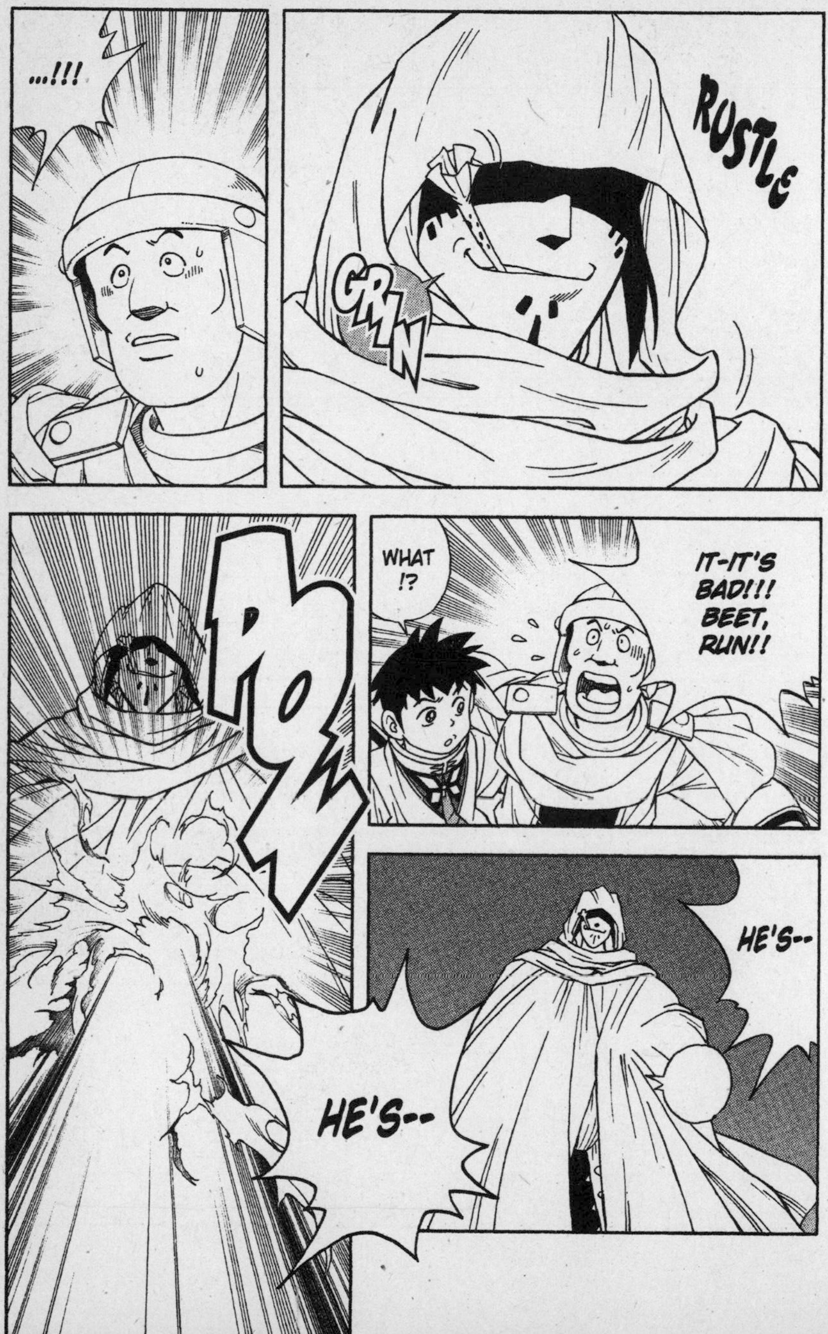
RUSTLE
GRIN
...!!!
IT-IT'S BAD!!! BEET, RUN!!
WHAT !?
HE'S--
HE'S--
POW

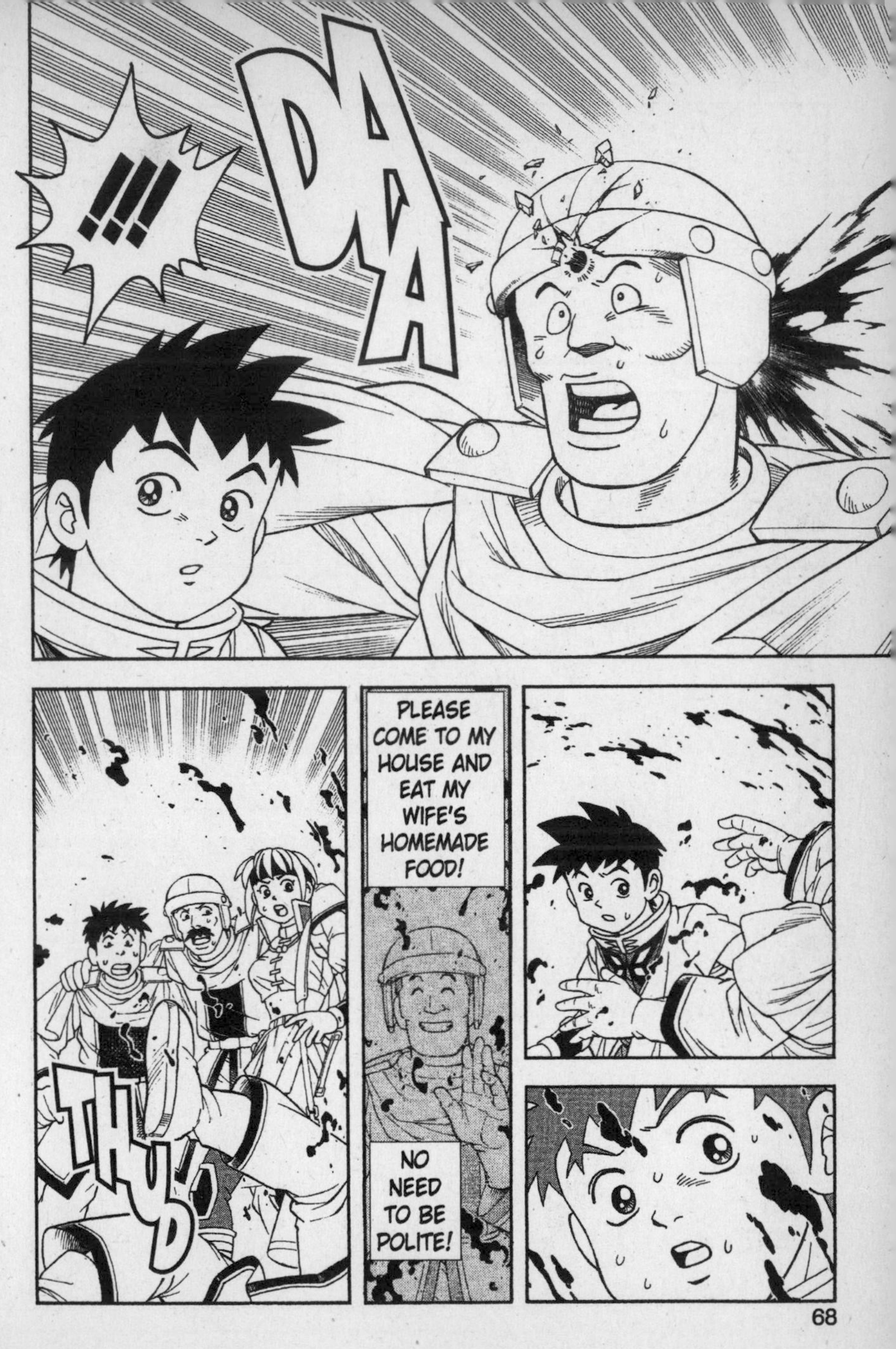
DA
!!!
PLEASE COME TO MY HOUSE AND EAT MY WIFE'S HOMEMADE FOOD!
NO NEED TO BE POLITE!
THUD!

READ THIS WAY

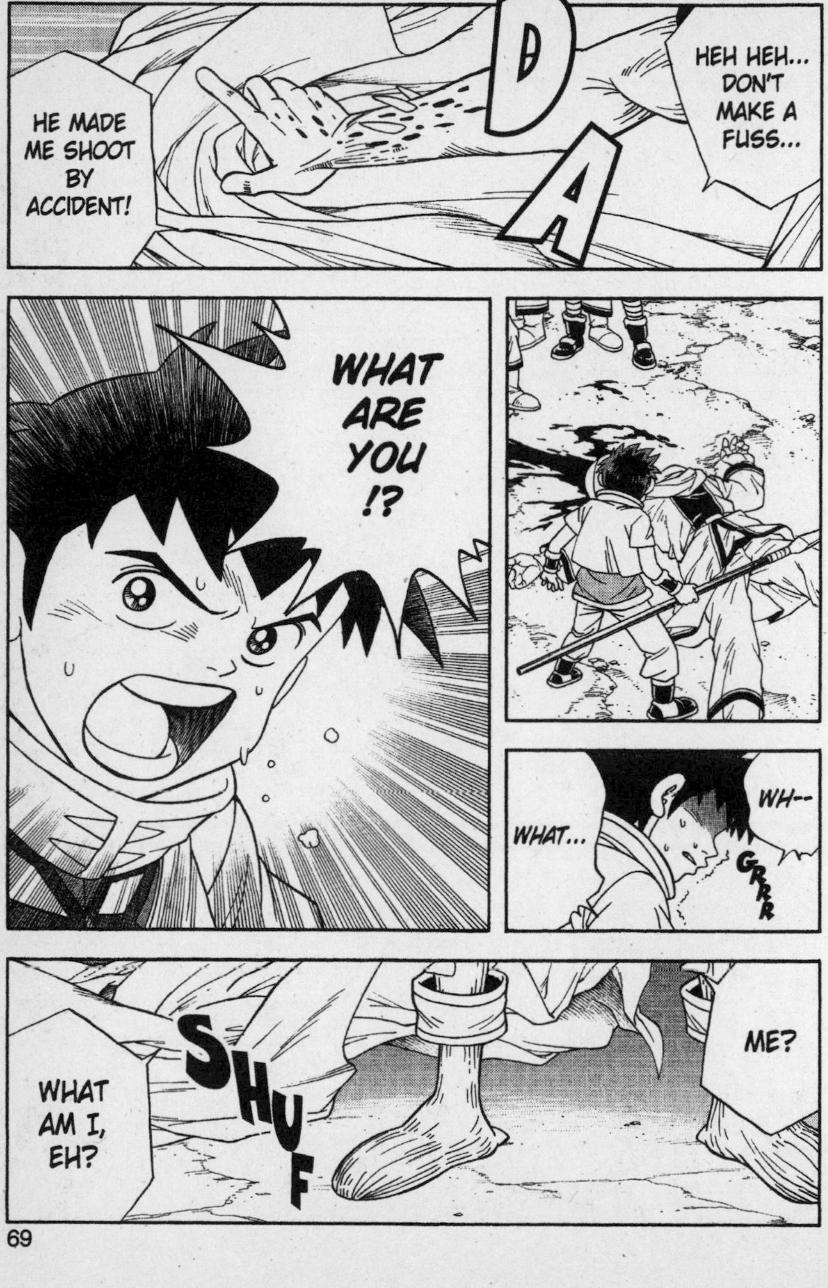

HEH HEH... DON'T MAKE A FUSS...
DA
HE MADE ME SHOOT BY ACCIDENT!
WH-- WHAT...
GRRR
WHAT ARE YOU !?
ME?
SHUF
WHAT AM I, EH?

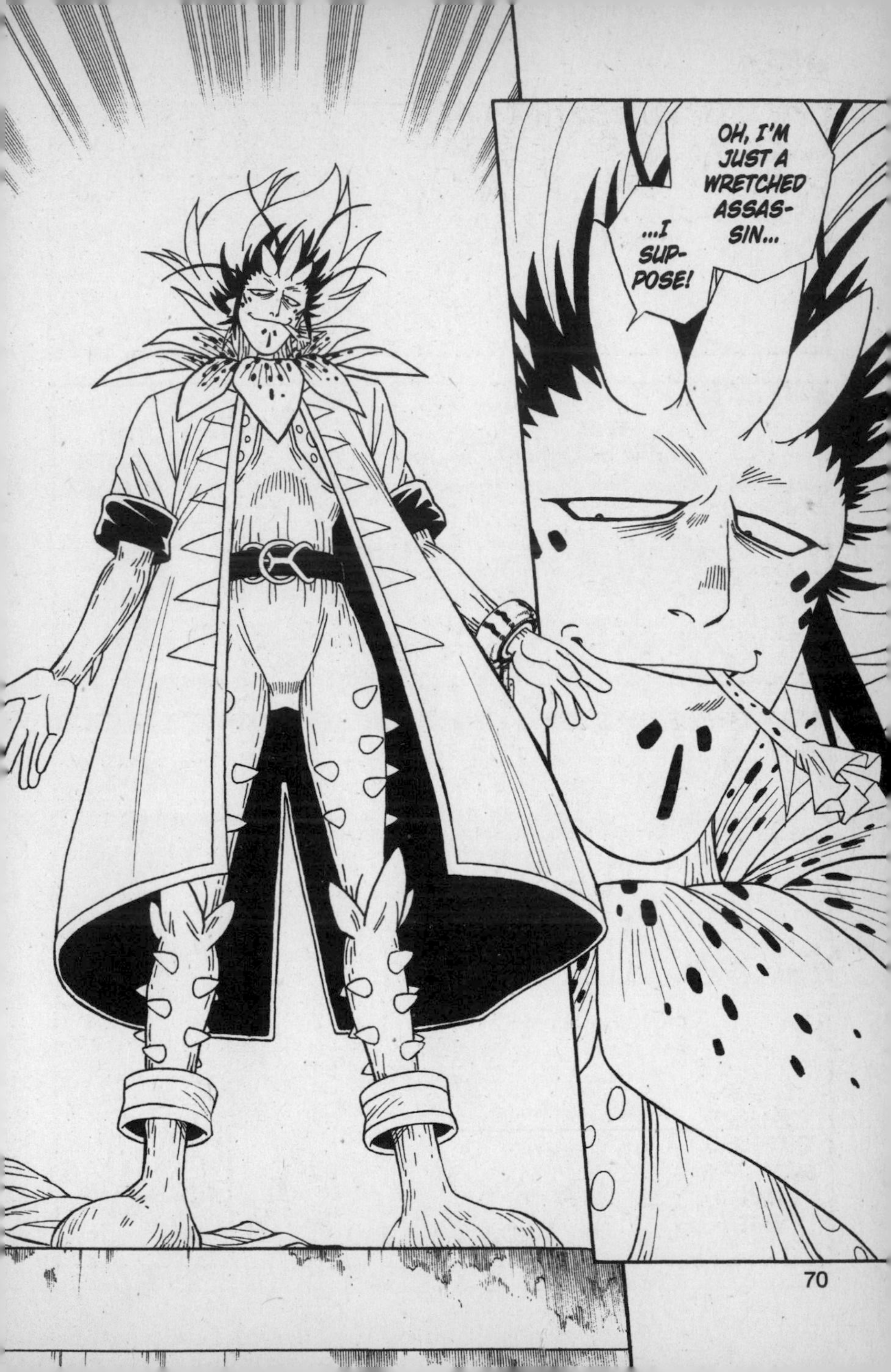
OH, I'M JUST A WRETCHED ASSAS- SIN...
...I SUP- POSE!

READ THIS WAY

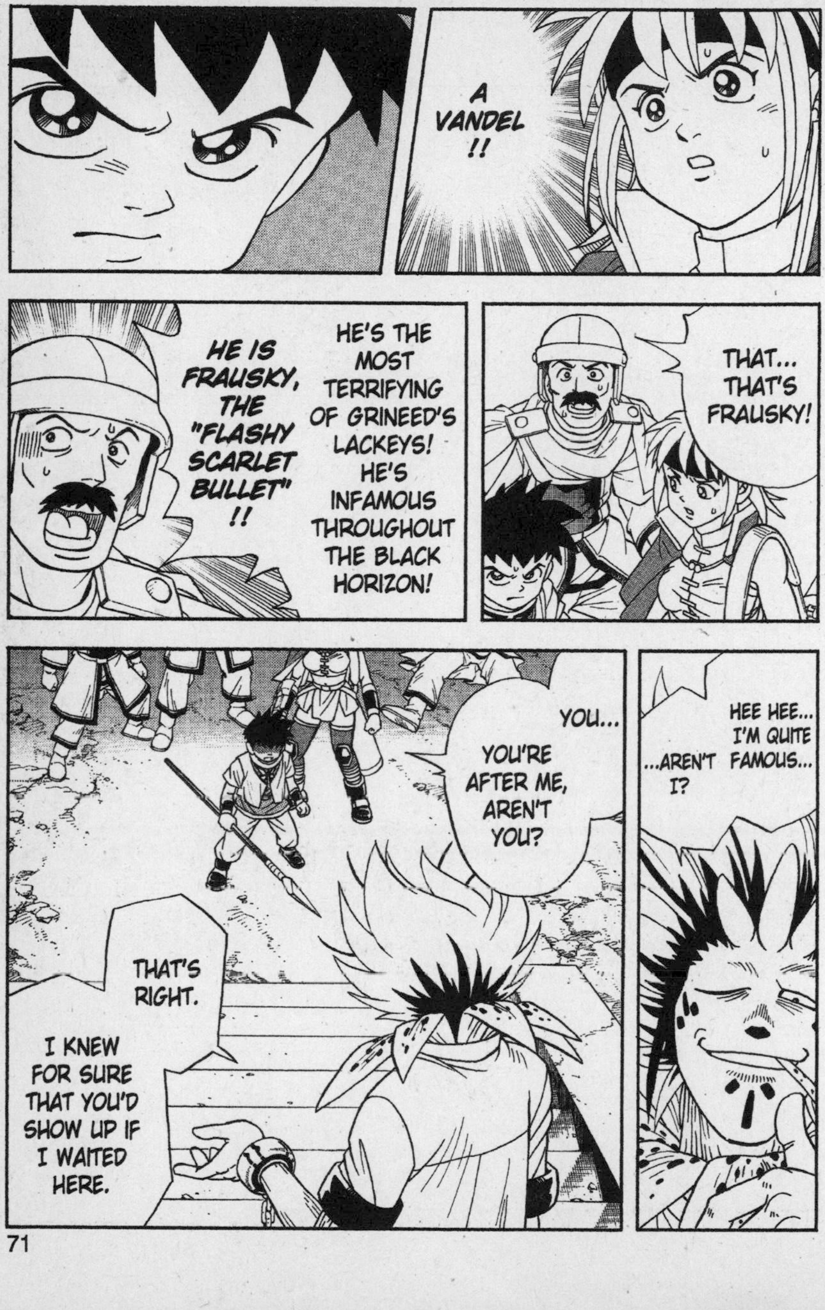
A VANDEL !!
THAT... THAT'S FRAUSKY!
HE'S THE MOST TERRIFYING OF GRINEED'S LACKEYS! HE'S INFAMOUS THROUGHOUT THE BLACK HORIZON!
HE IS FRAUSKY, THE "FLASHY SCARLET BULLET" !!
HEE HEE... I'M QUITE FAMOUS...
...AREN'T I?
YOU... YOU'RE AFTER ME, AREN'T YOU?
THAT'S RIGHT. I KNEW FOR SURE THAT YOU'D SHOW UP IF I WAITED HERE.

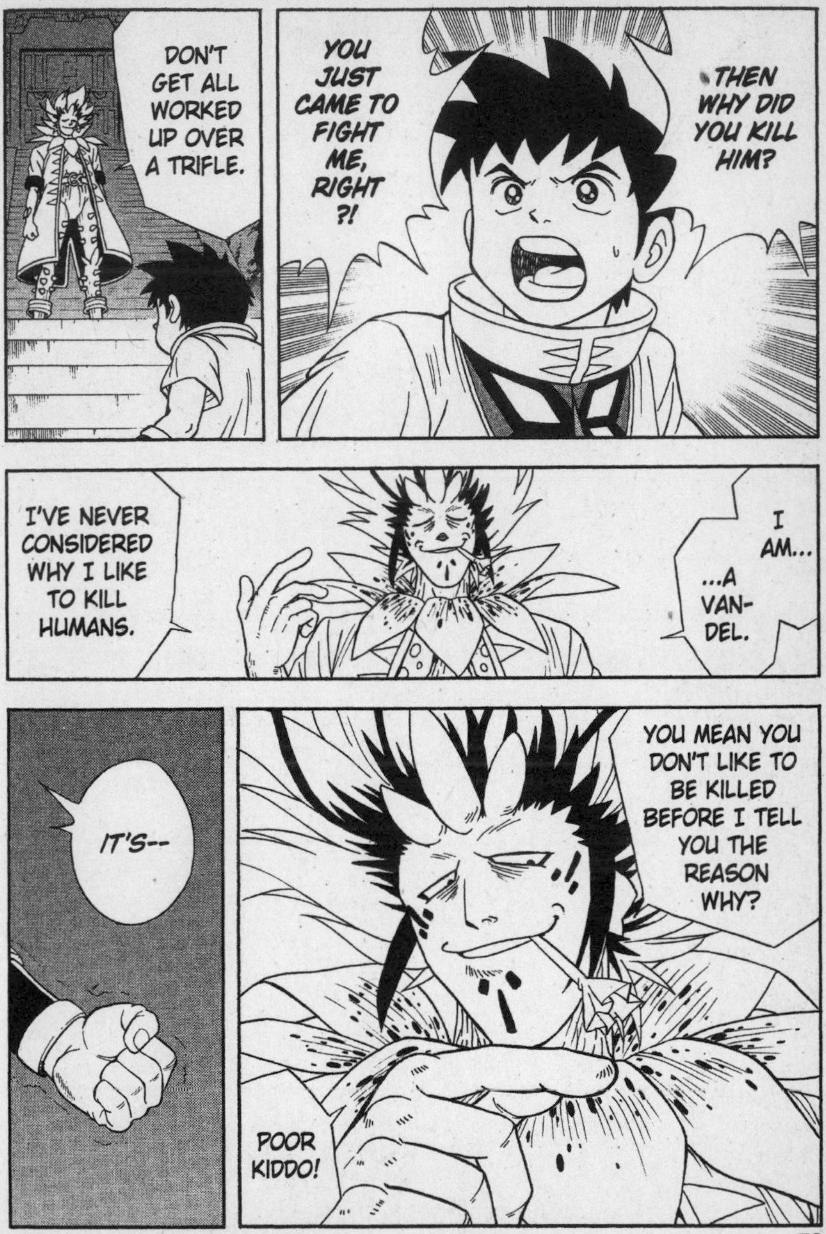
THEN WHY DID YOU KILL HIM?
YOU JUST CAME TO FIGHT ME, RIGHT ?!
DON'T GET ALL WORKED UP OVER A TRIFLE.
I AM...
...A VAN-DEL.
I'VE NEVER CONSIDERED WHY I LIKE TO KILL HUMANS.
YOU MEAN YOU DON'T LIKE TO BE KILLED BEFORE I TELL YOU THE REASON WHY?
POOR KIDDO!
IT'S--

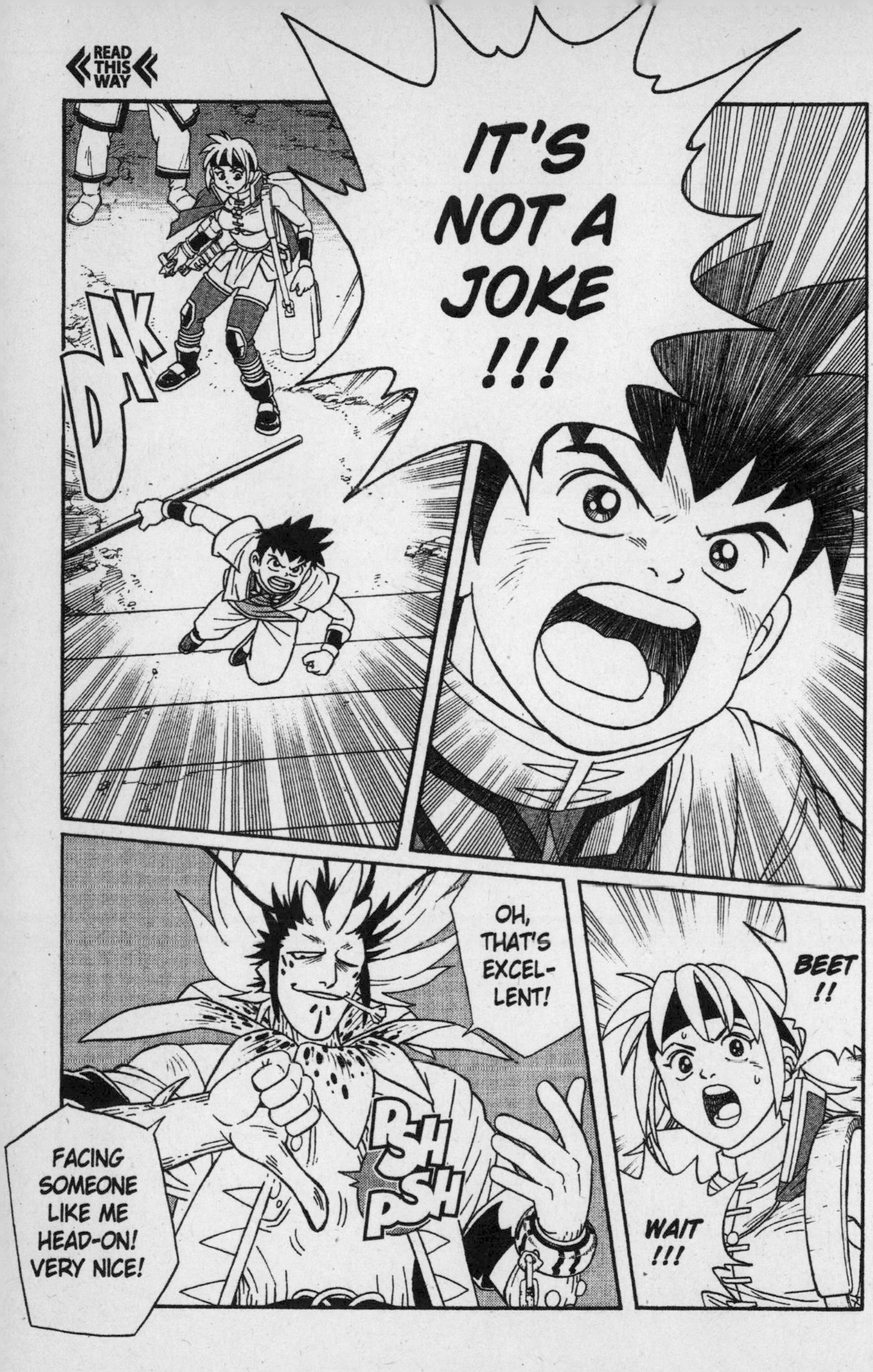
READ THIS WAY
IT'S NOT A JOKE !!!
DAK
BEET !!
WAIT !!!
OH, THAT'S EXCEL-LENT!
PSH PSH
FACING SOMEONE LIKE ME HEAD-ON! VERY NICE!

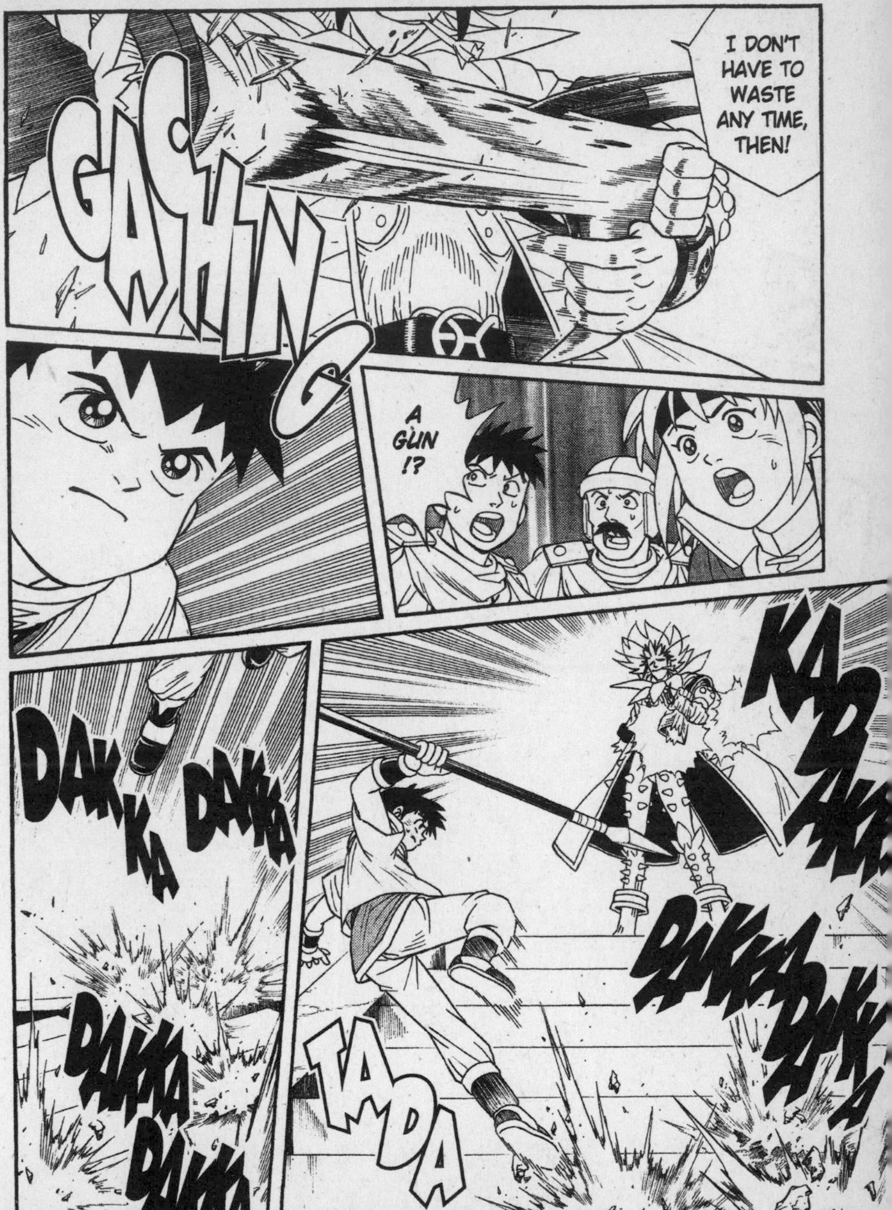
I DON'T HAVE TO WASTE ANY TIME, THEN!
GACHING
A GUN !?
TADA

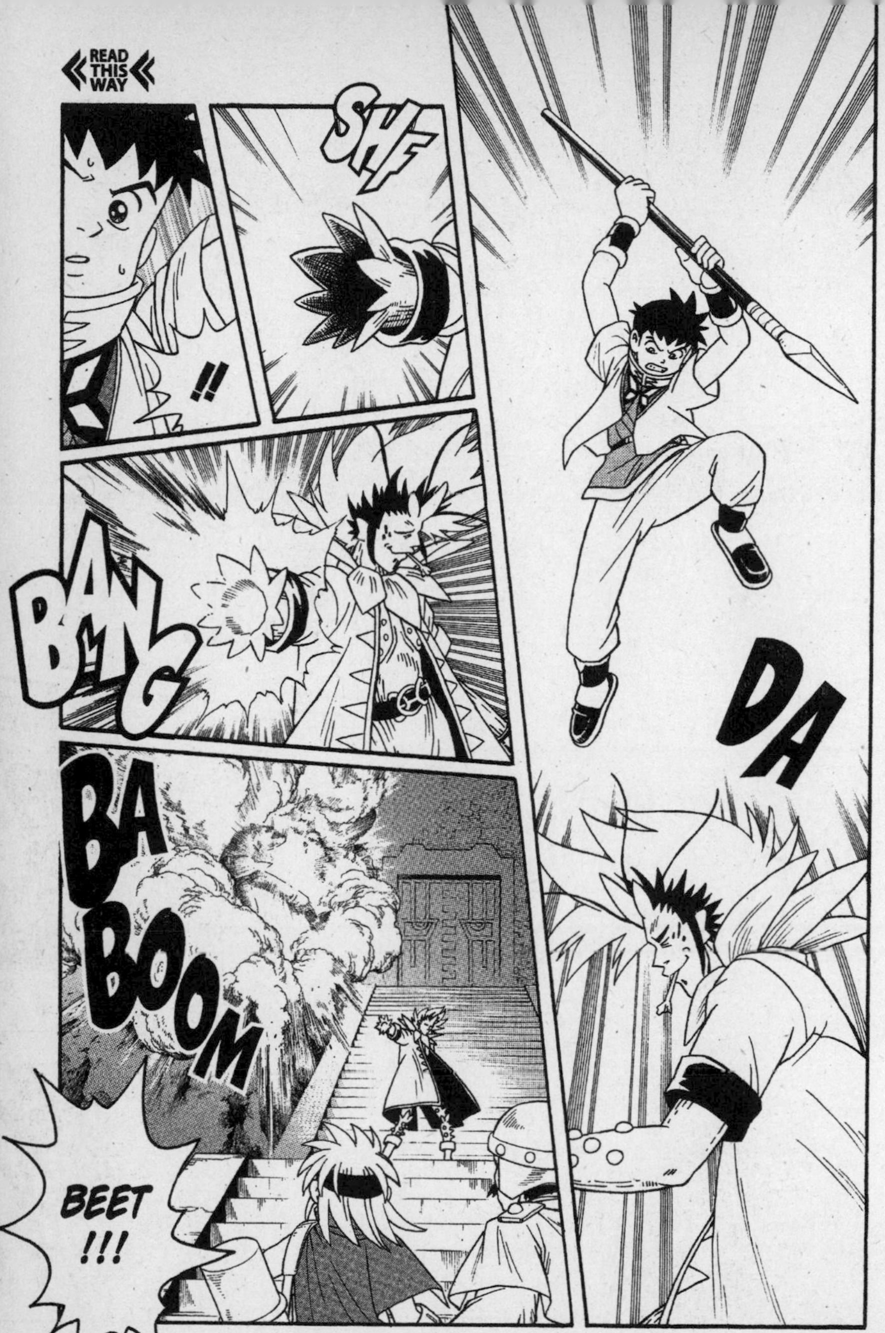
READ THIS WAY
DA
SHF
!!
BANG
BA BOOM
BEET !!!

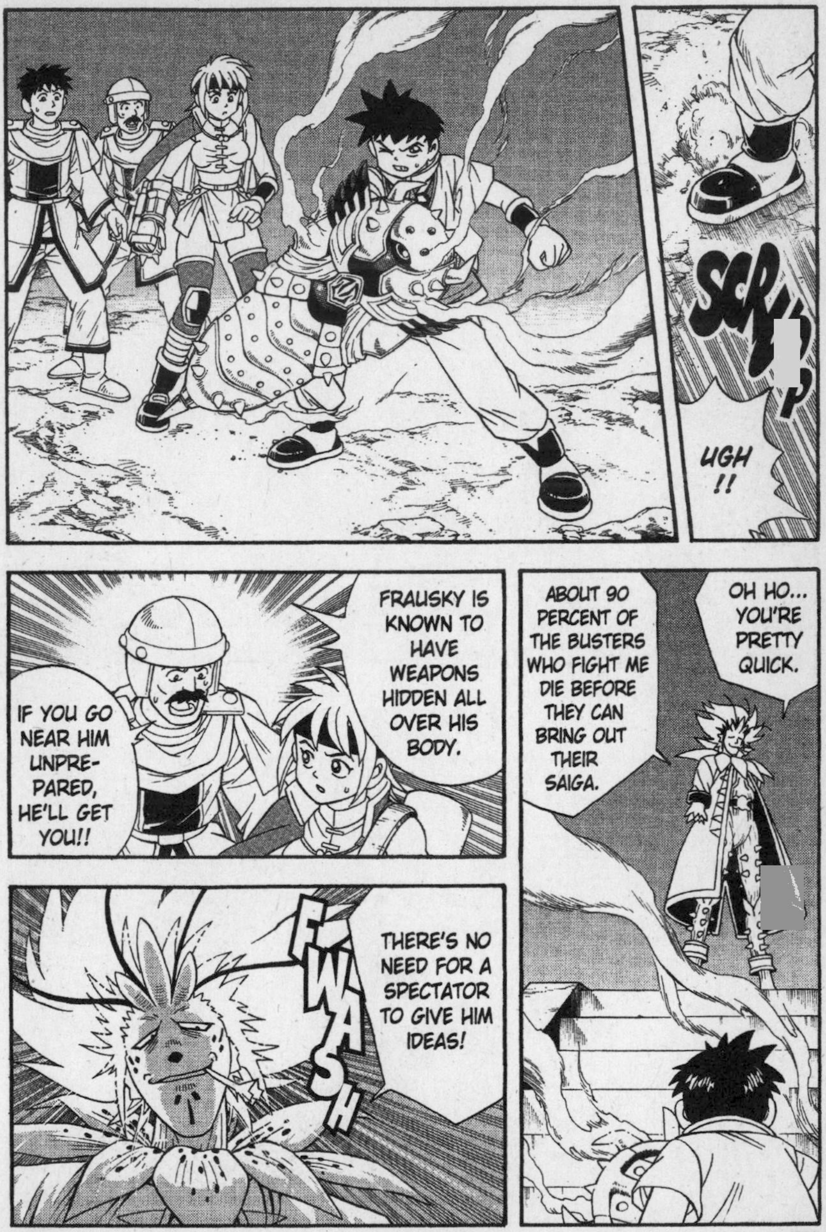
UGH !!
OH HO... YOU'RE PRETTY QUICK.
ABOUT 90 PERCENT OF THE BUSTERS WHO FIGHT ME DIE BEFORE THEY CAN BRING OUT THEIR SAIGA.
FRAUSKY IS KNOWN TO HAVE WEAPONS HIDDEN ALL OVER HIS BODY.
IF YOU GO NEAR HIM UNPRE-PARED, HE'LL GET YOU!!
FWASH
THERE'S NO NEED FOR A SPECTATOR TO GIVE HIM IDEAS!

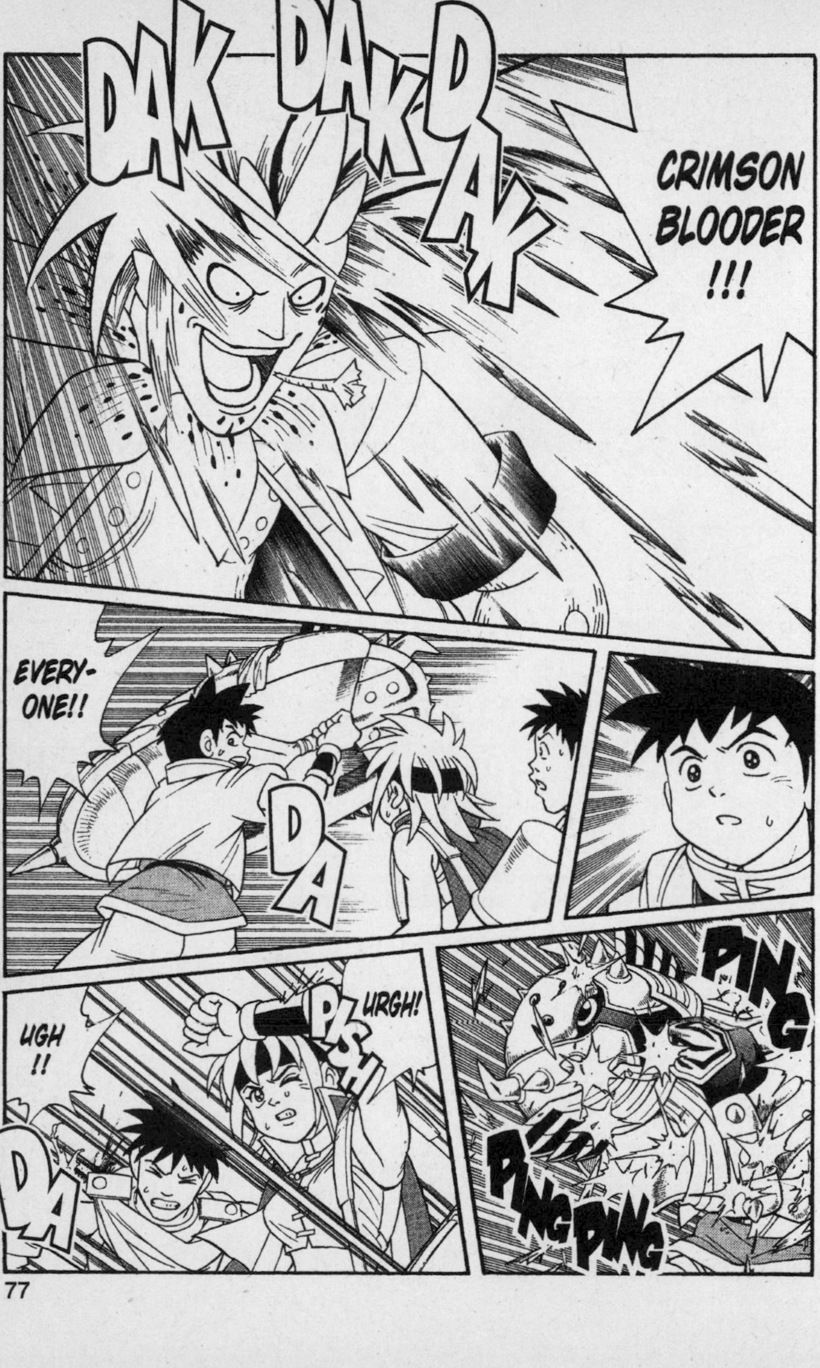
CRIMSON BLOODER !!!
DAK DAK DAK
EVERY-ONE!!
DA
PING
PING PING
URGH!
PISH
UGH !!
DA

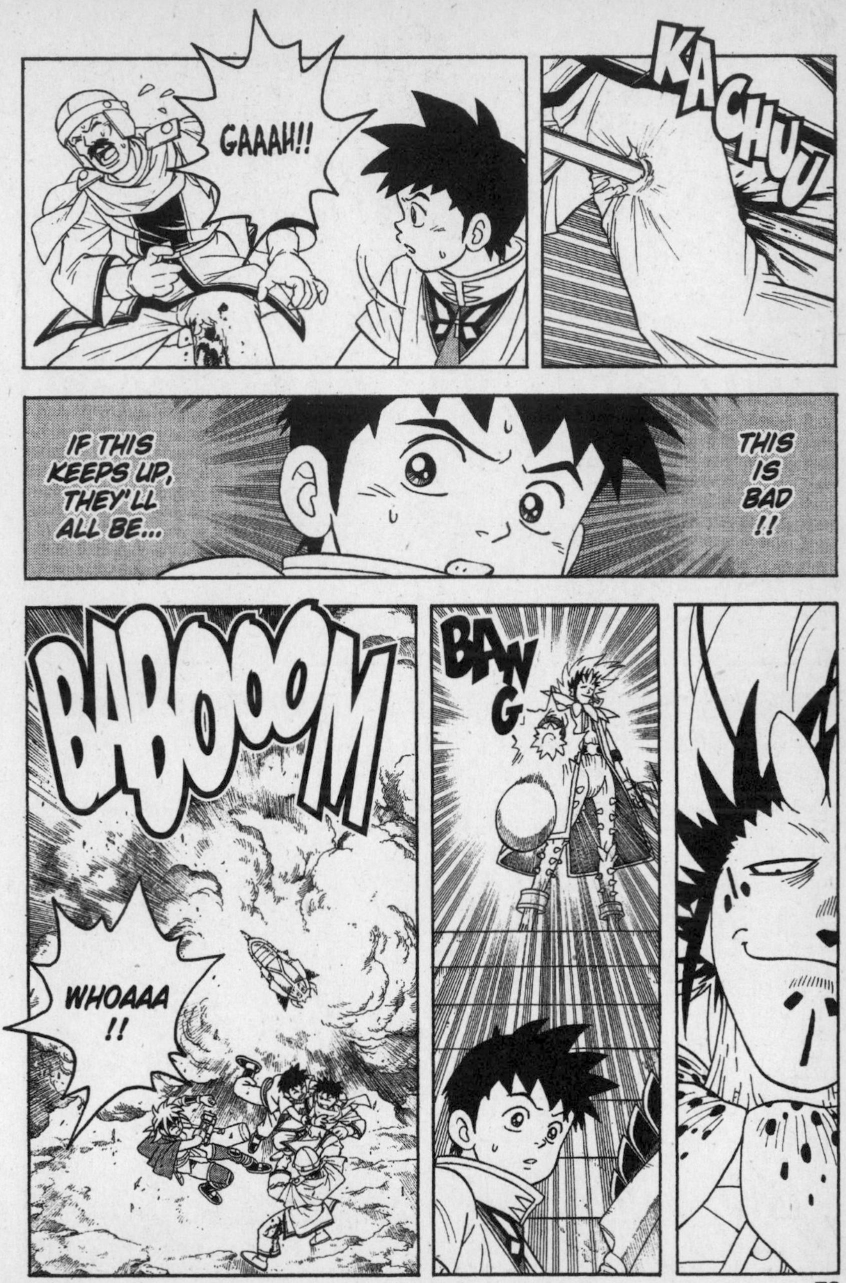
KACHUU
GAAAH!!
THIS IS BAD !!
IF THIS KEEPS UP, THEY'LL ALL BE...
BANG
BABOOOM
WHOAAA !!

READ THIS WAY

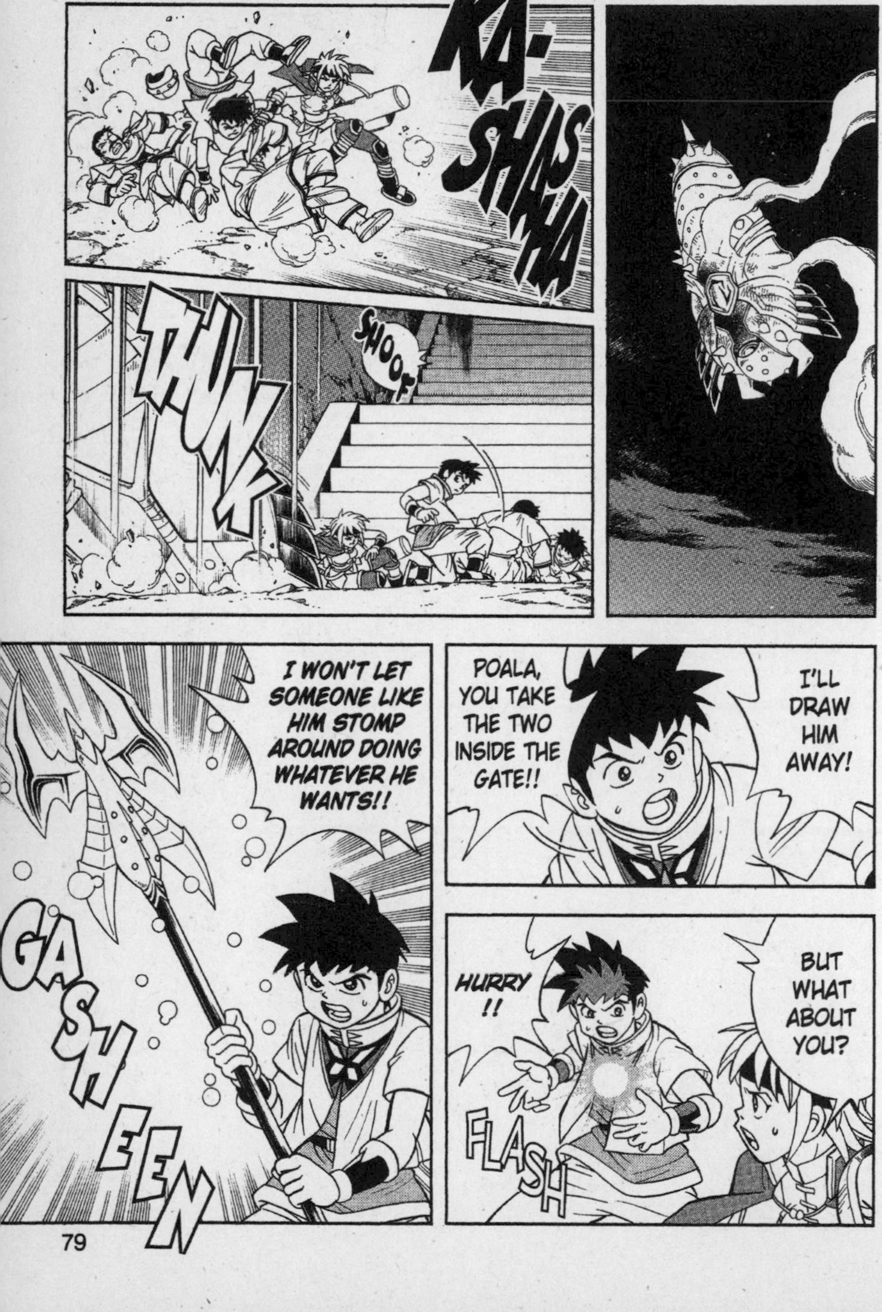
KA-SHASHA
THUNK
SHOOF
I'LL DRAW HIM AWAY!
POALA, YOU TAKE THE TWO INSIDE THE GATE!!
BUT WHAT ABOUT YOU?
HURRY!!
FLASH
I WON'T LET SOMEONE LIKE HIM STOMP AROUND DOING WHATEVER HE WANTS!!
GASHEEN

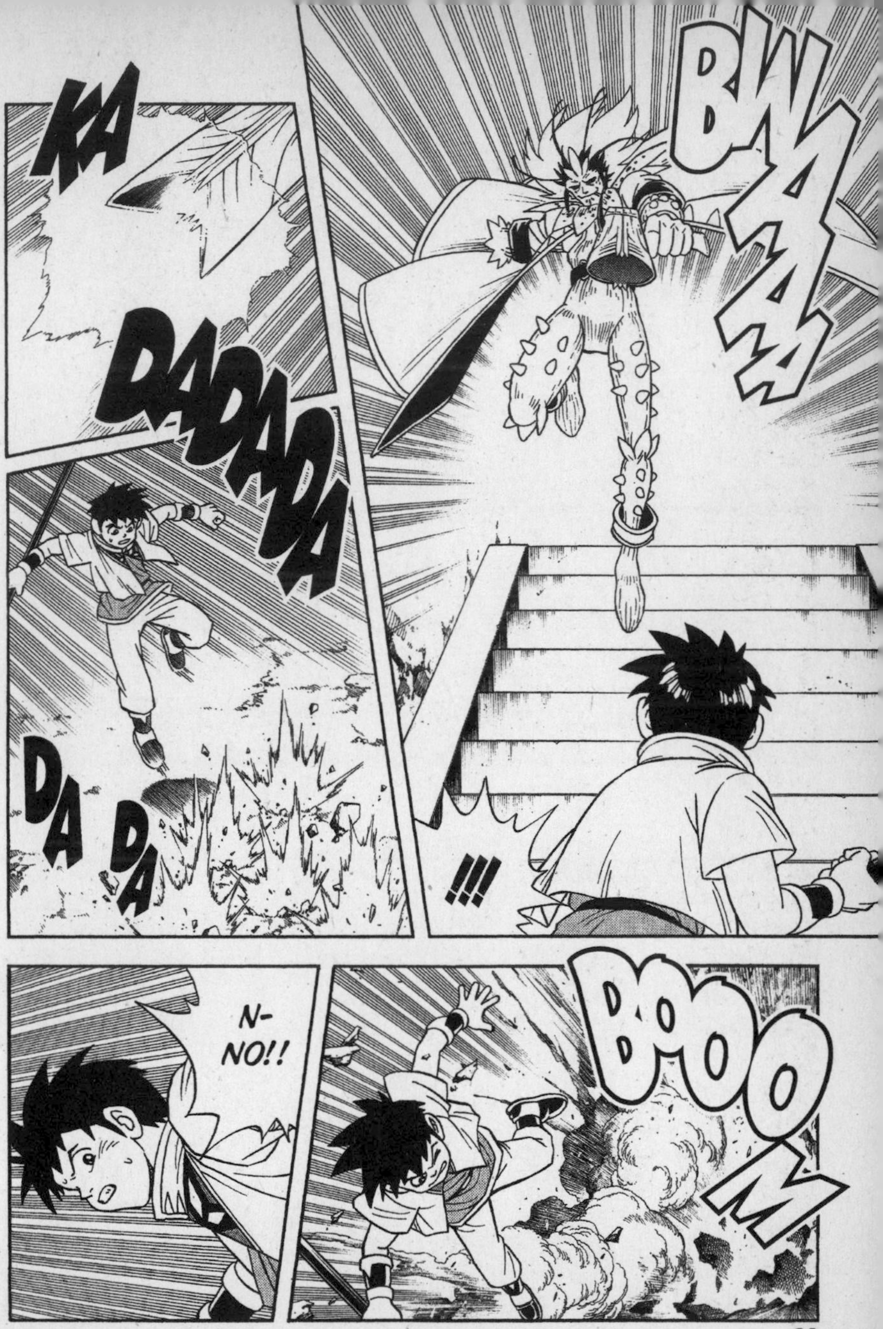
BWA
!!!!
KA
DADADADA
DA DA DA
BOOOM
N-
NO!!

READ THIS WAY

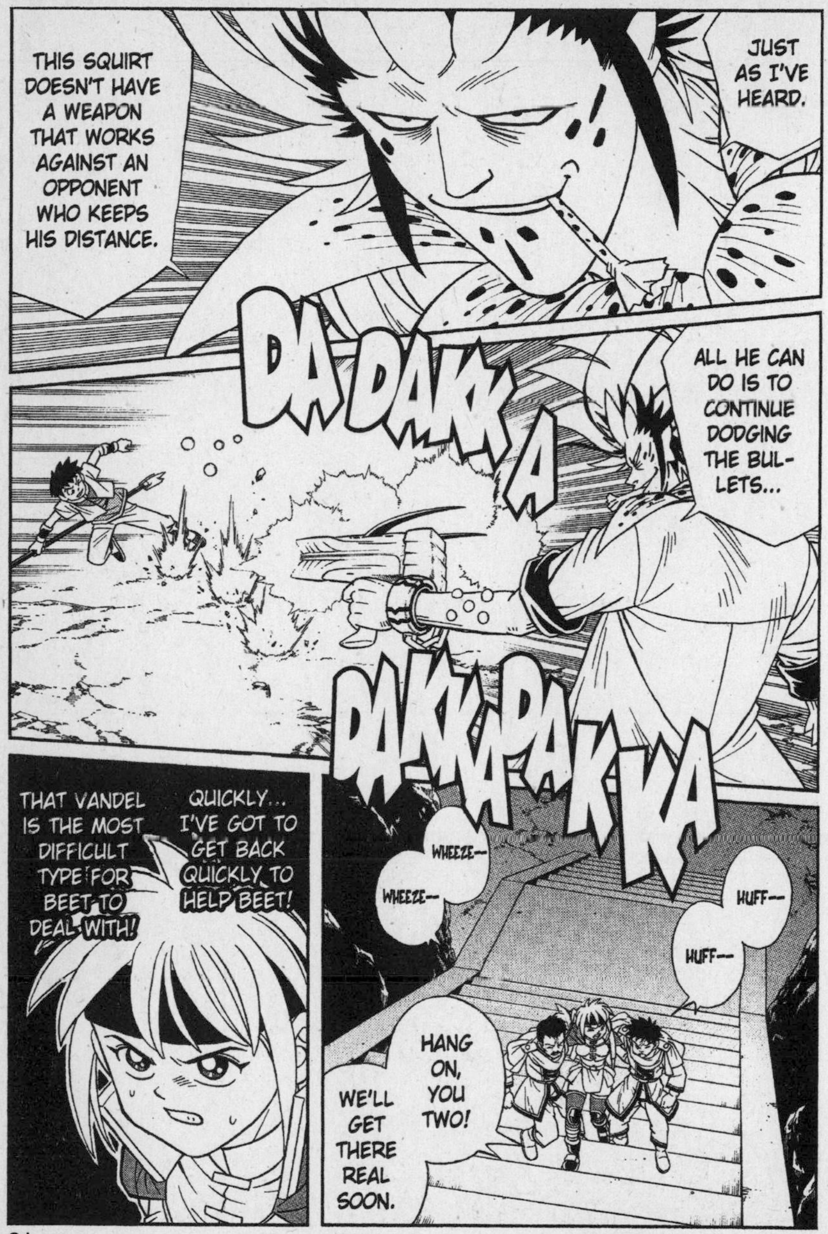
JUST AS I'VE HEARD.
THIS SQUIRT DOESN'T HAVE A WEAPON THAT WORKS AGAINST AN OPPONENT WHO KEEPS HIS DISTANCE.
DA DAKKA
ALL HE CAN DO IS TO CONTINUE DODGING THE BUL-LETS...
DA-KKA-DA-K-KA
HUFF--
HUFF--
WHEEZE--
WHEEZE--
HANG ON, YOU TWO!
WE'LL GET THERE REAL SOON.
QUICKLY... I'VE GOT TO GET BACK QUICKLY TO HELP BEET!
THAT VANDEL IS THE MOST DIFFICULT TYPE FOR BEET TO DEAL WITH!

DADAK

ABOUT TIME.

KA-CHAK

CHING

WHOA!!

AH!

thuck

TAK

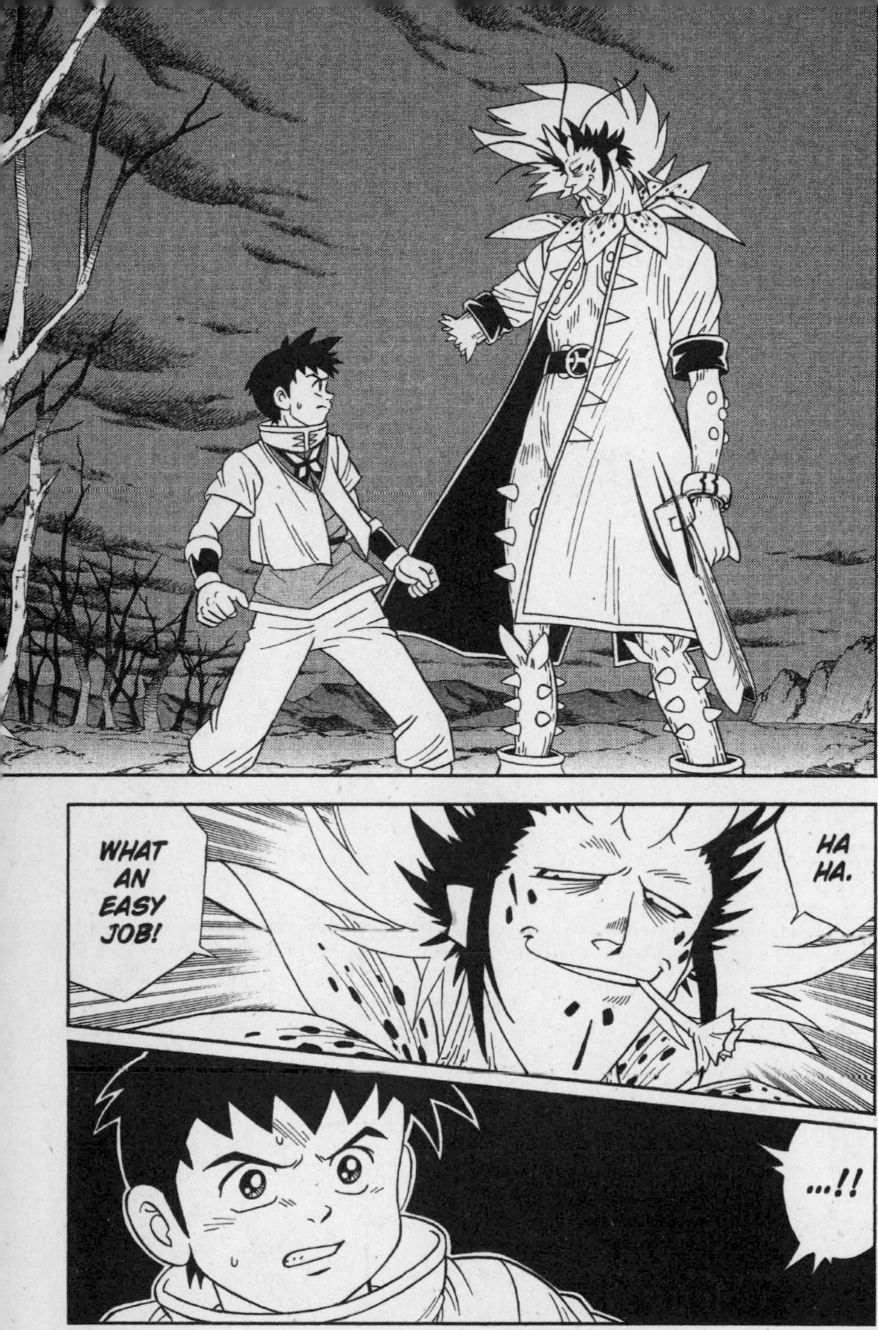
HA HA.
WHAT AN EASY JOB!
...!!

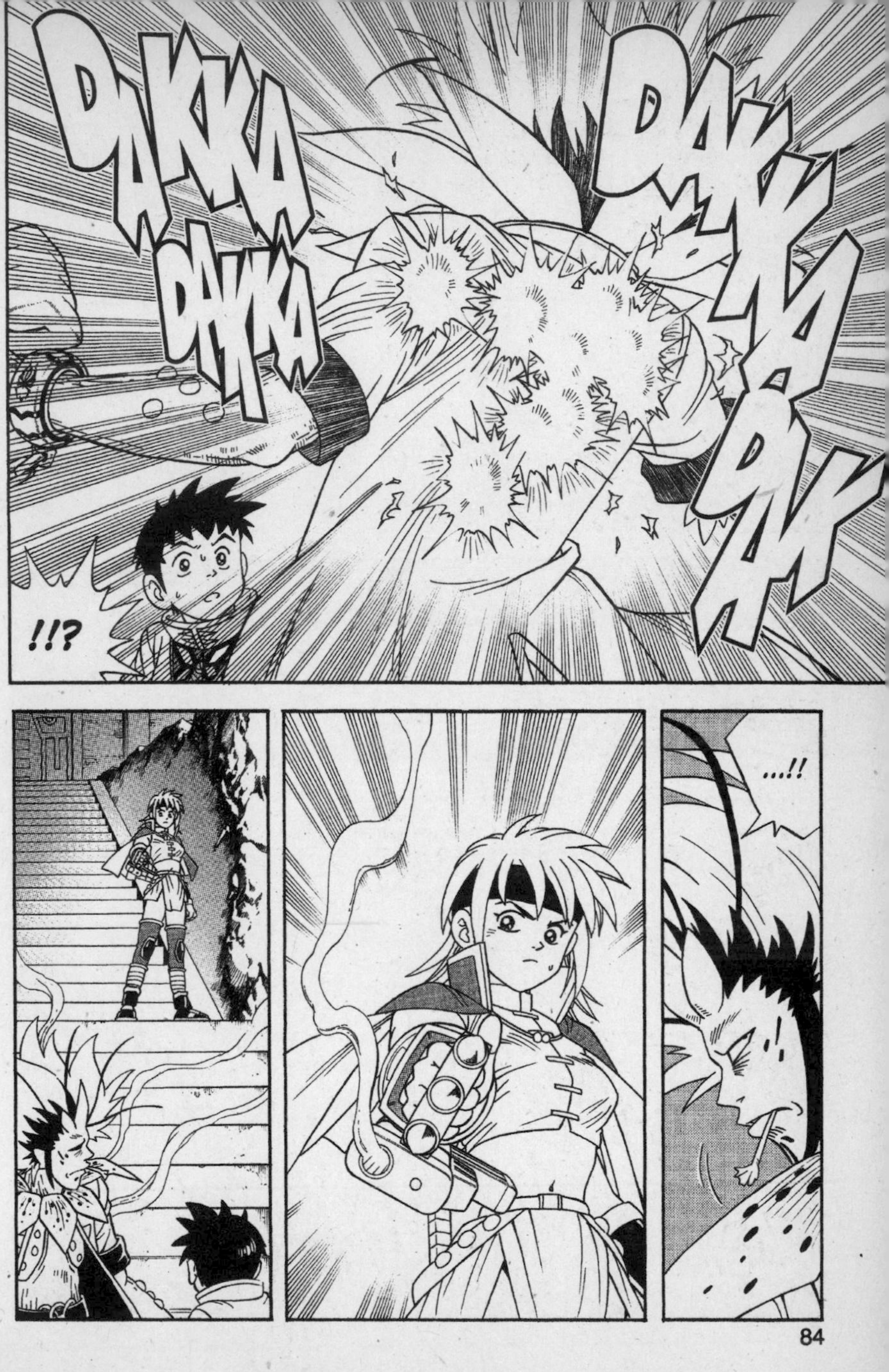
DAKKA DAKKA
DAKKA DAKKA
!!?
...!!

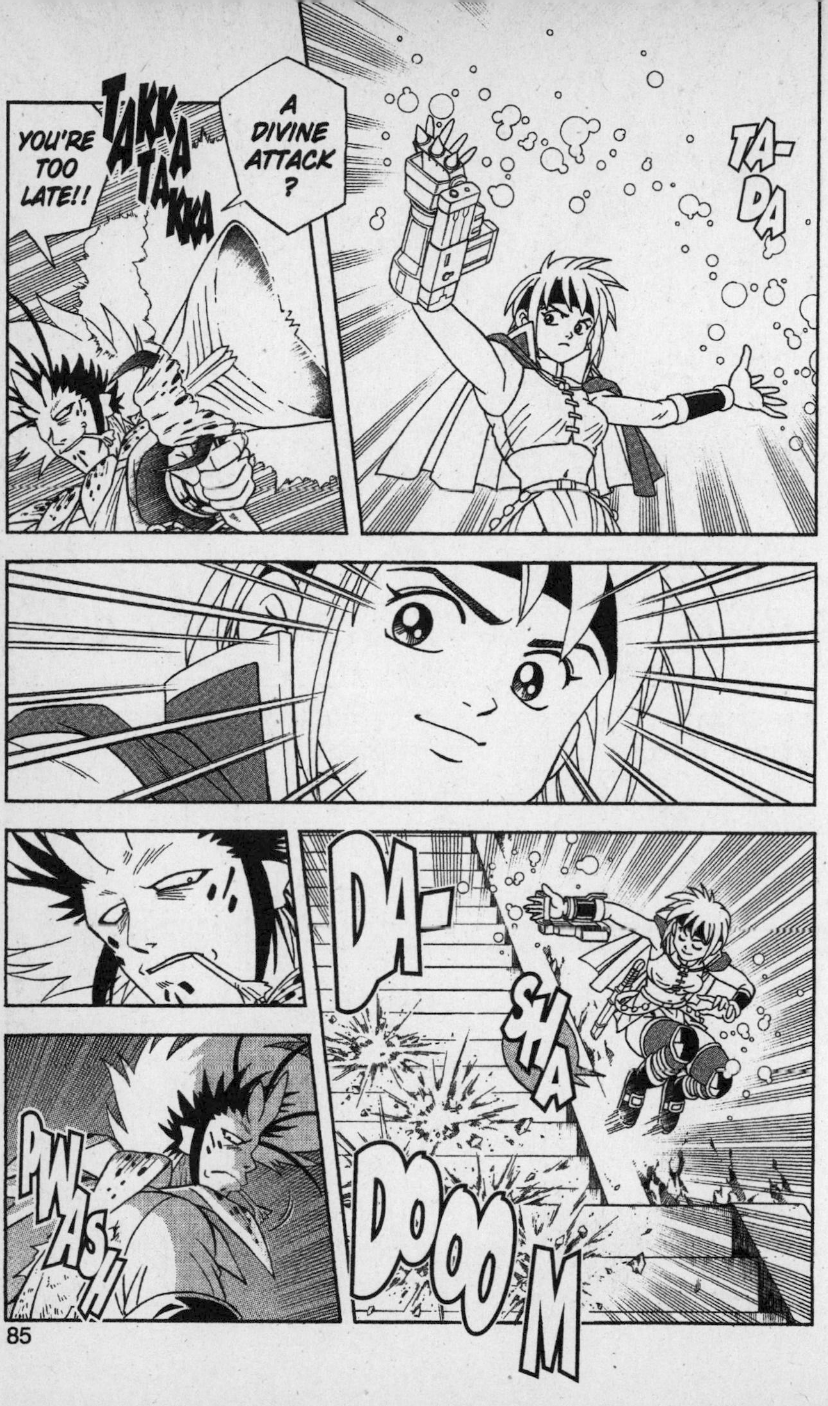
TA-DA
A DIVINE ATTACK?
TAKKA TAKKA
YOU'RE TOO LATE!!
DA-SHA
DOOOM
PWASH

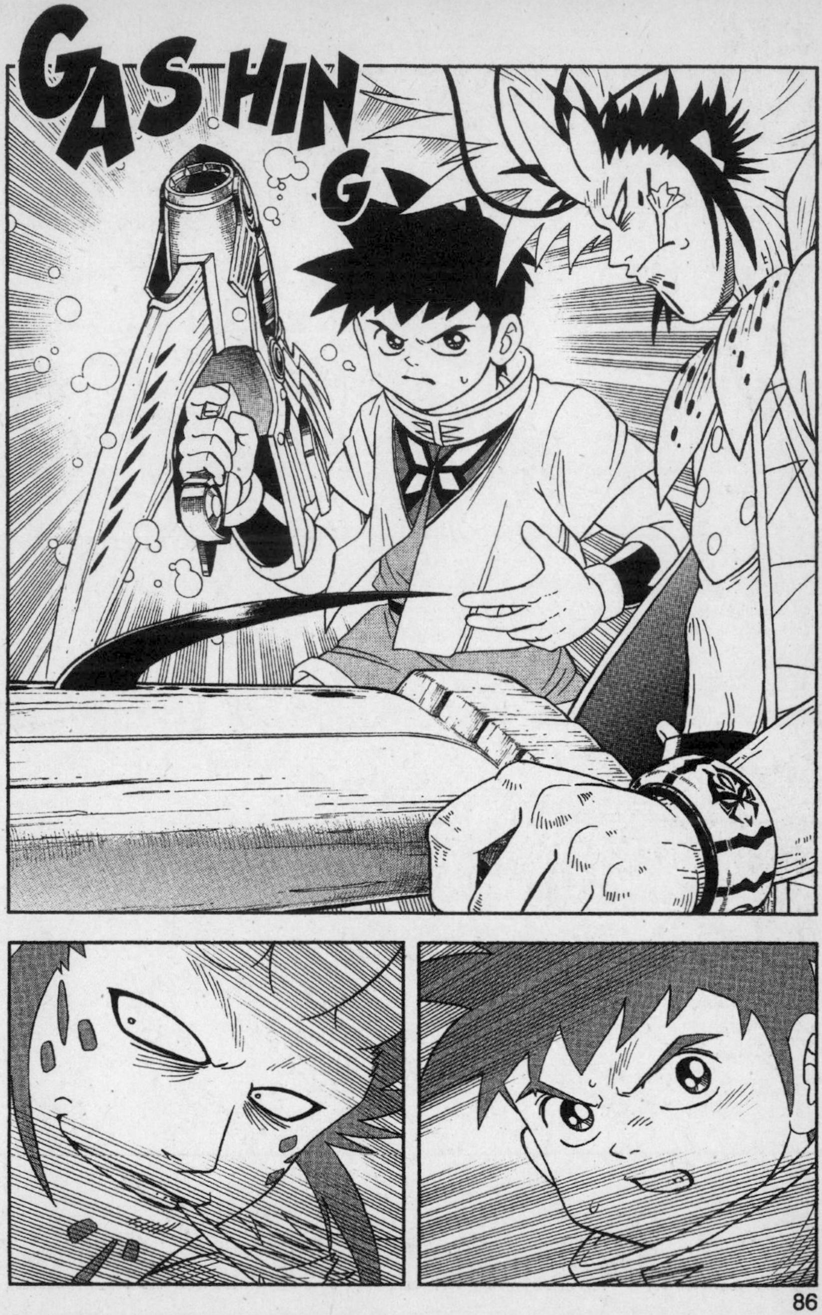
GASHING

READ THIS WAY

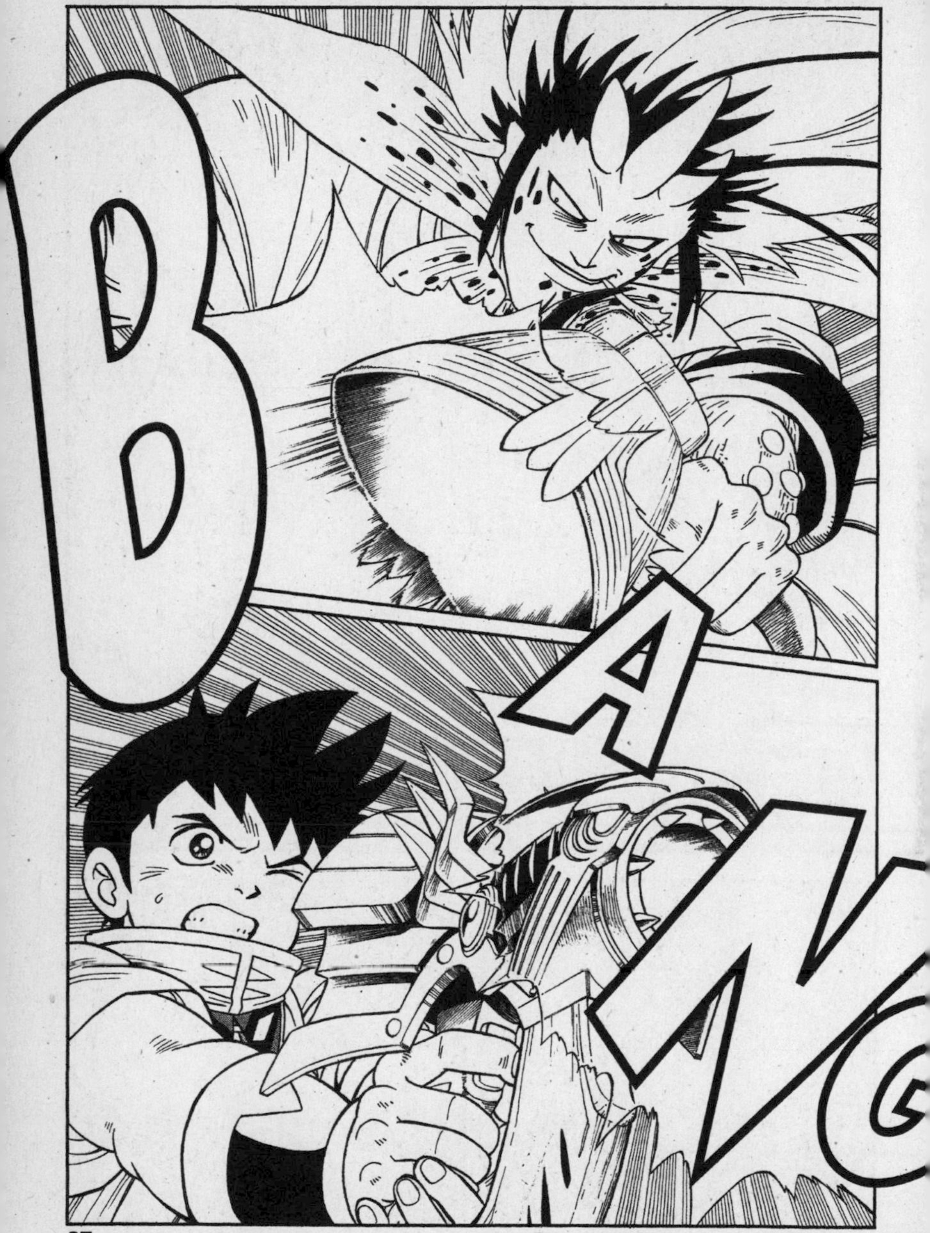
BANG

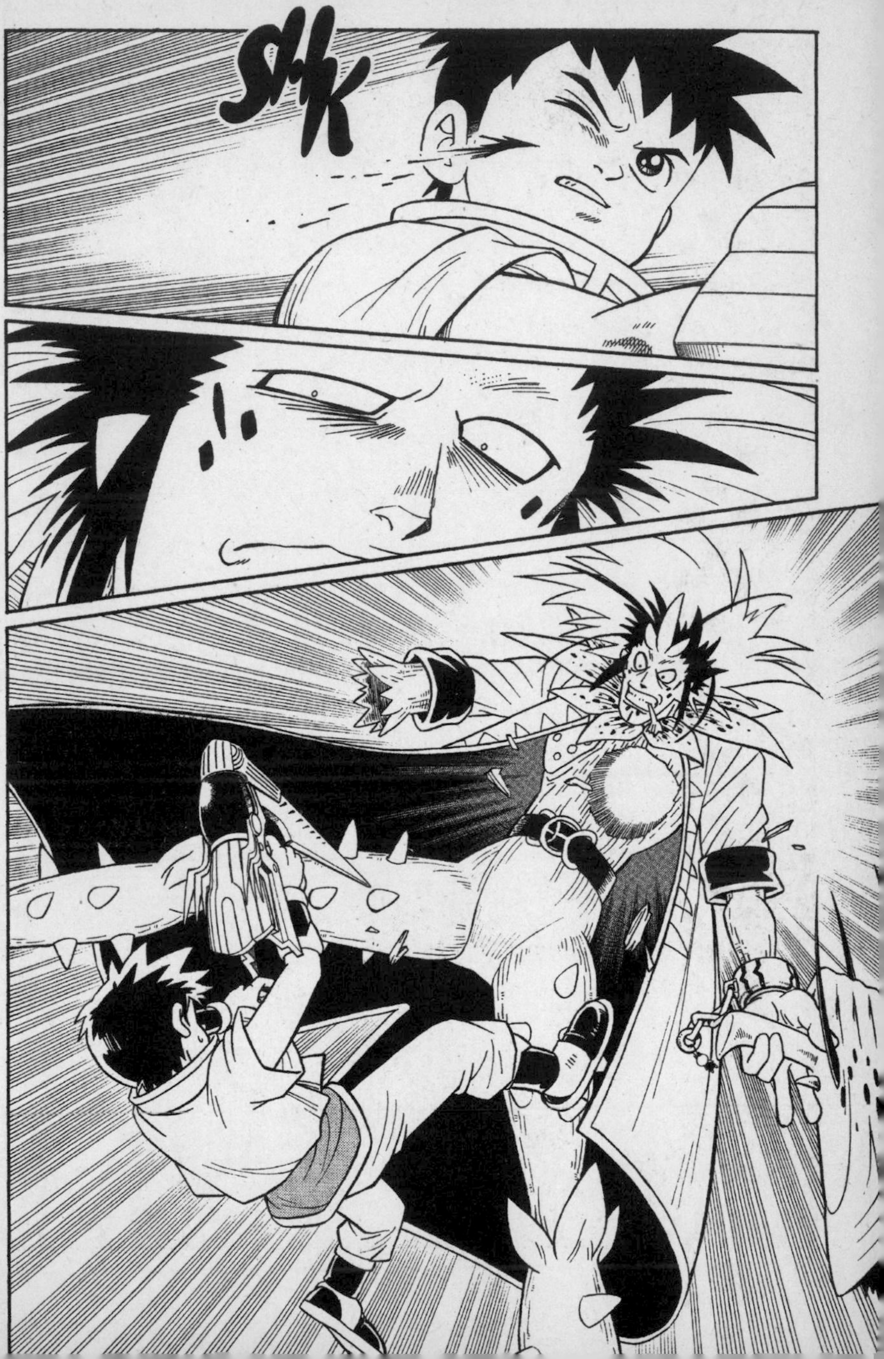
SHK

READ THIS WAY

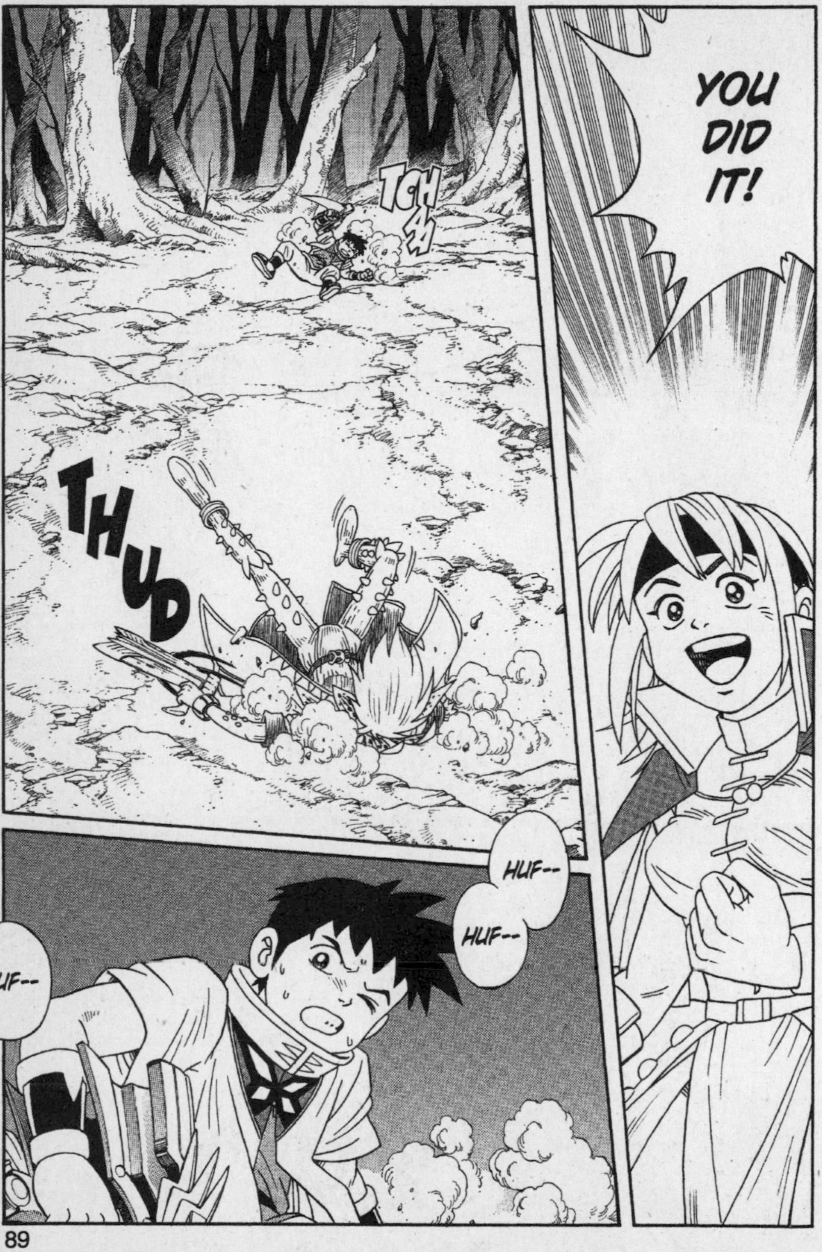
YOU DID IT!
TCH
THUD
HUF--
HUF--
HUF--

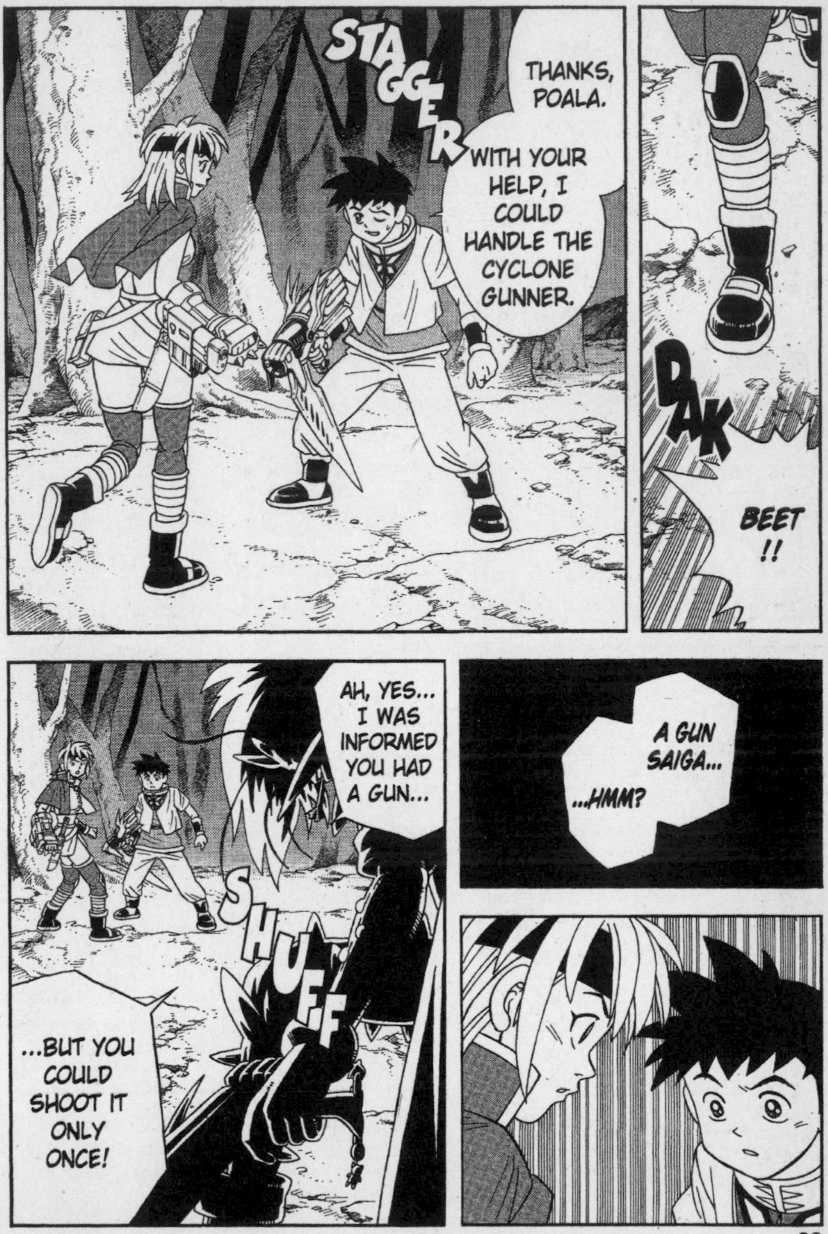
DAK
BEET !!
STAGGER
THANKS, POALA.
WITH YOUR HELP, I COULD HANDLE THE CYCLONE GUNNER.
A GUN SAIGA...
...HMM?
AH, YES... I WAS INFORMED YOU HAD A GUN...
SHUFF
...BUT YOU COULD SHOOT IT ONLY ONCE!

READ THIS WAY

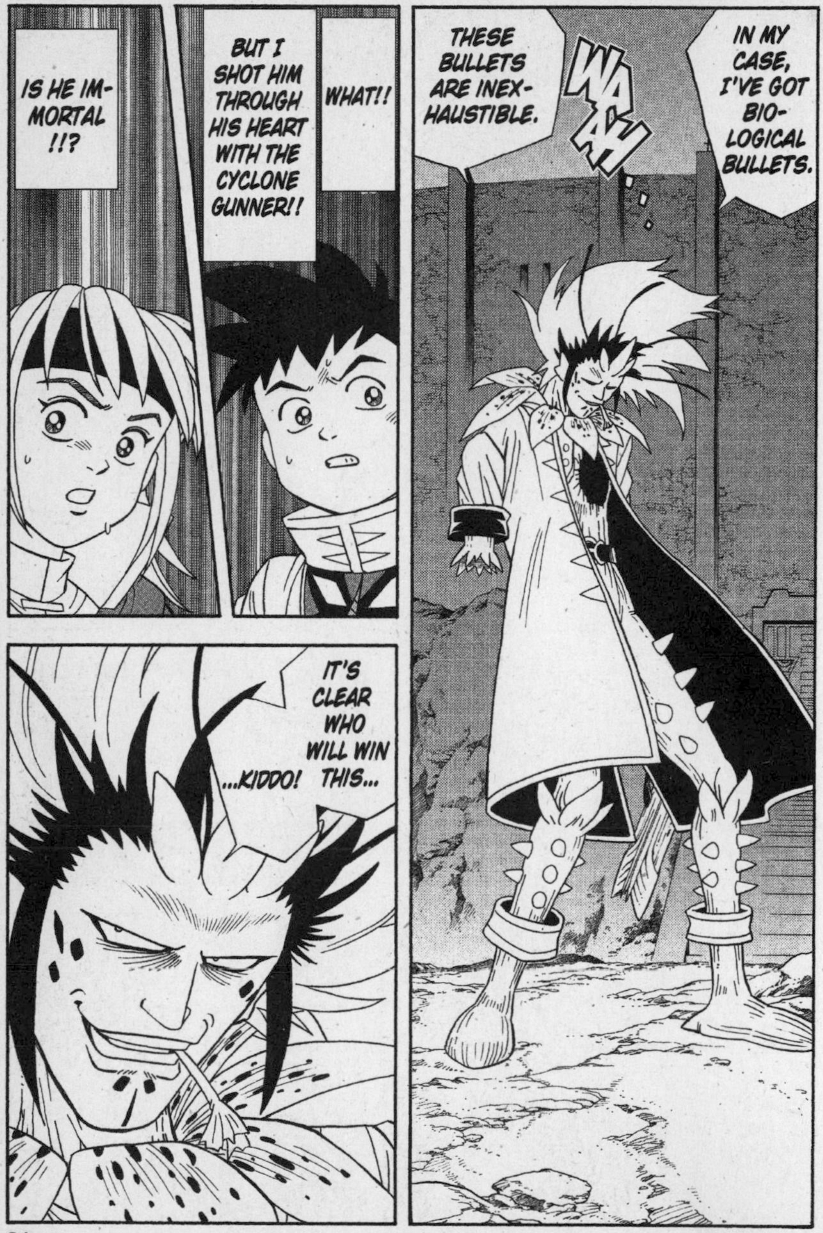
IN MY CASE, I'VE GOT BIO-LOGICAL BULLETS.
WAAH
THESE BULLETS ARE INEX-HAUSTIBLE.
WHAT!!
BUT I SHOT HIM THROUGH HIS HEART WITH THE CYCLONE GUNNER!!
IS HE IM-MORTAL !!?
IT'S CLEAR WHO WILL WIN THIS...
...KIDDO!

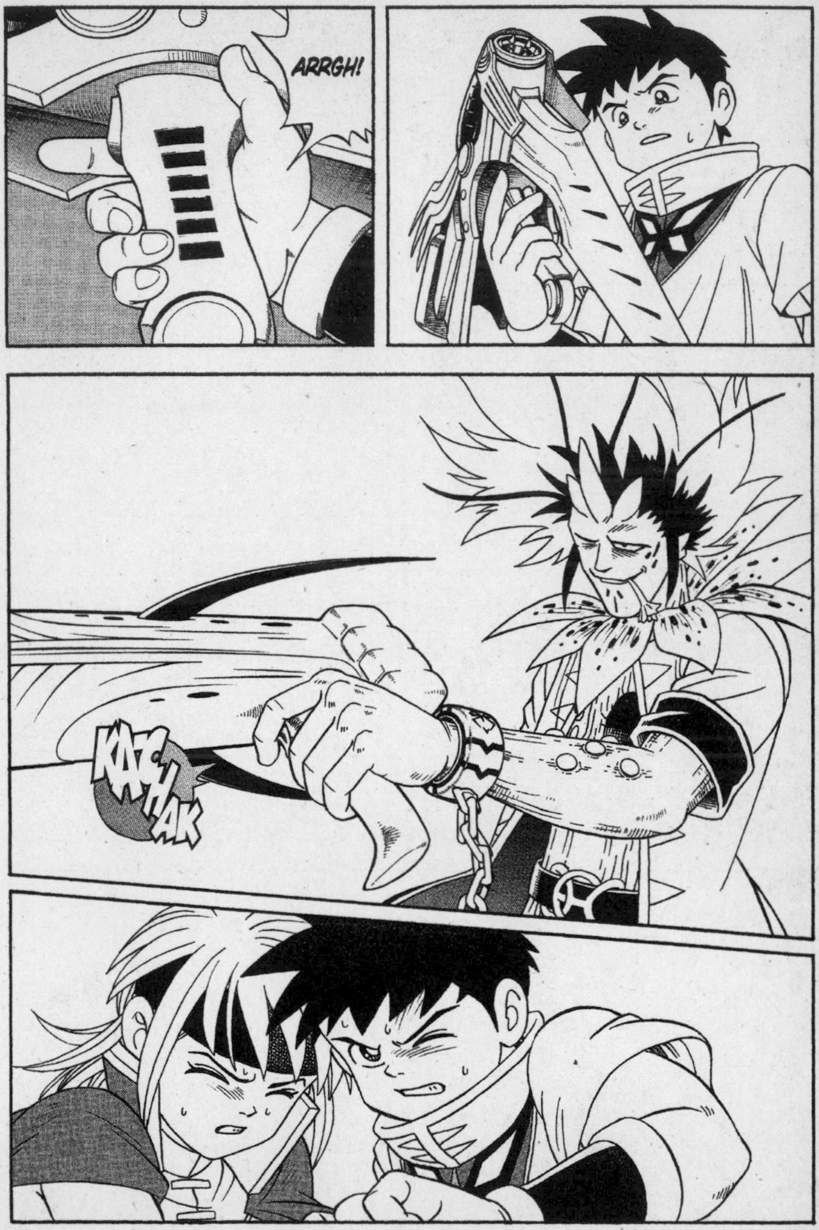
ARRGH!
KACHAK

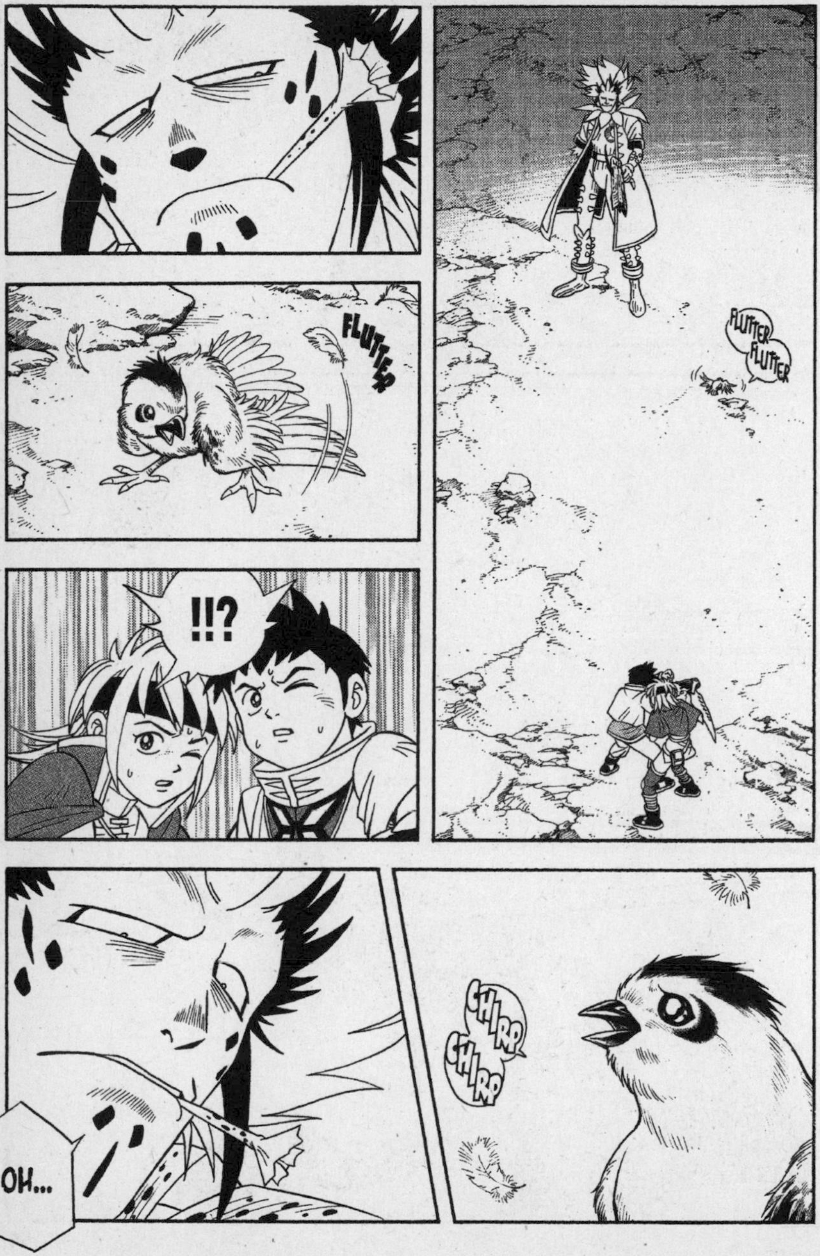
FLUTTER FLUTTER
FLUTTER
!!?
CHIRP CHIRP
OH...

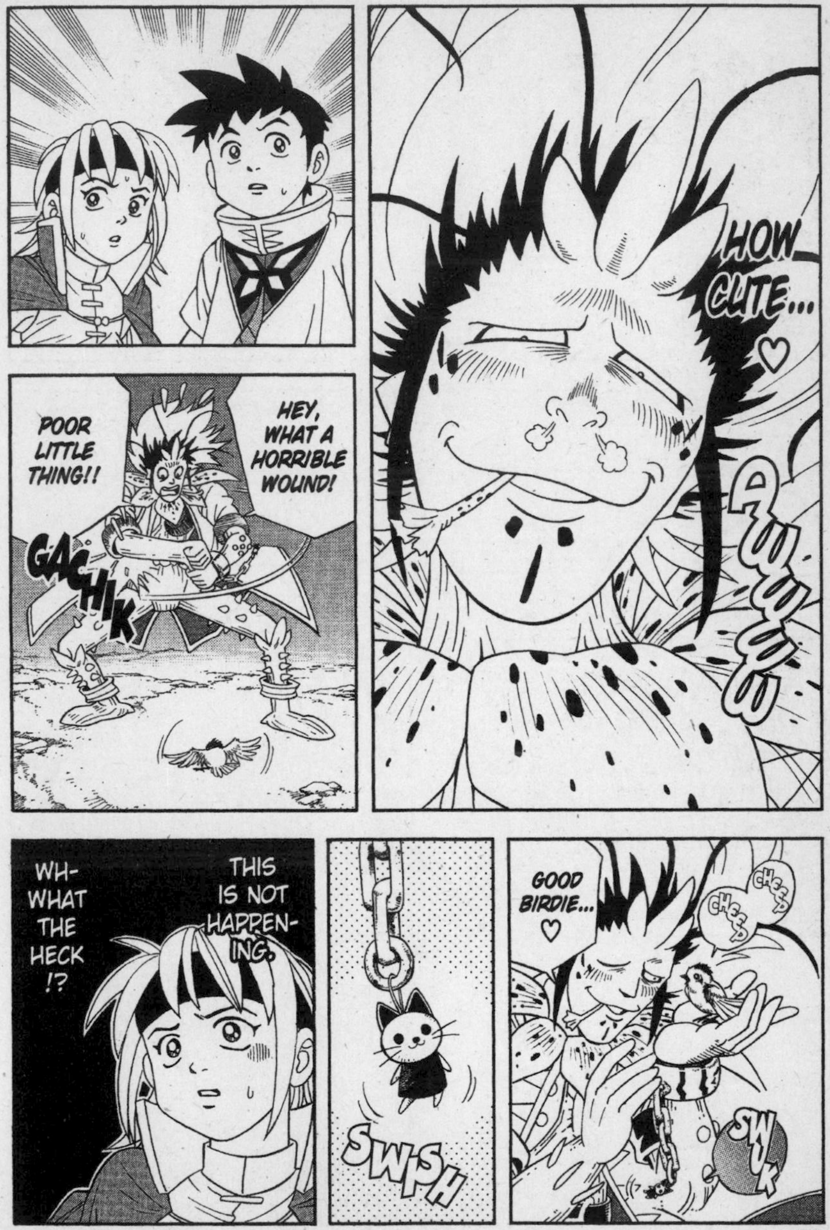
HOW CUTE... ♥
AWWWW
HEY, WHAT A HORRIBLE WOUND!
POOR LITTLE THING!!
GACHIK
GOOD BIRDIE... ♥
CHEEP
CHEEP
SWUK
SWISH
THIS IS NOT HAPPENING.
WH-WHAT THE HECK!?

READ THIS WAY

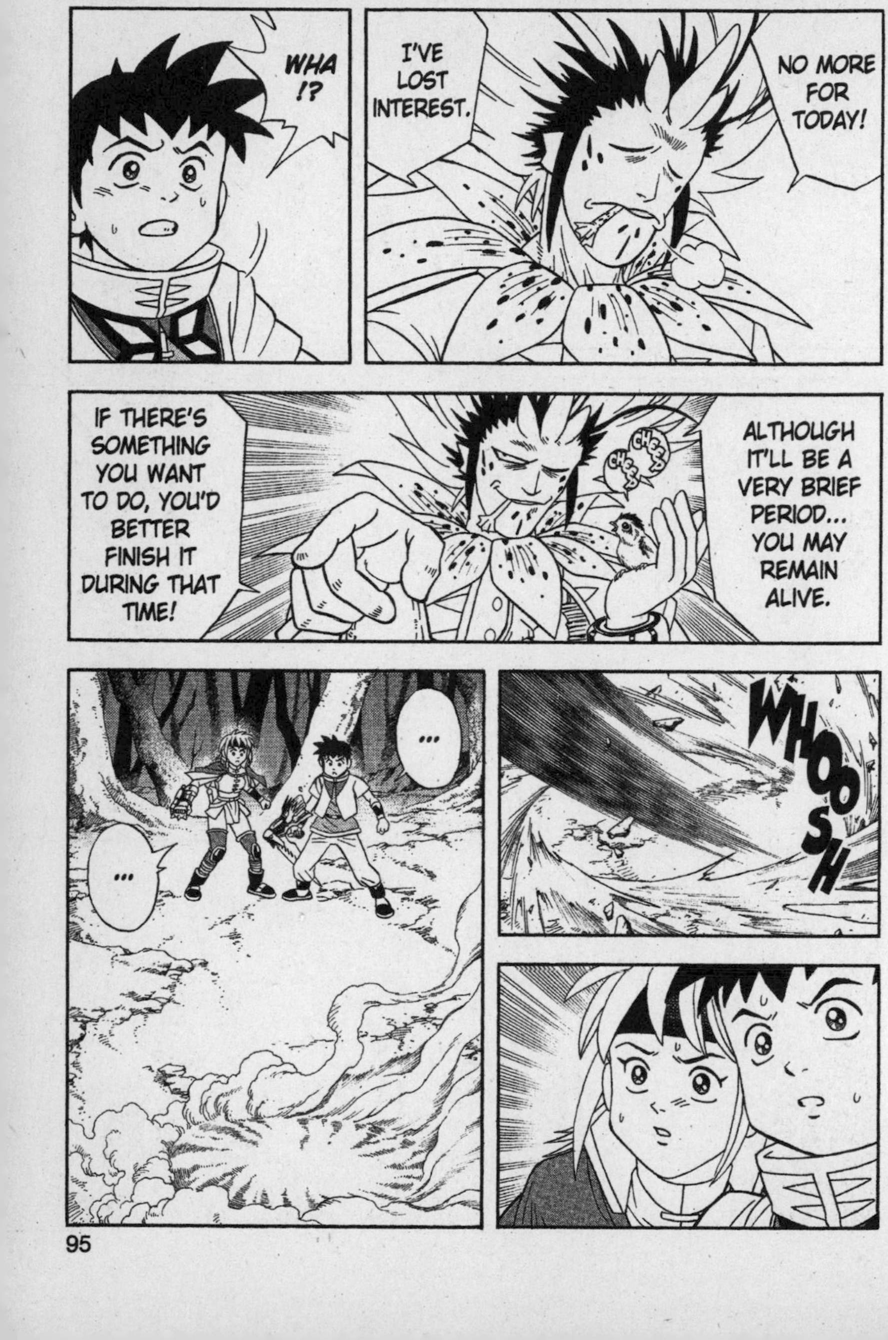

NO MORE FOR TODAY!
I'VE LOST INTEREST.
WHA !?
ALTHOUGH IT'LL BE A VERY BRIEF PERIOD... YOU MAY REMAIN ALIVE.
CHEEP CHEEP
IF THERE'S SOMETHING YOU WANT TO DO, YOU'D BETTER FINISH IT DURING THAT TIME!
WHOOSH
...
...

WE ONLY ESCAPED BECAUSE THAT VANDEL HAS A WEIRD PERSONALITY.

YEAH.

TAK

NOPE.

STILL...

...HE'S STRONG!

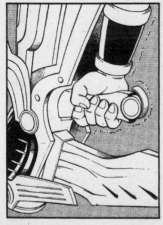

I--

READ THIS WAY

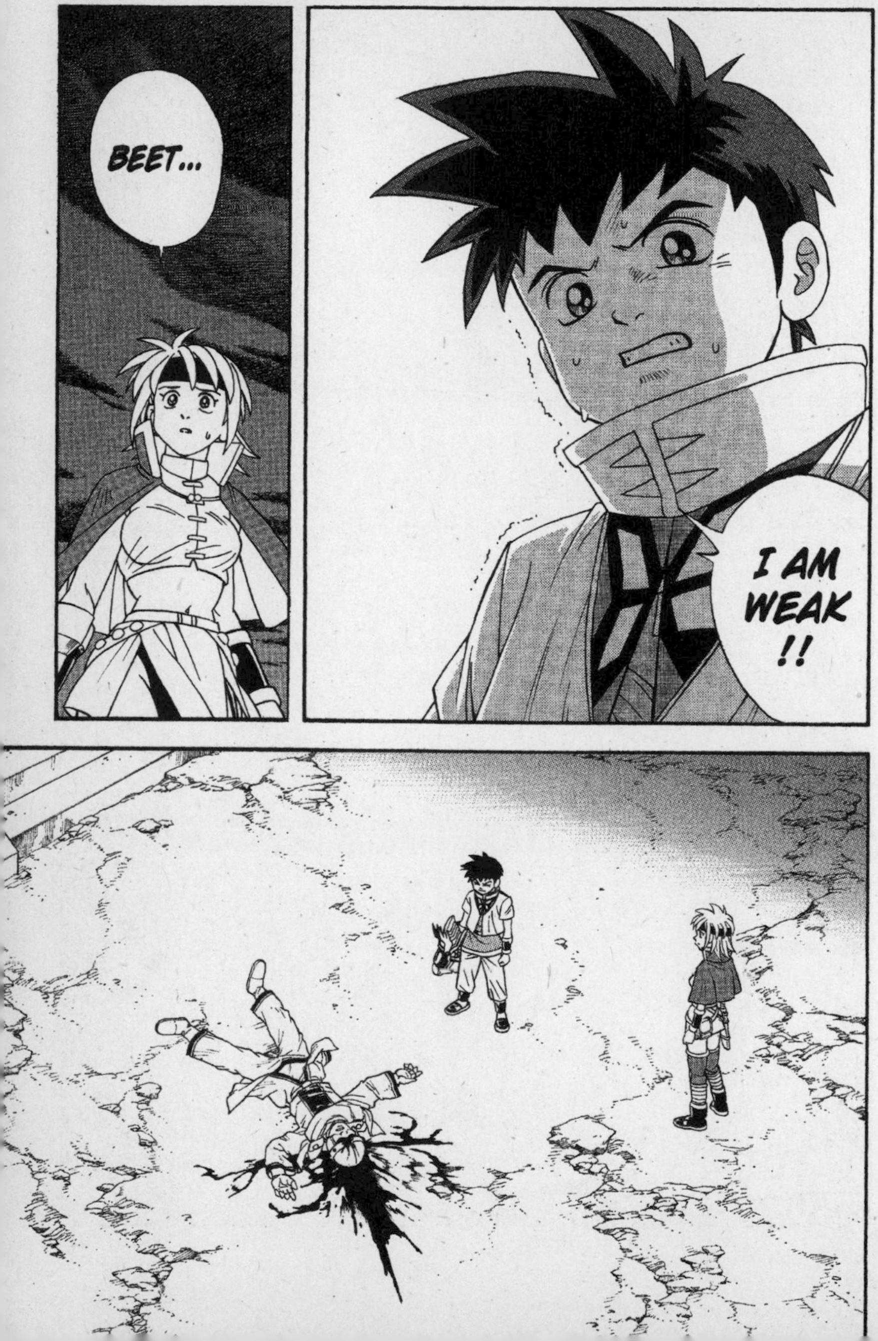
I AM WEAK !!
BEET...

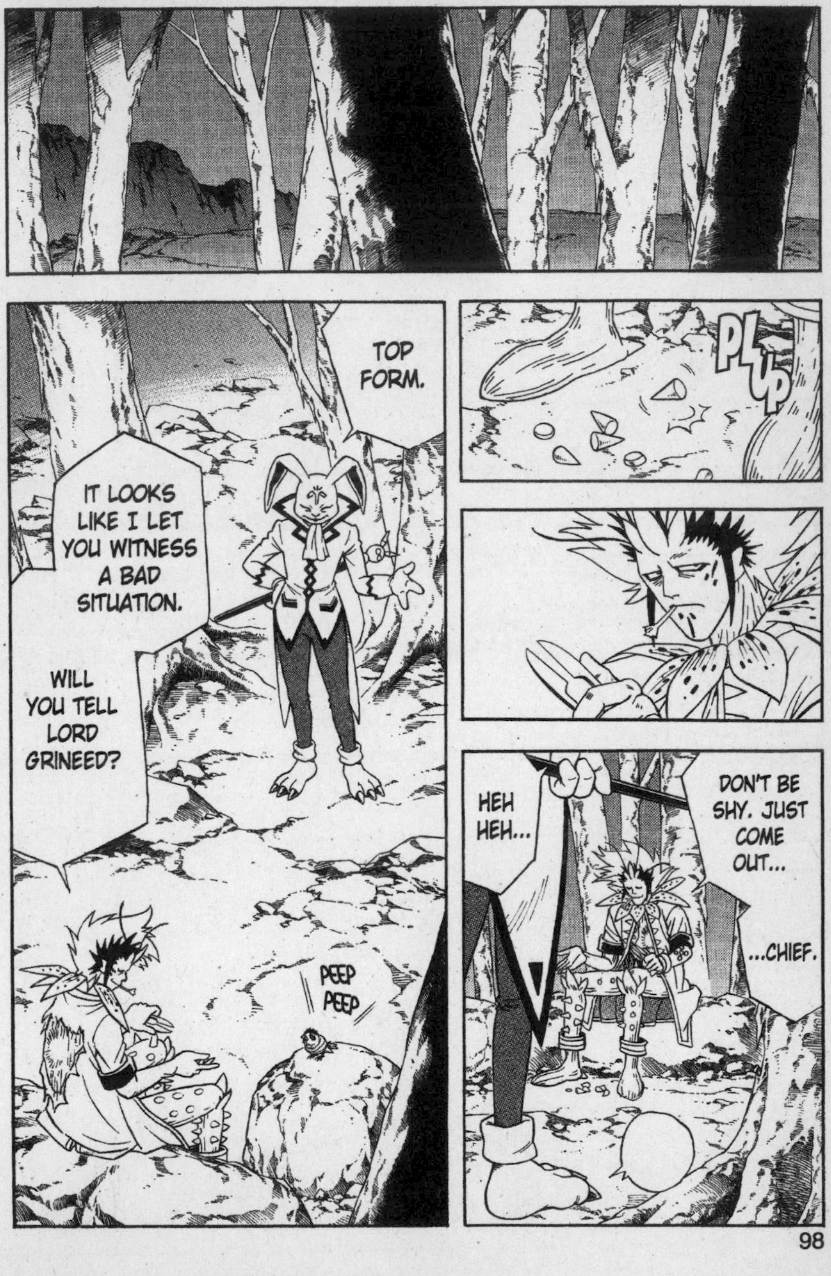
PLUP
DON'T BE SHY. JUST COME OUT...
HEH HEH...
...CHIEF.
TOP FORM.
IT LOOKS LIKE I LET YOU WITNESS A BAD SITUATION.
WILL YOU TELL LORD GRINEED?
PEEP PEEP

READ THIS WAY

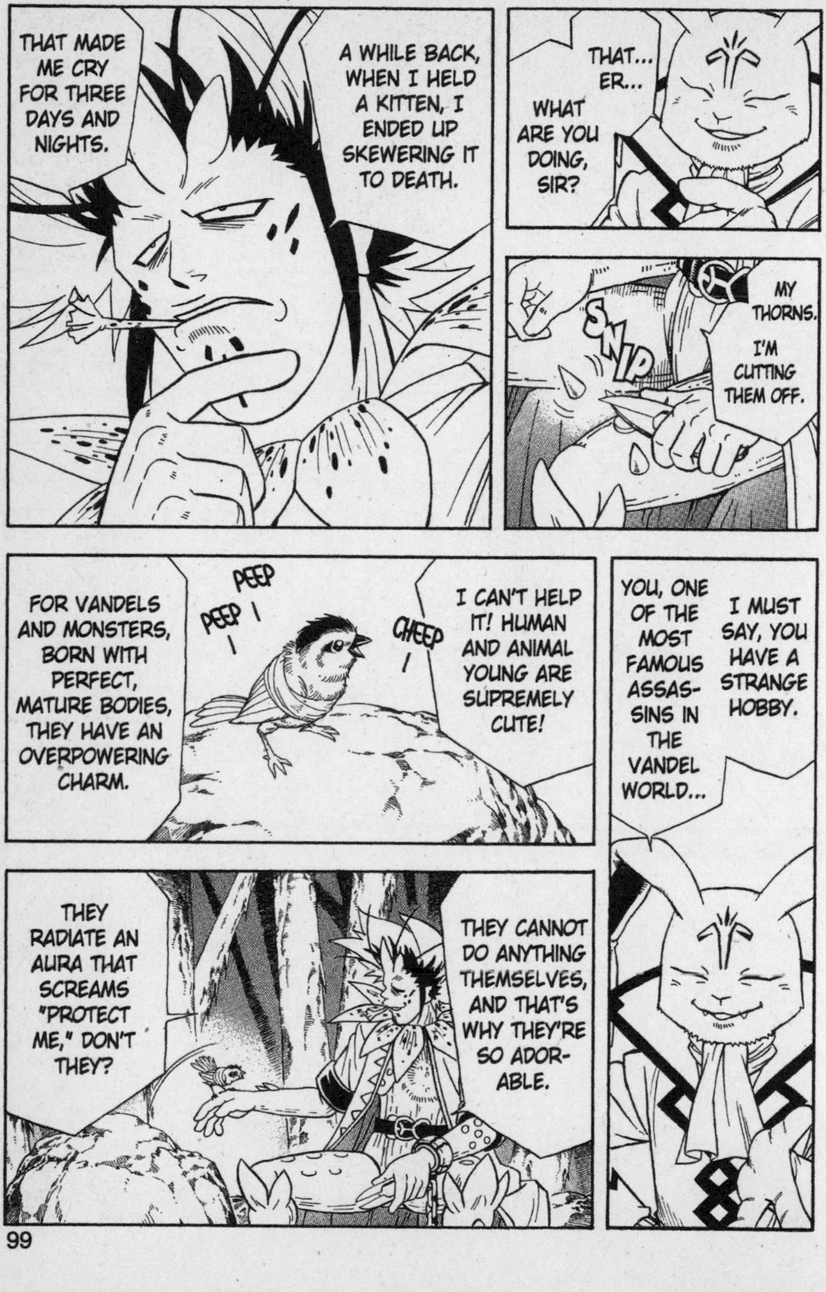
THAT... ER...
WHAT ARE YOU DOING, SIR?
SNIP
MY THORNS.
I'M CUTTING THEM OFF.
A WHILE BACK, WHEN I HELD A KITTEN, I ENDED UP SKEWERING IT TO DEATH.
THAT MADE ME CRY FOR THREE DAYS AND NIGHTS.
I MUST SAY, YOU HAVE A STRANGE HOBBY.
YOU, ONE OF THE MOST FAMOUS ASSAS-SINS IN THE VANDEL WORLD...
I CAN'T HELP IT! HUMAN AND ANIMAL YOUNG ARE SUPREMELY CUTE!
CHEEP
PEEP
PEEP
FOR VANDELS AND MONSTERS, BORN WITH PERFECT, MATURE BODIES, THEY HAVE AN OVERPOWERING CHARM.
THEY CANNOT DO ANYTHING THEMSELVES, AND THAT'S WHY THEY'RE SO ADOR-ABLE.
THEY RADIATE AN AURA THAT SCREAMS "PROTECT ME," DON'T THEY?

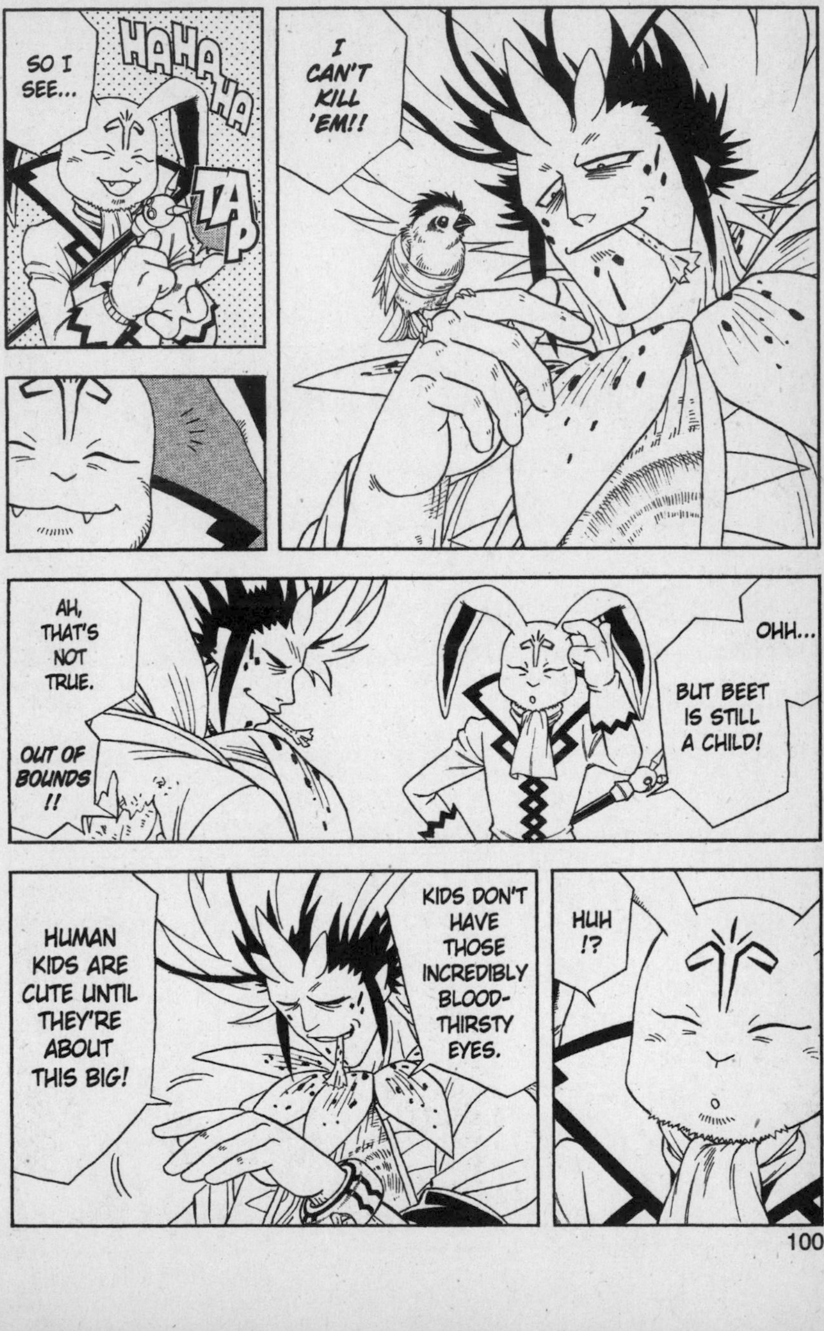
I CAN'T KILL 'EM!!
SO I SEE...
HAHAHAHA
TAP
OHH...
BUT BEET IS STILL A CHILD!
AH, THAT'S NOT TRUE.
OUT OF BOUNDS!!
HUH!?
KIDS DON'T HAVE THOSE INCREDIBLY BLOOD-THIRSTY EYES.
HUMAN KIDS ARE CUTE UNTIL THEY'RE ABOUT THIS BIG!

READ THIS WAY

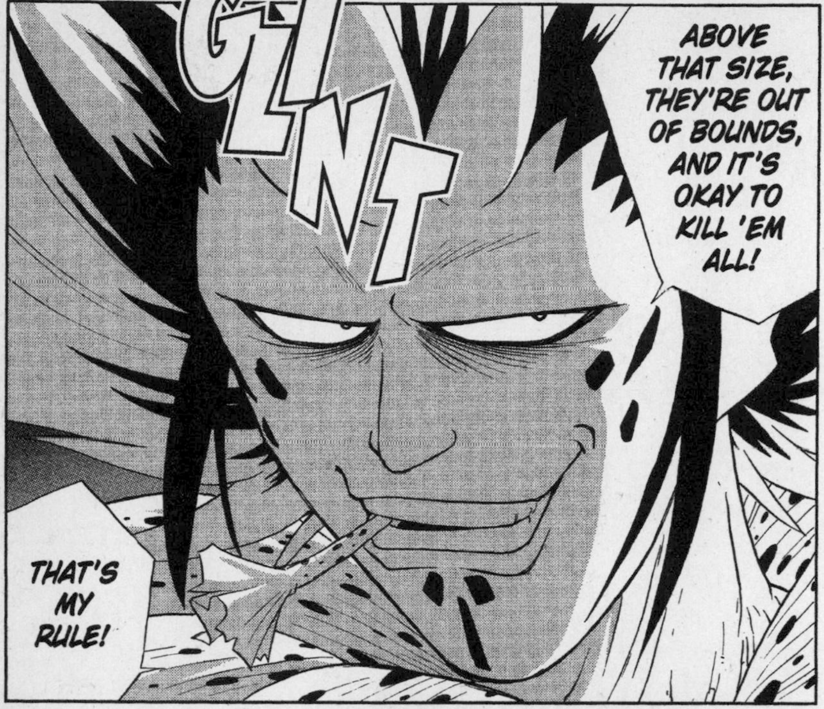
GLINT
ABOVE THAT SIZE, THEY'RE OUT OF BOUNDS, AND IT'S OKAY TO KILL 'EM ALL!
THAT'S MY RULE!

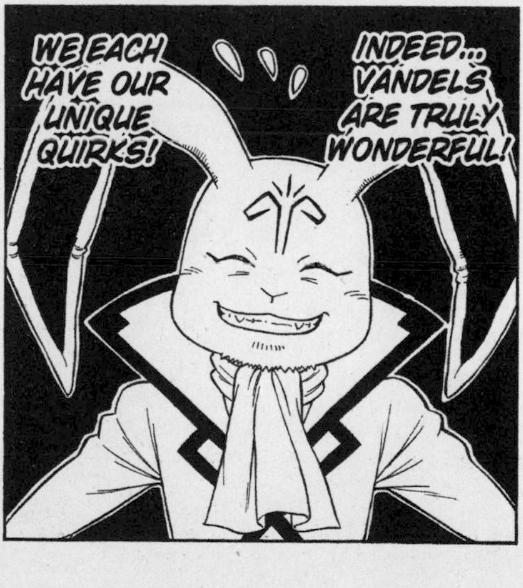
INDEED... VANDELS ARE TRULY WONDERFUL!
WE EACH HAVE OUR UNIQUE QUIRKS!

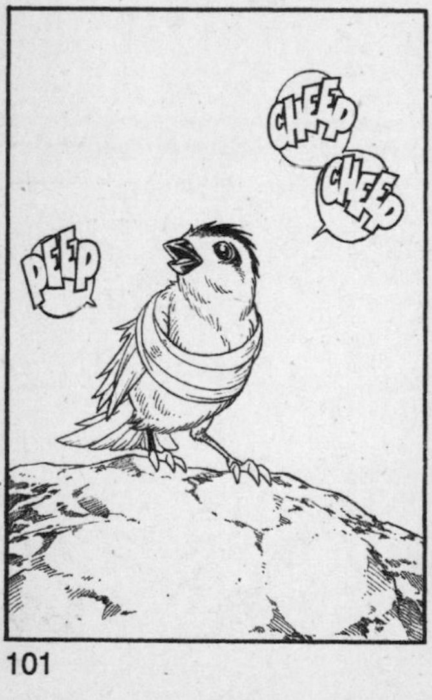
CHEEP
CHEEP
PEEP

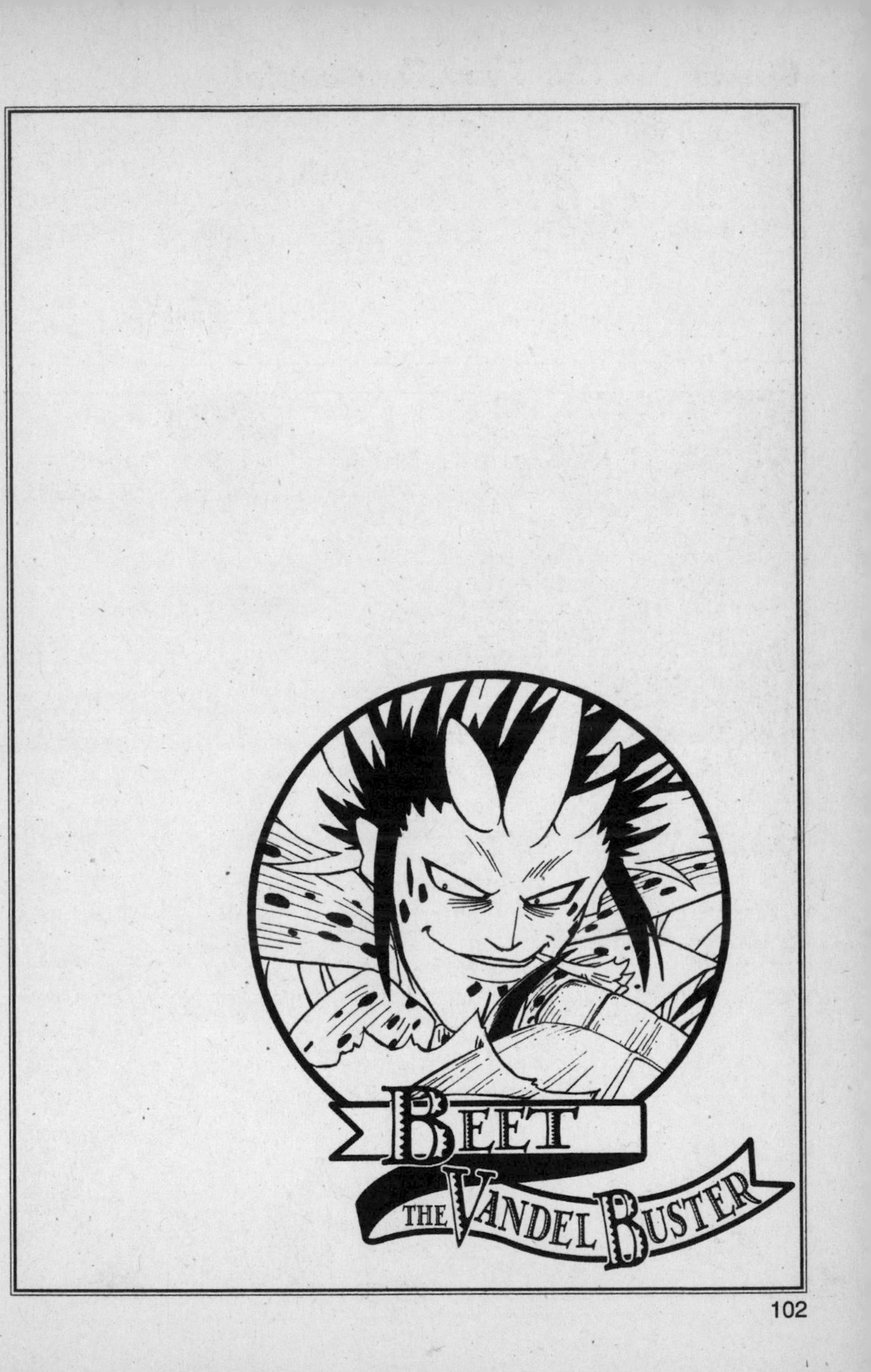
BEET
THE VANDEL BUSTER

Chapter 13: The Third Teammate!

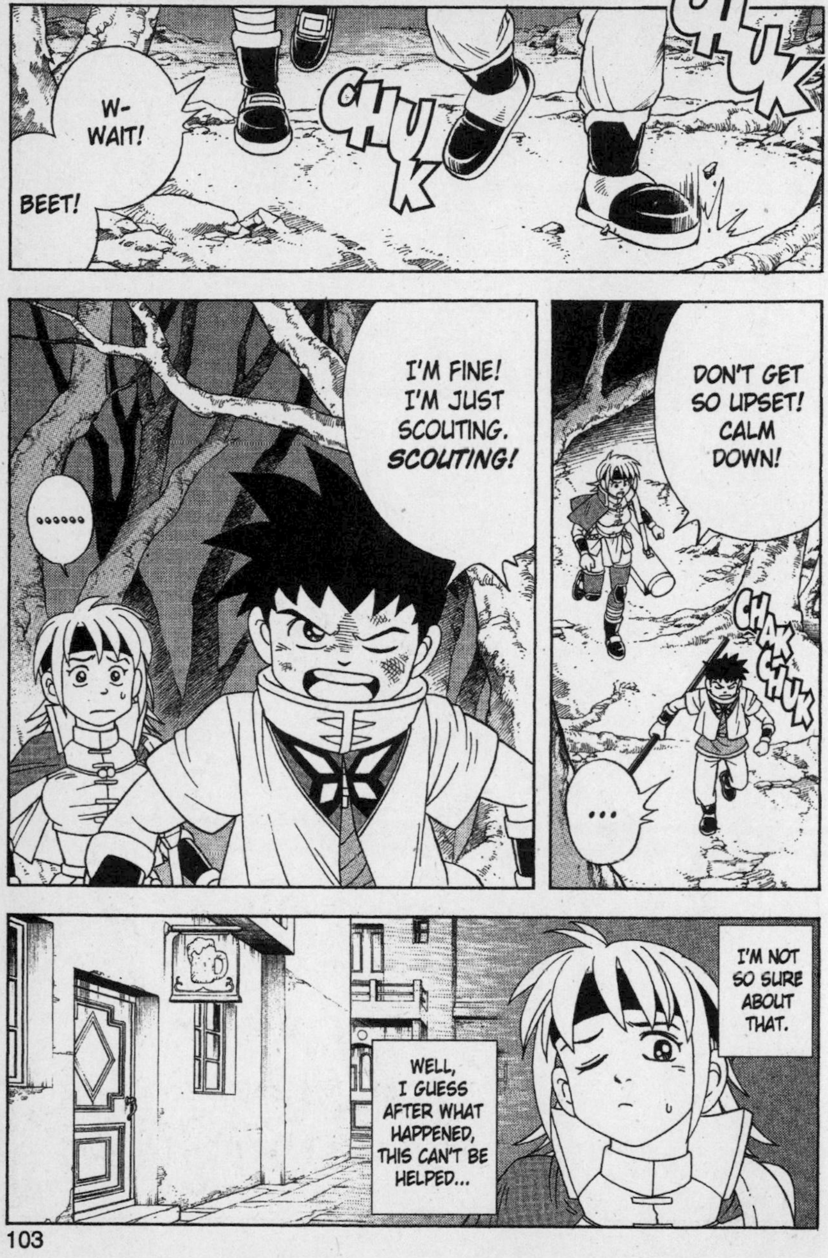
CHUK
CHUK
W-WAIT!
BEET!
DON'T GET SO UPSET! CALM DOWN!
CHAK CHUK
...
I'M FINE! I'M JUST SCOUTING. *SCOUTING!*
......
I'M NOT SO SURE ABOUT THAT.
WELL, I GUESS AFTER WHAT HAPPENED, THIS CAN'T BE HELPED...

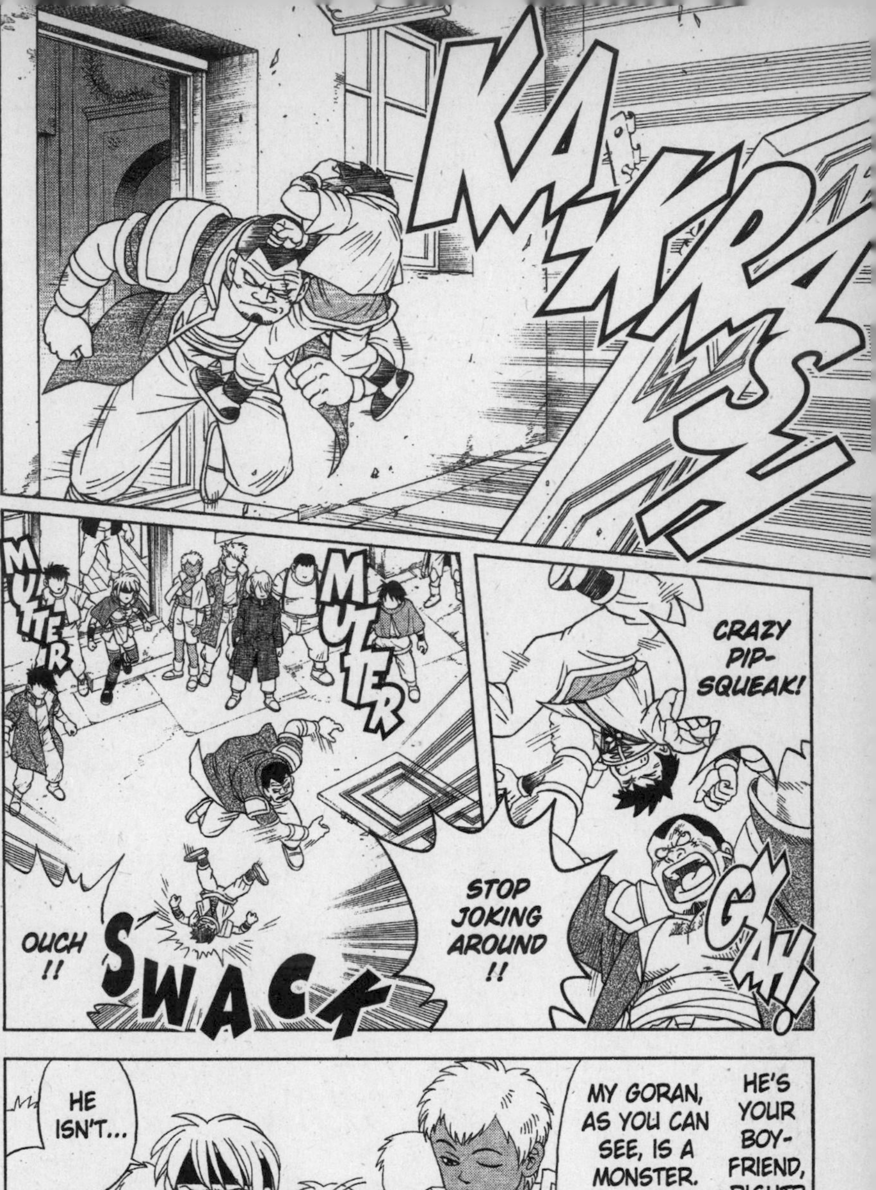
KAKRASH!
CRAZY PIP-SQUEAK!
GAH!
STOP JOKING AROUND!!
MUTTER
MUTTER
SWACK
OUCH!!
HE'S YOUR BOY-FRIEND, RIGHT?
MY GORAN, AS YOU CAN SEE, IS A MONSTER. YOUR BOY'LL GET KILLED IF YOU DON'T STEP IN.
HE ISN'T...
...MY BOY-FRIEND.

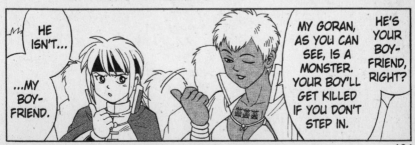

READ THIS WAY

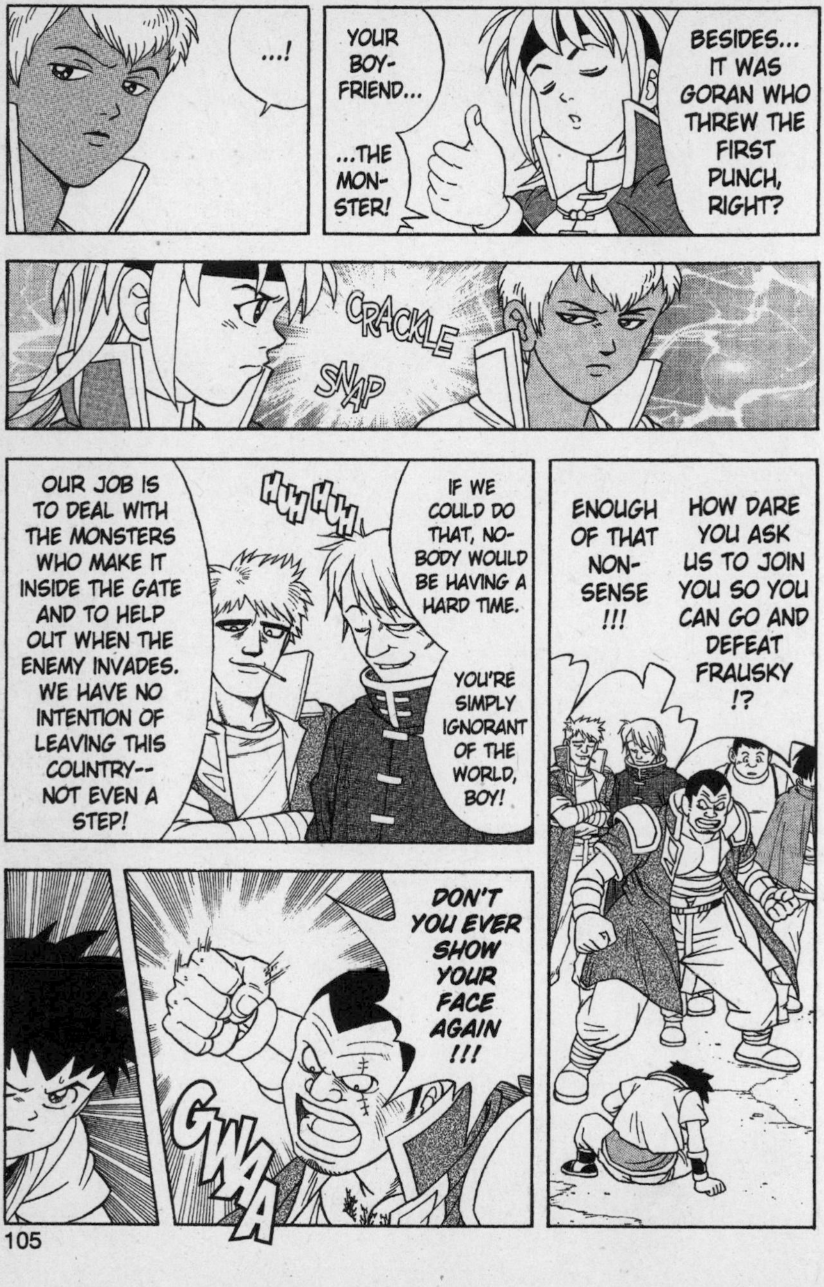
BESIDES... IT WAS GORAN WHO THREW THE FIRST PUNCH, RIGHT?
YOUR BOY-FRIEND...
...THE MON-STER!
...!
CRACKLE
SNAP
HOW DARE YOU ASK US TO JOIN YOU SO YOU CAN GO AND DEFEAT FRAUSKY !?
ENOUGH OF THAT NON-SENSE !!!
IF WE COULD DO THAT, NO-BODY WOULD BE HAVING A HARD TIME.
HUH HUH
YOU'RE SIMPLY IGNORANT OF THE WORLD, BOY!
OUR JOB IS TO DEAL WITH THE MONSTERS WHO MAKE IT INSIDE THE GATE AND TO HELP OUT WHEN THE ENEMY INVADES. WE HAVE NO INTENTION OF LEAVING THIS COUNTRY-- NOT EVEN A STEP!
DON'T YOU EVER SHOW YOUR FACE AGAIN !!!
GWAA

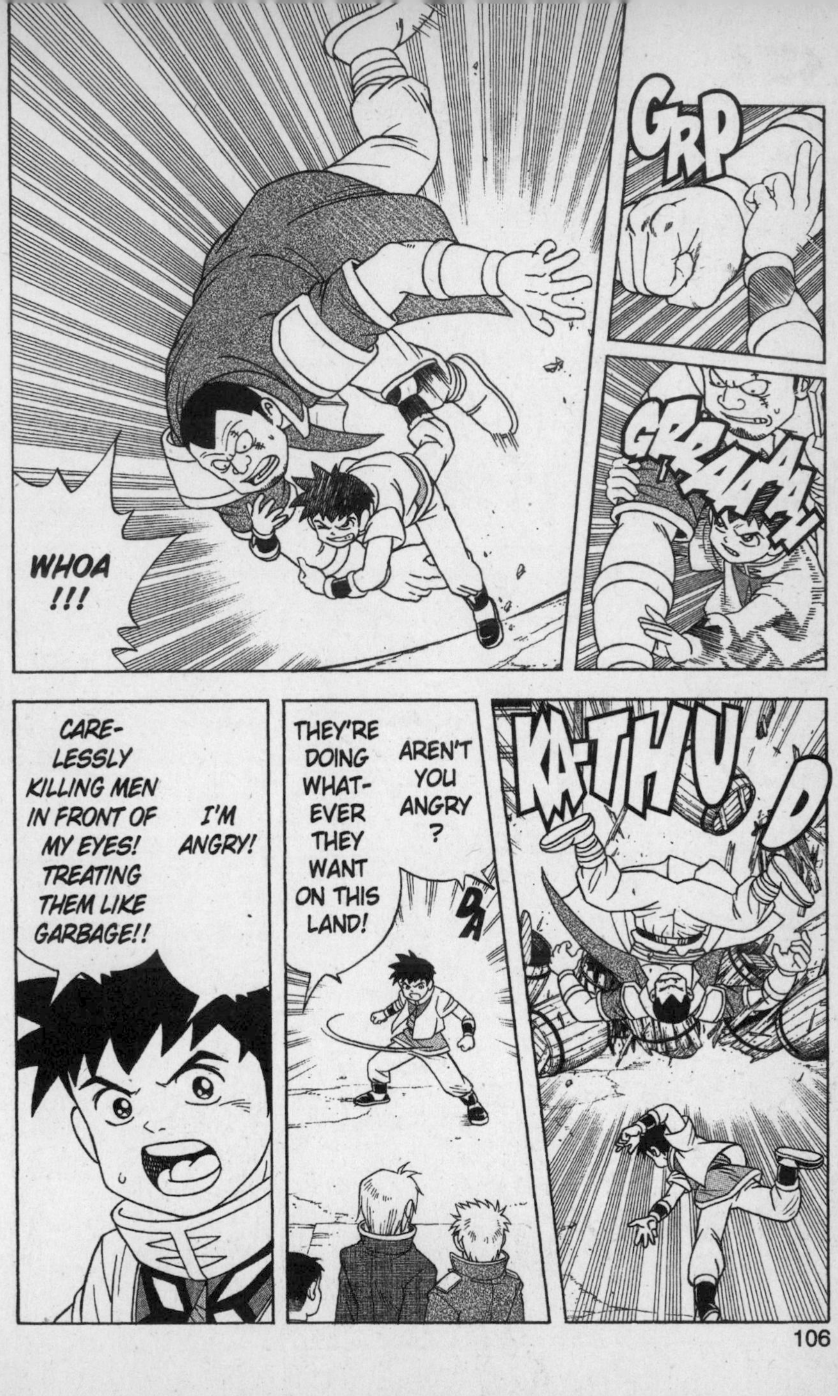
GRP
GREAAAH
WHOA !!!
KA-THUD
DA
THEY'RE DOING WHAT-EVER THEY WANT ON THIS LAND! AREN'T YOU ANGRY?
CARE-LESSLY KILLING MEN IN FRONT OF MY EYES! TREATING THEM LIKE GARBAGE!! I'M ANGRY!

READ THIS WAY

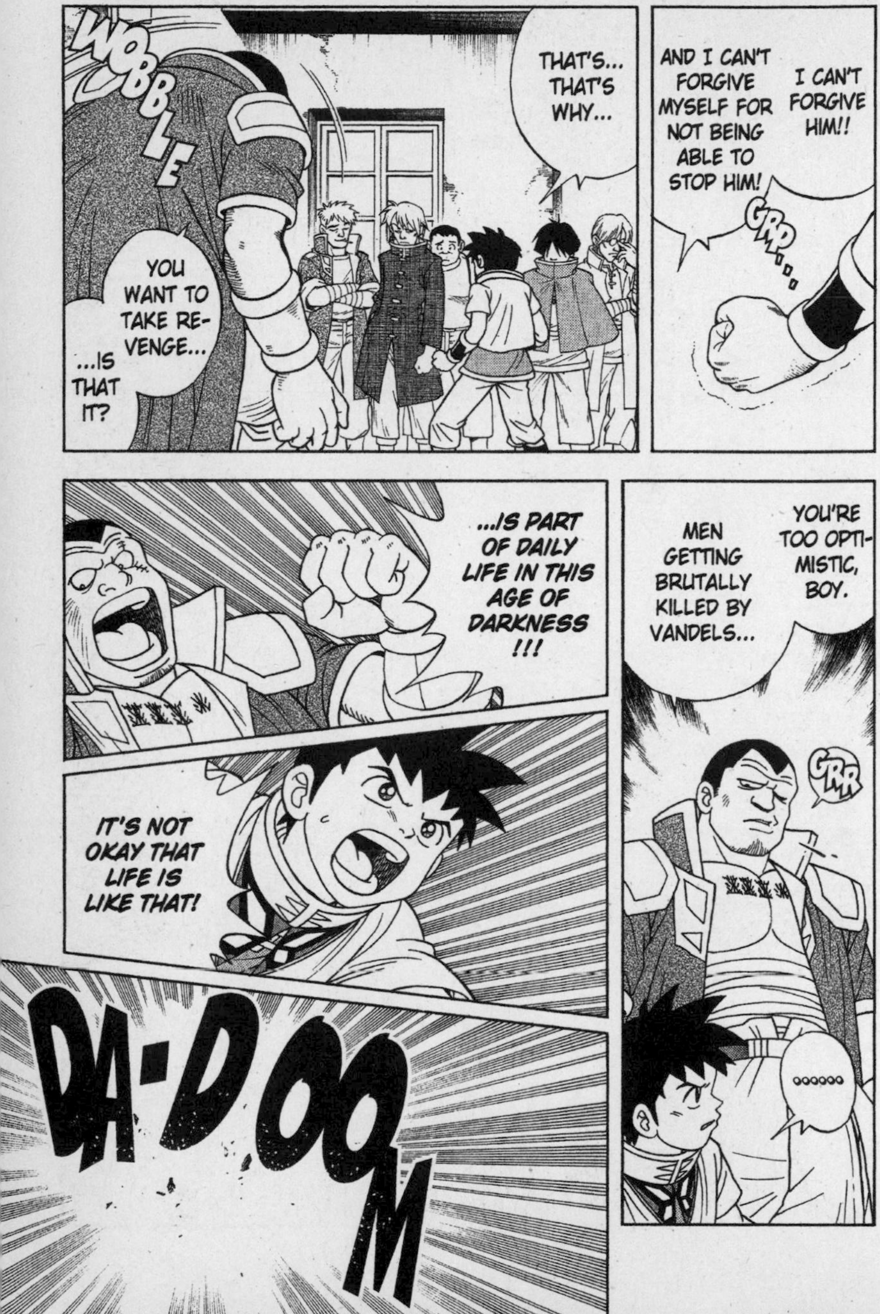
I CAN'T FORGIVE HIM!!
AND I CAN'T FORGIVE MYSELF FOR NOT BEING ABLE TO STOP HIM!
GRP...
THAT'S... THAT'S WHY...
WOBBLE
YOU WANT TO TAKE RE-VENGE...
...IS THAT IT?
YOU'RE TOO OPTI-MISTIC, BOY.
MEN GETTING BRUTALLY KILLED BY VANDELS...
GRR
......
...IS PART OF DAILY LIFE IN THIS AGE OF DARKNESS!!!
IT'S NOT OKAY THAT LIFE IS LIKE THAT!
DA-DOOM

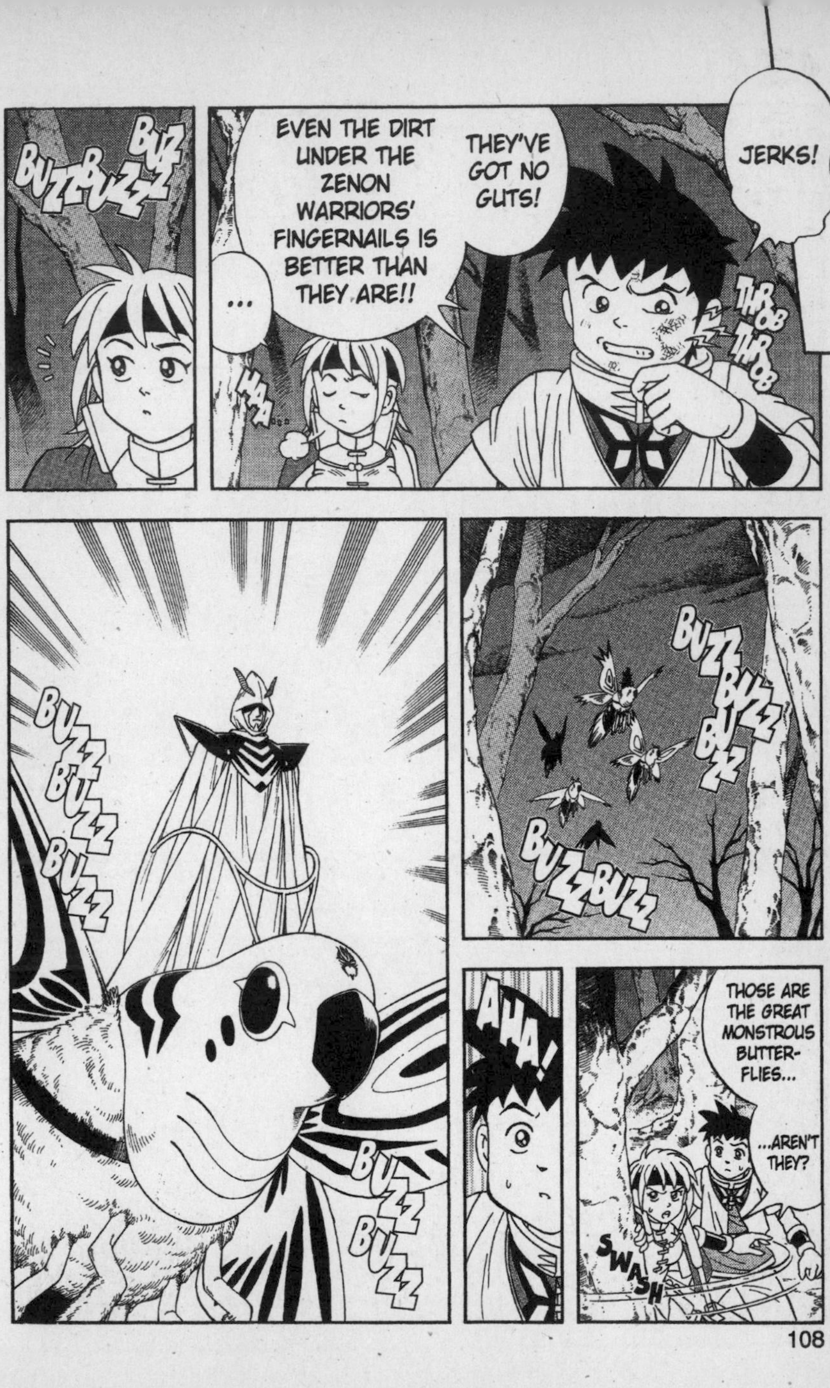
JERKS!
THEY'VE GOT NO GUTS!
EVEN THE DIRT UNDER THE ZENON WARRIORS' FINGERNAILS IS BETTER THAN THEY ARE!!
THROB THROB
...
HAA
BUZZ BUZZZ BUZZZ
BUZZ BUZZZ BUZZ
BUZZZ BUZZ
THOSE ARE THE GREAT MONSTROUS BUTTER-FLIES...
...AREN'T THEY?
SWASH
AHA!
BUZZZ BUZZZ BUZZZ
BUZZZ BUZZZ

READ THIS WAY

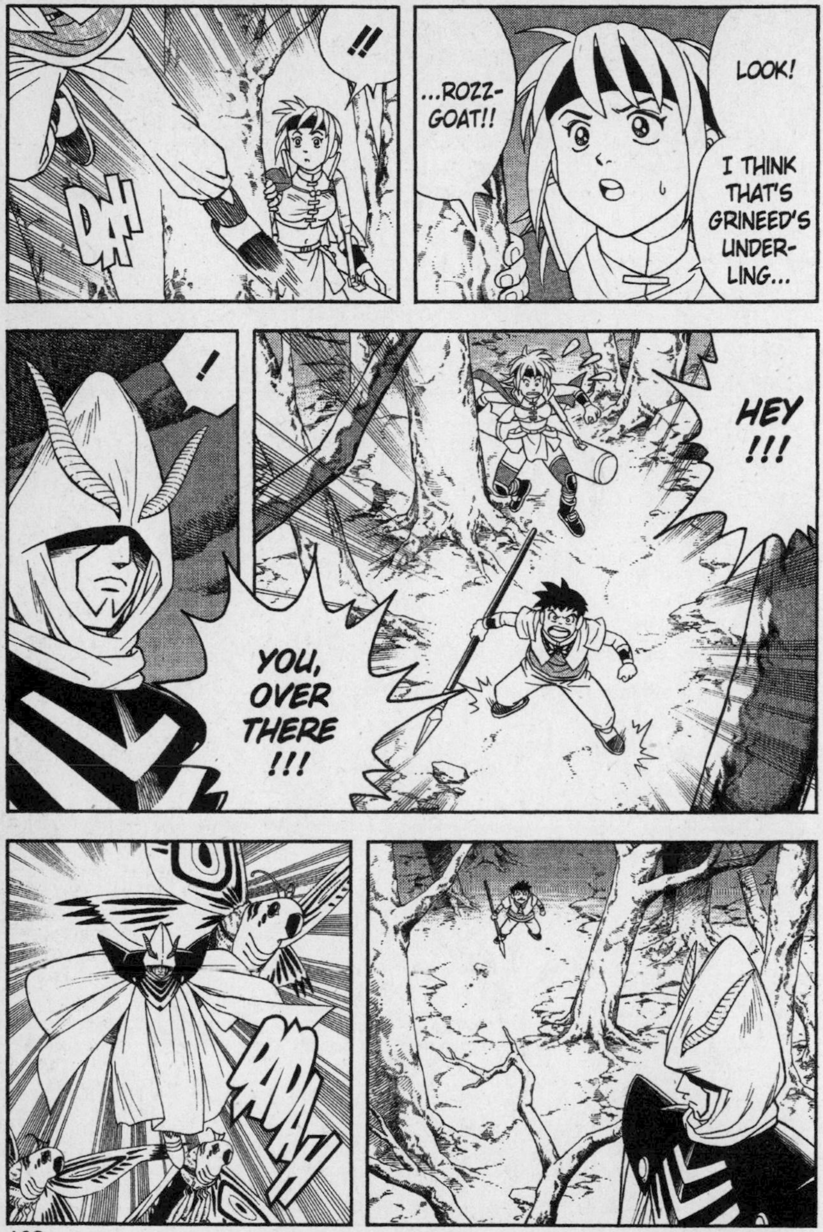
LOOK!
I THINK THAT'S GRINEED'S UNDER-LING...
...ROZZ-GOAT!!
!!
DAH
HEY!!!
YOU, OVER THERE!!!
!
PAPAH

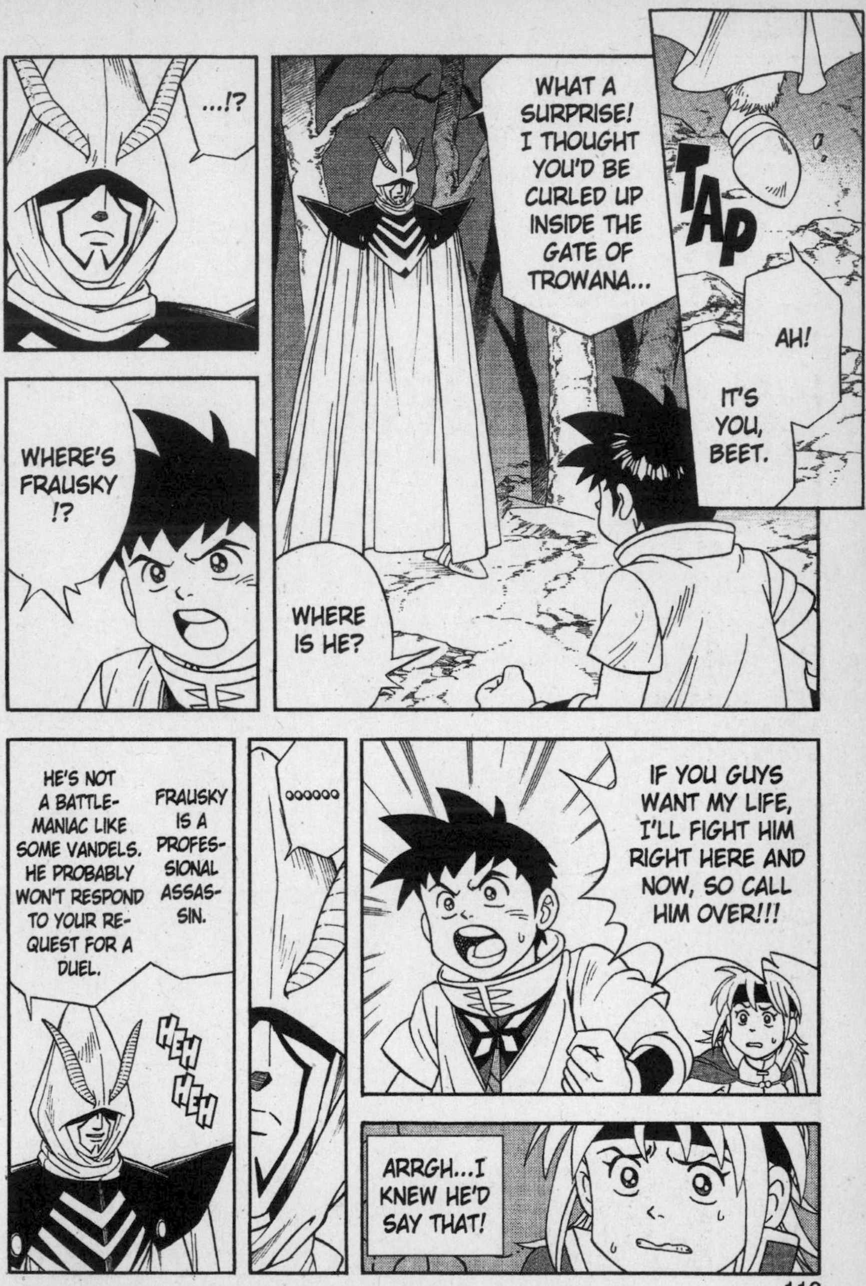
TAP
AH!
IT'S YOU, BEET.
WHAT A SURPRISE! I THOUGHT YOU'D BE CURLED UP INSIDE THE GATE OF TROWANA...
WHERE IS HE?
...!?
WHERE'S FRAUSKY !?
IF YOU GUYS WANT MY LIFE, I'LL FIGHT HIM RIGHT HERE AND NOW, SO CALL HIM OVER!!!
ARRGH...I KNEW HE'D SAY THAT!
......
FRAUSKY IS A PROFES- SIONAL ASSAS- SIN.
HE'S NOT A BATTLE- MANIAC LIKE SOME VANDELS. HE PROBABLY WON'T RESPOND TO YOUR RE- QUEST FOR A DUEL.
HEH HEH

READ THIS WAY

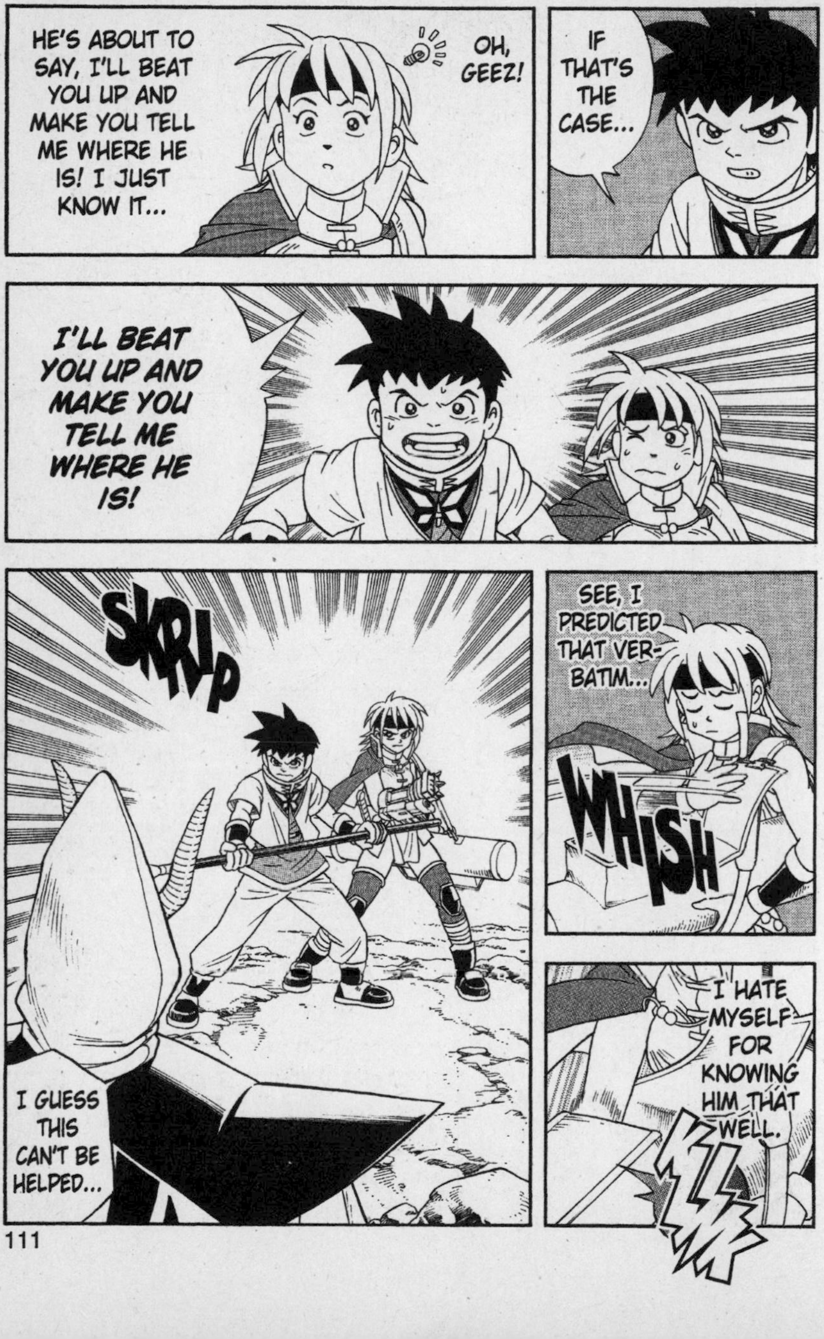

IF THAT'S THE CASE...
OH, GEEZ!
HE'S ABOUT TO SAY, I'LL BEAT YOU UP AND MAKE YOU TELL ME WHERE HE IS! I JUST KNOW IT...
I'LL BEAT YOU UP AND MAKE YOU TELL ME WHERE HE IS!
SEE, I PREDICTED THAT VER-BATIM...
WHISH
I HATE MYSELF FOR KNOWING HIM THAT WELL.
SKRIIP
I GUESS THIS CAN'T BE HELPED...

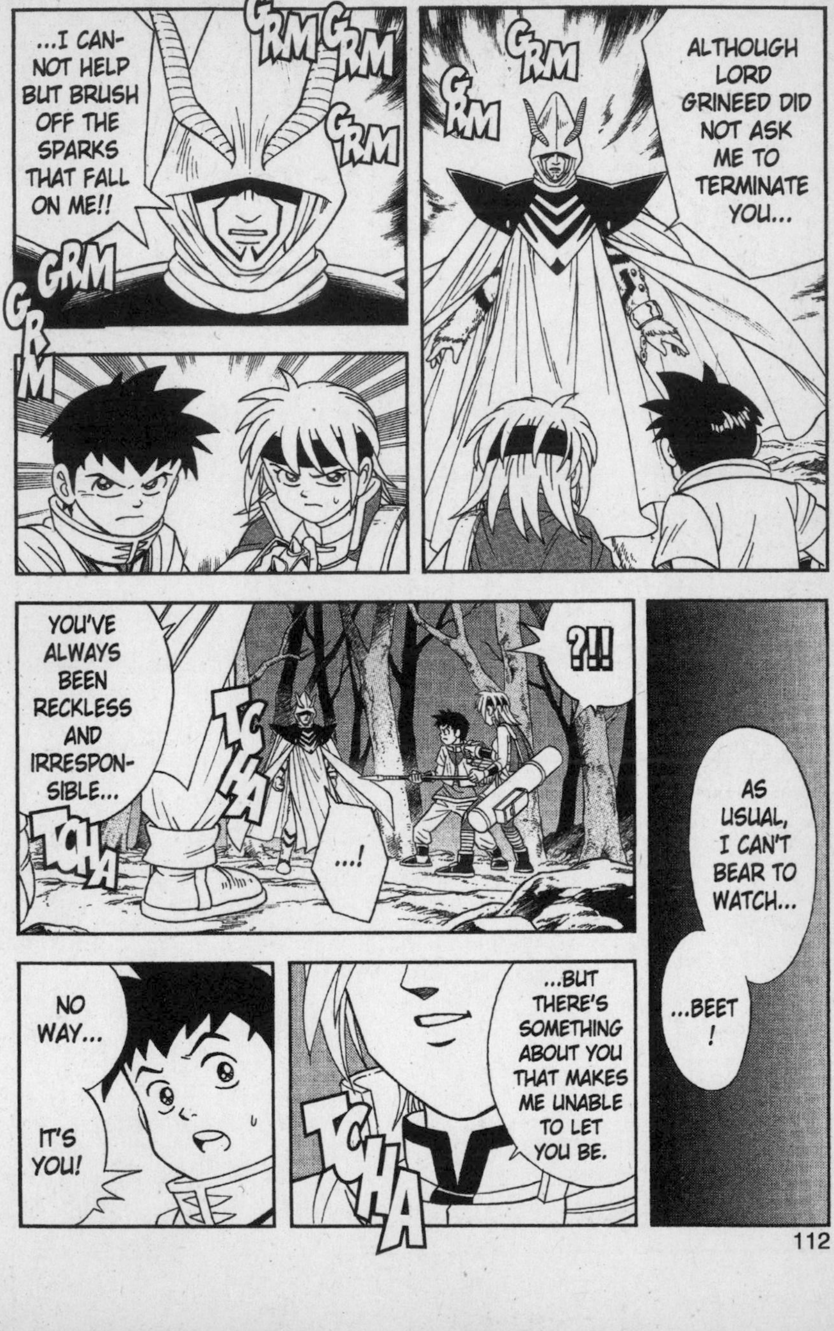
GRM
GRM
ALTHOUGH LORD GRINEED DID NOT ASK ME TO TERMINATE YOU...
GRM GRM
GRM
...I CAN-NOT HELP BUT BRUSH OFF THE SPARKS THAT FALL ON ME!!
GRM
GRM
AS USUAL, I CAN'T BEAR TO WATCH...
...BEET!
?!!
YOU'VE ALWAYS BEEN RECKLESS AND IRRESPON-SIBLE...
TCHA
...!
TCHA
...BUT THERE'S SOMETHING ABOUT YOU THAT MAKES ME UNABLE TO LET YOU BE.
TCHA
NO WAY...
IT'S YOU!

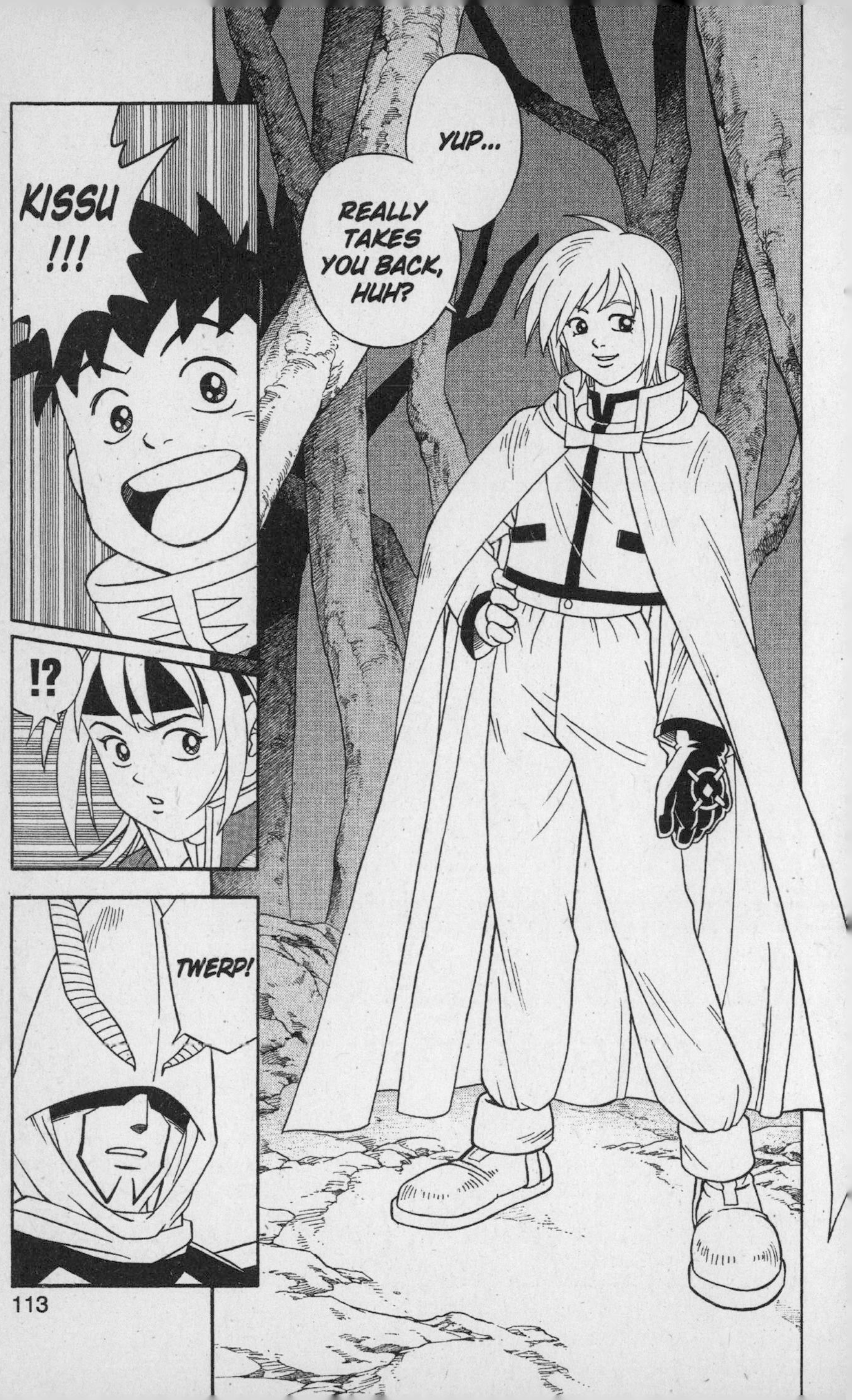
YUP...
REALLY TAKES YOU BACK, HUH?
KISSU !!!
!?
TWERP!

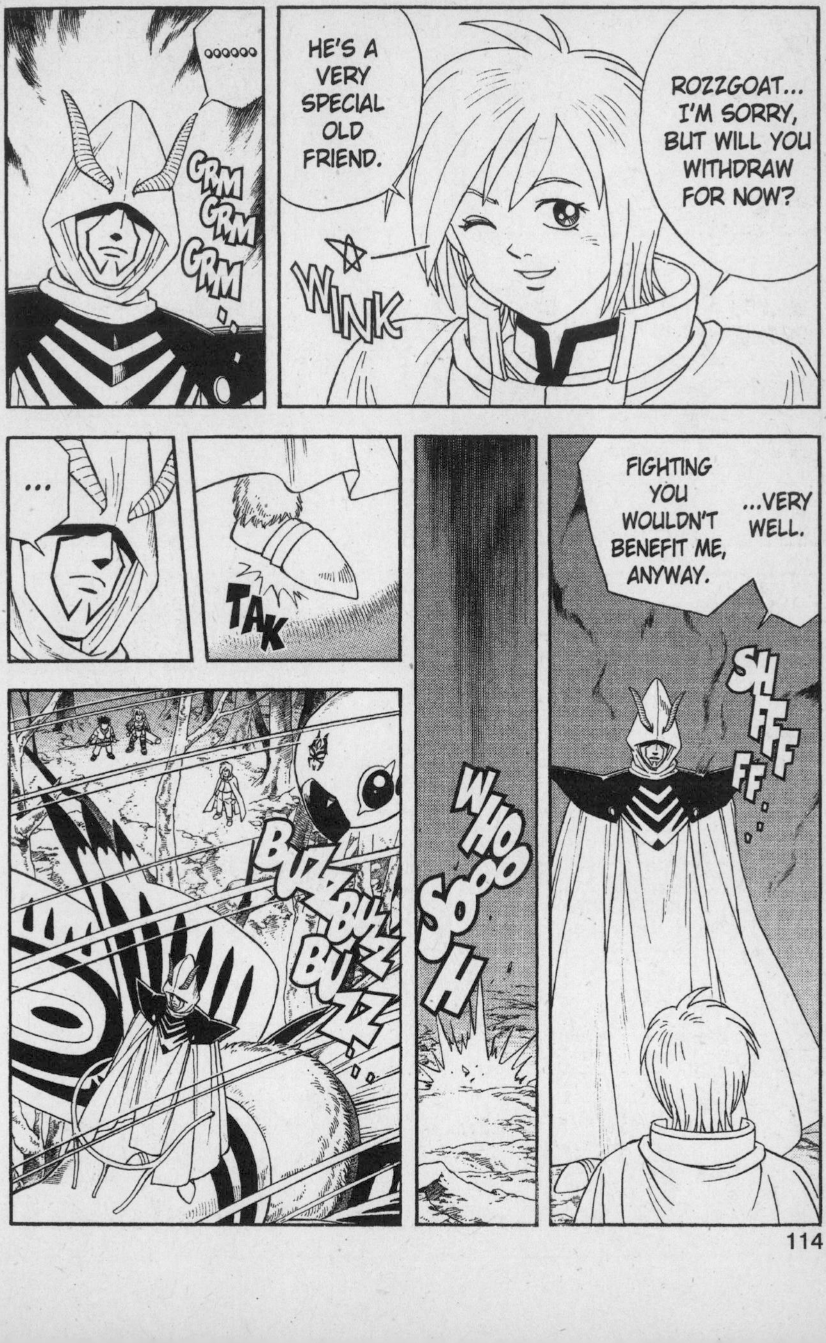
ROZZGOAT... I'M SORRY, BUT WILL YOU WITHDRAW FOR NOW?
HE'S A VERY SPECIAL OLD FRIEND.
WINK
oooooo
GRM GRM GRM
...VERY WELL.
FIGHTING YOU WOULDN'T BENEFIT ME, ANYWAY.
SHFFFFF
WHOOSOOOSH
TAK
...
BUZZ BUZZ BUZZ

READ THIS WAY

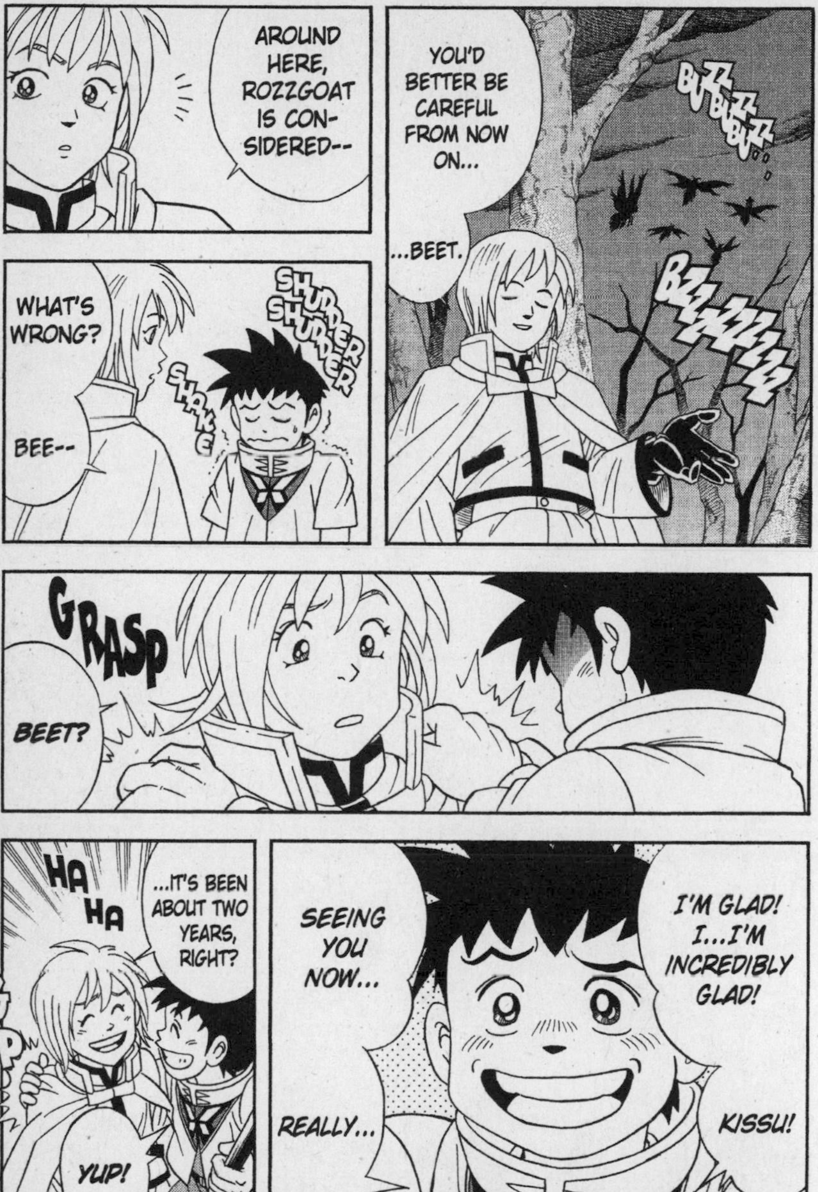
YOU'D BETTER BE CAREFUL FROM NOW ON...
...BEET.
BUZZ BUBUZZZ
BZZZZZZZZZ
AROUND HERE, ROZZGOAT IS CON-SIDERED--
SHUDDER SHUDDER
SHAKE
WHAT'S WRONG?
BEE--
GRASP
BEET?
I'M GLAD! I...I'M INCREDIBLY GLAD!
SEEING YOU NOW...
KISSU!
REALLY...
...IT'S BEEN ABOUT TWO YEARS, RIGHT?
HA HA
GRIP
YUP!

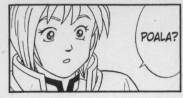

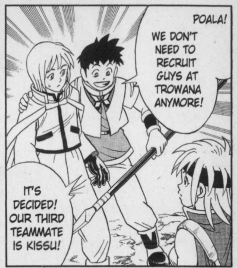

POALA!
WE DON'T NEED TO RECRUIT GUYS AT TROWANA ANYMORE!
IT'S DECIDED! OUR THIRD TEAMMATE IS KISSU!
POALA?
AH!
YOUR FUTURE WIFE, I BELIEVE!
HAVE YOU TOLD EVERYONE THAT?
YOU IDIOT!
DON'T BE EMBARRASSED.
I ENVY BEET FOR HAVING A PARTNER AS WONDERFUL AS YOU.
GOOD FORTUNE TO YOU... ♡
SHUU
YOWZA
KISS
WH-WHAT THE HECK!?
HE'S A PRETTY DEMONSTRATIVE GUY!!

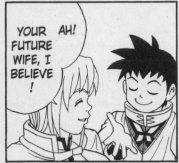

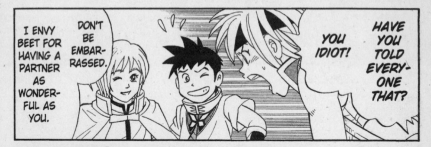

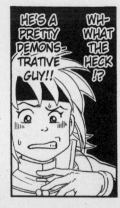

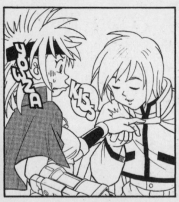

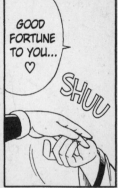

READ THIS WAY

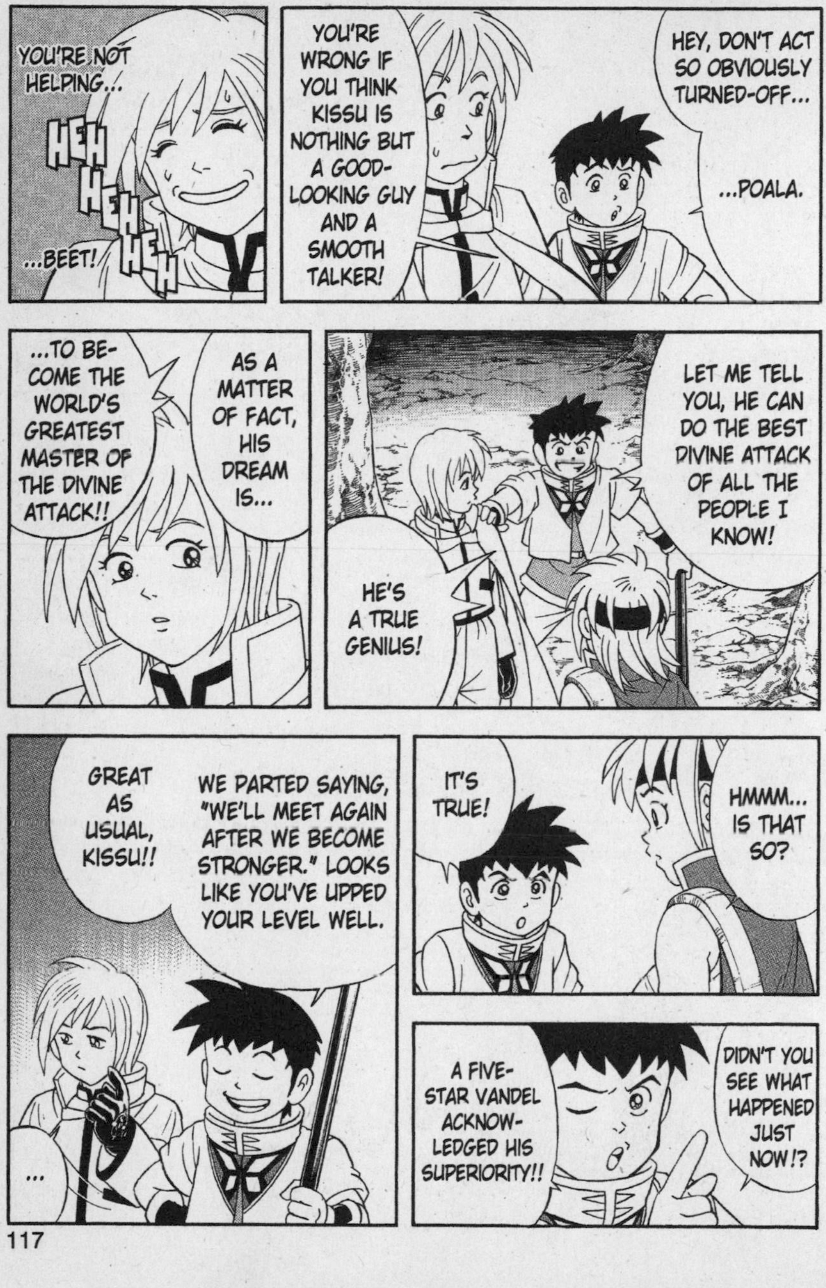
HEY, DON'T ACT SO OBVIOUSLY TURNED-OFF...
...POALA.
YOU'RE WRONG IF YOU THINK KISSU IS NOTHING BUT A GOOD-LOOKING GUY AND A SMOOTH TALKER!
YOU'RE NOT HELPING...
HEH HEH HEH HEH
...BEET!
LET ME TELL YOU, HE CAN DO THE BEST DIVINE ATTACK OF ALL THE PEOPLE I KNOW!
HE'S A TRUE GENIUS!
AS A MATTER OF FACT, HIS DREAM IS...
...TO BE-COME THE WORLD'S GREATEST MASTER OF THE DIVINE ATTACK!!
HMMM... IS THAT SO?
IT'S TRUE!
DIDN'T YOU SEE WHAT HAPPENED JUST NOW!?
A FIVE-STAR VANDEL ACKNOW-LEDGED HIS SUPERIORITY!!
WE PARTED SAYING, "WE'LL MEET AGAIN AFTER WE BECOME STRONGER." LOOKS LIKE YOU'VE UPPED YOUR LEVEL WELL.
GREAT AS USUAL, KISSU!!
...

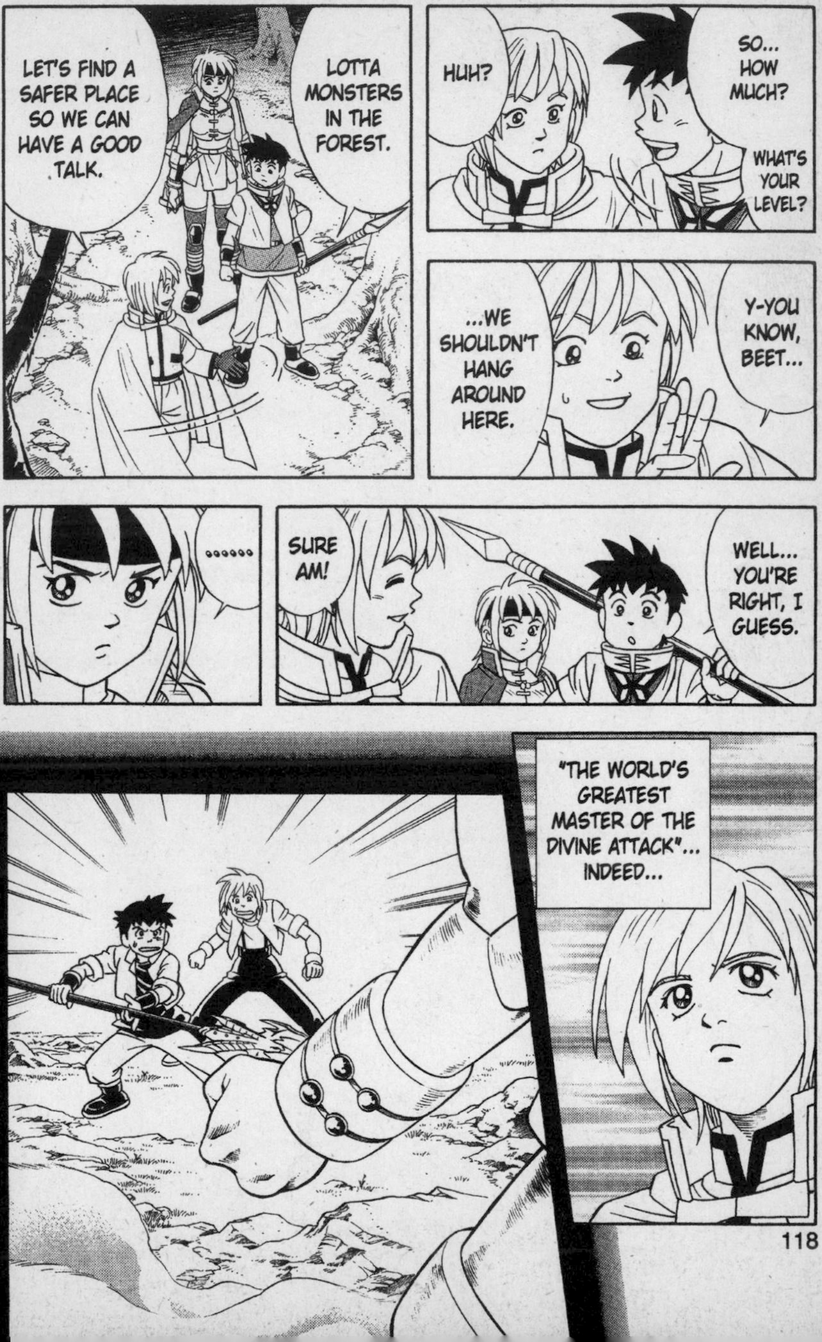
SO... HOW MUCH?
WHAT'S YOUR LEVEL?
HUH?
Y-YOU KNOW, BEET...
...WE SHOULDN'T HANG AROUND HERE.
LOTTA MONSTERS IN THE FOREST.
LET'S FIND A SAFER PLACE SO WE CAN HAVE A GOOD TALK.
WELL... YOU'RE RIGHT, I GUESS.
SURE AM!
......
"THE WORLD'S GREATEST MASTER OF THE DIVINE ATTACK"... INDEED...

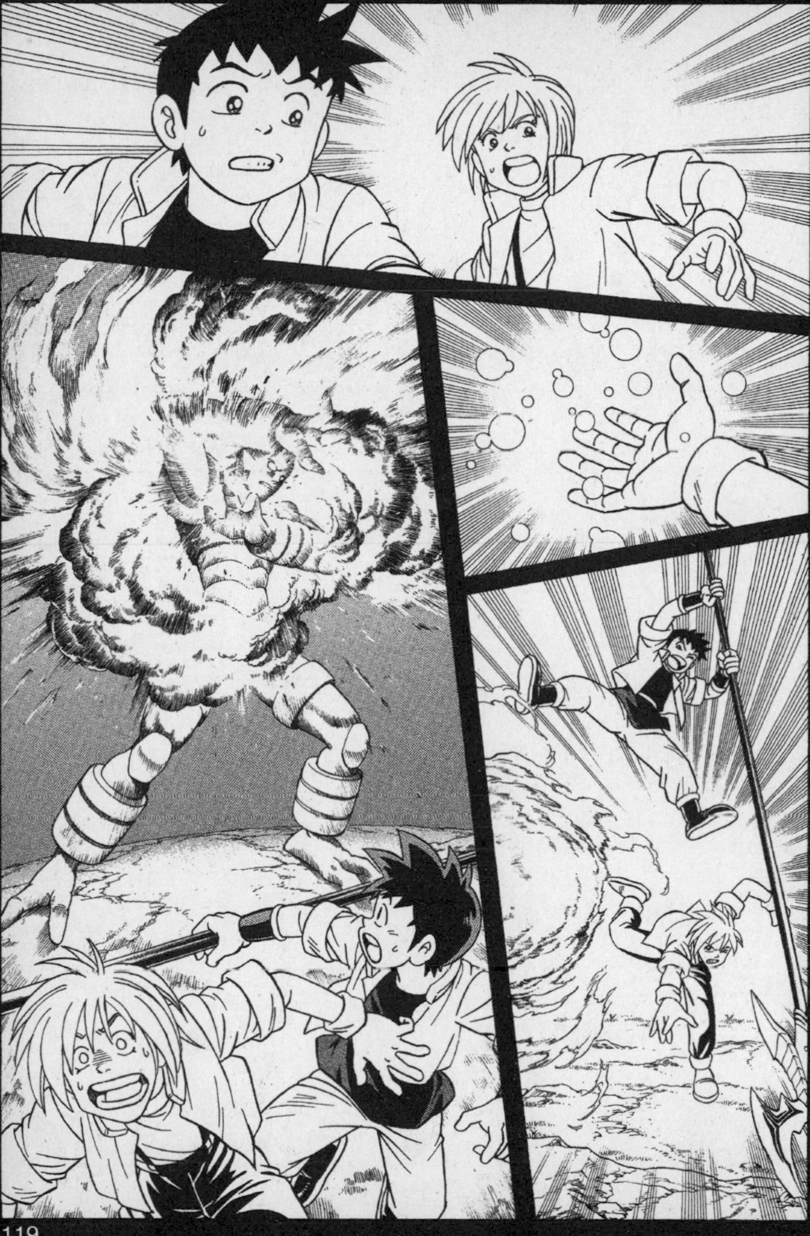

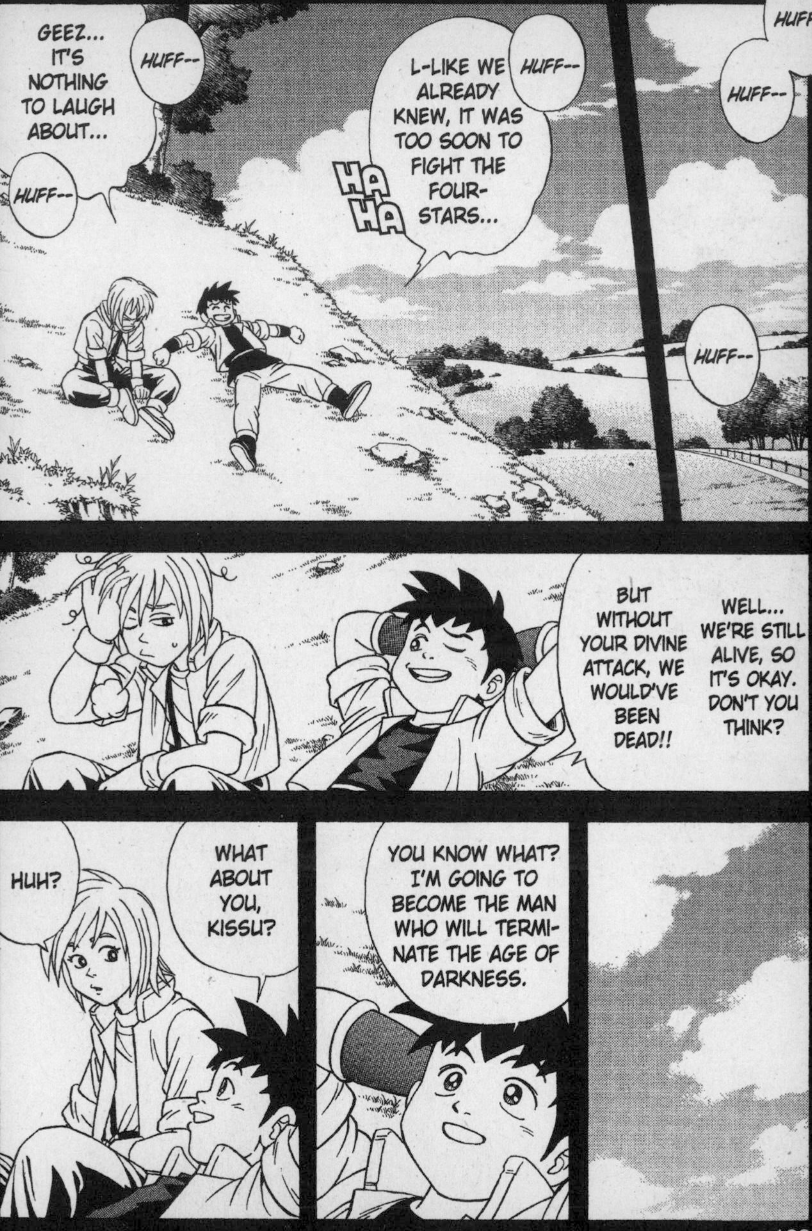

HUFF--
HUFF--
HUFF--
HUFF--
L-LIKE WE ALREADY KNEW, IT WAS TOO SOON TO FIGHT THE FOUR-STARS...
HA HA
HUFF--
GEEZ... IT'S NOTHING TO LAUGH ABOUT...
HUFF--
WELL... WE'RE STILL ALIVE, SO IT'S OKAY. DON'T YOU THINK?
BUT WITHOUT YOUR DIVINE ATTACK, WE WOULD'VE BEEN DEAD!!
YOU KNOW WHAT? I'M GOING TO BECOME THE MAN WHO WILL TERMINATE THE AGE OF DARKNESS.
WHAT ABOUT YOU, KISSU?
HUH?

READ THIS WAY

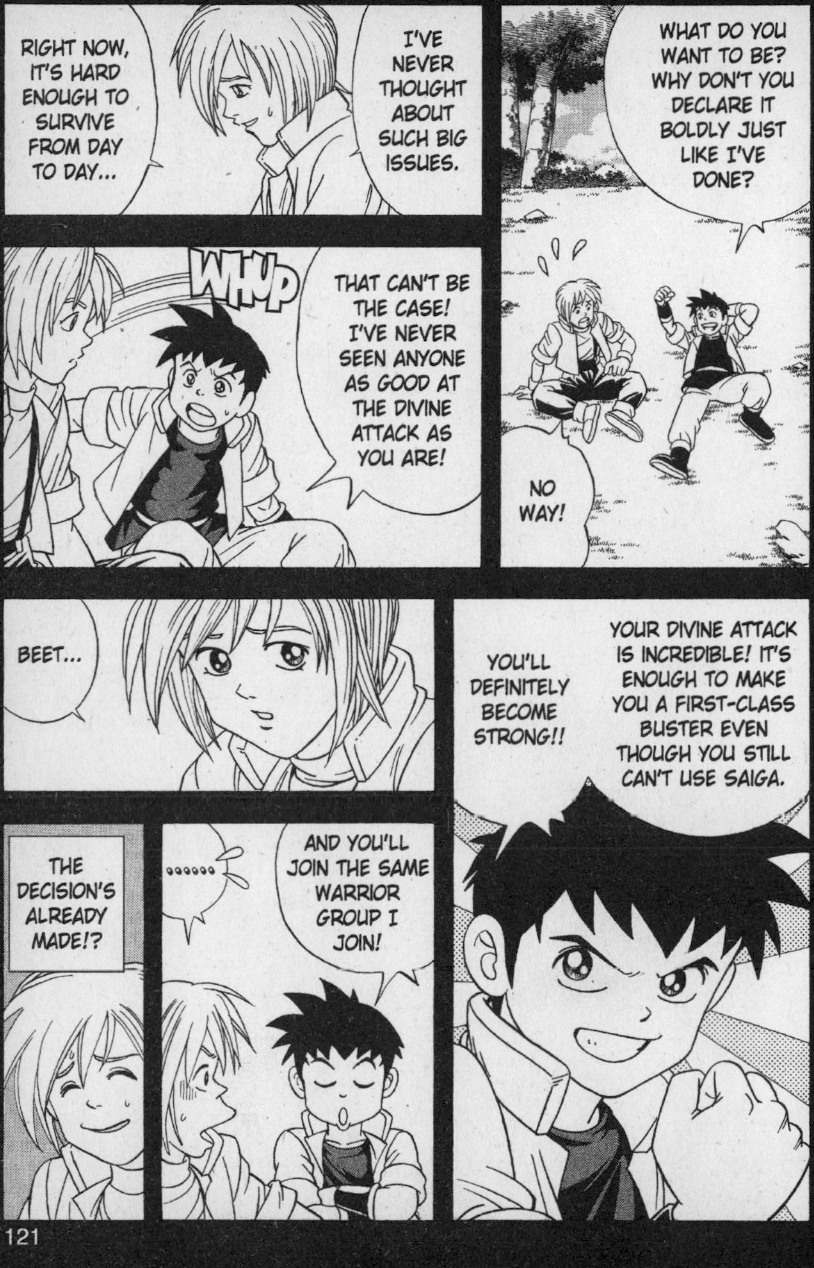

WHAT DO YOU WANT TO BE? WHY DON'T YOU DECLARE IT BOLDLY JUST LIKE I'VE DONE?
NO WAY!
I'VE NEVER THOUGHT ABOUT SUCH BIG ISSUES.
RIGHT NOW, IT'S HARD ENOUGH TO SURVIVE FROM DAY TO DAY...
THAT CAN'T BE THE CASE! I'VE NEVER SEEN ANYONE AS GOOD AT THE DIVINE ATTACK AS YOU ARE!
WHUP
YOUR DIVINE ATTACK IS INCREDIBLE! IT'S ENOUGH TO MAKE YOU A FIRST-CLASS BUSTER EVEN THOUGH YOU STILL CAN'T USE SAIGA.
YOU'LL DEFINITELY BECOME STRONG!!
BEET...
AND YOU'LL JOIN THE SAME WARRIOR GROUP I JOIN!
......
THE DECISION'S ALREADY MADE!?

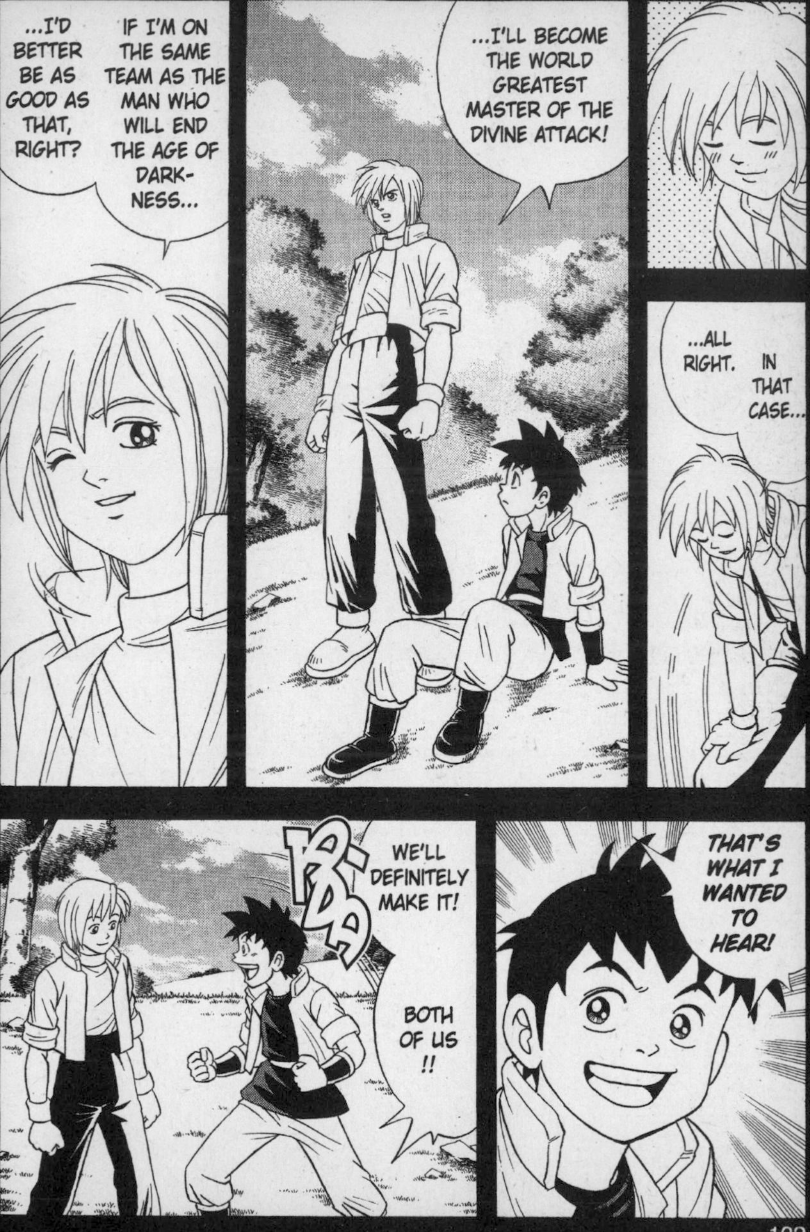
...ALL RIGHT.
IN THAT CASE...
...I'LL BECOME THE WORLD GREATEST MASTER OF THE DIVINE ATTACK!
IF I'M ON THE SAME TEAM AS THE MAN WHO WILL END THE AGE OF DARKNESS...
...I'D BETTER BE AS GOOD AS THAT, RIGHT?
THAT'S WHAT I WANTED TO HEAR!
WE'LL DEFINITELY MAKE IT!
BOTH OF US !!

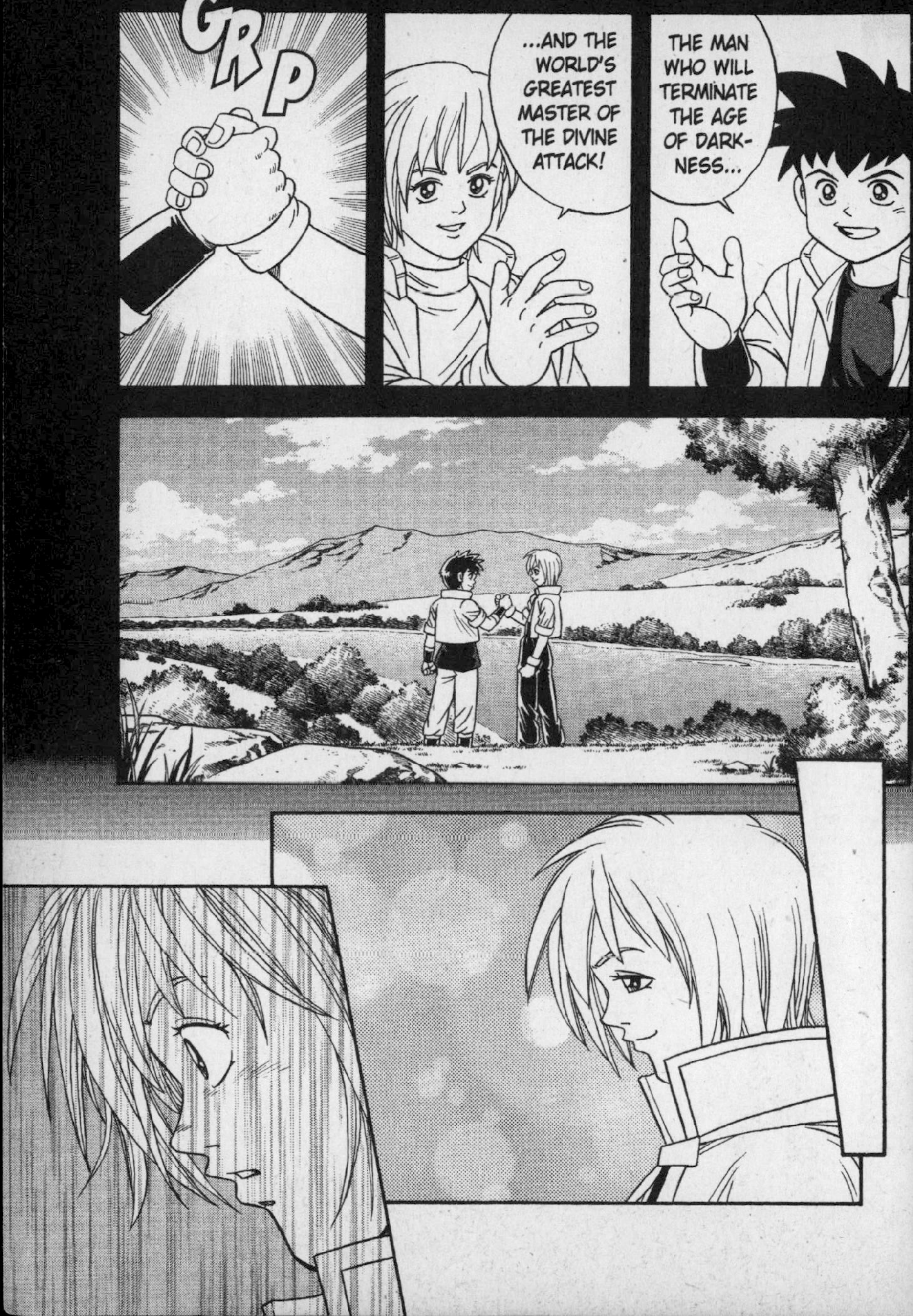
THE MAN WHO WILL TERMINATE THE AGE OF DARK- NESS...
...AND THE WORLD'S GREATEST MASTER OF THE DIVINE ATTACK!
GRP

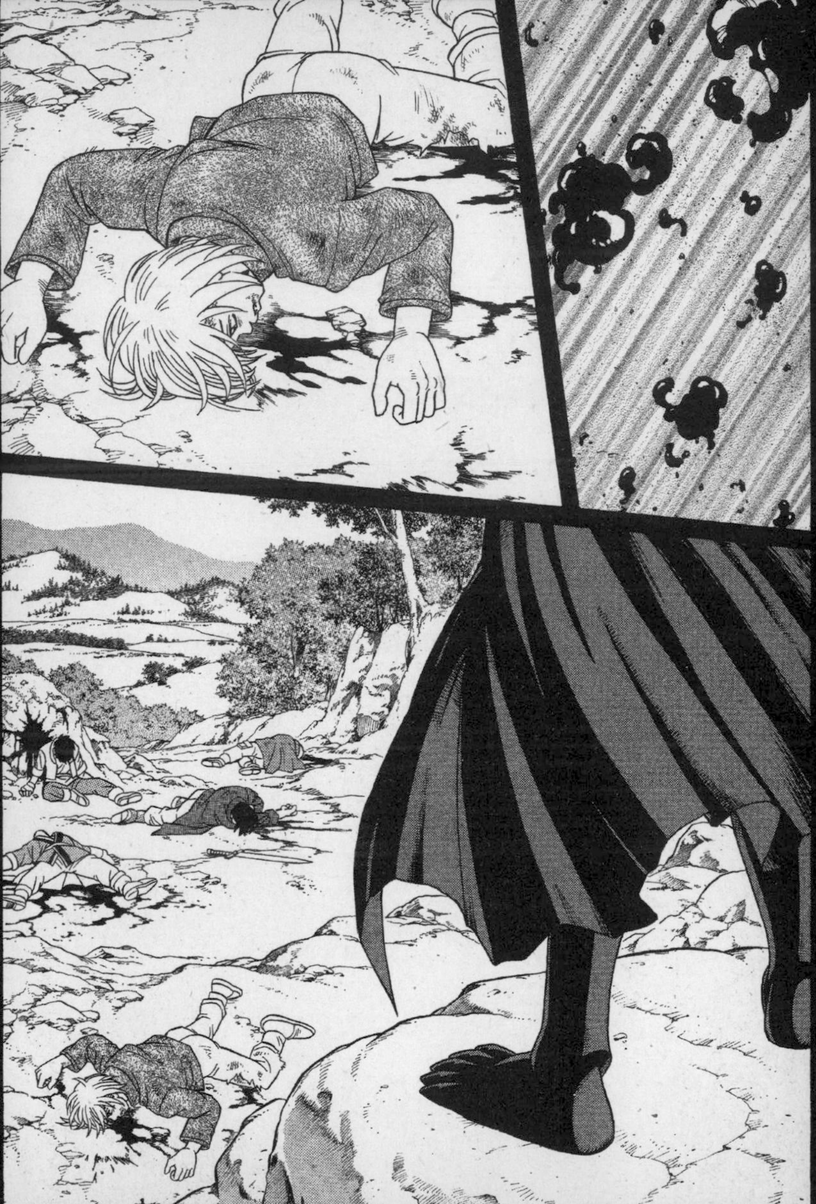

READ THIS WAY

UGH!!
WHAT'S WRONG?
!!
N- NO...
...NO- THING...

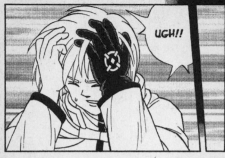

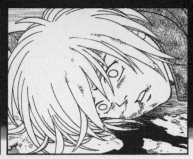

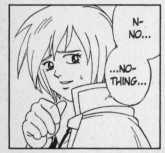

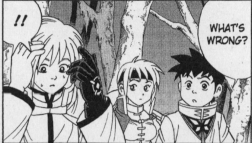

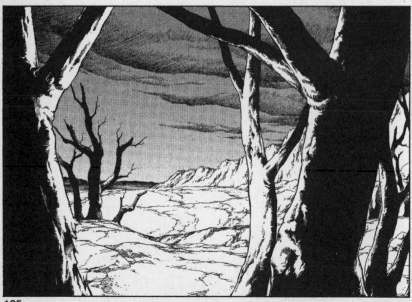

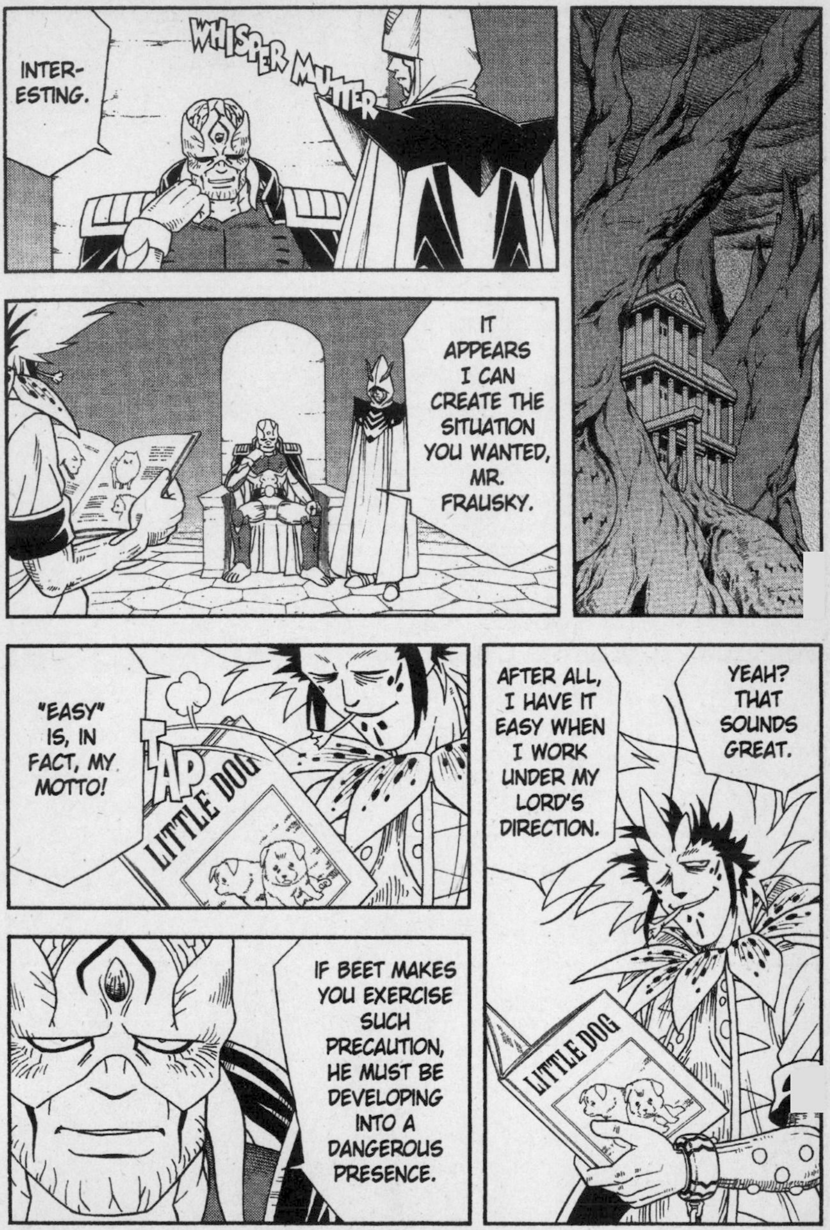

WHISPER MUTTER
INTER-ESTING.
IT APPEARS I CAN CREATE THE SITUATION YOU WANTED, MR. FRAUSKY.
YEAH? THAT SOUNDS GREAT.
AFTER ALL, I HAVE IT EASY WHEN I WORK UNDER MY LORD'S DIRECTION.
LITTLE DOG
"EASY" IS, IN FACT, MY MOTTO!
TAP
LITTLE DOG
IF BEET MAKES YOU EXERCISE SUCH PRECAUTION, HE MUST BE DEVELOPING INTO A DANGEROUS PRESENCE.

READ THIS WAY

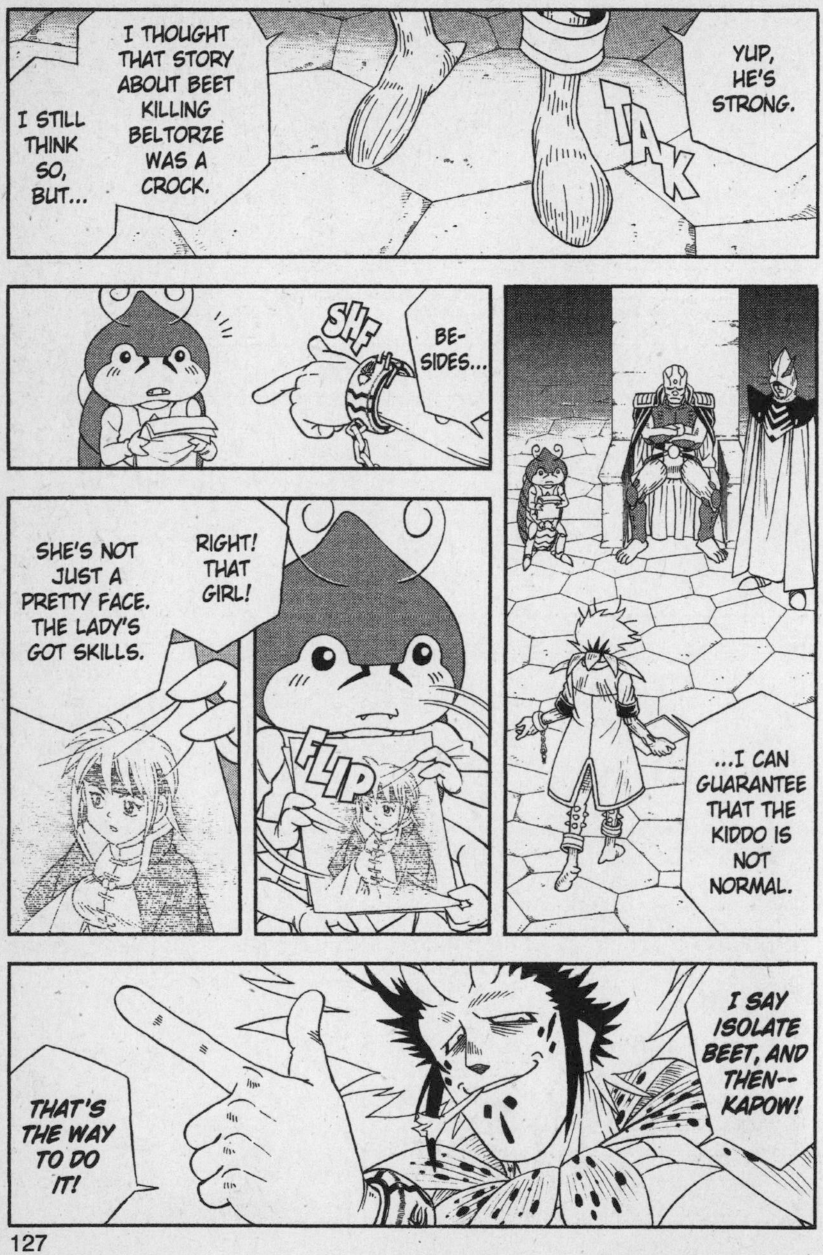

YUP, HE'S STRONG.
TAK
I THOUGHT THAT STORY ABOUT BEET KILLING BELTORZE WAS A CROCK.
I STILL THINK SO, BUT...
BE-SIDES...
SHF
...I CAN GUARANTEE THAT THE KIDDO IS NOT NORMAL.
RIGHT! THAT GIRL!
FLIP
SHE'S NOT JUST A PRETTY FACE. THE LADY'S GOT SKILLS.
I SAY ISOLATE BEET, AND THEN--KAPOW!
THAT'S THE WAY TO DO IT!

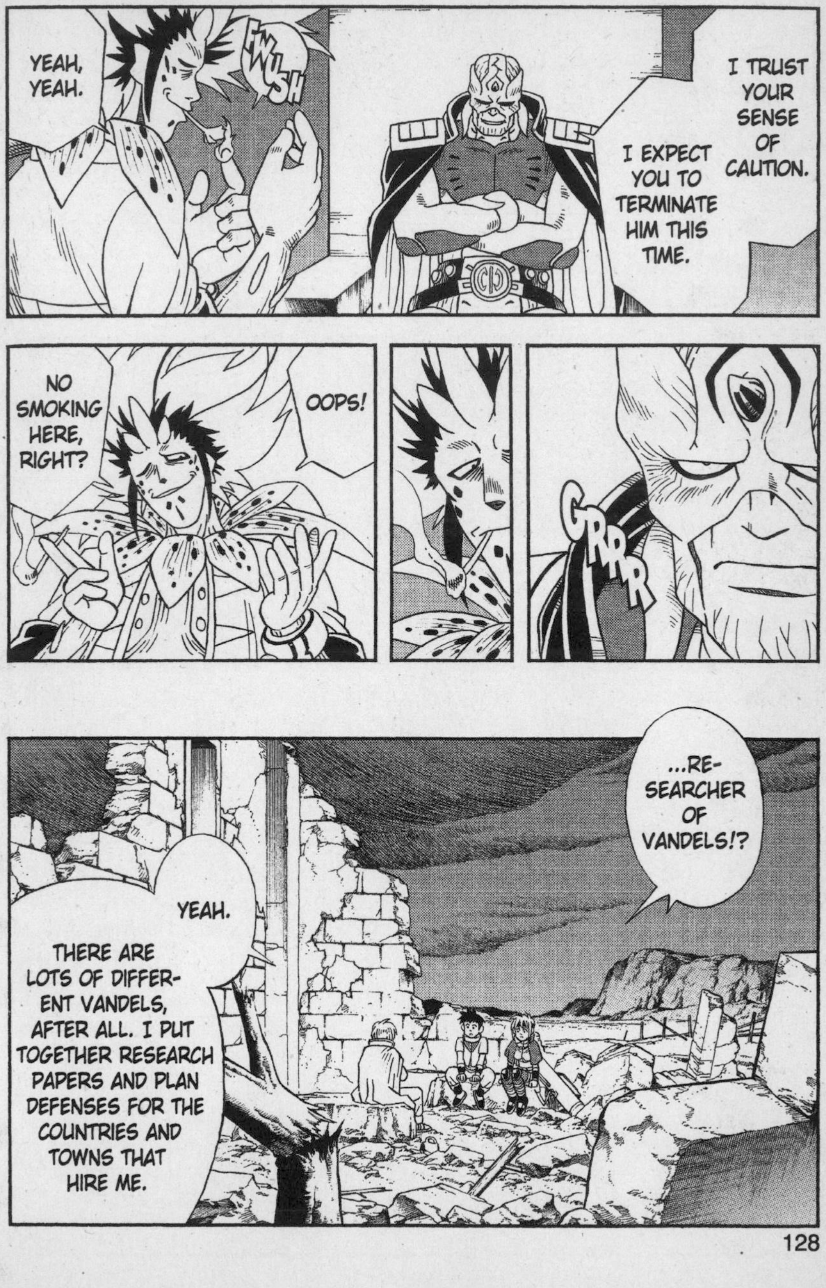
I TRUST YOUR SENSE OF CAUTION.
I EXPECT YOU TO TERMINATE HIM THIS TIME.
FWUSH
YEAH, YEAH.
GRRRR
OOPS!
NO SMOKING HERE, RIGHT?
...RESEARCHER OF VANDELS!?
YEAH.
THERE ARE LOTS OF DIFFERENT VANDELS, AFTER ALL. I PUT TOGETHER RESEARCH PAPERS AND PLAN DEFENSES FOR THE COUNTRIES AND TOWNS THAT HIRE ME.

READ THIS WAY

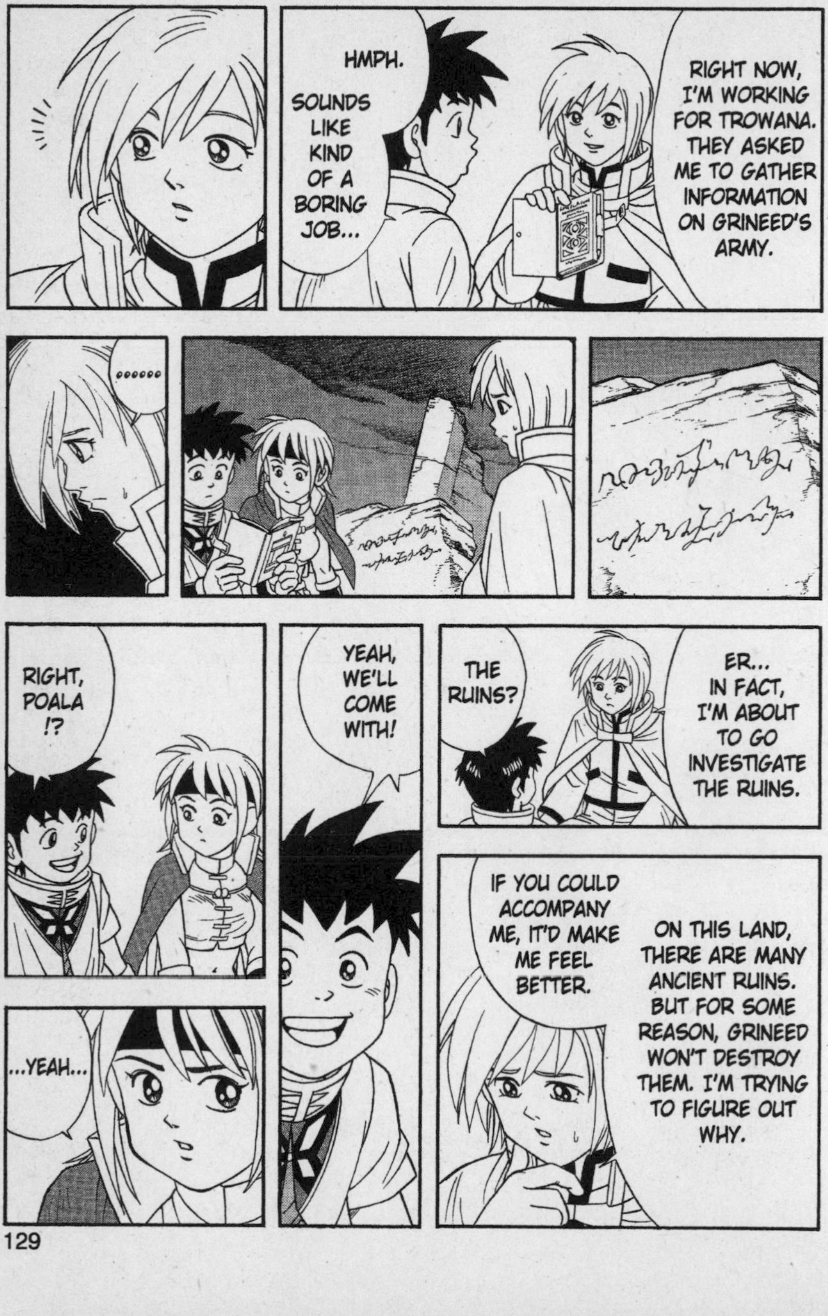

RIGHT NOW, I'M WORKING FOR TROWANA. THEY ASKED ME TO GATHER INFORMATION ON GRINEED'S ARMY.
HMPH.
SOUNDS LIKE KIND OF A BORING JOB...
......
ER... IN FACT, I'M ABOUT TO GO INVESTIGATE THE RUINS.
THE RUINS?
ON THIS LAND, THERE ARE MANY ANCIENT RUINS. BUT FOR SOME REASON, GRINEED WON'T DESTROY THEM. I'M TRYING TO FIGURE OUT WHY.
IF YOU COULD ACCOMPANY ME, IT'D MAKE ME FEEL BETTER.
YEAH, WE'LL COME WITH!
RIGHT, POALA !?
...YEAH...

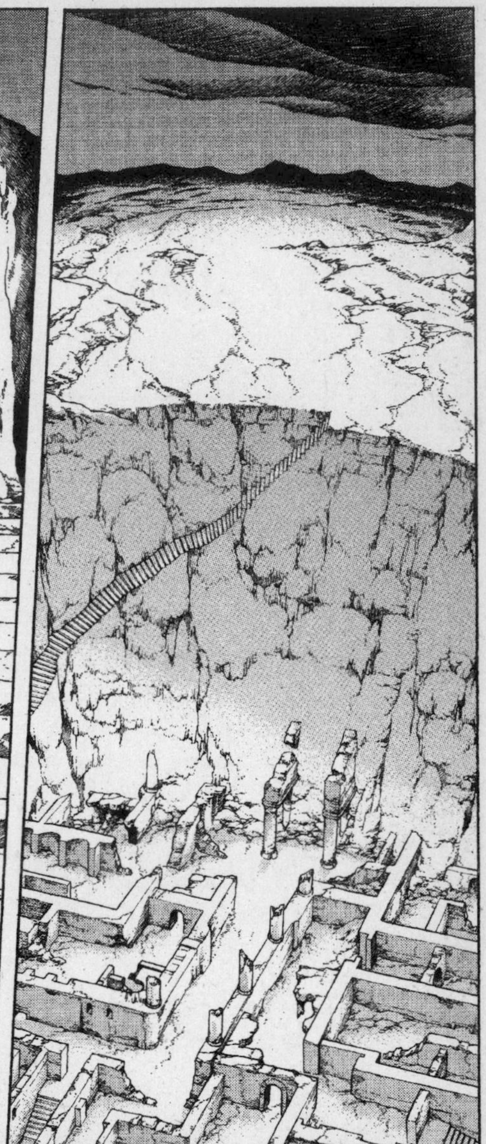

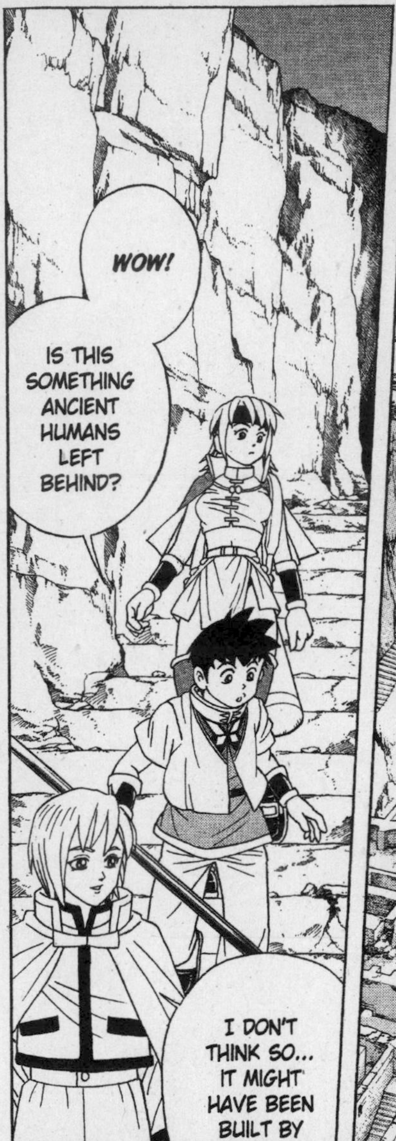
WOW!
IS THIS SOMETHING ANCIENT HUMANS LEFT BEHIND?
I DON'T THINK SO... IT MIGHT HAVE BEEN BUILT BY VANDELS.

READ THIS WAY

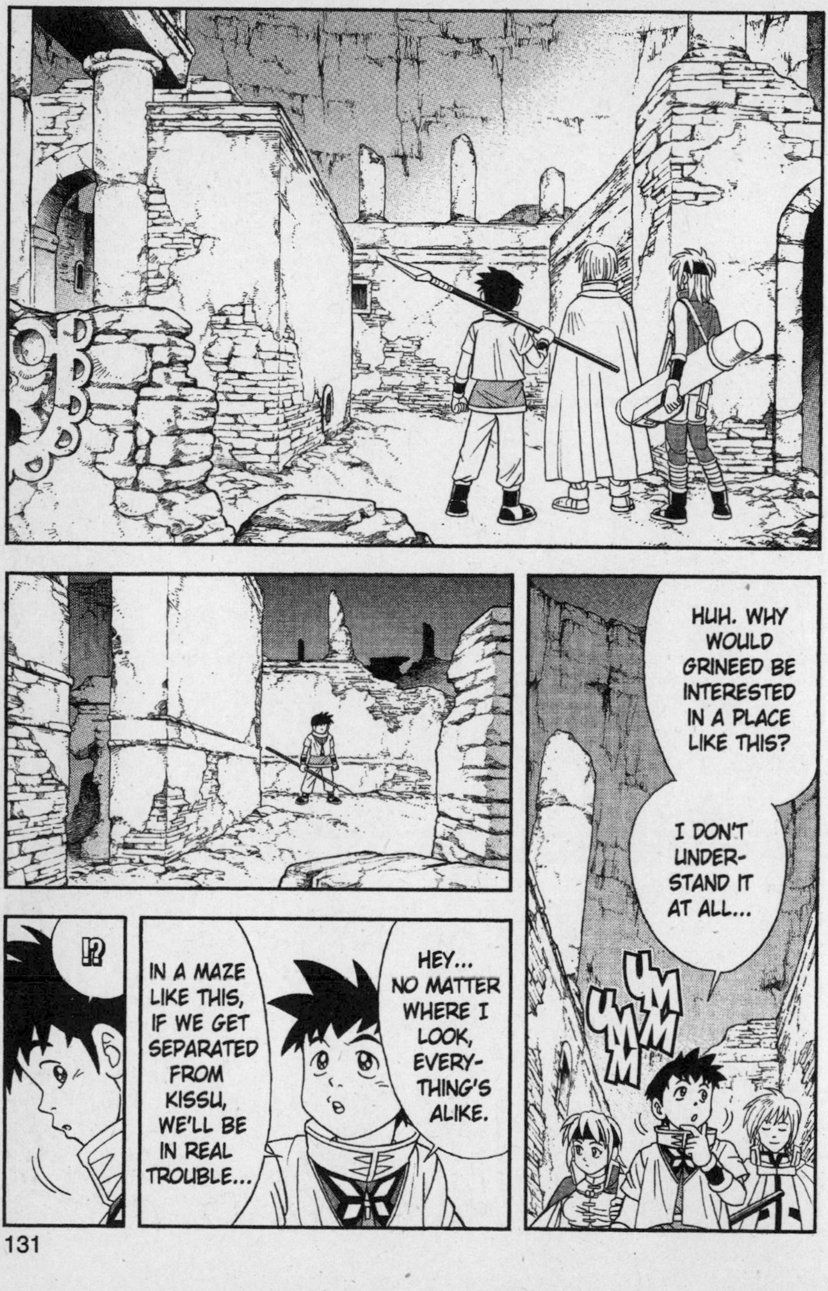
HUH. WHY WOULD GRINEED BE INTERESTED IN A PLACE LIKE THIS?
I DON'T UNDER-STAND IT AT ALL...
UMM
UMM
HEY... NO MATTER WHERE I LOOK, EVERY-THING'S ALIKE.
IN A MAZE LIKE THIS, IF WE GET SEPARATED FROM KISSU, WE'LL BE IN REAL TROUBLE...
!?

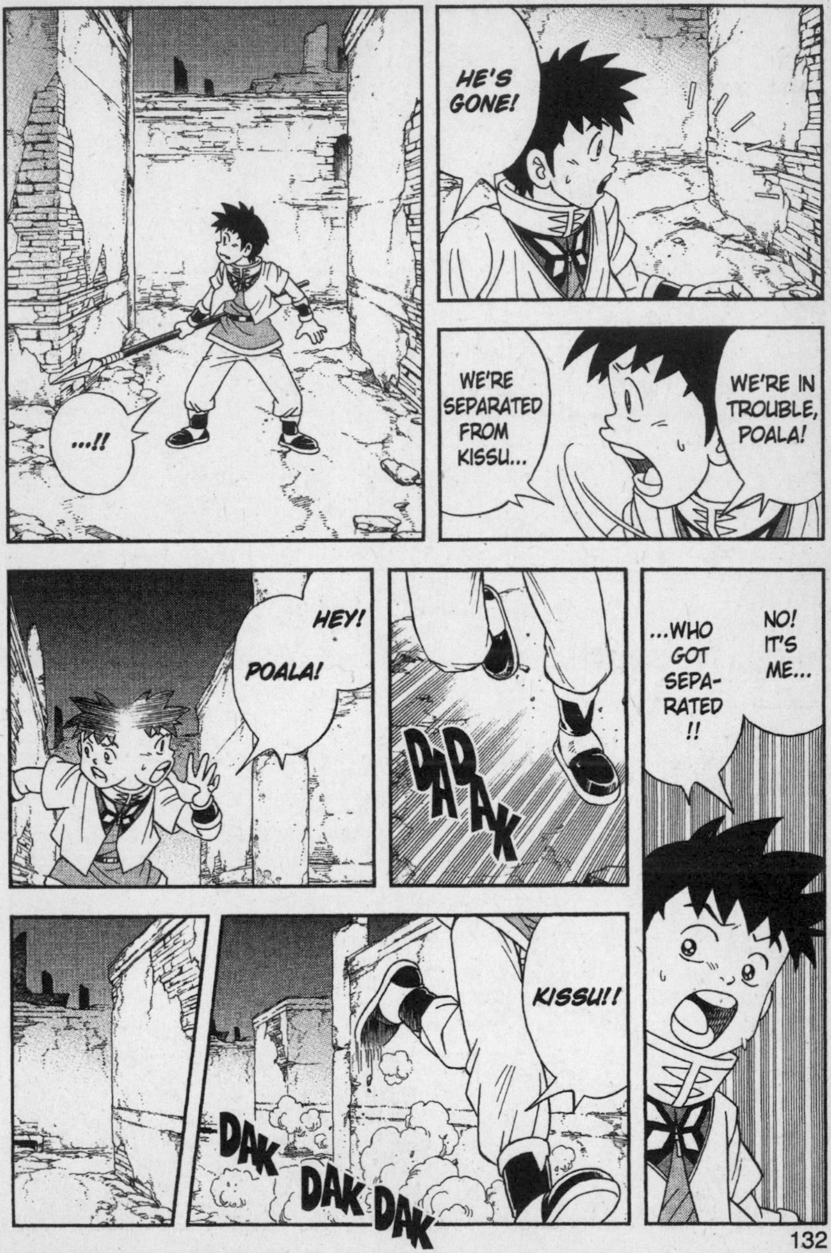
HE'S GONE!
WE'RE IN TROUBLE, POALA!
WE'RE SEPARATED FROM KISSU...
...!!
NO! IT'S ME...
...WHO GOT SEPA-RATED !!
DADAK
HEY!
POALA!
KISSU!!
DAK
DAK
DAK

READ THIS WAY

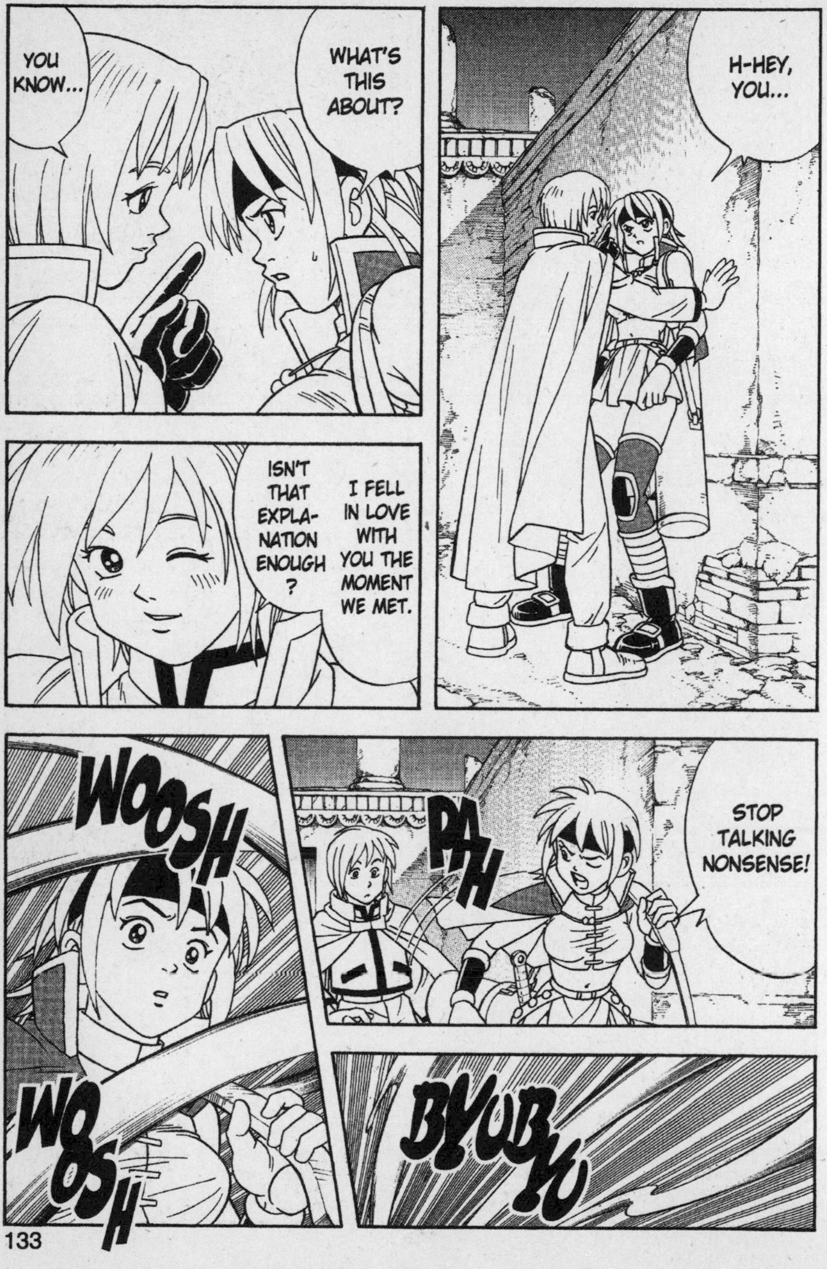

H-HEY, YOU...
WHAT'S THIS ABOUT?
YOU KNOW...
I FELL IN LOVE WITH YOU THE MOMENT WE MET.
ISN'T THAT EXPLANATION ENOUGH?
STOP TALKING NONSENSE!
PAH
BYUBYU
WOOSH
WOOSH

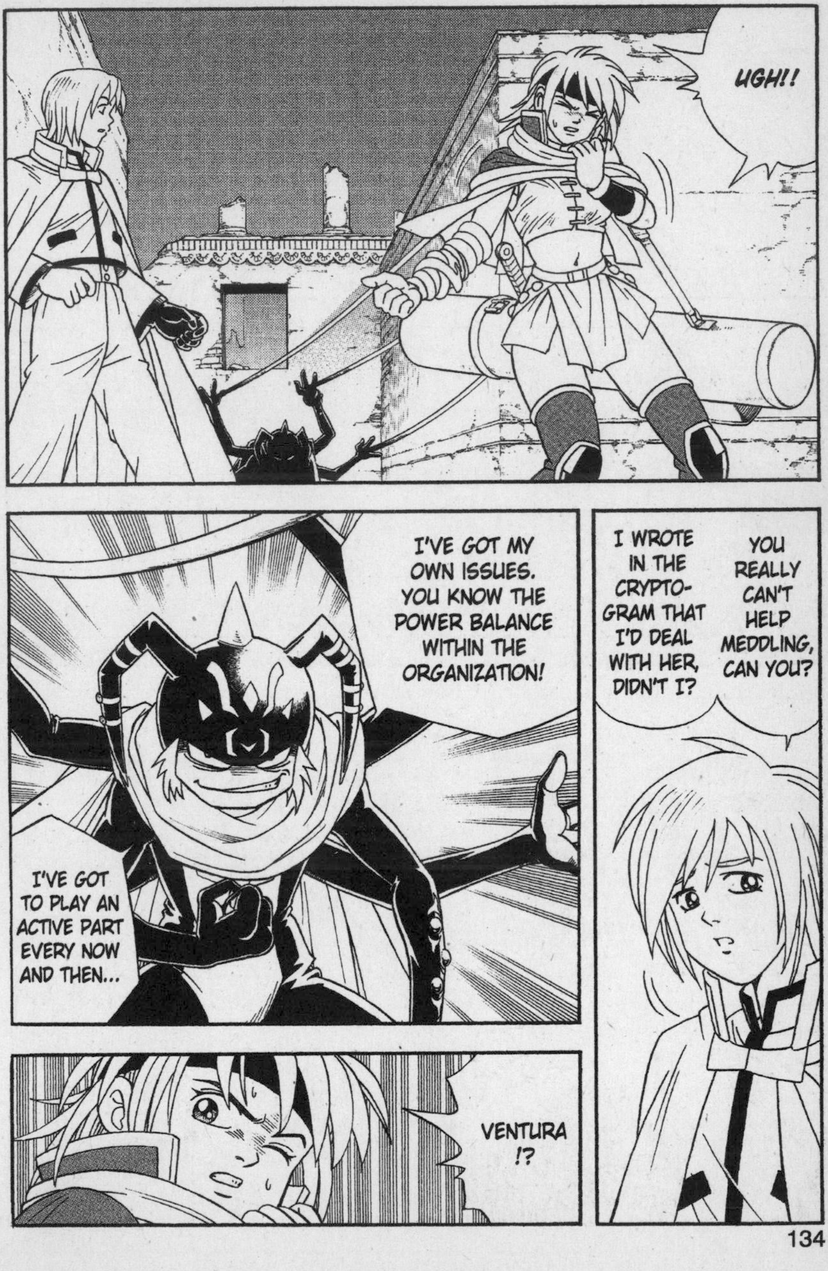
UGH!!
YOU REALLY CAN'T HELP MEDDLING, CAN YOU?
I WROTE IN THE CRYPTO-GRAM THAT I'D DEAL WITH HER, DIDN'T I?
I'VE GOT MY OWN ISSUES. YOU KNOW THE POWER BALANCE WITHIN THE ORGANIZATION!
I'VE GOT TO PLAY AN ACTIVE PART EVERY NOW AND THEN...
VENTURA !?

READ THIS WAY

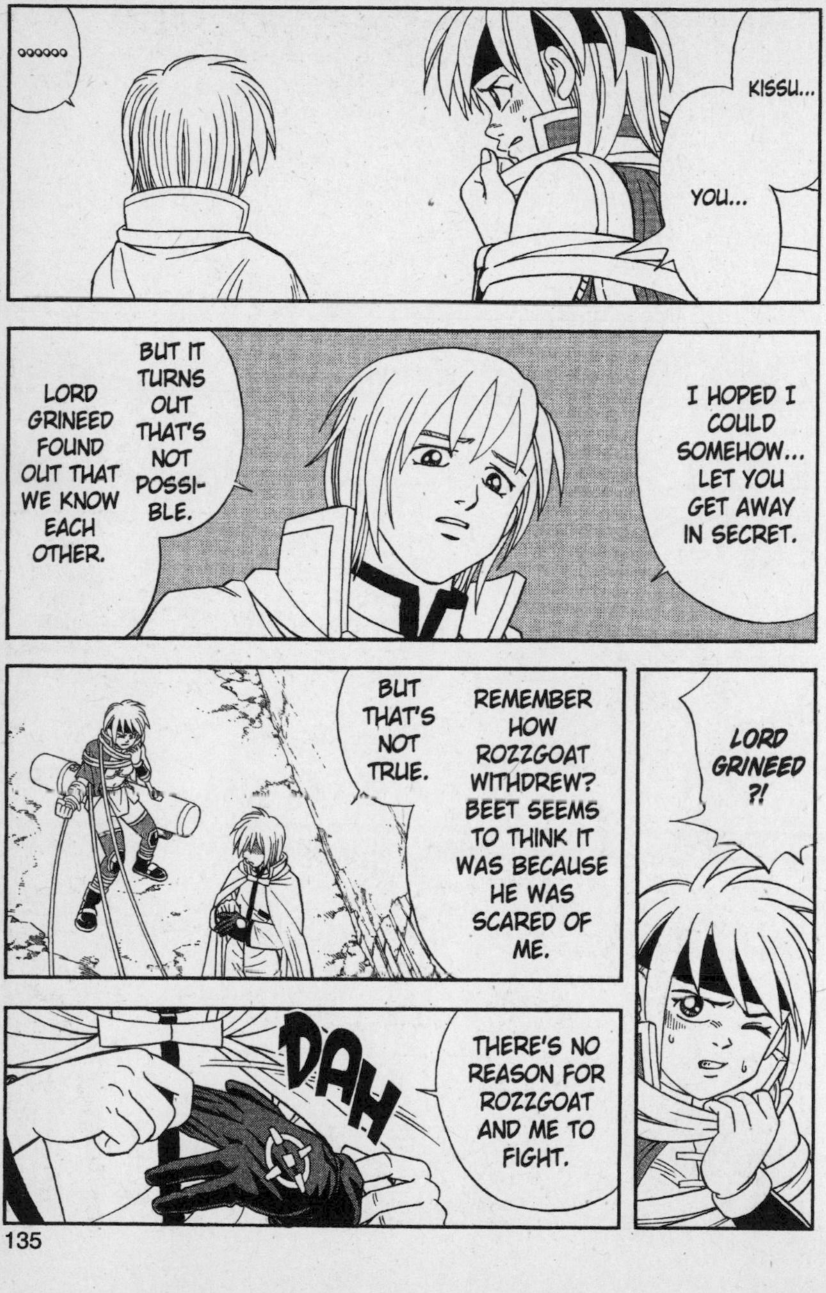
KISSU...
YOU...
......
I HOPED I COULD SOMEHOW... LET YOU GET AWAY IN SECRET.
BUT IT TURNS OUT THAT'S NOT POSSI-BLE.
LORD GRINEED FOUND OUT THAT WE KNOW EACH OTHER.
LORD GRINEED ?!
REMEMBER HOW ROZZGOAT WITHDREW? BEET SEEMS TO THINK IT WAS BECAUSE HE WAS SCARED OF ME.
BUT THAT'S NOT TRUE.
THERE'S NO REASON FOR ROZZGOAT AND ME TO FIGHT.
DAH

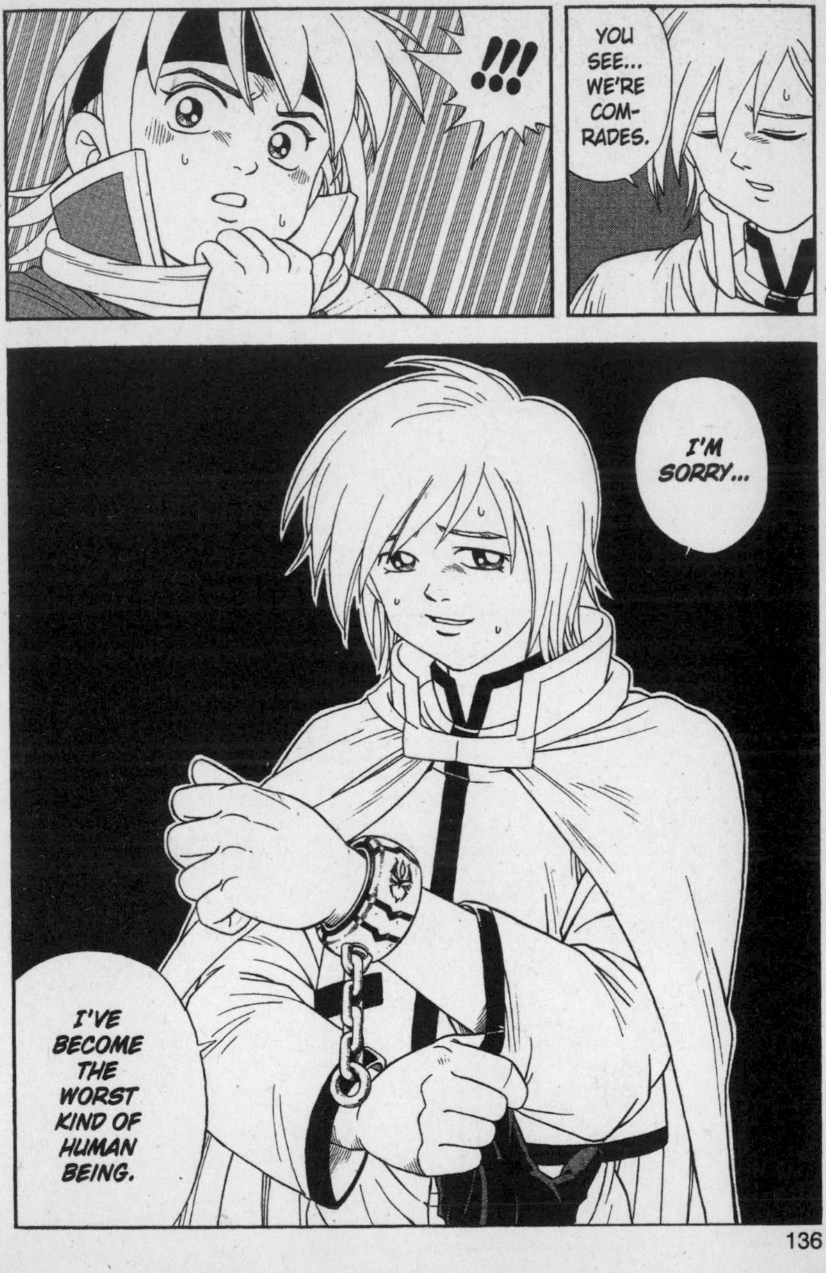
YOU SEE... WE'RE COM- RADES.
!!!
I'M SORRY...
I'VE BECOME THE WORST KIND OF HUMAN BEING.

READ THIS WAY

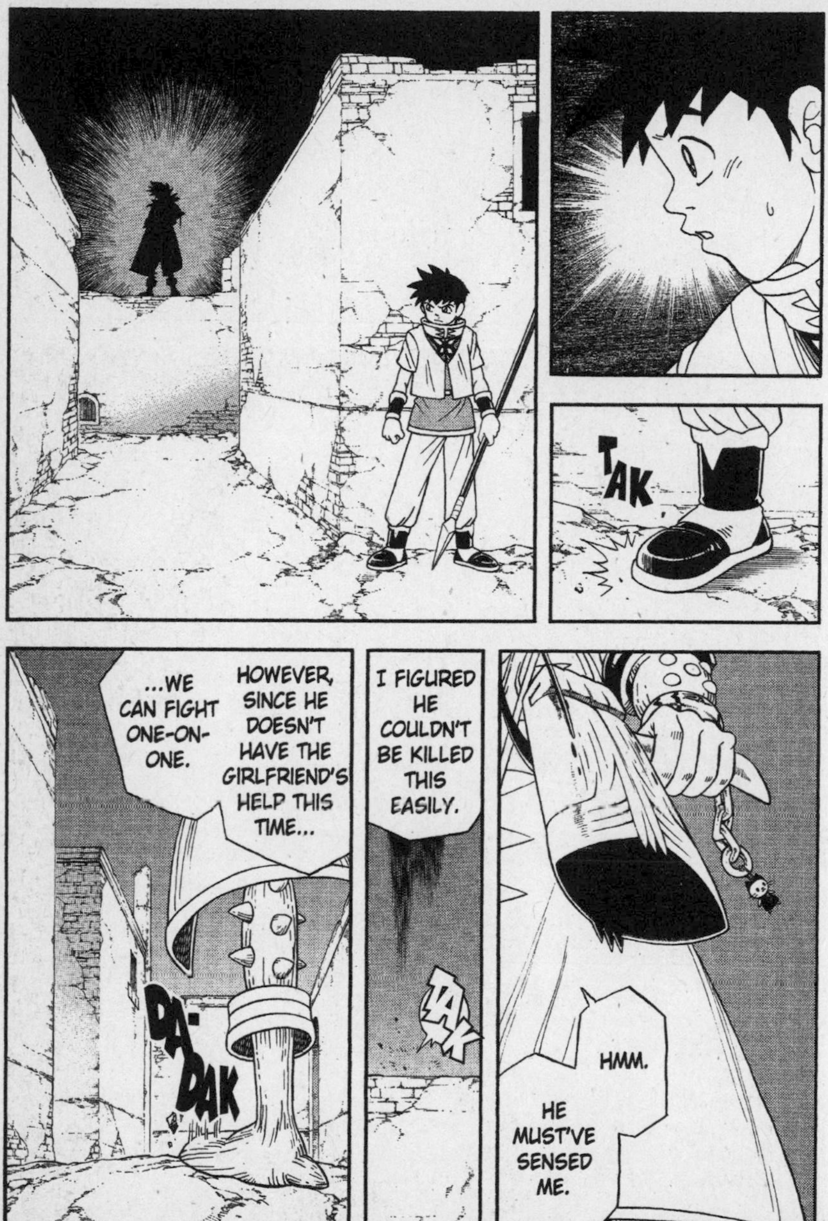

TAK
HMM.
HE MUST'VE SENSED ME.
I FIGURED HE COULDN'T BE KILLED THIS EASILY.
TAK
HOWEVER, SINCE HE DOESN'T HAVE THE GIRLFRIEND'S HELP THIS TIME...
...WE CAN FIGHT ONE-ON-ONE.
DA-DAK

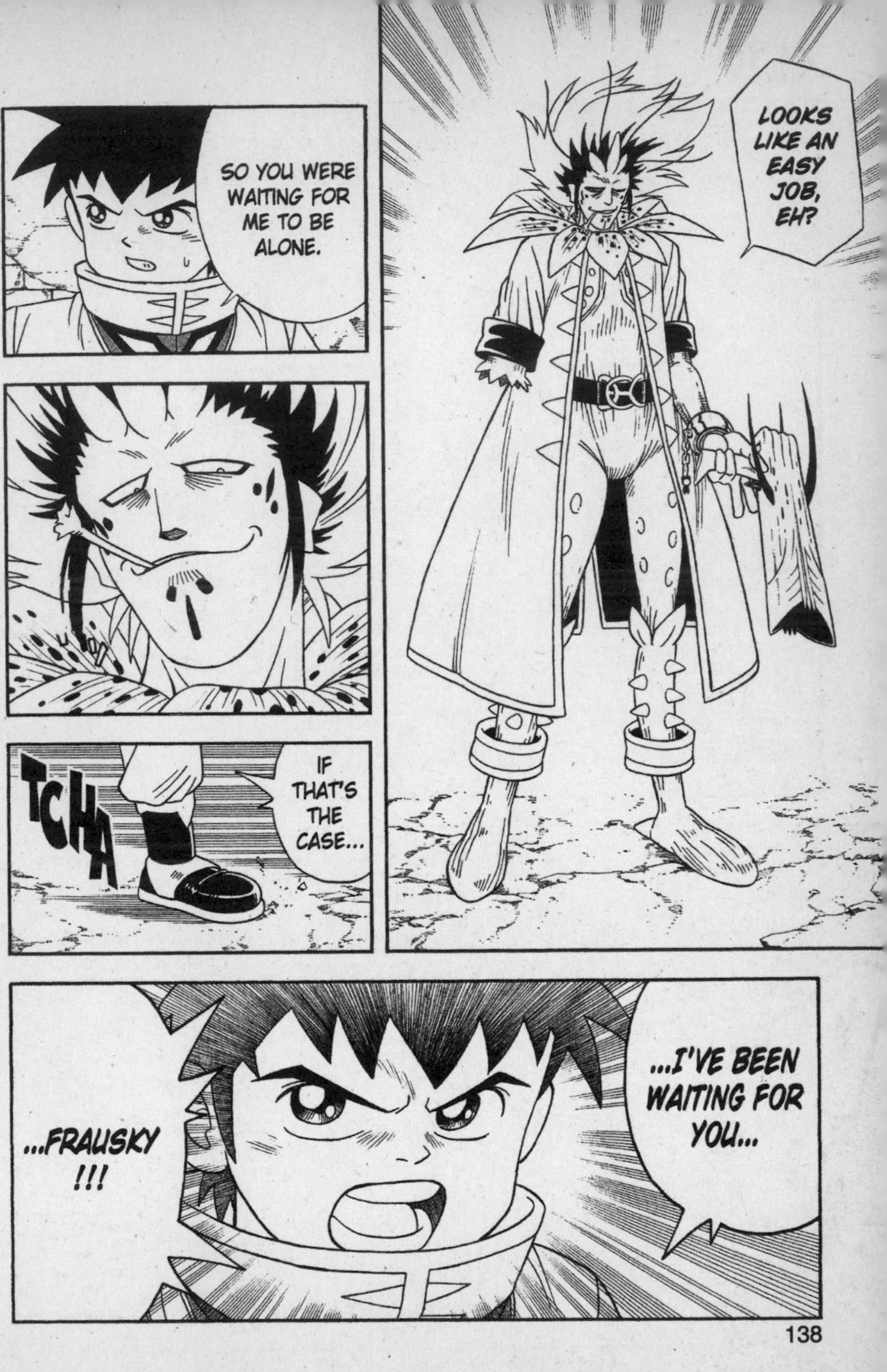
LOOKS LIKE AN EASY JOB, EH?
SO YOU WERE WAITING FOR ME TO BE ALONE.
TCHA
IF THAT'S THE CASE...
...I'VE BEEN WAITING FOR YOU...
...FRAUSKY !!!

READ THIS WAY

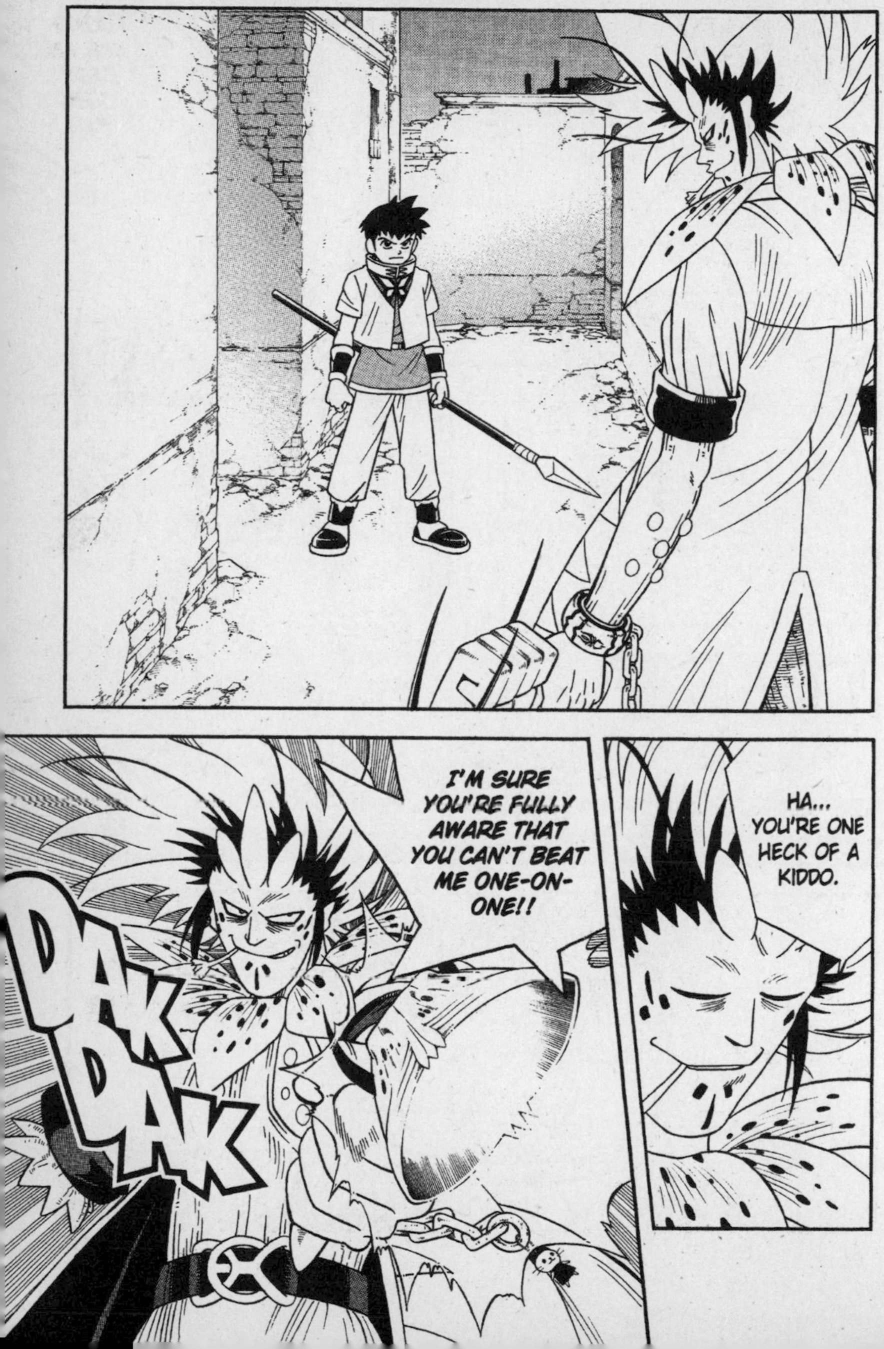
HA... YOU'RE ONE HECK OF A KIDDO.
I'M SURE YOU'RE FULLY AWARE THAT YOU CAN'T BEAT ME ONE-ON-ONE!!
DAK DAK

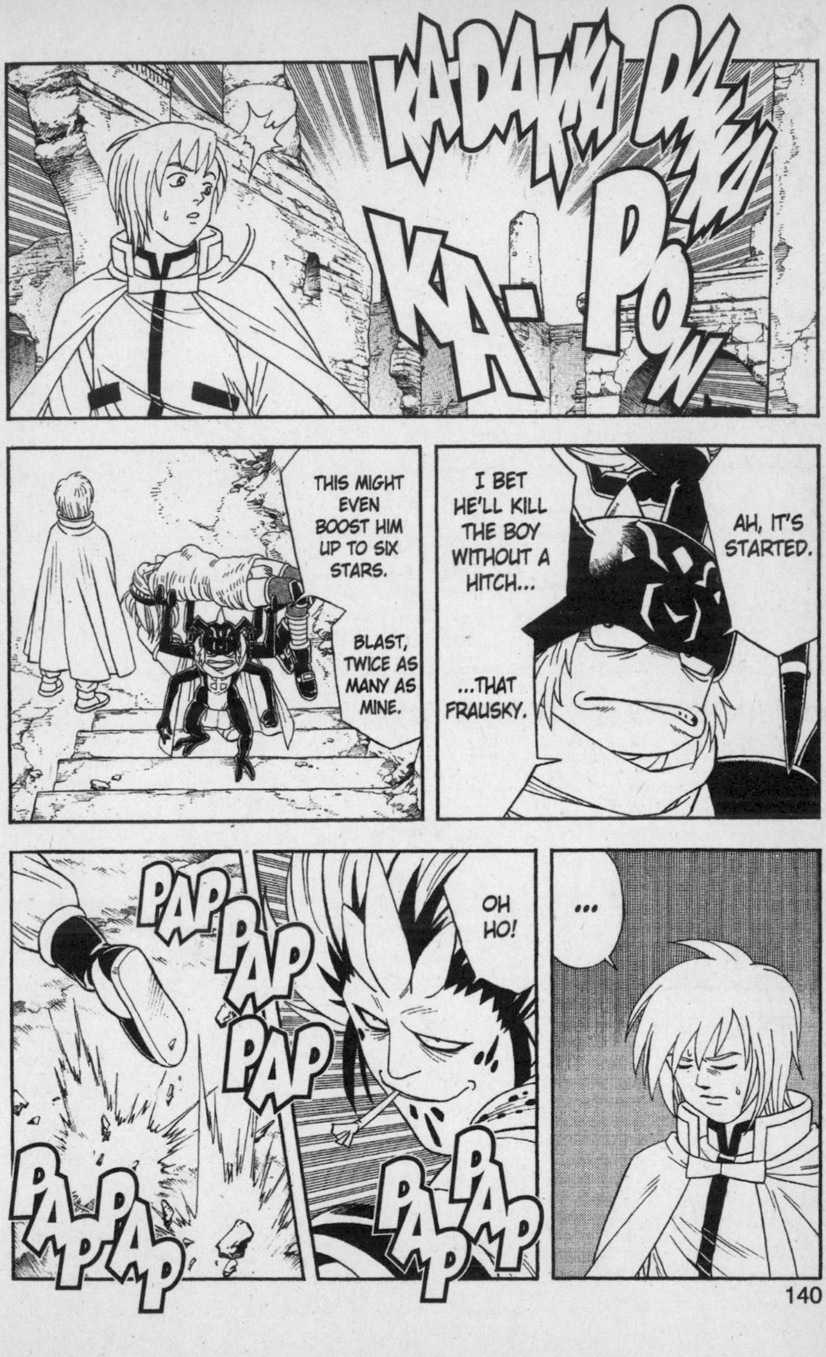
KA-DAKKA DA-KA
KA-POW
AH, IT'S STARTED.
I BET HE'LL KILL THE BOY WITHOUT A HITCH...
...THAT FRAUSKY.
THIS MIGHT EVEN BOOST HIM UP TO SIX STARS.
BLAST, TWICE AS MANY AS MINE.
...
OH HO!
PAP PAP PAP PAP
PAP PAP PAP
PAPAPAP

READ THIS WAY

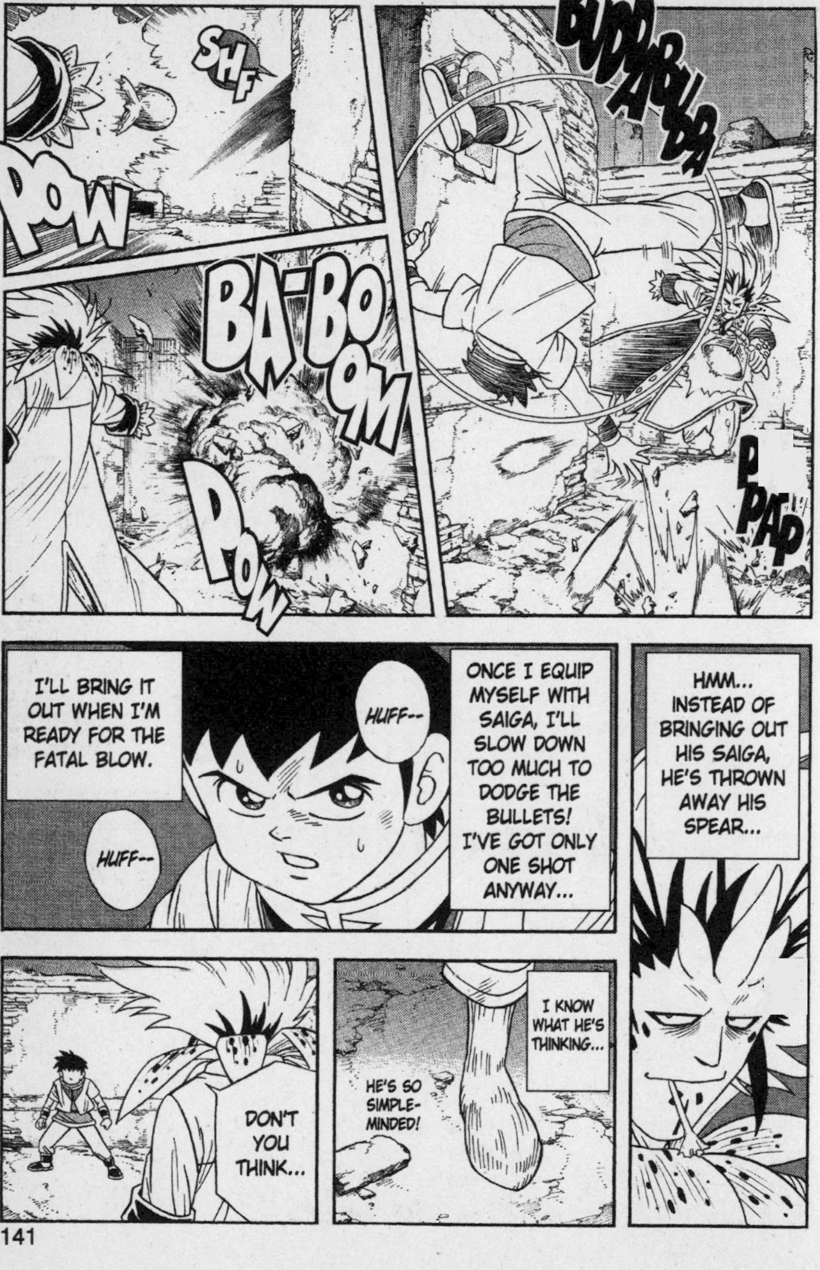
BUDDABUDDA
PAP
SHF
POW
BA-BOOM
POW
HMM... INSTEAD OF BRINGING OUT HIS SAIGA, HE'S THROWN AWAY HIS SPEAR...
ONCE I EQUIP MYSELF WITH SAIGA, I'LL SLOW DOWN TOO MUCH TO DODGE THE BULLETS! I'VE GOT ONLY ONE SHOT ANYWAY...
HUFF--
I'LL BRING IT OUT WHEN I'M READY FOR THE FATAL BLOW.
HUFF--
I KNOW WHAT HE'S THINKING...
HE'S SO SIMPLE-MINDED!
DON'T YOU THINK...

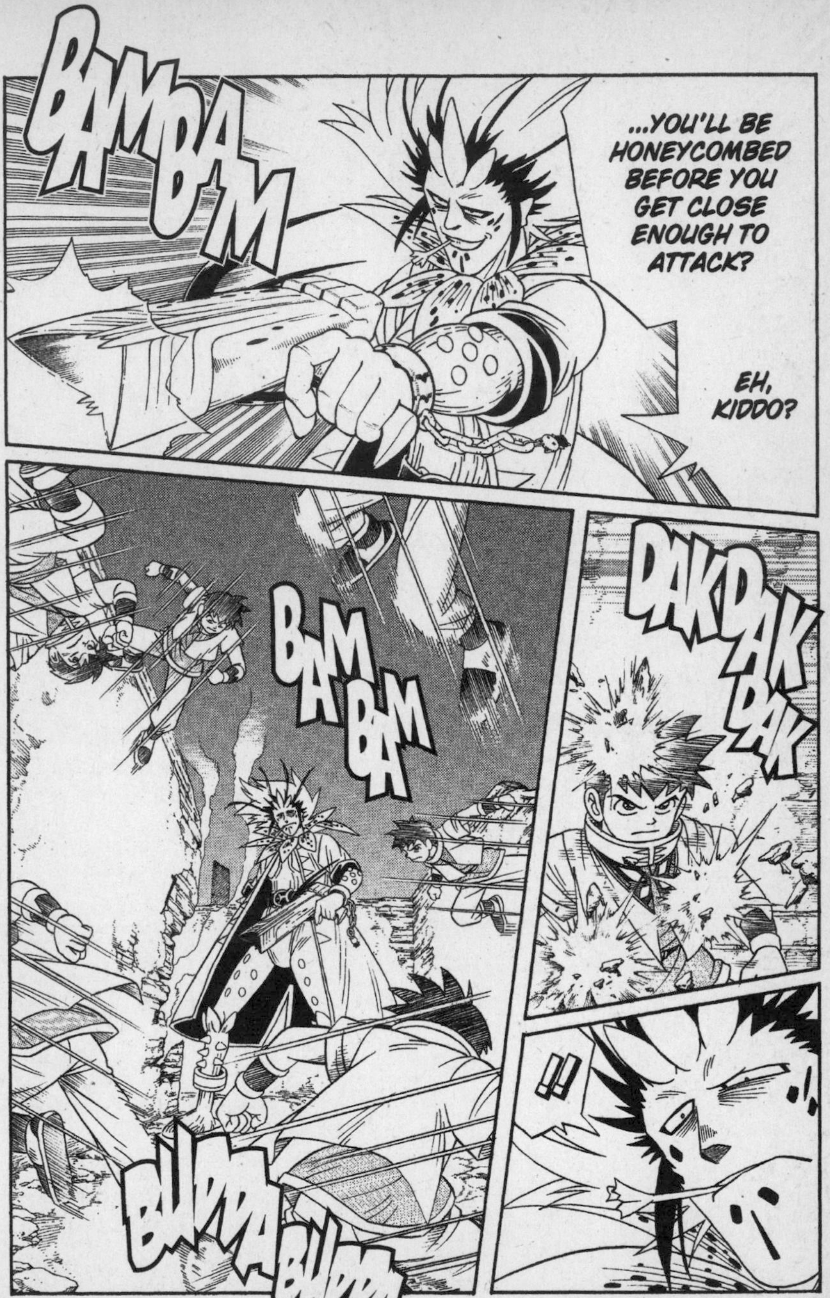
BAMBAM
...YOU'LL BE HONEYCOMBED BEFORE YOU GET CLOSE ENOUGH TO ATTACK?
EH, KIDDO?
DAK DAK DAK DAK
!!
BAM BAM BAM BAM
BUDDA BUDDA

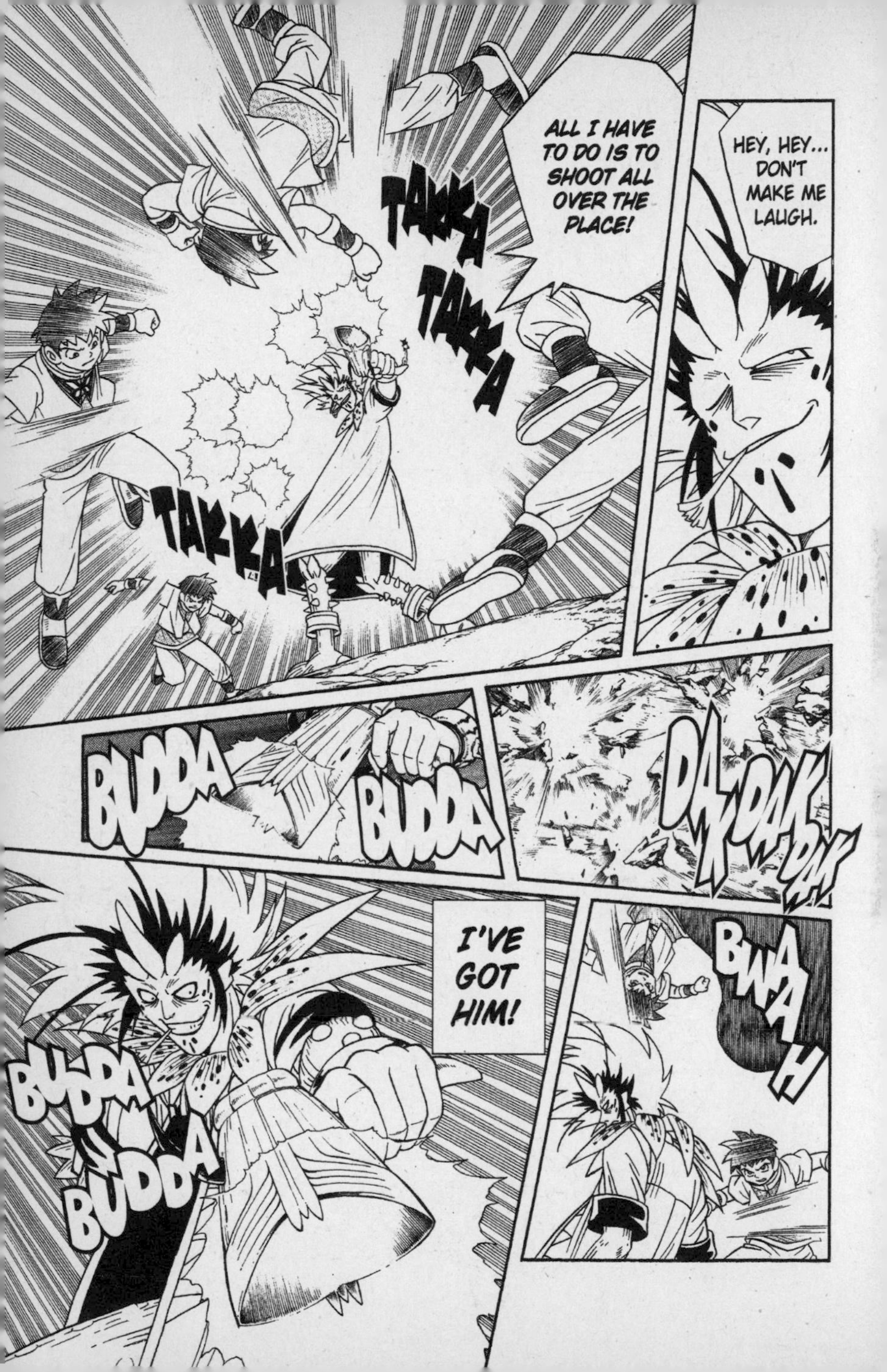
HEY, HEY... DON'T MAKE ME LAUGH.
ALL I HAVE TO DO IS TO SHOOT ALL OVER THE PLACE!
TAKKA TAKKA TAKKA
TAKKA
DA DAK DAK
BUDDA BUDDA
BWAAH
I'VE GOT HIM!
BUDDA BUDDA

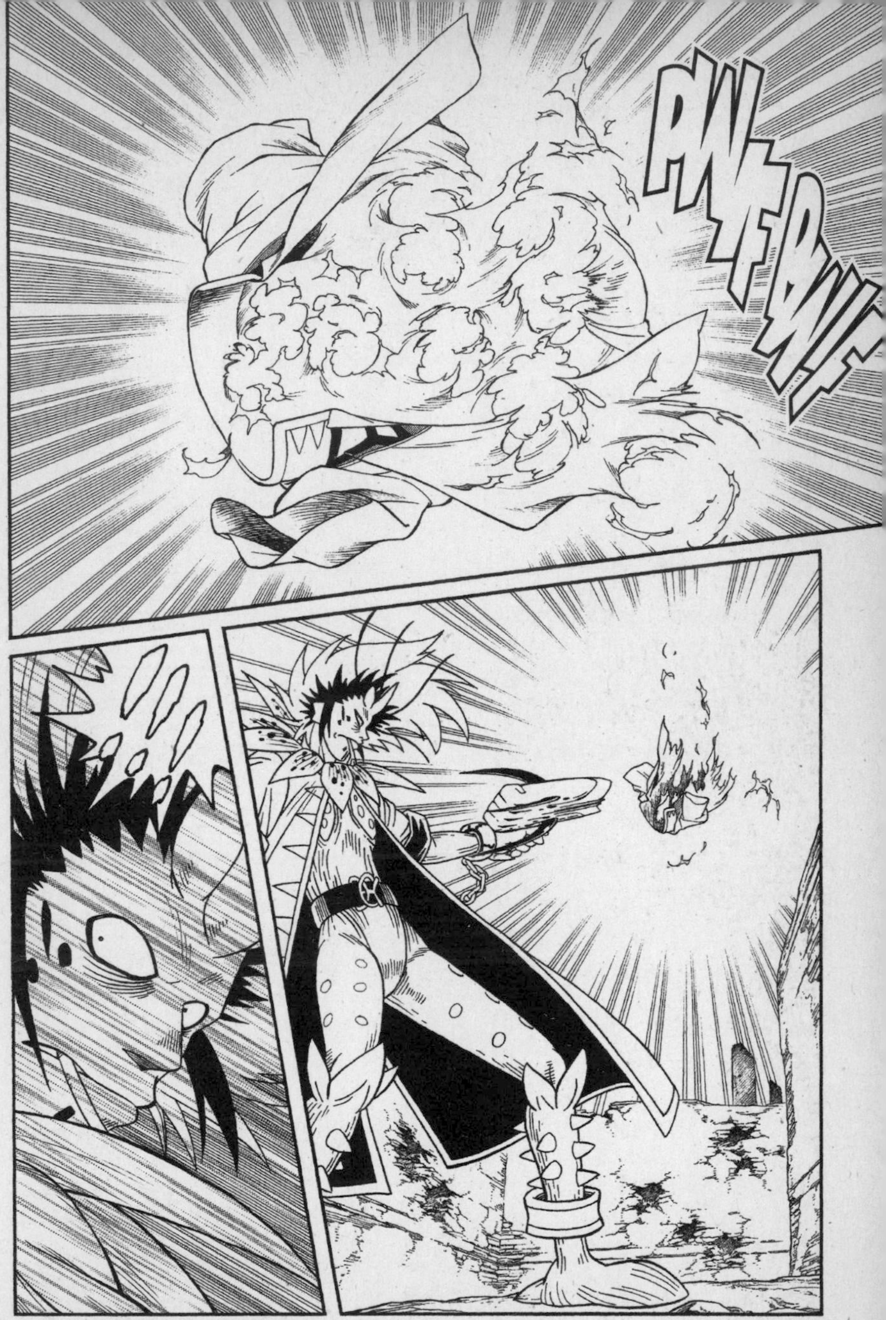

READ THIS WAY

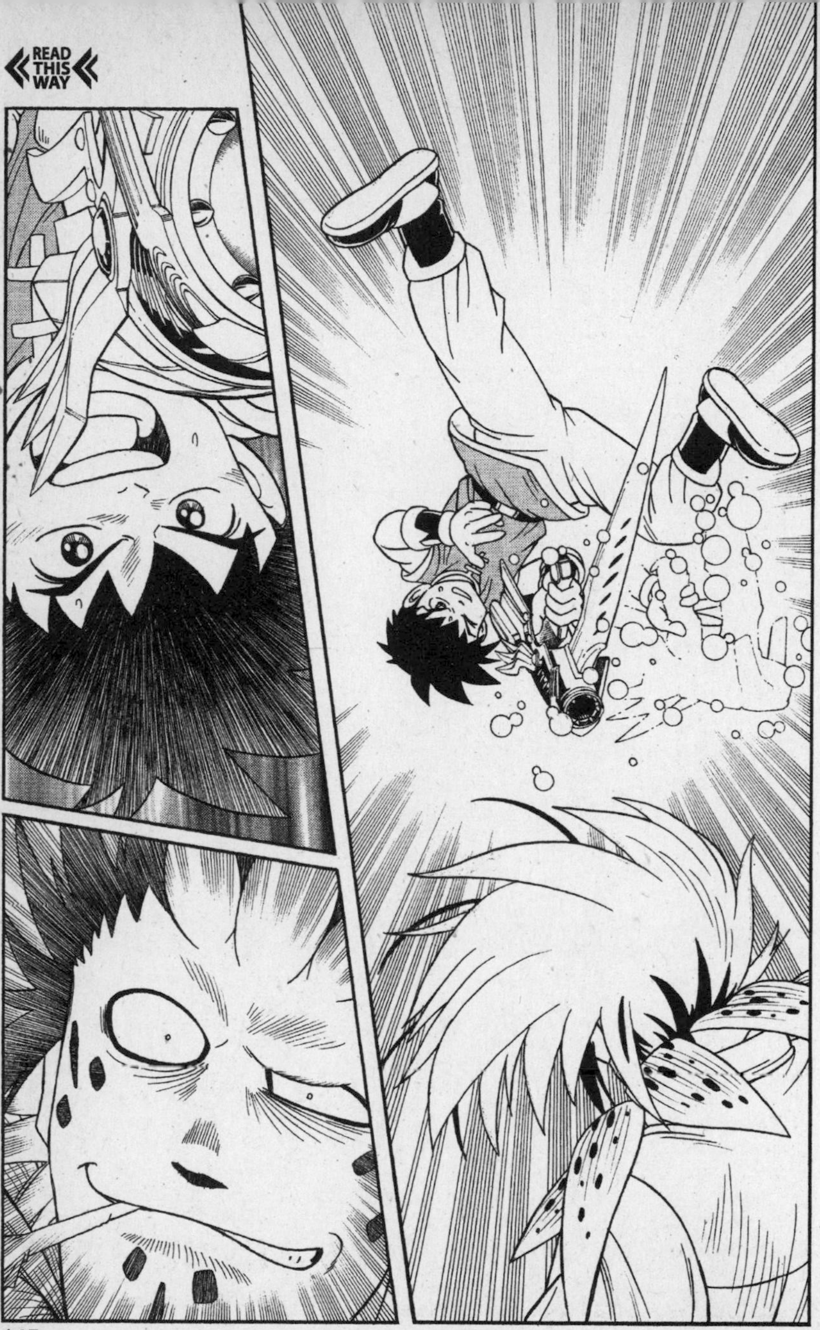

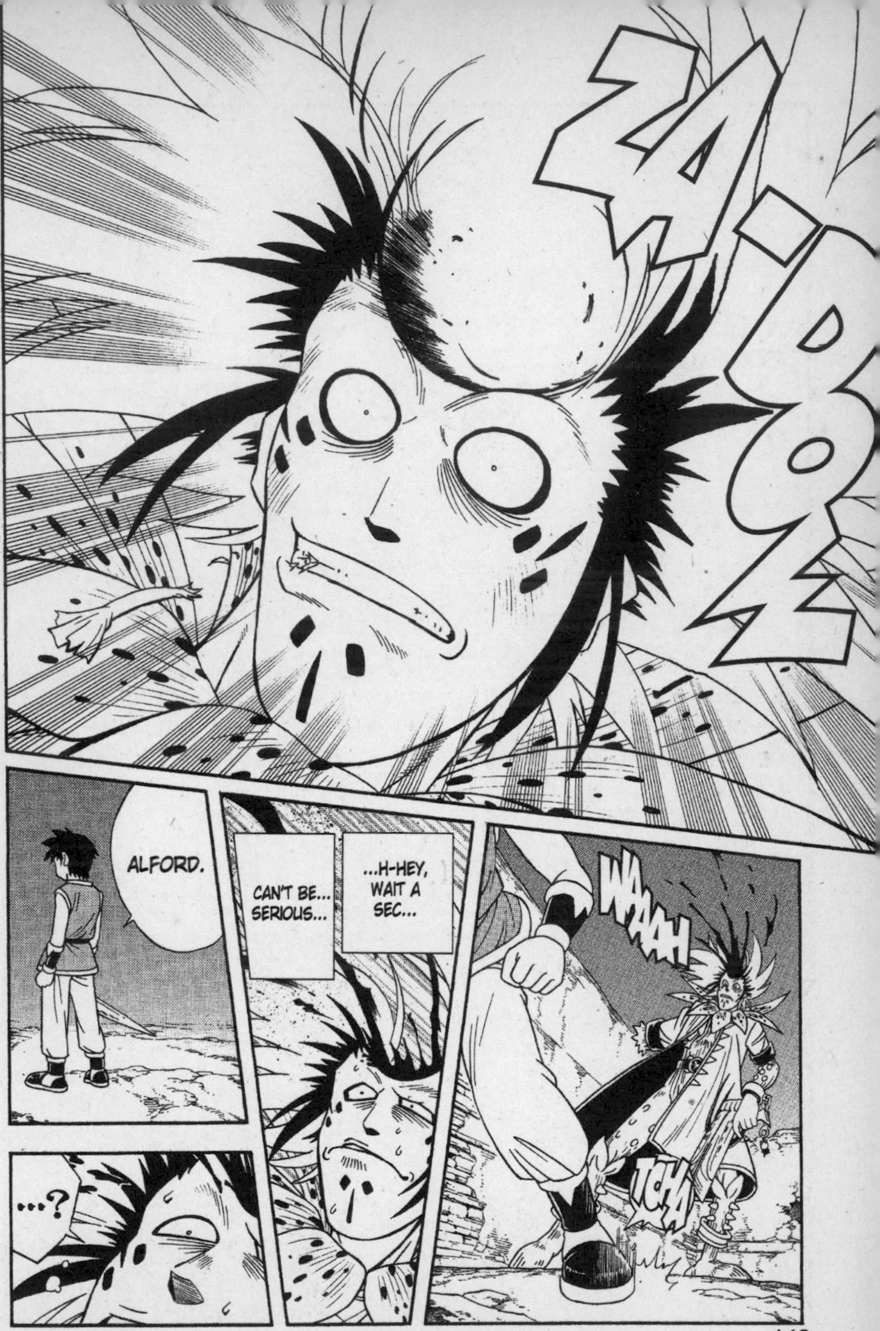
ZA-DOOM
WAAAH
TCHA
...H-HEY, WAIT A SEC...
CAN'T BE... SERIOUS...
ALFORD.
...?

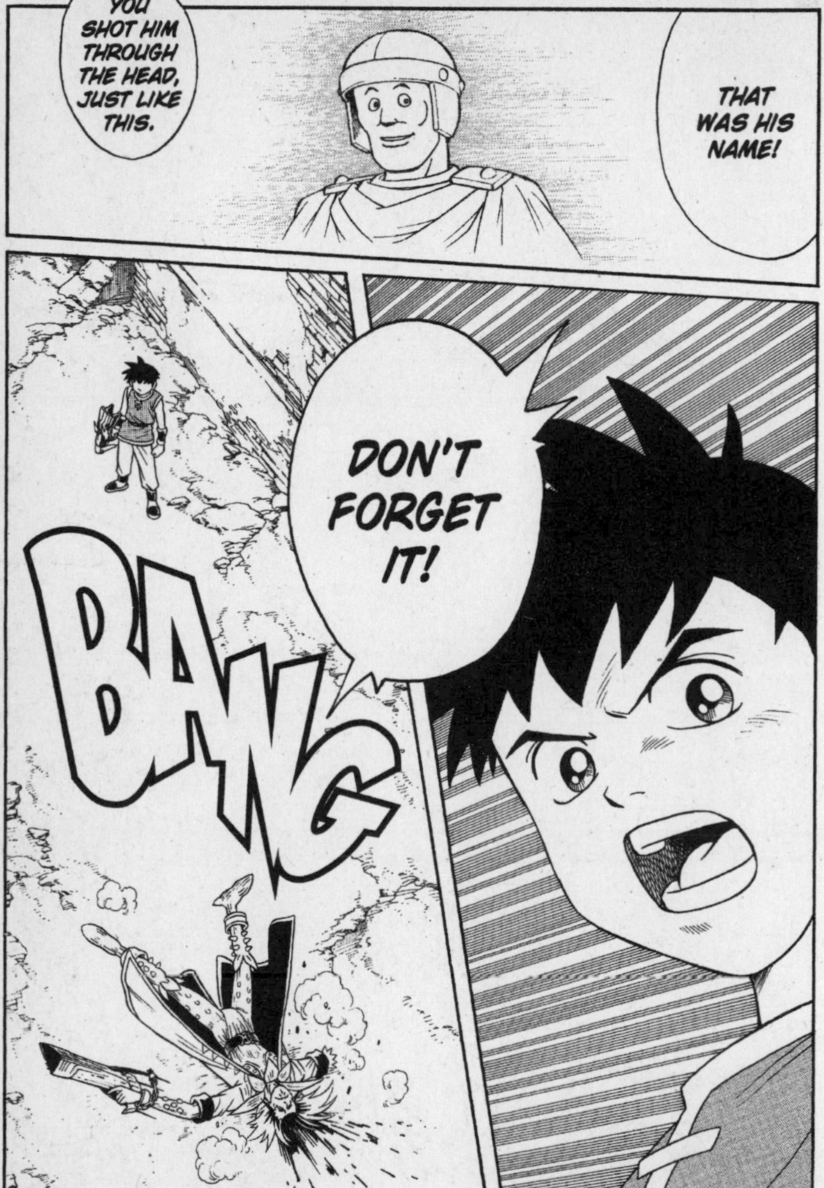
THAT WAS HIS NAME!
YOU SHOT HIM THROUGH THE HEAD, JUST LIKE THIS.
DON'T FORGET IT!
BANG

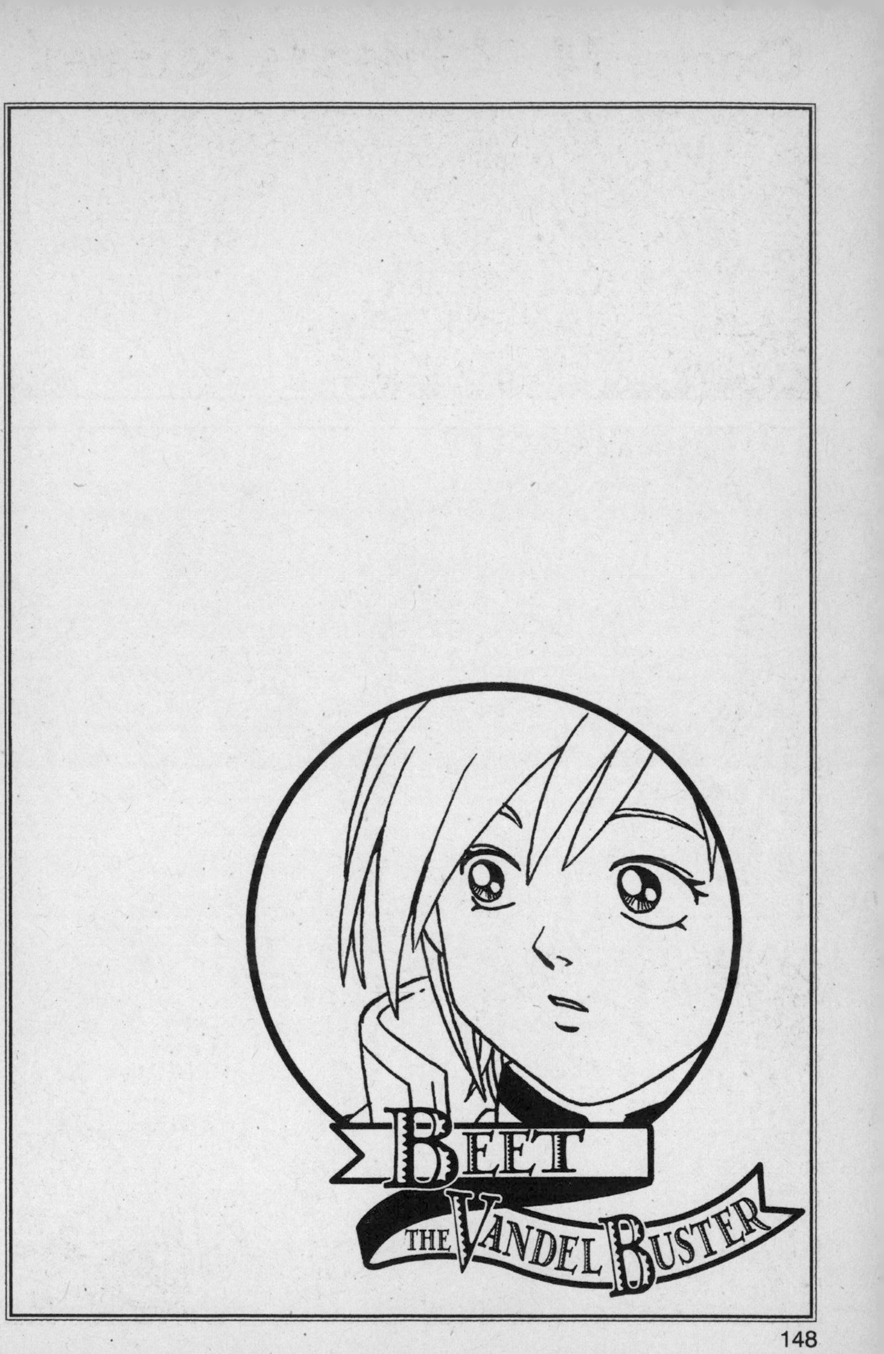
BEET
THE VANDEL BUSTER

Chapter 14: A Friend's Betrayal

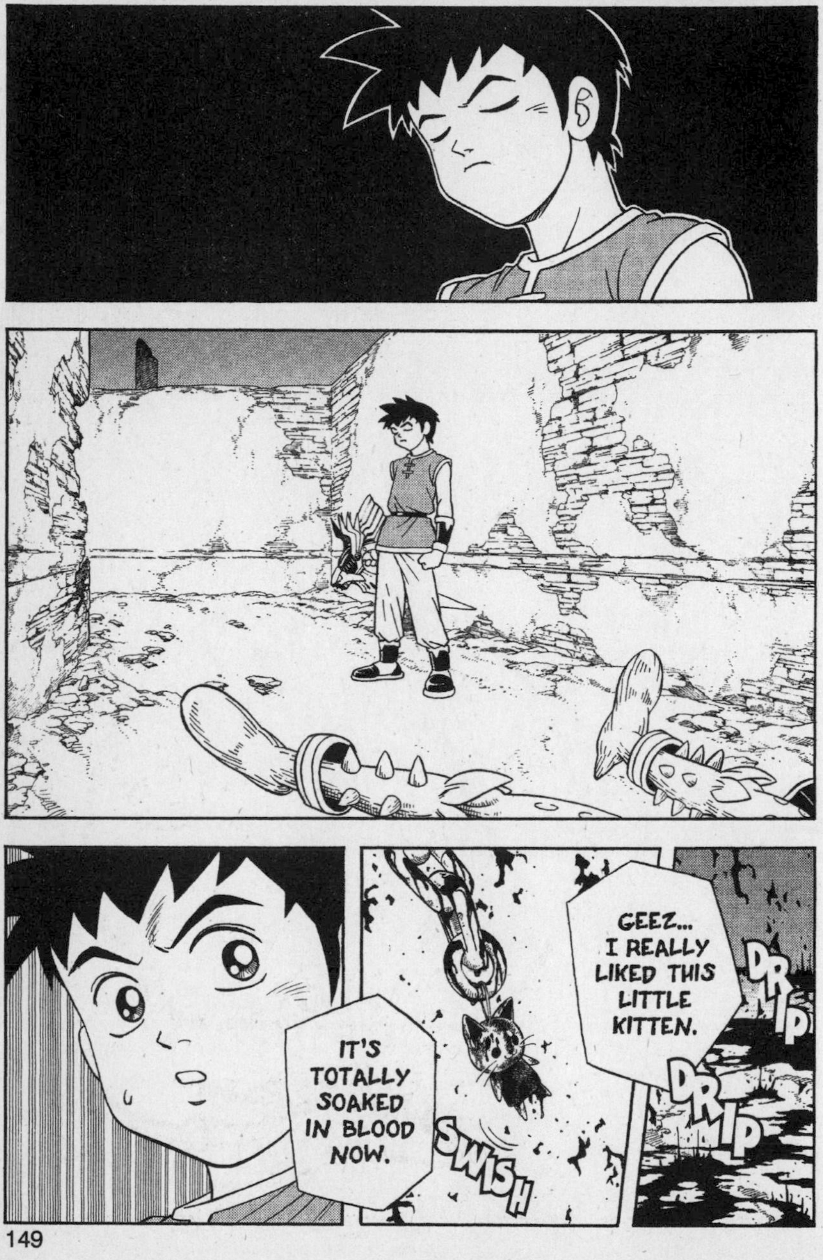
DRIP
DRIP
GEEZ... I REALLY LIKED THIS LITTLE KITTEN.
IT'S TOTALLY SOAKED IN BLOOD NOW.
SWISH

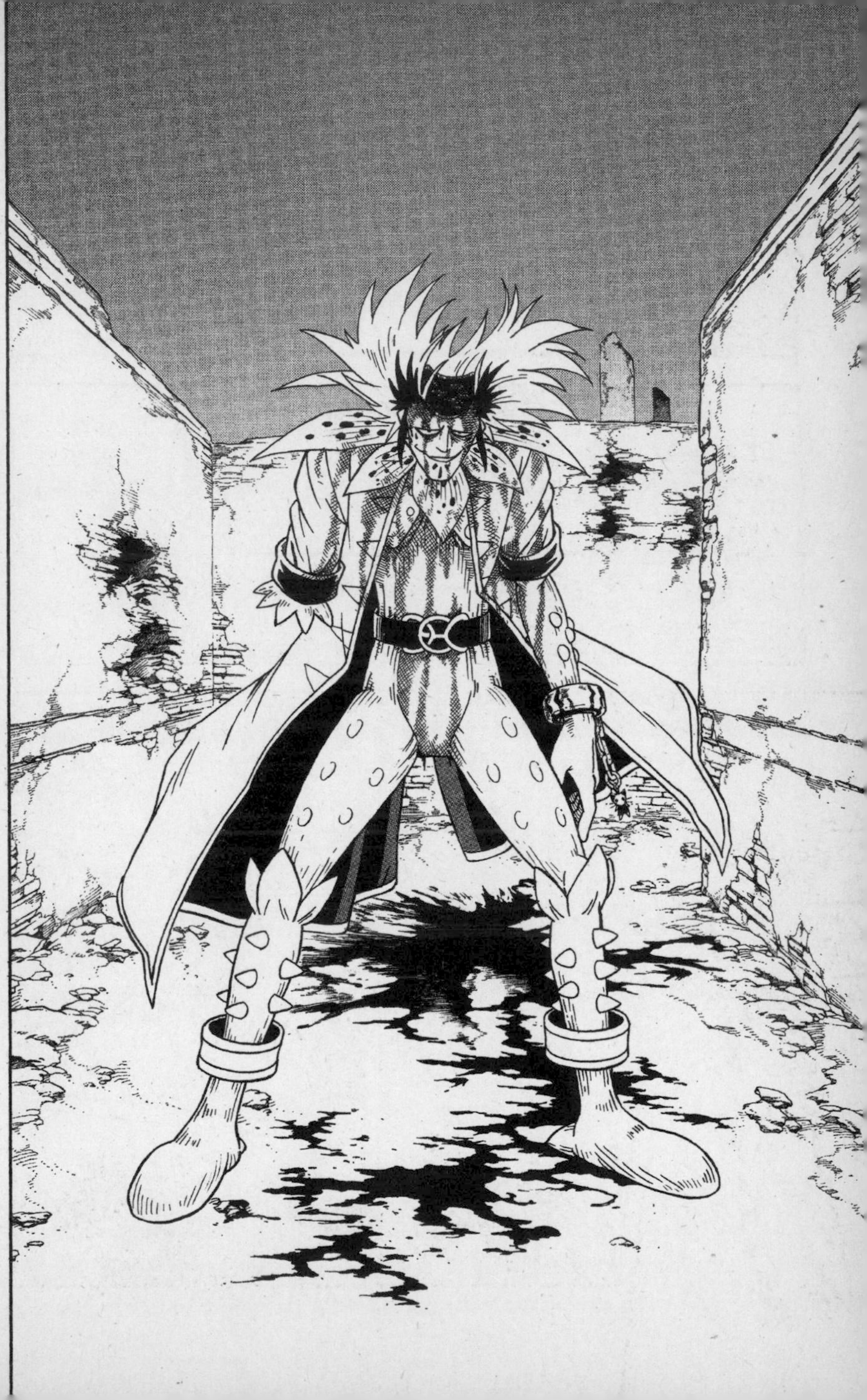

READ THIS WAY

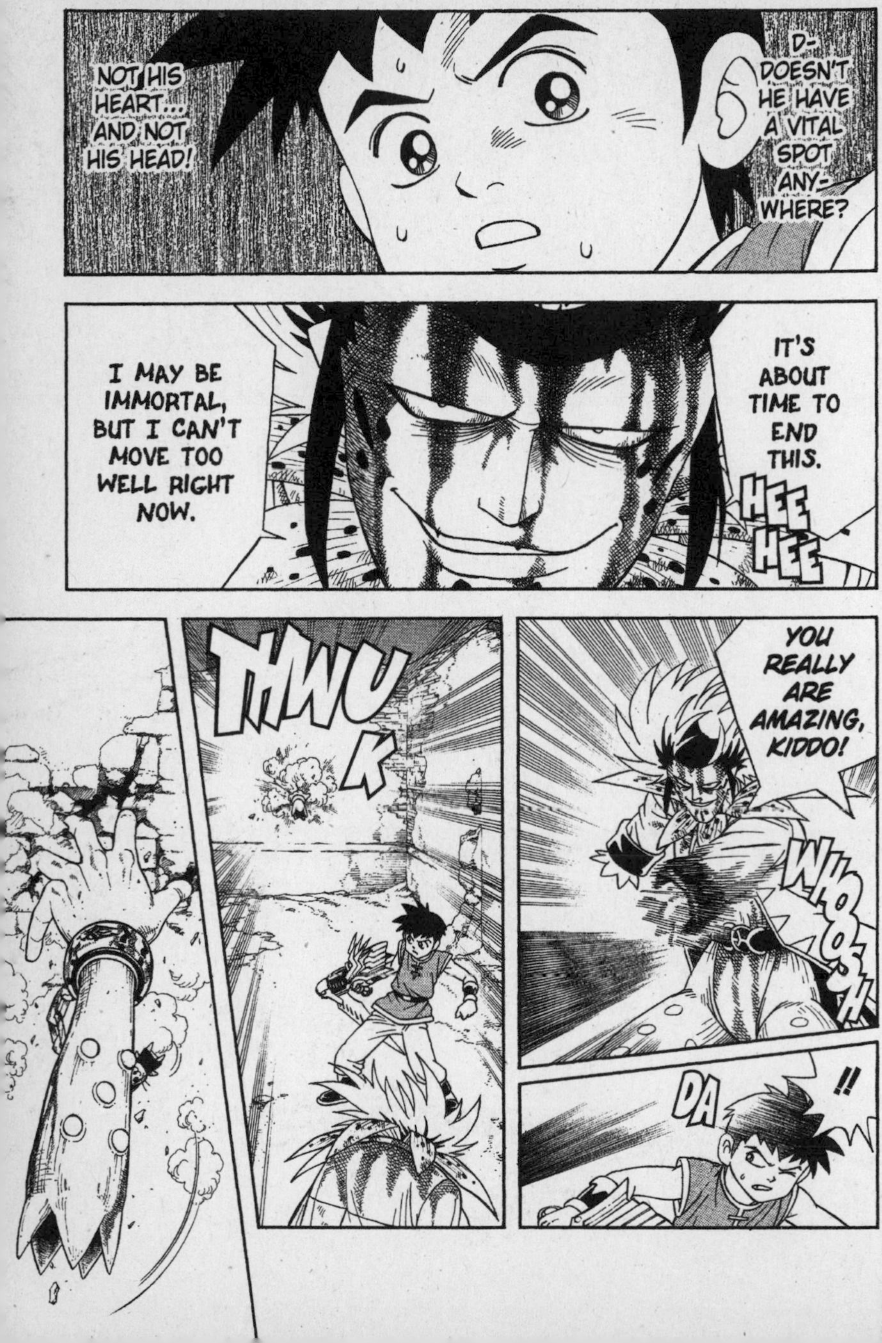

D-DOESN'T HE HAVE A VITAL SPOT ANY-WHERE?
NOT HIS HEART... AND NOT HIS HEAD!
IT'S ABOUT TIME TO END THIS.
HEE HEE
I MAY BE IMMORTAL, BUT I CAN'T MOVE TOO WELL RIGHT NOW.
YOU REALLY ARE AMAZING, KIDDO!
WHOOSH
DA !!
THWUK

WHIP

SWISH

!!

AS A GIFT FOR YOU TO TAKE TO HELL...

...LET ME TELL YOU SOMETHING INTERESTING.

TAP

ZUMMMM

FOR SOME VANDELS... BRAINS AND HEARTS ARE JUST ORGANS TO SUPPORT THEIR BATTLE STRENGTH.

!?

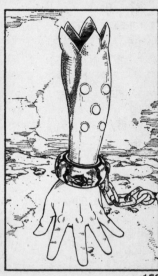

READ THIS WAY

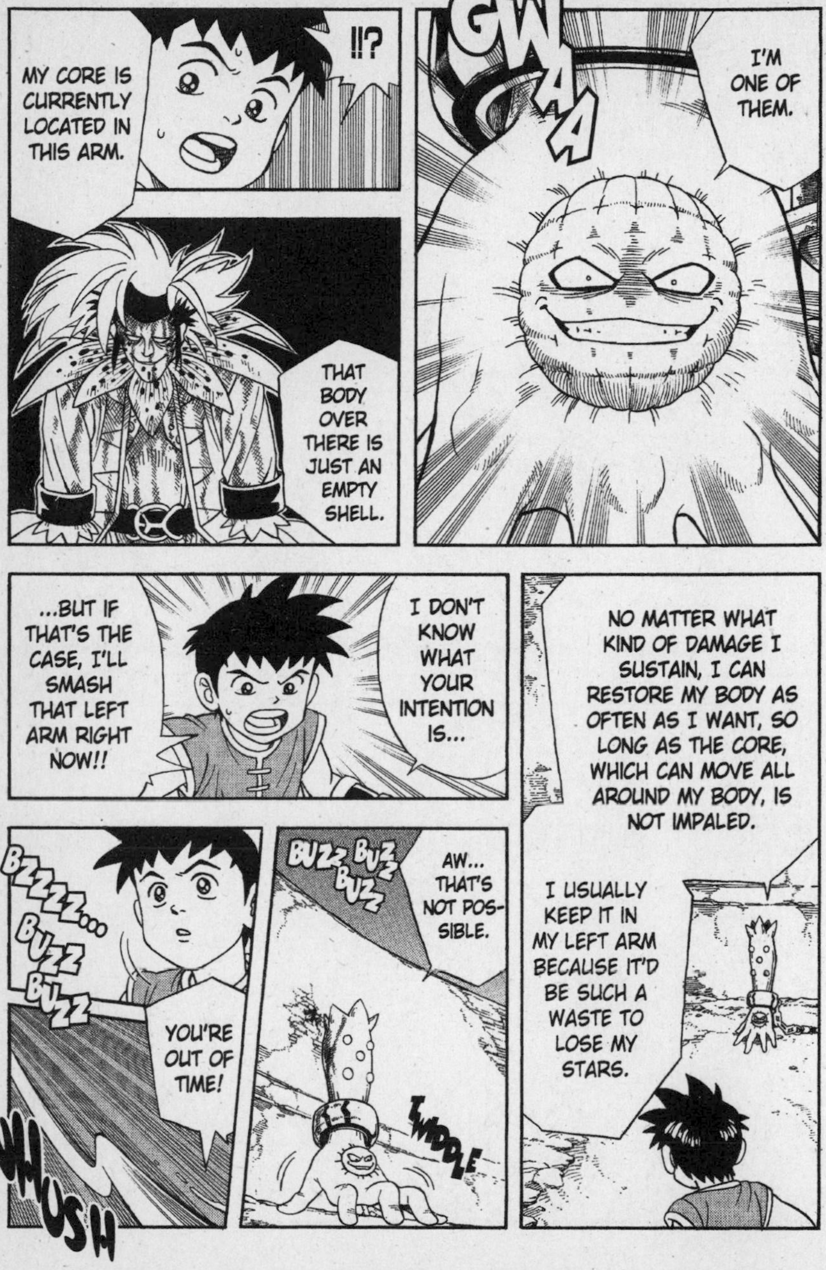
GWAA
I'M ONE OF THEM.
!!?
MY CORE IS CURRENTLY LOCATED IN THIS ARM.
THAT BODY OVER THERE IS JUST AN EMPTY SHELL.
NO MATTER WHAT KIND OF DAMAGE I SUSTAIN, I CAN RESTORE MY BODY AS OFTEN AS I WANT, SO LONG AS THE CORE, WHICH CAN MOVE ALL AROUND MY BODY, IS NOT IMPALED.
I USUALLY KEEP IT IN MY LEFT ARM BECAUSE IT'D BE SUCH A WASTE TO LOSE MY STARS.
I DON'T KNOW WHAT YOUR INTENTION IS...
...BUT IF THAT'S THE CASE, I'LL SMASH THAT LEFT ARM RIGHT NOW!!
BUZZ BUZZ BUZZ
AW... THAT'S NOT POS-SIBLE.
TWIDDLE
BZZZZ... BUZZ BUZZ
YOU'RE OUT OF TIME!
WHUSH

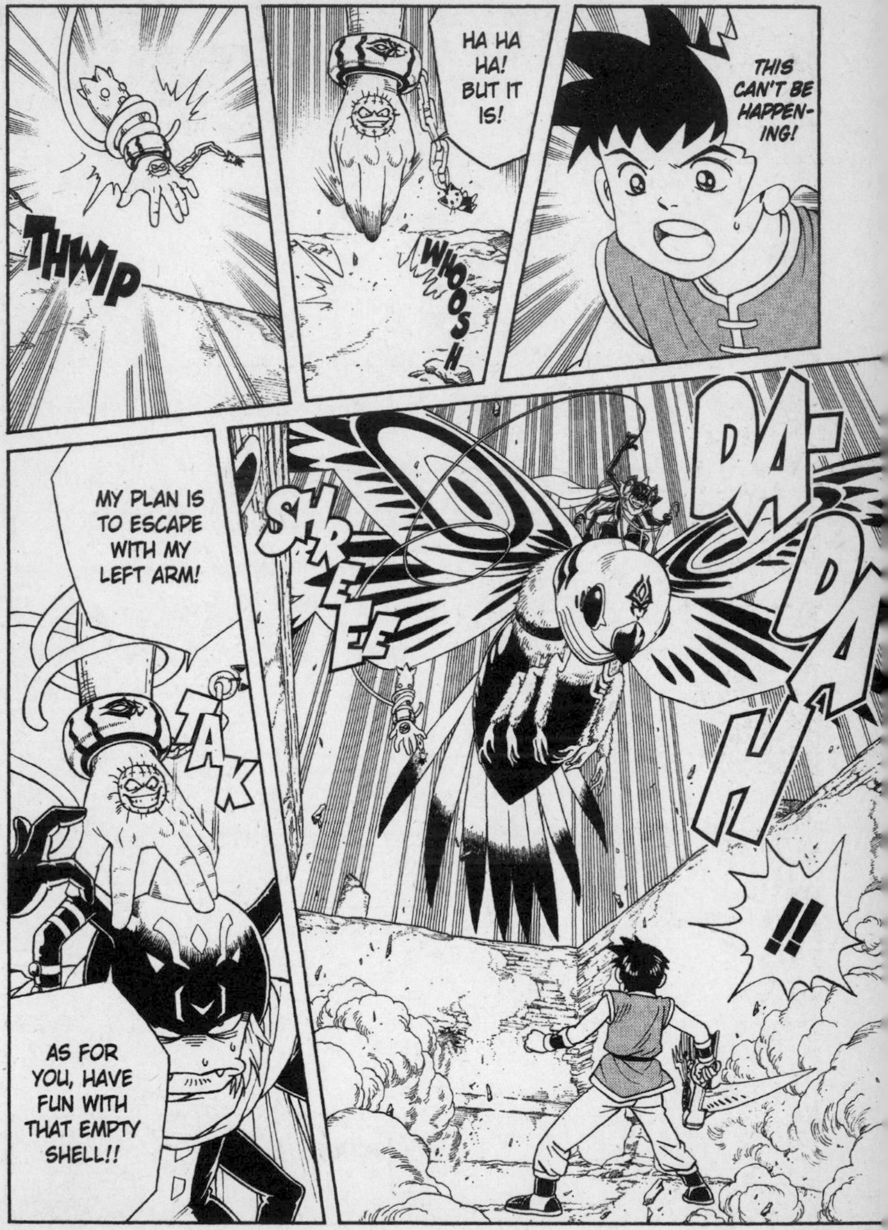
THIS CAN'T BE HAPPEN-ING!
HA HA HA! BUT IT IS!
WHOOSH
THWIP
DA-DA-DA-H!!
SHREEEE
MY PLAN IS TO ESCAPE WITH MY LEFT ARM!
TAK
AS FOR YOU, HAVE FUN WITH THAT EMPTY SHELL!!

READ THIS WAY

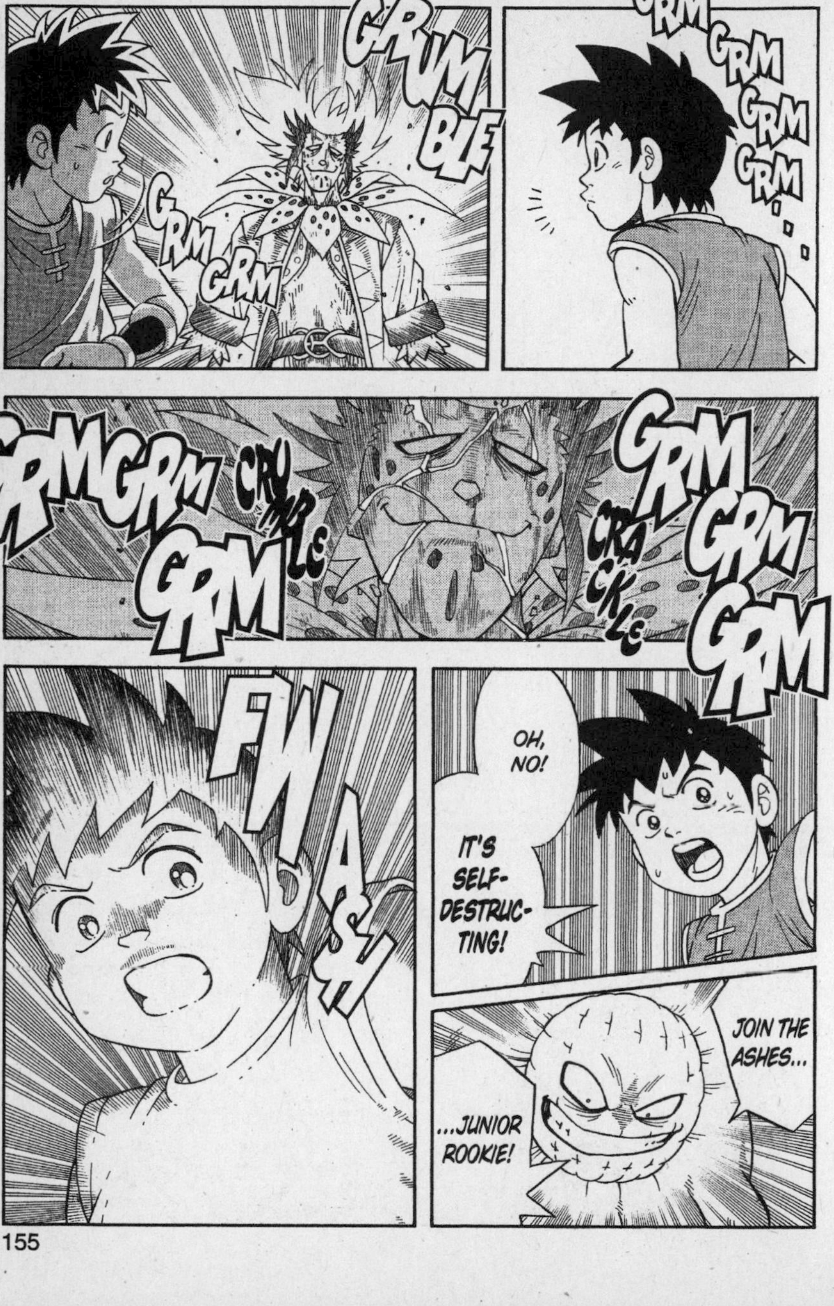
GRM GRM GRM GRM...
GRUMBLE
GRM GRM
GRM GRM GRM GRM
CRACKLE
CRUMBLE
GRMGRM GRM
OH, NO!
IT'S SELF-DESTRUCTING!
JOIN THE ASHES...
...JUNIOR ROOKIE!
FWASH

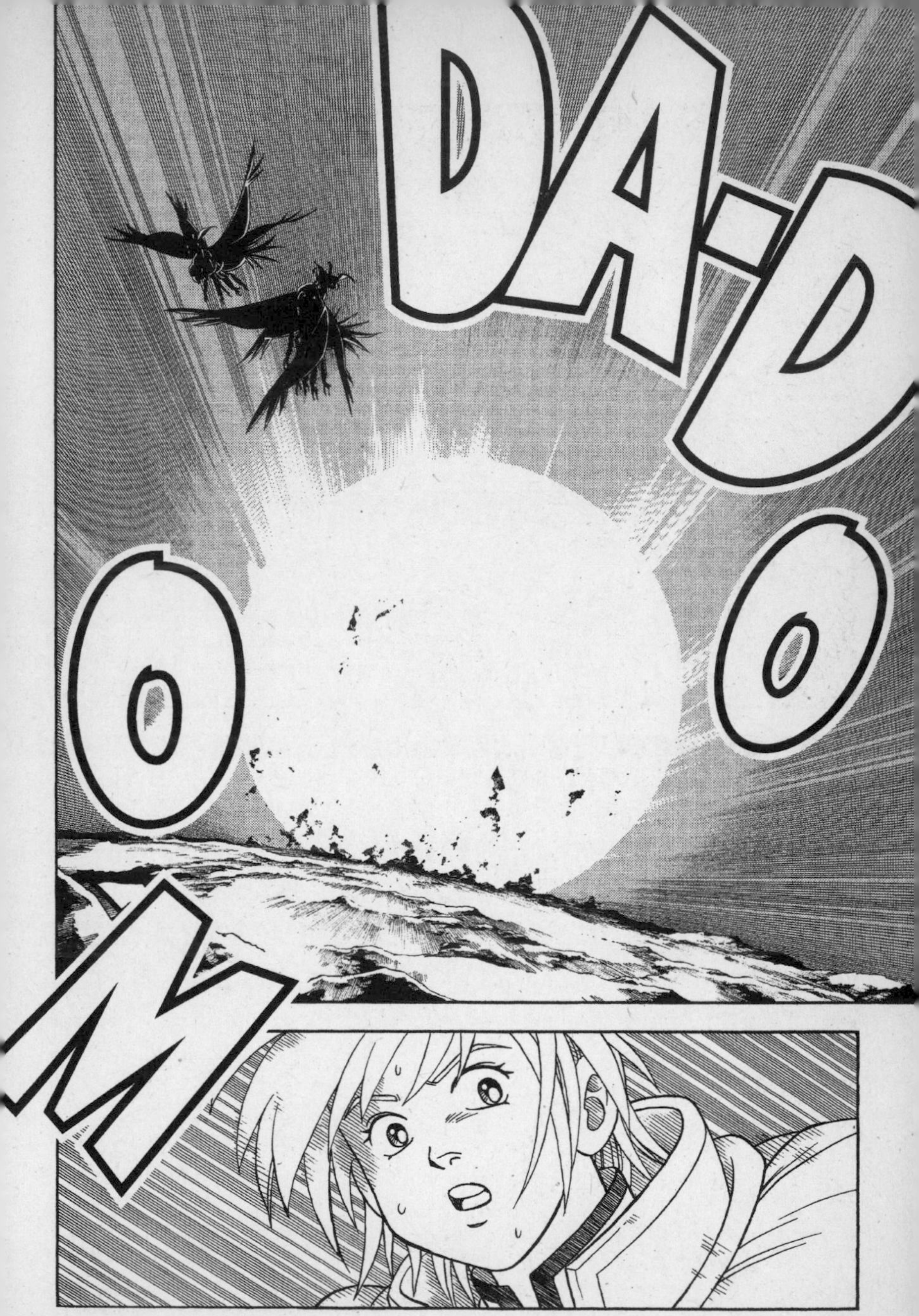
DA-DOOM

READ THIS WAY

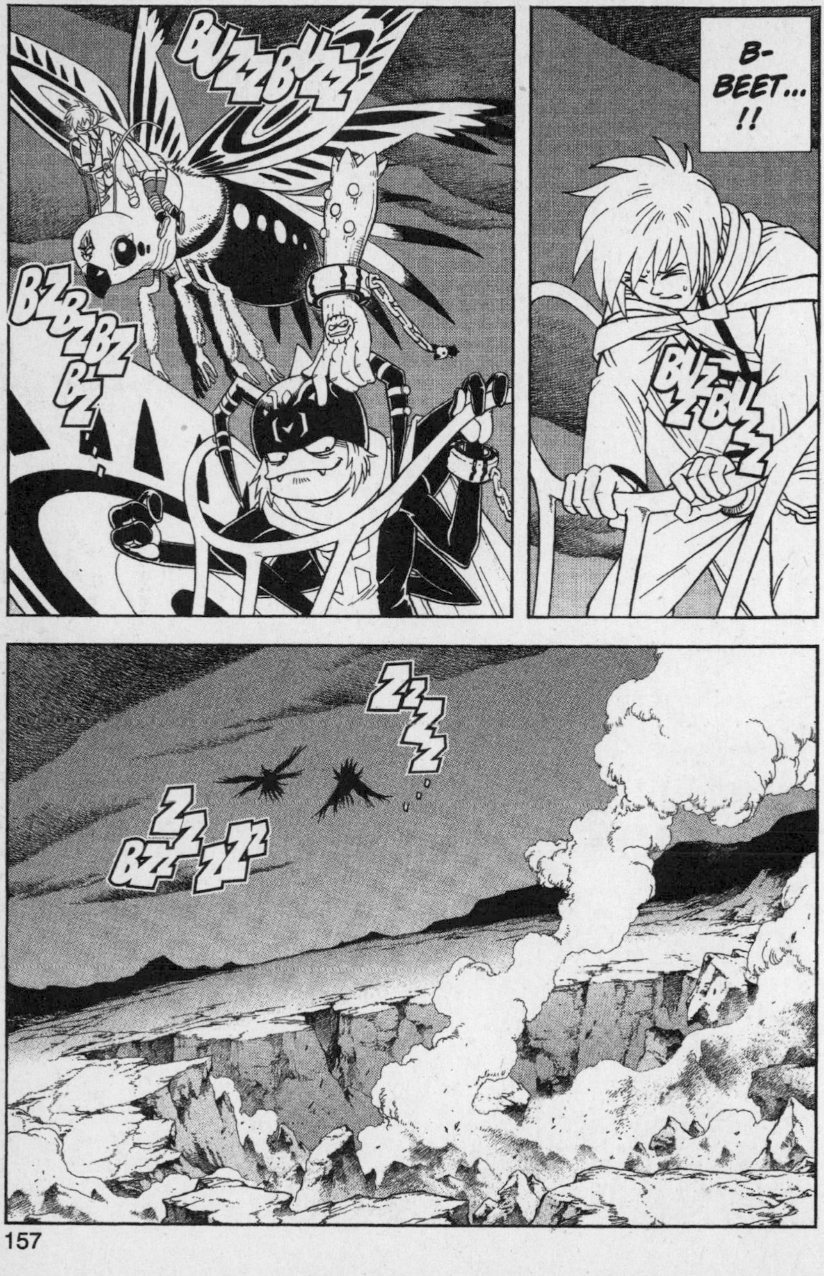
B-
BEET...
!!
BUZZ-BUZZZ
BUZZBUZZ
BZBZBZBZ
ZZZZ
ZZ
BZZZZZ

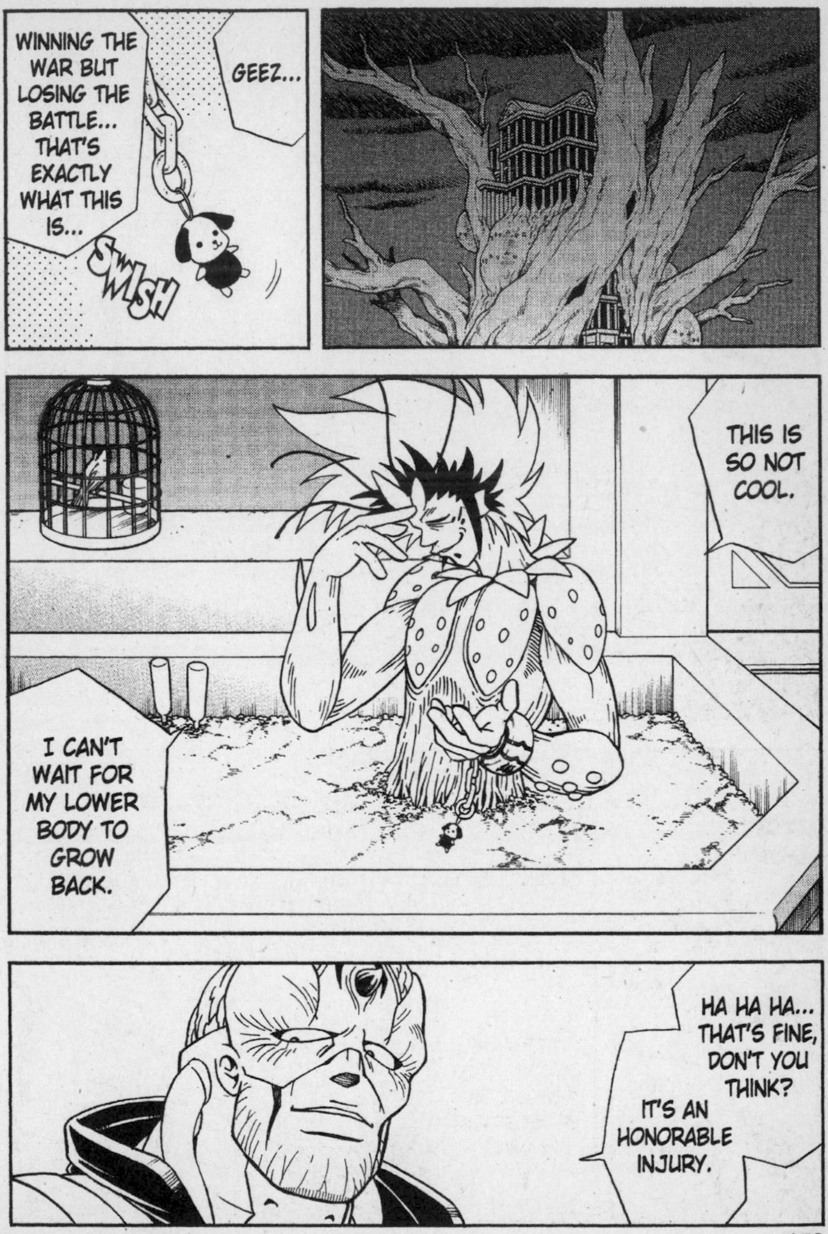
GEEZ...
WINNING THE WAR BUT LOSING THE BATTLE... THAT'S EXACTLY WHAT THIS IS...
SWISH
THIS IS SO NOT COOL.
I CAN'T WAIT FOR MY LOWER BODY TO GROW BACK.
HA HA HA... THAT'S FINE, DON'T YOU THINK?
IT'S AN HONORABLE INJURY.

READ THIS WAY

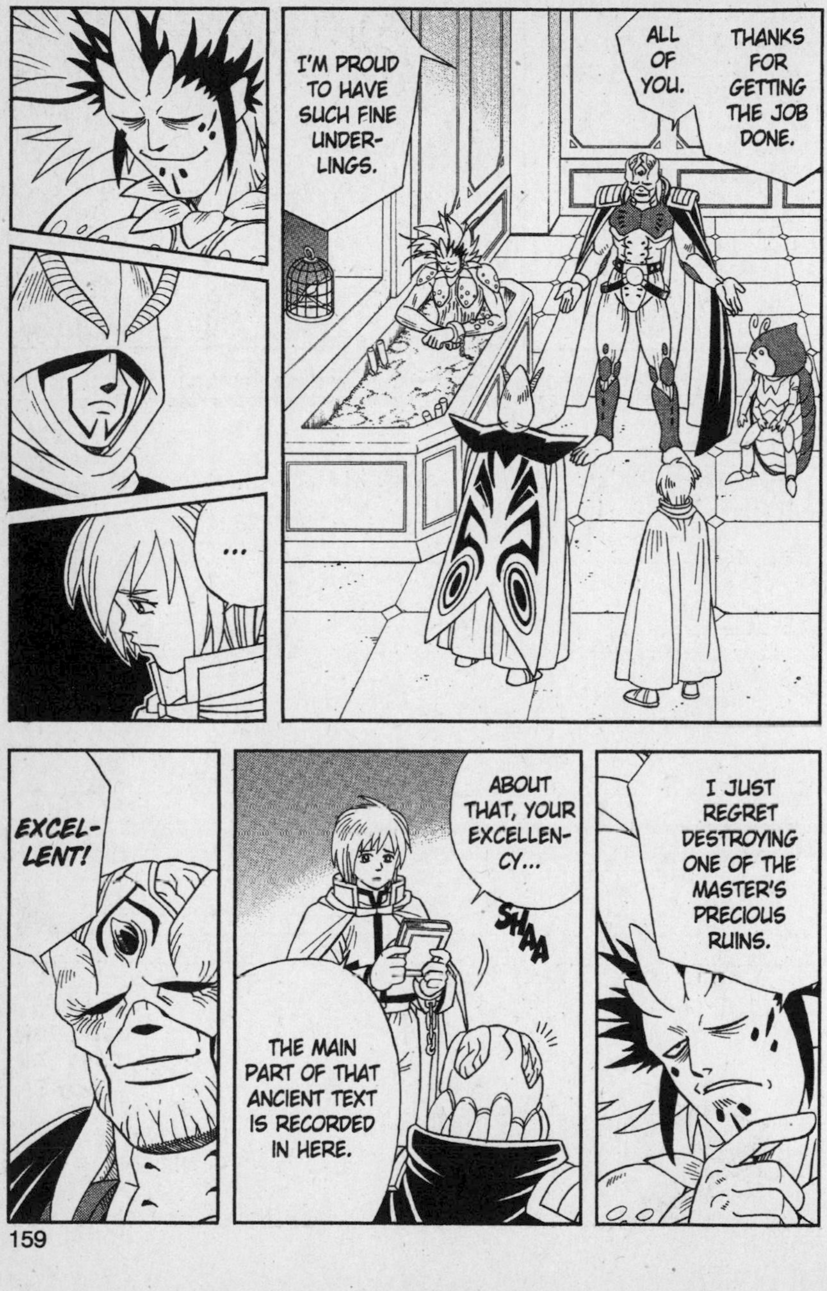
THANKS FOR GETTING THE JOB DONE.
ALL OF YOU.
I'M PROUD TO HAVE SUCH FINE UNDER-LINGS.
...
I JUST REGRET DESTROYING ONE OF THE MASTER'S PRECIOUS RUINS.
ABOUT THAT, YOUR EXCELLEN-CY...
SHAA
THE MAIN PART OF THAT ANCIENT TEXT IS RECORDED IN HERE.
EXCEL-LENT!

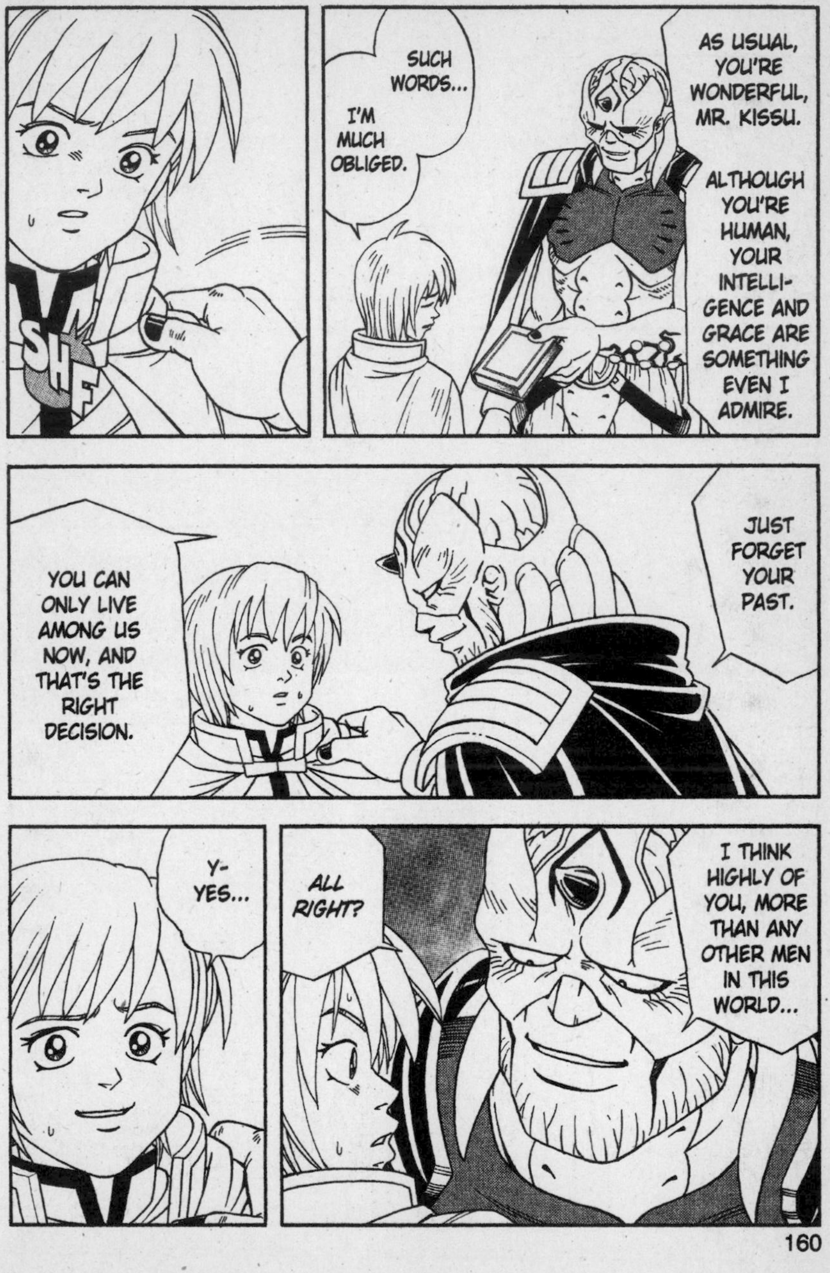
AS USUAL, YOU'RE WONDERFUL, MR. KISSU.
ALTHOUGH YOU'RE HUMAN, YOUR INTELLIGENCE AND GRACE ARE SOMETHING EVEN I ADMIRE.
SUCH WORDS...
I'M MUCH OBLIGED.
SHF
JUST FORGET YOUR PAST.
YOU CAN ONLY LIVE AMONG US NOW, AND THAT'S THE RIGHT DECISION.
I THINK HIGHLY OF YOU, MORE THAN ANY OTHER MEN IN THIS WORLD...
ALL RIGHT?
Y-YES...

READ THIS WAY

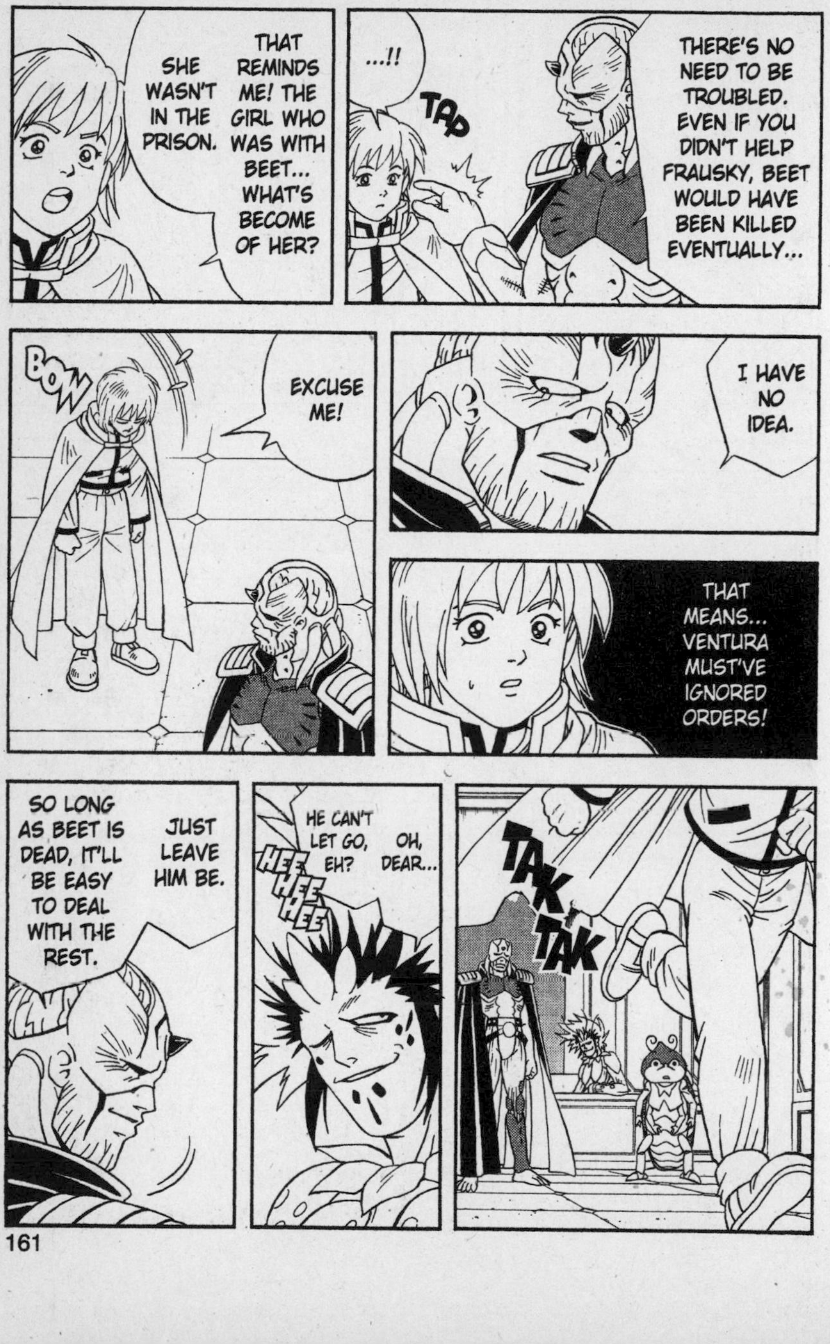

THERE'S NO NEED TO BE TROUBLED. EVEN IF YOU DIDN'T HELP FRAUSKY, BEET WOULD HAVE BEEN KILLED EVENTUALLY...
TAP
...!!
THAT REMINDS ME! THE GIRL WHO WAS WITH BEET... WHAT'S BECOME OF HER?
SHE WASN'T IN THE PRISON.
I HAVE NO IDEA.
THAT MEANS... VENTURA MUST'VE IGNORED ORDERS!
EXCUSE ME!
BOW
TAK TAK
OH, DEAR...
HE CAN'T LET GO, EH?
HEE HEE HEE
JUST LEAVE HIM BE.
SO LONG AS BEET IS DEAD, IT'LL BE EASY TO DEAL WITH THE REST.

MR. ROZZ-GOAT.
YES!
I'M ENTERING THE CHAMBER. YOU'RE IN CHARGE.
UNDER-STOOD.
IT'S ABOUT THAT "GREAT UNDERTAKING OF THE CENTURY," RIGHT?
SINCE BEET IS DEAD, I'M SURE HE'LL FOCUS ON THAT FOR A WHILE.
ALREADY DEAD...
...I HOPE.
...?
HMPH... DON'T BE RIDICULOUS.
CHAK
NO ONE CAN SURVIVE THAT SELF-BLAST OF YOURS.

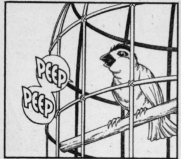

READ THIS WAY

PEEP
PEEP
SHF
WHY DID I DO THAT?
FOR SOME REASON, I LET IT ESCAPE...

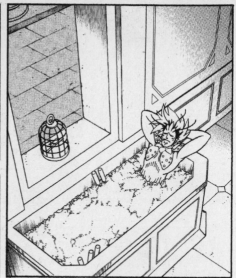

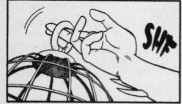

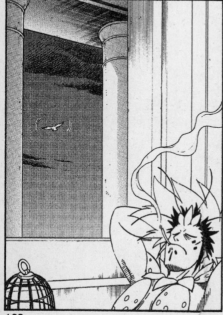

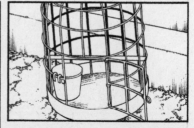

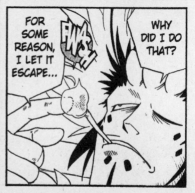

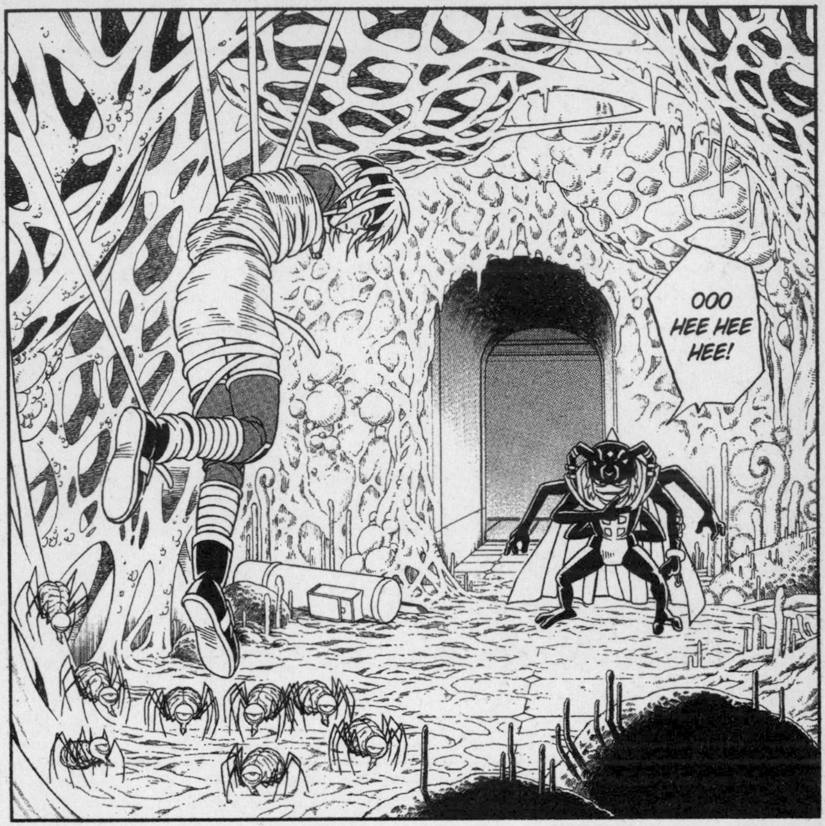
OOO HEE HEE HEE!

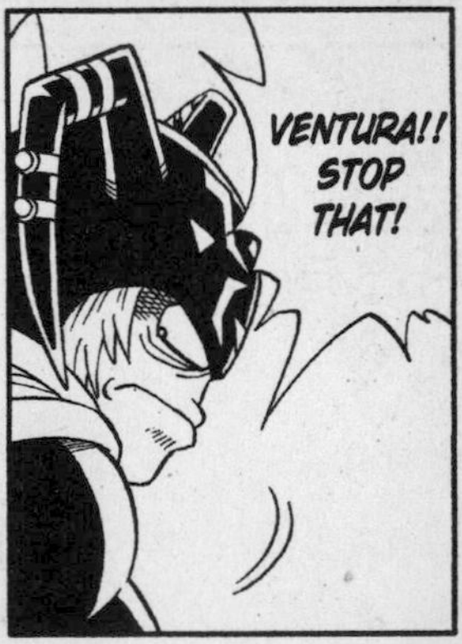
VENTURA!! STOP THAT!

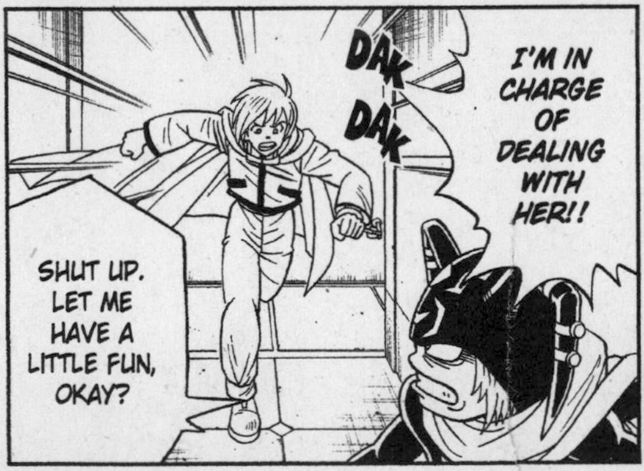
I'M IN CHARGE OF DEALING WITH HER!!
DAK DAK
SHUT UP. LET ME HAVE A LITTLE FUN, OKAY?

READ THIS WAY

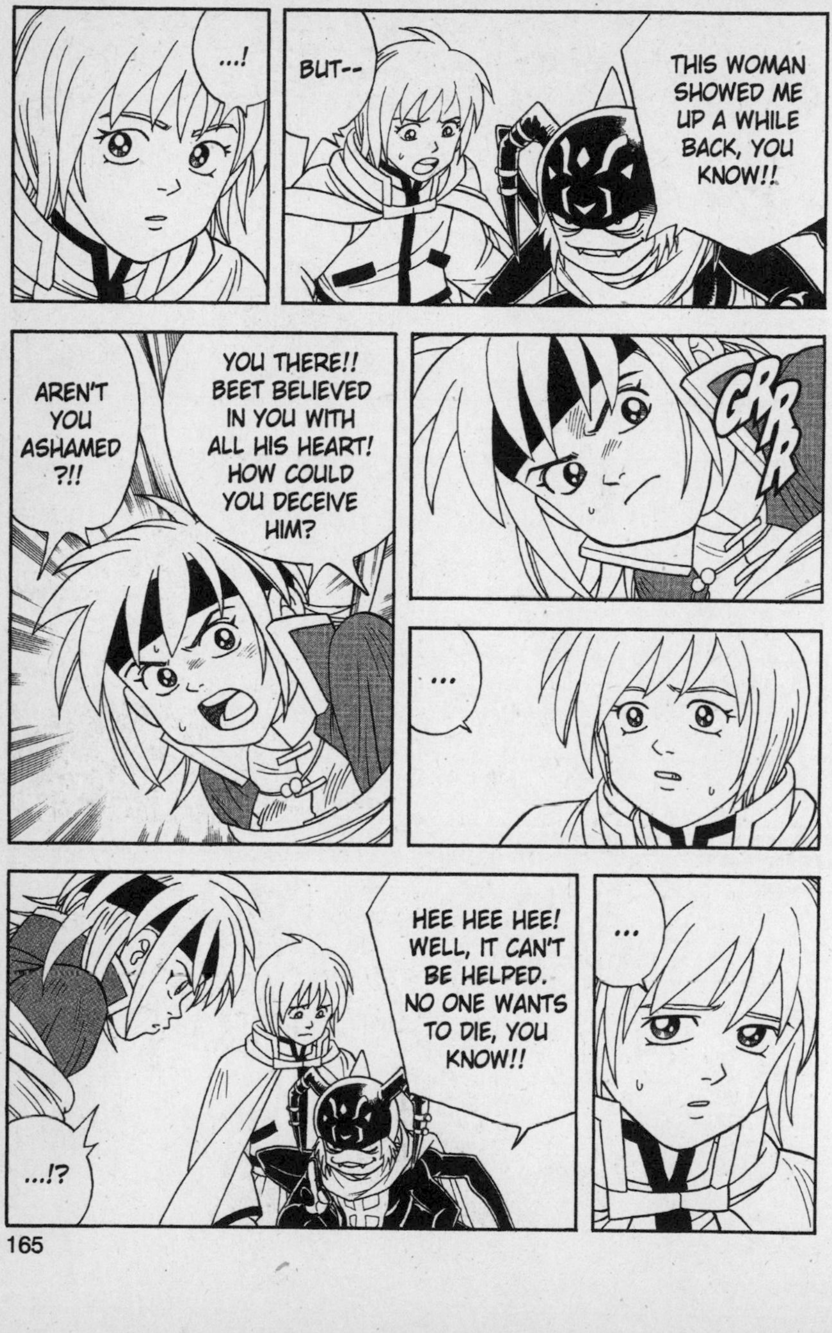
THIS WOMAN SHOWED ME UP A WHILE BACK, YOU KNOW!!
BUT--
...!
GRRR
...
YOU THERE!! BEET BELIEVED IN YOU WITH ALL HIS HEART! HOW COULD YOU DECEIVE HIM?
AREN'T YOU ASHAMED?!!
...
HEE HEE HEE! WELL, IT CAN'T BE HELPED. NO ONE WANTS TO DIE, YOU KNOW!!
...!?

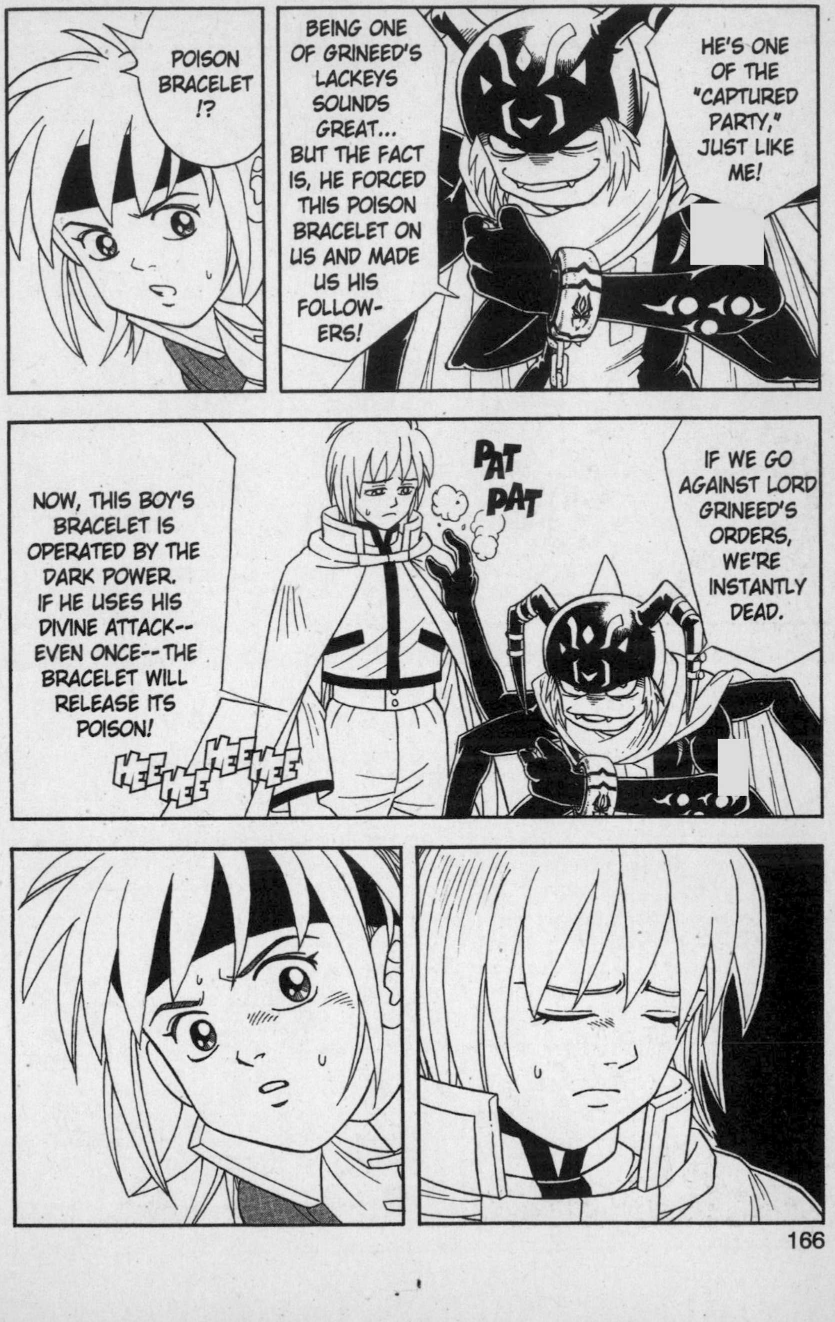
HE'S ONE OF THE "CAPTURED PARTY," JUST LIKE ME!
BEING ONE OF GRINEED'S LACKEYS SOUNDS GREAT... BUT THE FACT IS, HE FORCED THIS POISON BRACELET ON US AND MADE US HIS FOLLOW-ERS!
POISON BRACELET !?
IF WE GO AGAINST LORD GRINEED'S ORDERS, WE'RE INSTANTLY DEAD.
PAT PAT
NOW, THIS BOY'S BRACELET IS OPERATED BY THE DARK POWER. IF HE USES HIS DIVINE ATTACK-- EVEN ONCE--THE BRACELET WILL RELEASE ITS POISON!
HEE HEE HEE HEE

READ THIS WAY

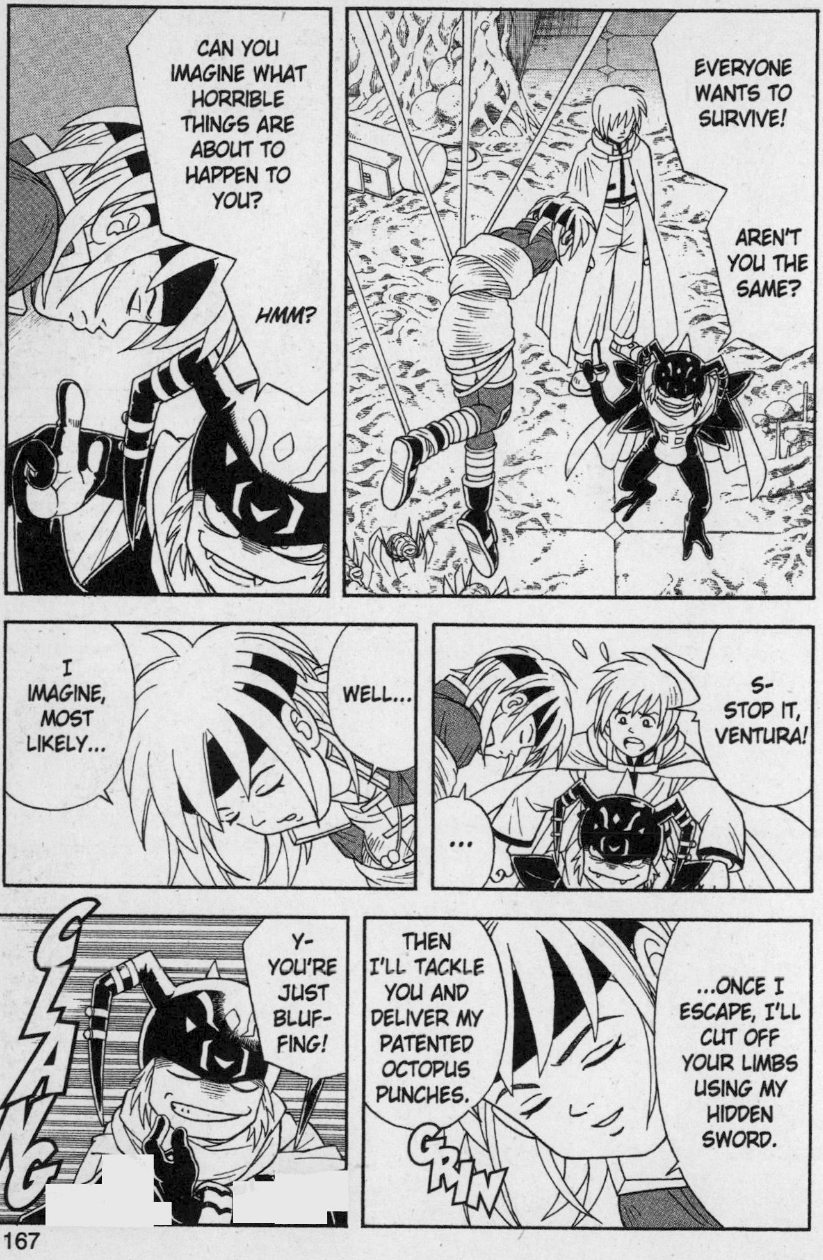
EVERYONE WANTS TO SURVIVE!
AREN'T YOU THE SAME?
CAN YOU IMAGINE WHAT HORRIBLE THINGS ARE ABOUT TO HAPPEN TO YOU?
HMM?
S- STOP IT, VENTURA!
...
WELL...
I IMAGINE, MOST LIKELY...
...ONCE I ESCAPE, I'LL CUT OFF YOUR LIMBS USING MY HIDDEN SWORD.
THEN I'LL TACKLE YOU AND DELIVER MY PATENTED OCTOPUS PUNCHES.
GRIN
Y- YOU'RE JUST BLUF- FING!
CLANG

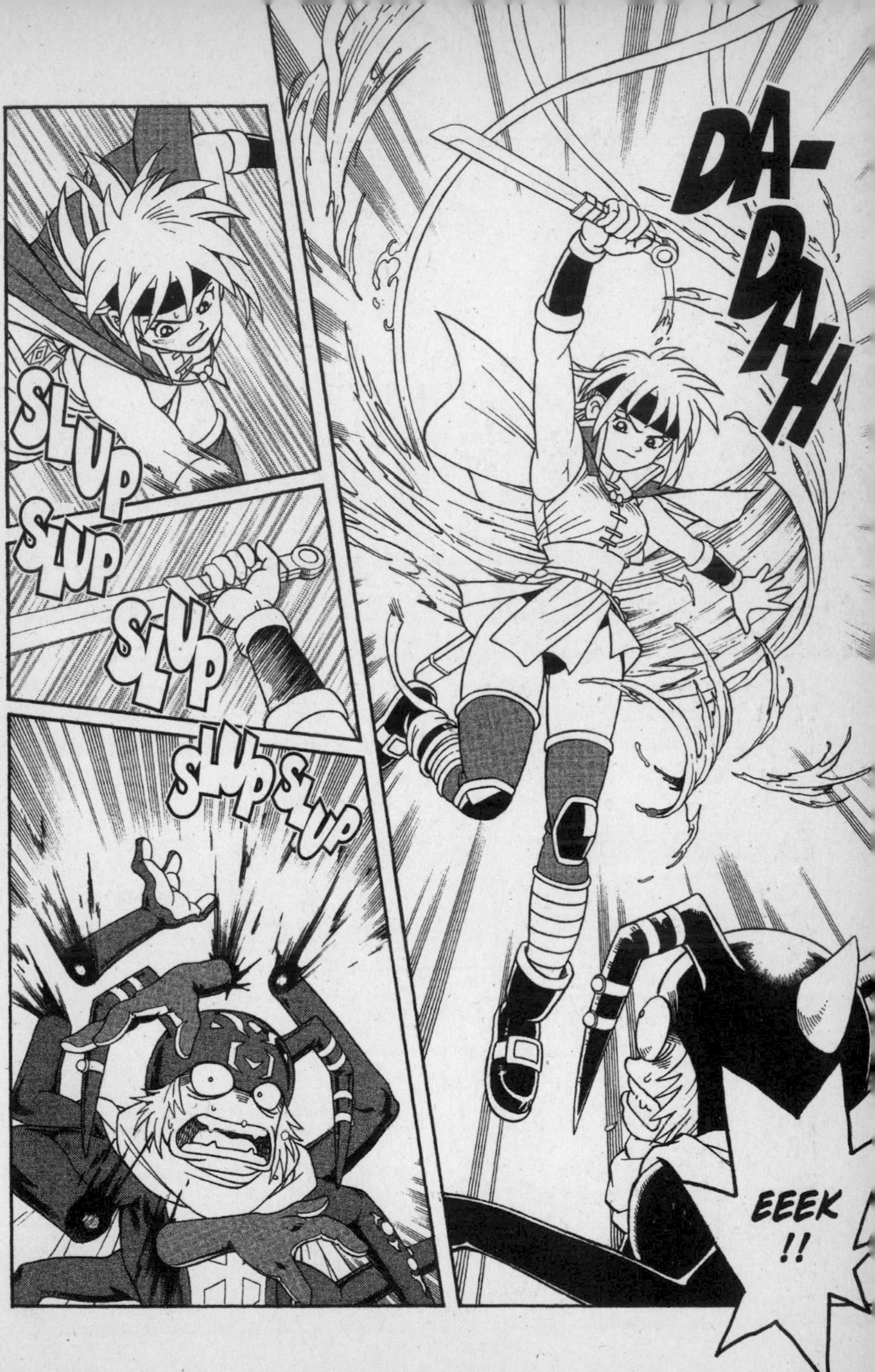
DA-DAH!
EEEK!!
SLUP
SLUP
SLUP
SLUP
SLUP

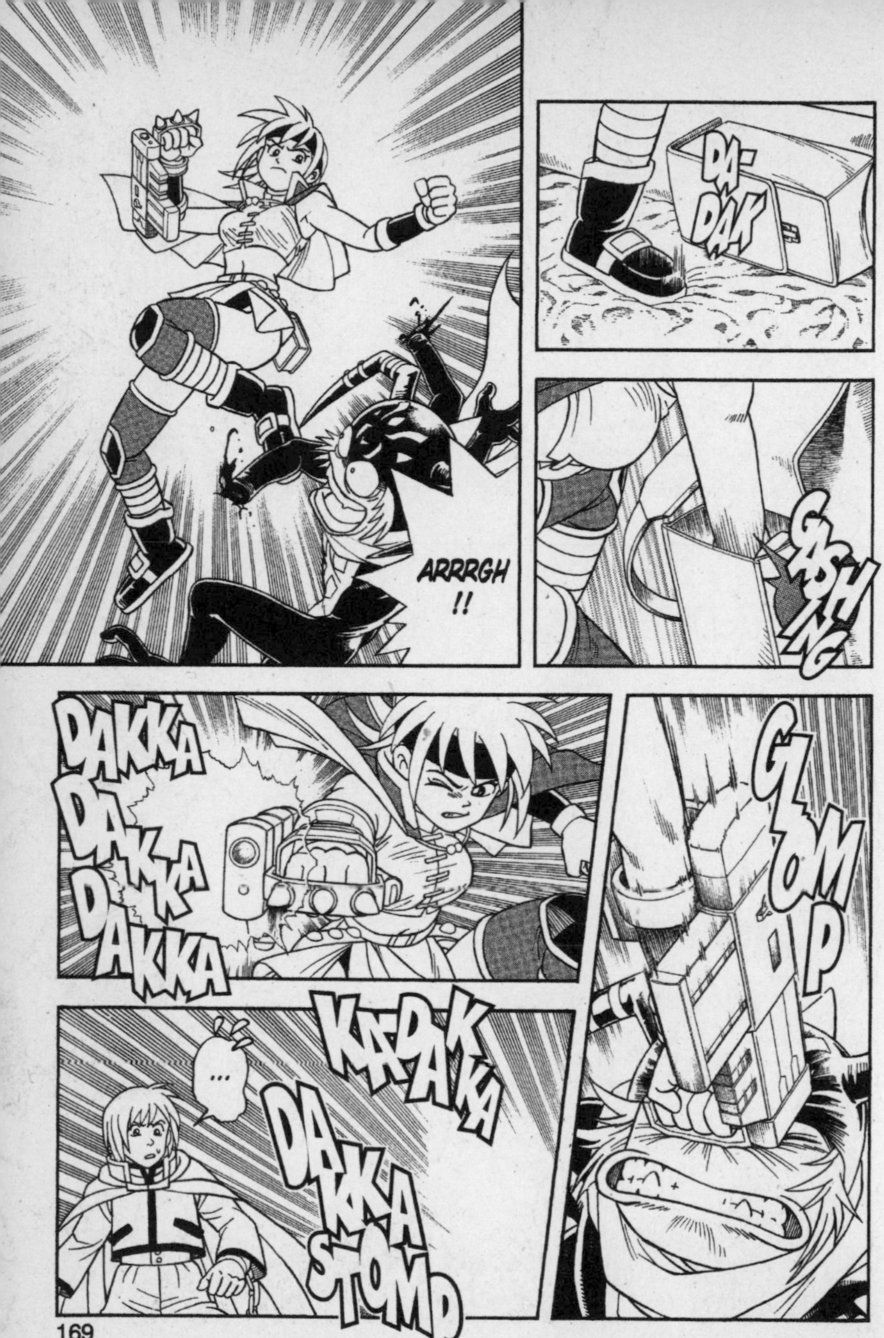
DA-DAK
GASHING
ARRRGH!!
GLOMP
DAKKA DAKKA DAKKA DAKKA
...
KADAKKA
DAKKA STOMP

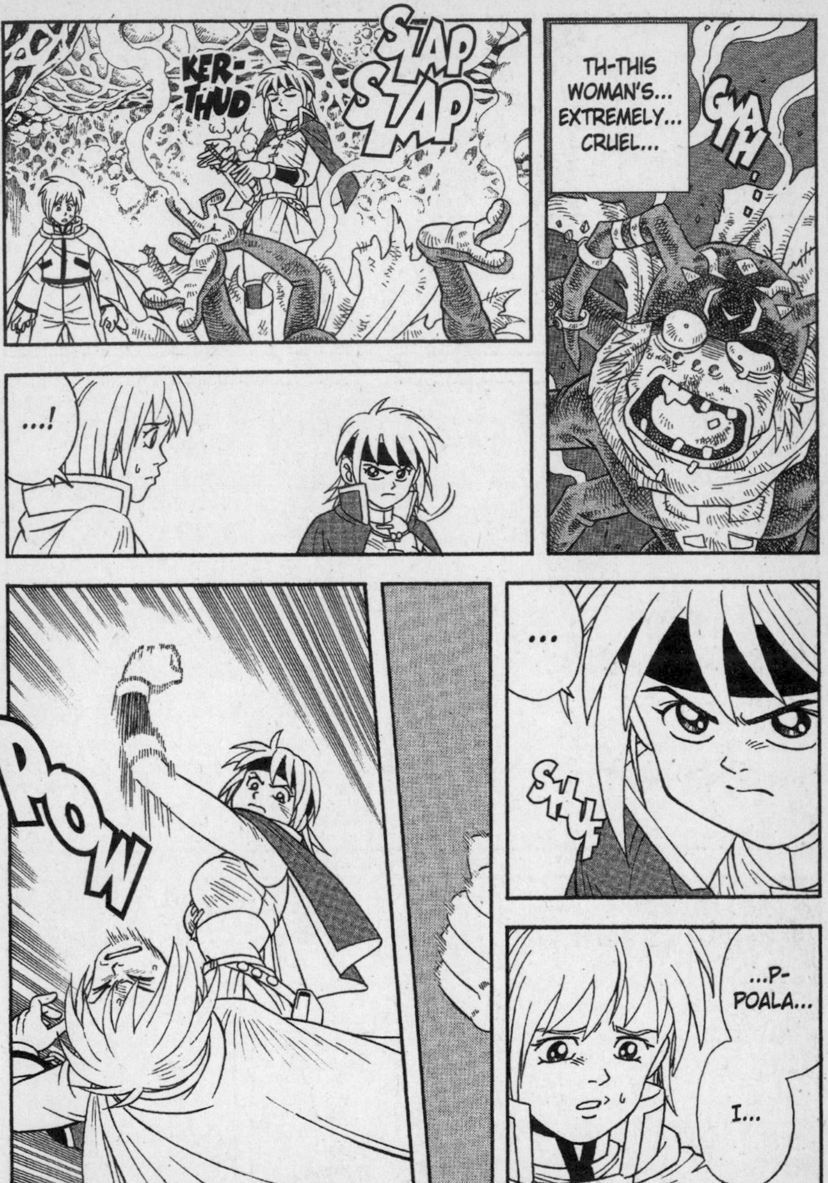
TH-THIS WOMAN'S... EXTREMELY... CRUEL...
GWAH
KER-THUD
SLAP SLAP
...!
...
SHUF
...P-POALA...
I...
POW

READ THIS WAY

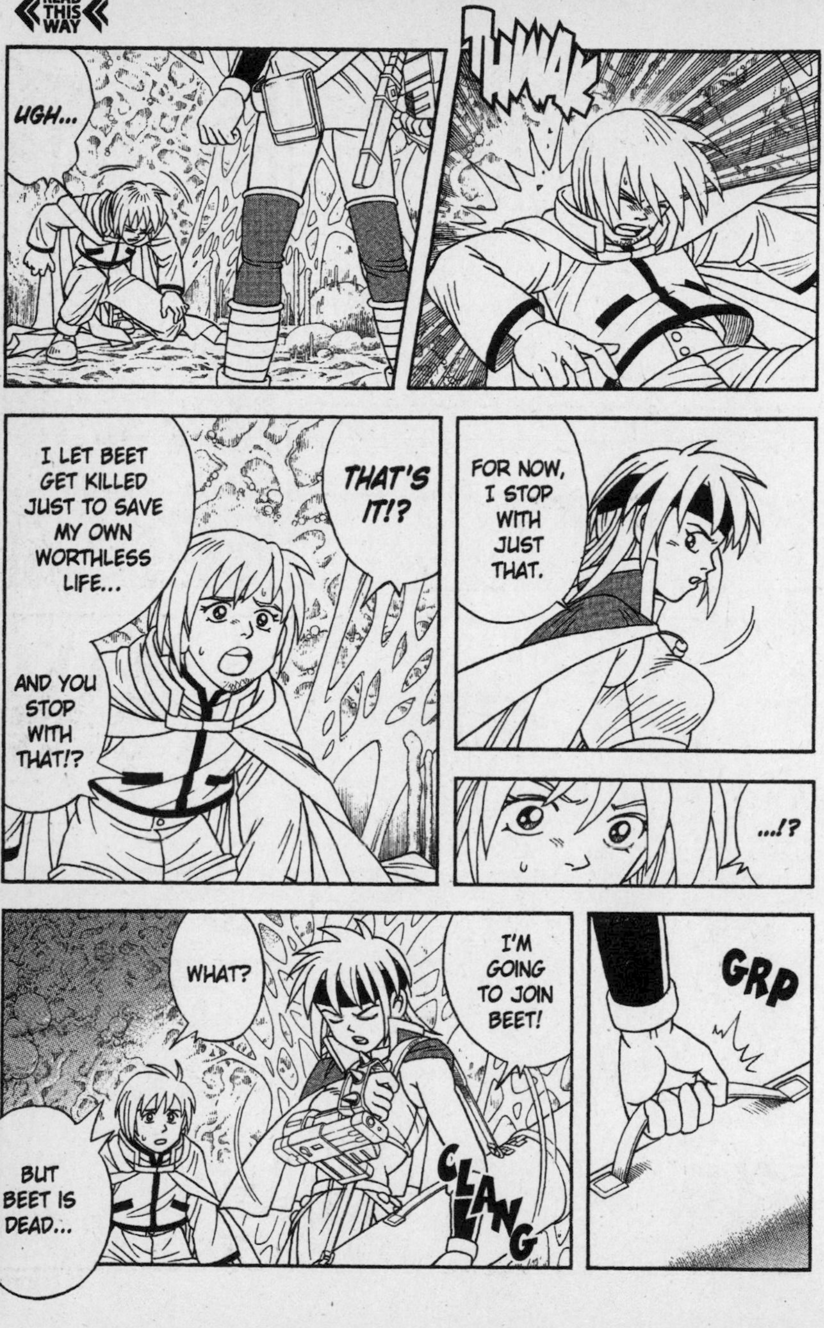
THWAK
UGH...
FOR NOW, I STOP WITH JUST THAT.
...!?
THAT'S IT!?
I LET BEET GET KILLED JUST TO SAVE MY OWN WORTHLESS LIFE...
AND YOU STOP WITH THAT!?
GRP
I'M GOING TO JOIN BEET!
WHAT?
CLANG
BUT BEET IS DEAD...

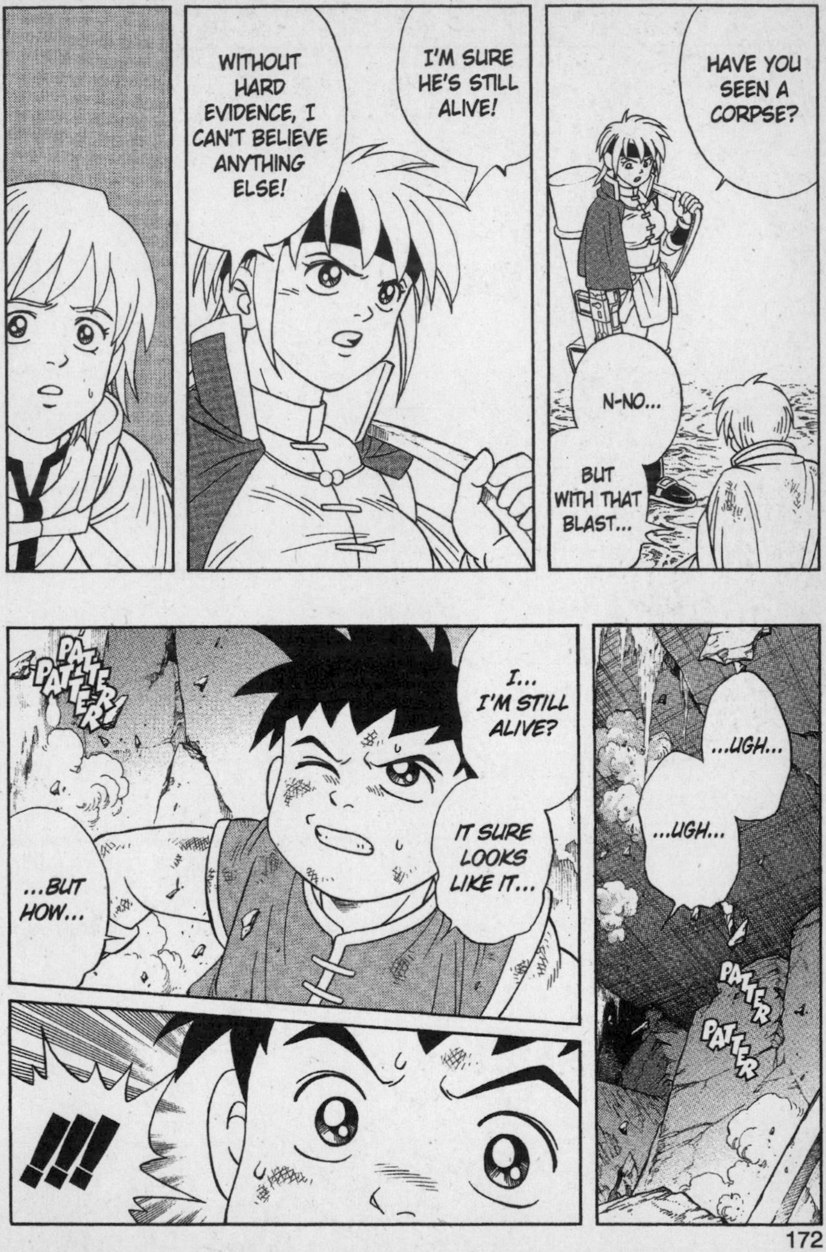
HAVE YOU SEEN A CORPSE?
N-NO...
BUT WITH THAT BLAST...
I'M SURE HE'S STILL ALIVE!
WITHOUT HARD EVIDENCE, I CAN'T BELIEVE ANYTHING ELSE!
...UGH...
...UGH...
PATTER PATTER
I... I'M STILL ALIVE?
IT SURE LOOKS LIKE IT...
...BUT HOW...
PATTER PATTER!
!!!

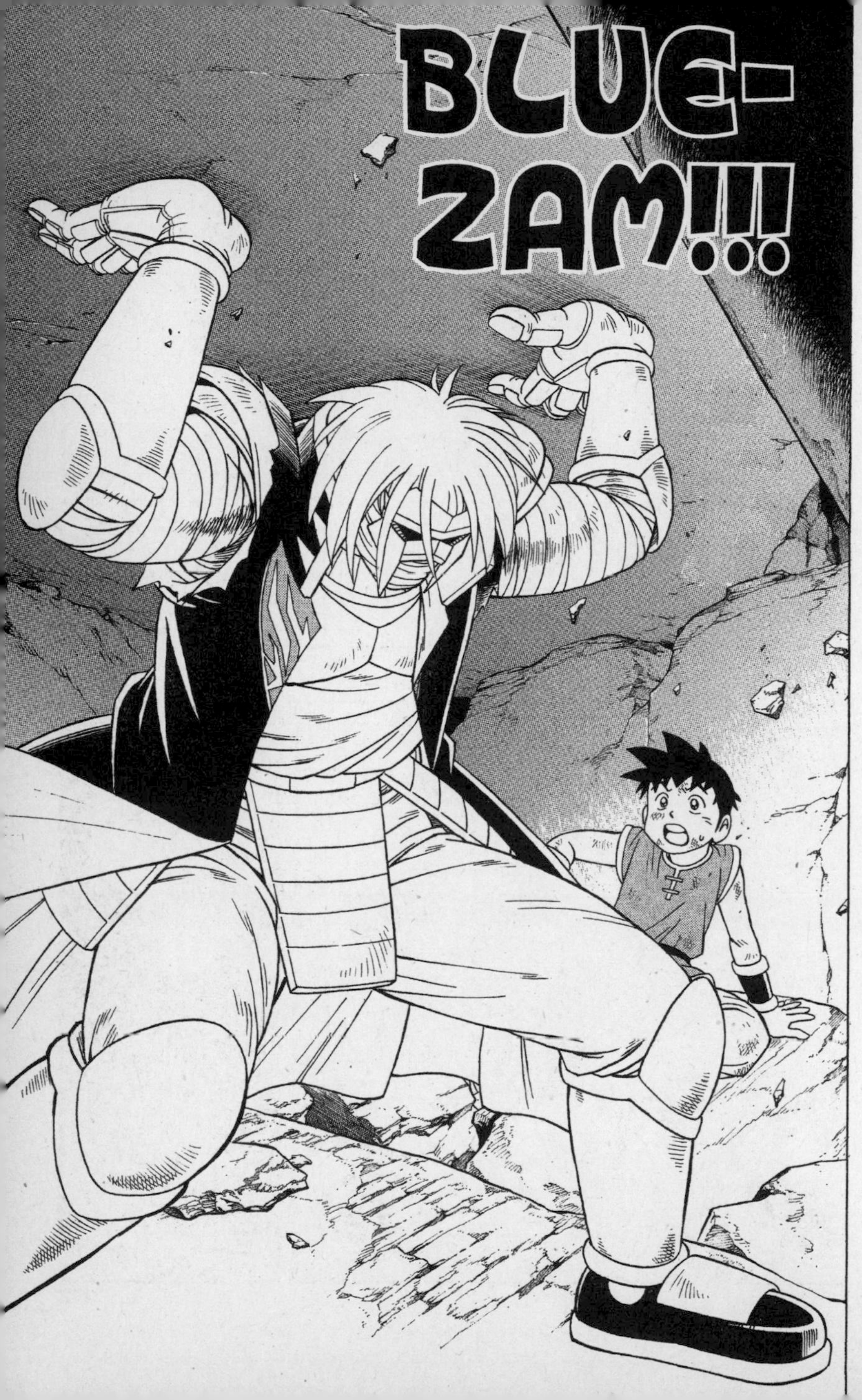
BLUG-
ZAM!!!

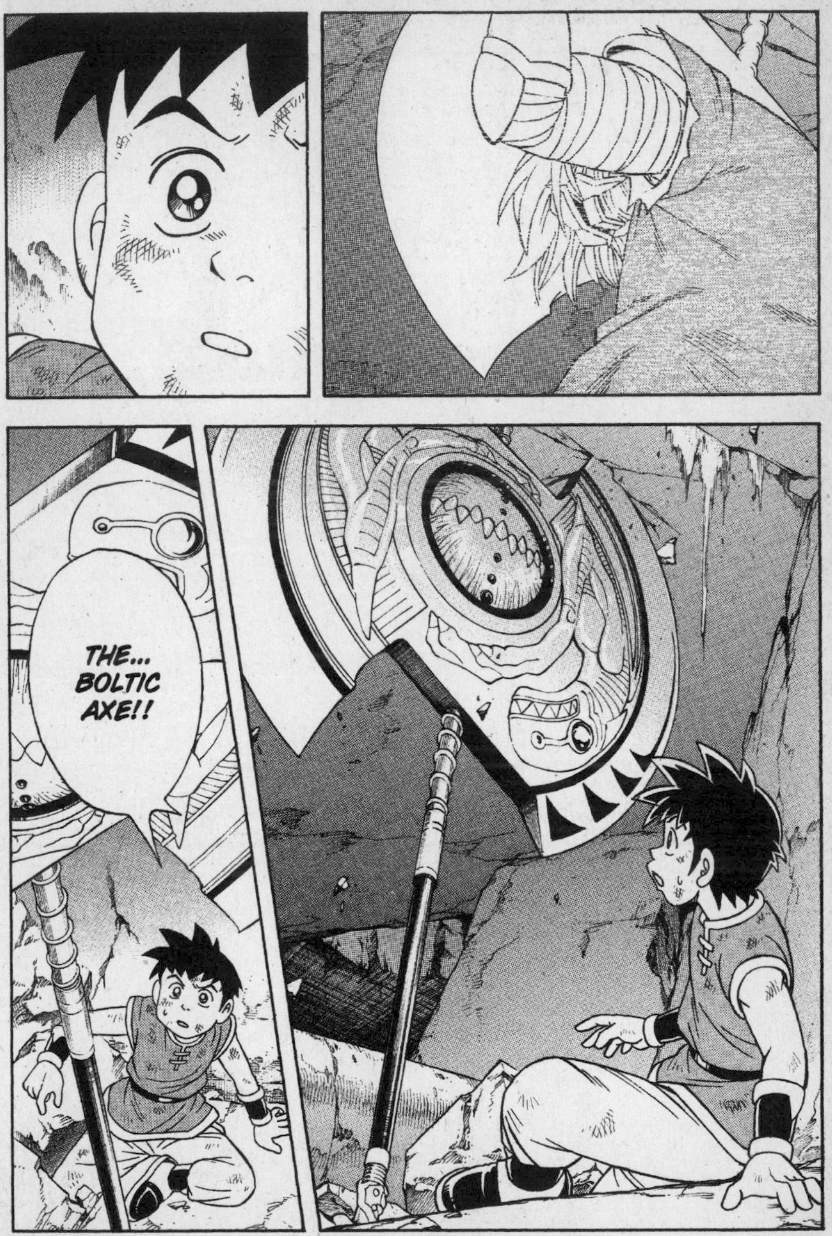
THE... BOLTIC AXE!!

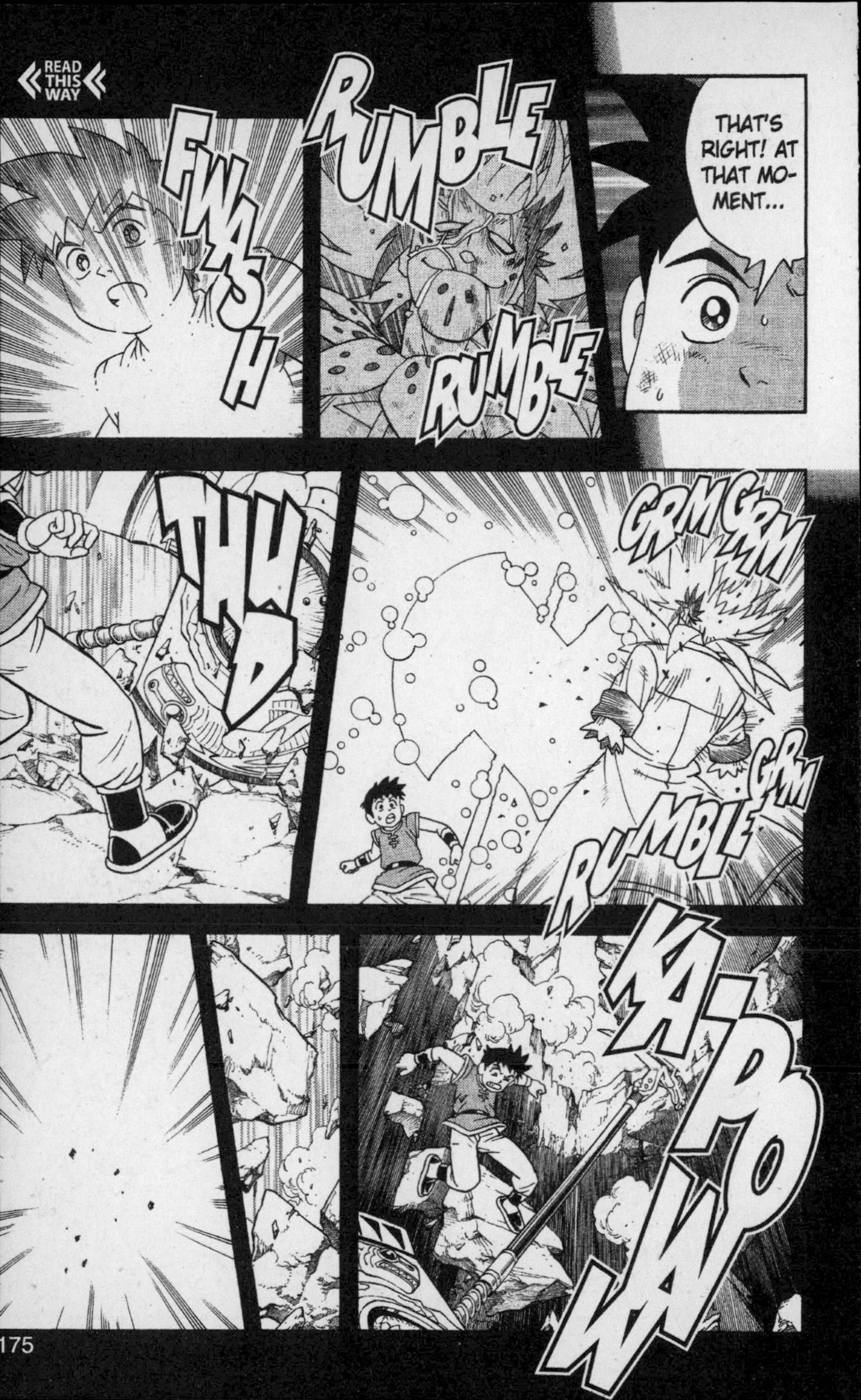
READ THIS WAY
THAT'S RIGHT! AT THAT MOMENT...
RUMBLE
RUMBLE
FWASH
GRM GRM
GRM
RUMBLE
THUD
KAPOW

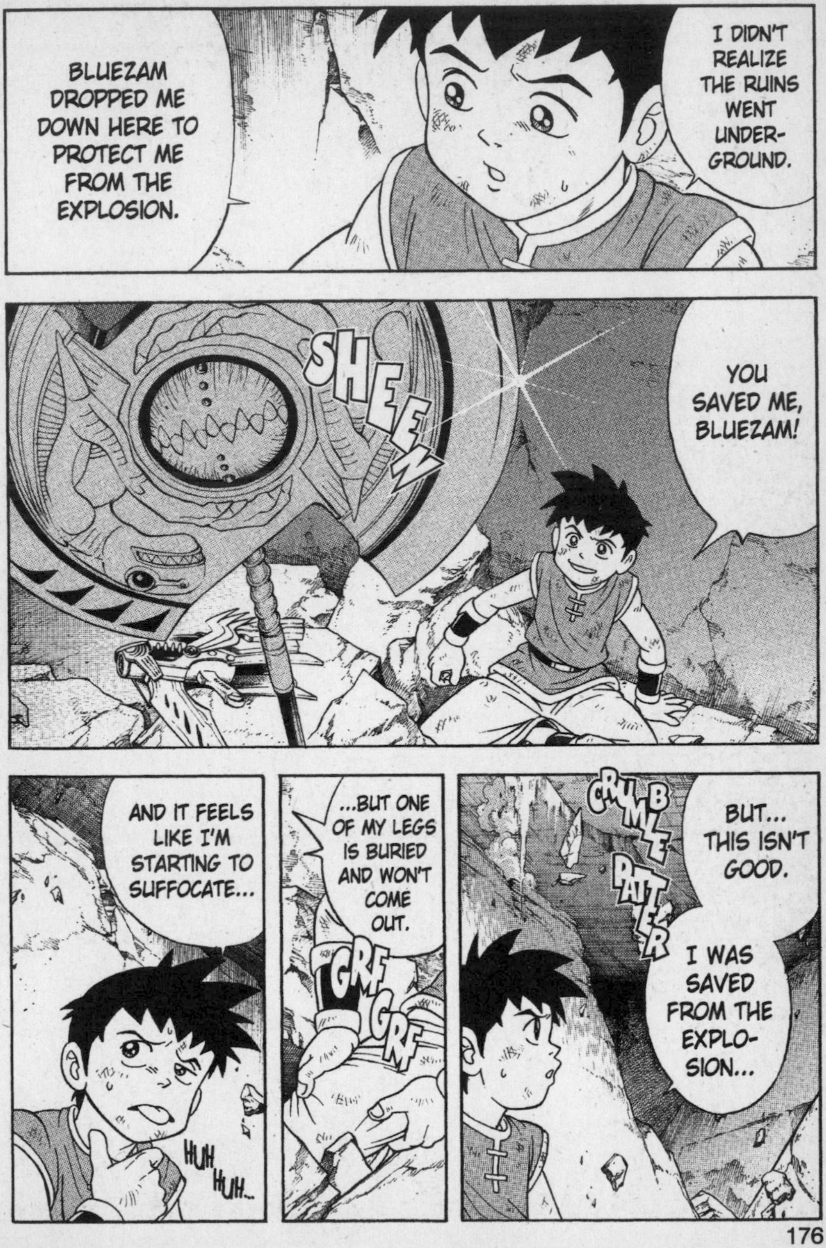
I DIDN'T REALIZE THE RUINS WENT UNDERGROUND.
BLUEZAM DROPPED ME DOWN HERE TO PROTECT ME FROM THE EXPLOSION.
YOU SAVED ME, BLUEZAM!
SHEEN
CRUMBLE
BUT... THIS ISN'T GOOD.
PATTER
I WAS SAVED FROM THE EXPLOSION...
...BUT ONE OF MY LEGS IS BURIED AND WON'T COME OUT.
GRF GRF
AND IT FEELS LIKE I'M STARTING TO SUFFOCATE...
HUH HUH...

READ THIS WAY

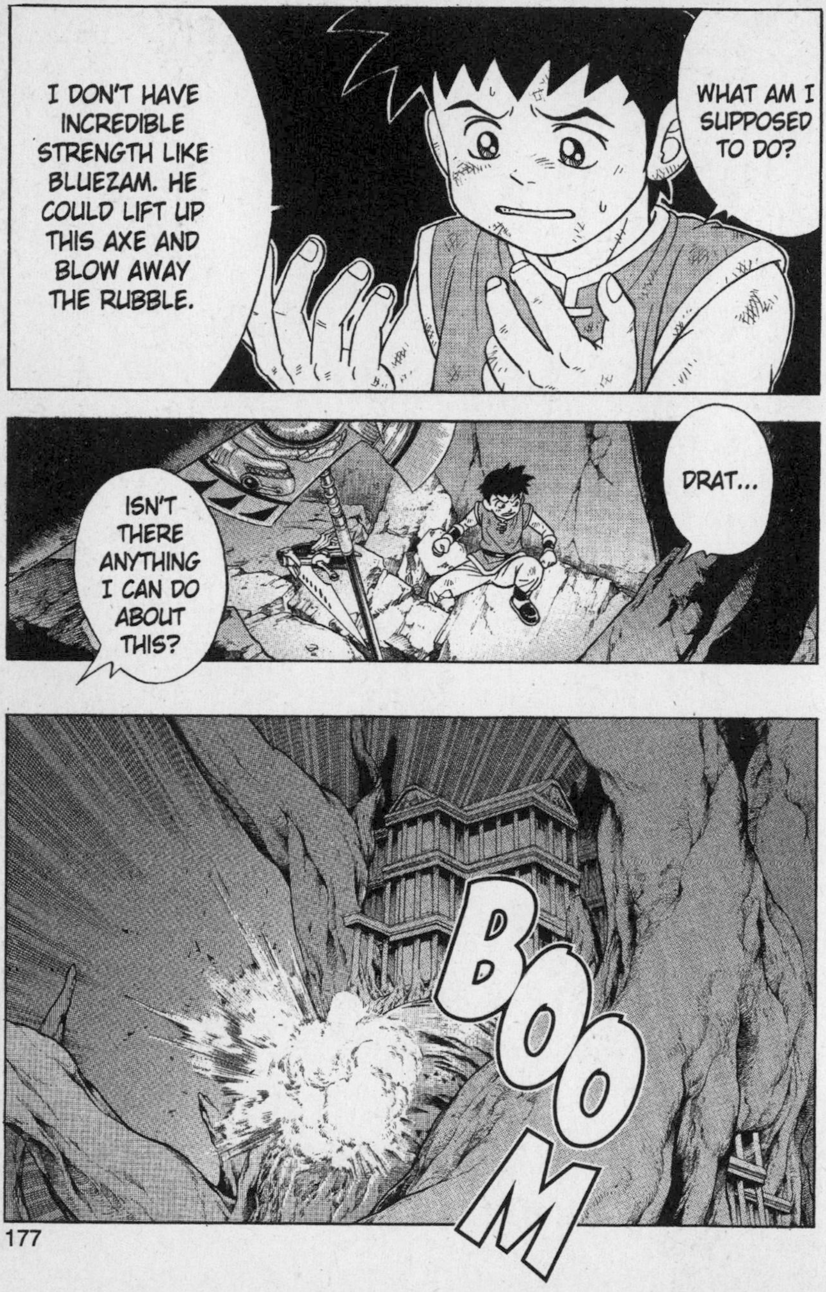
WHAT AM I SUPPOSED TO DO?
I DON'T HAVE INCREDIBLE STRENGTH LIKE BLUEZAM. HE COULD LIFT UP THIS AXE AND BLOW AWAY THE RUBBLE.
DRAT...
ISN'T THERE ANYTHING I CAN DO ABOUT THIS?
BOOM

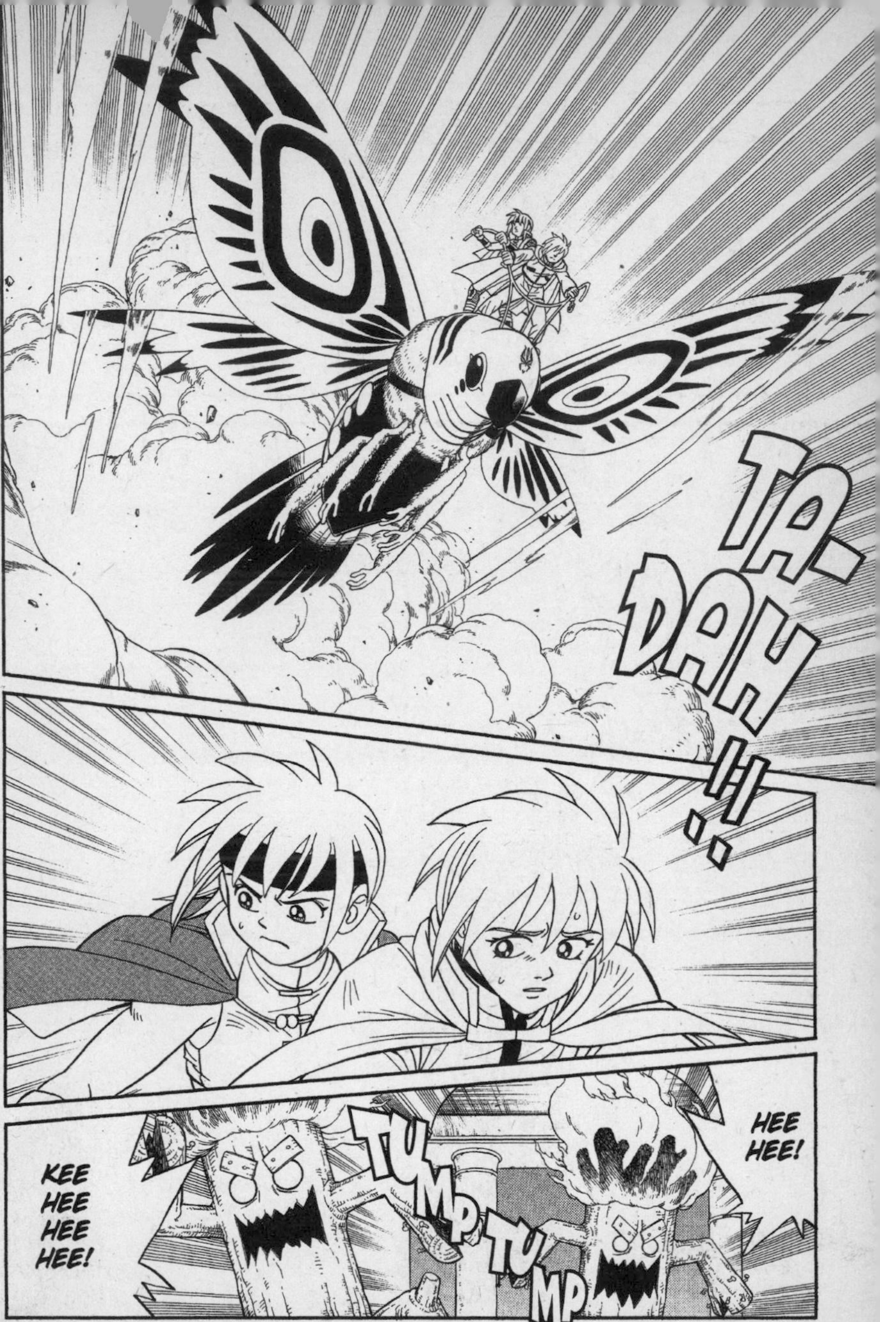
TA-DAH!!!
HEE HEE!
TUMP TUMP TUMP
KEE HEE HEE HEE!

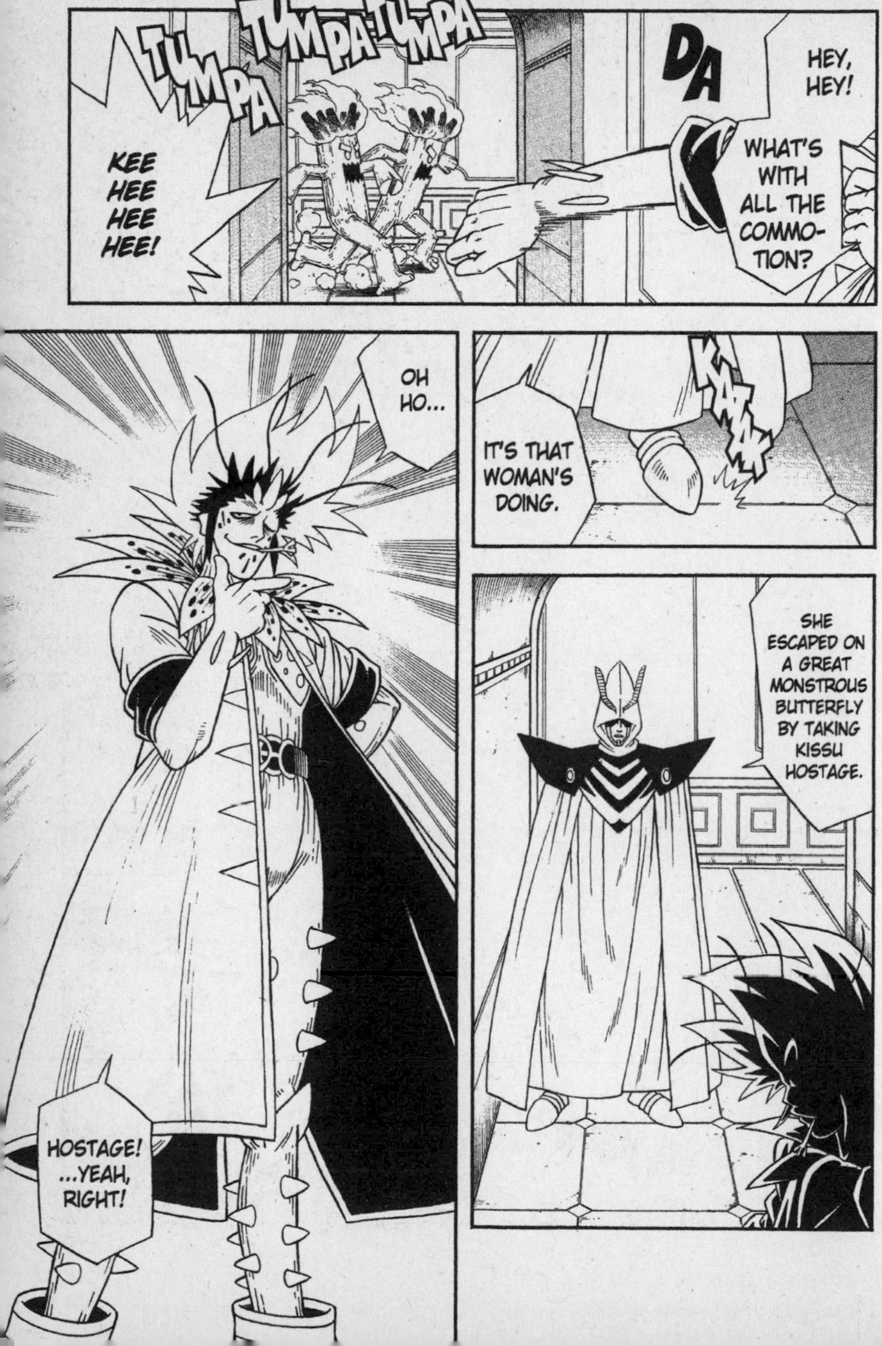
DA
HEY, HEY!
WHAT'S WITH ALL THE COMMOTION?
TUMPA TUMPA
TUMPA
KEE HEE HEE HEE!
KATAK
IT'S THAT WOMAN'S DOING.
SHE ESCAPED ON A GREAT MONSTROUS BUTTERFLY BY TAKING KISSU HOSTAGE.
OH HO...
HOSTAGE! ...YEAH, RIGHT!

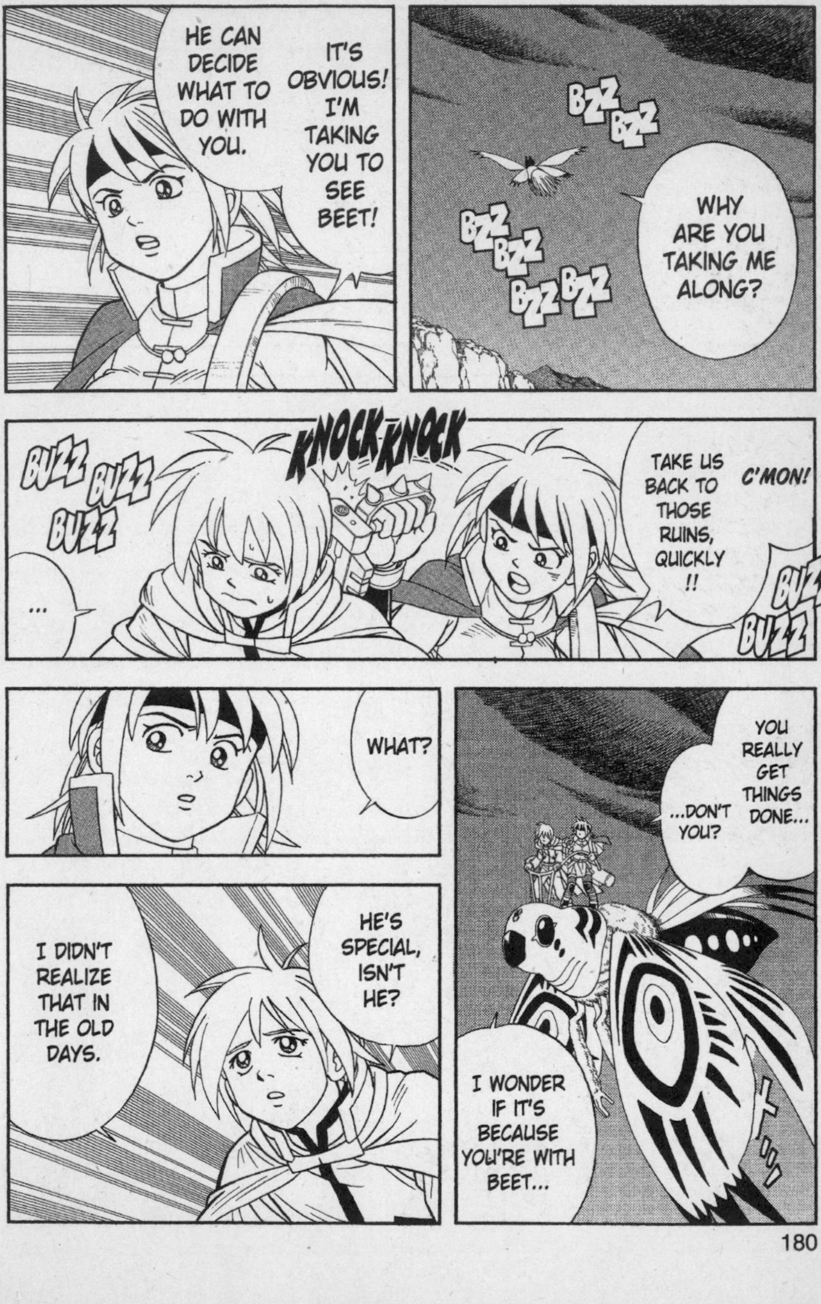
BZZ BZZ
BZZ BZZ BZZ BZZ
WHY ARE YOU TAKING ME ALONG?
IT'S OBVIOUS! I'M TAKING YOU TO SEE BEET!
HE CAN DECIDE WHAT TO DO WITH YOU.
BUZZ BUZZ
C'MON!
TAKE US BACK TO THOSE RUINS, QUICKLY !!
KNOCK-KNOCK
BUZZ BUZZ BUZZ
...
YOU REALLY GET THINGS DONE...
...DON'T YOU?
I WONDER IF IT'S BECAUSE YOU'RE WITH BEET...
WHAT?
HE'S SPECIAL, ISN'T HE?
I DIDN'T REALIZE THAT IN THE OLD DAYS.

READ THIS WAY

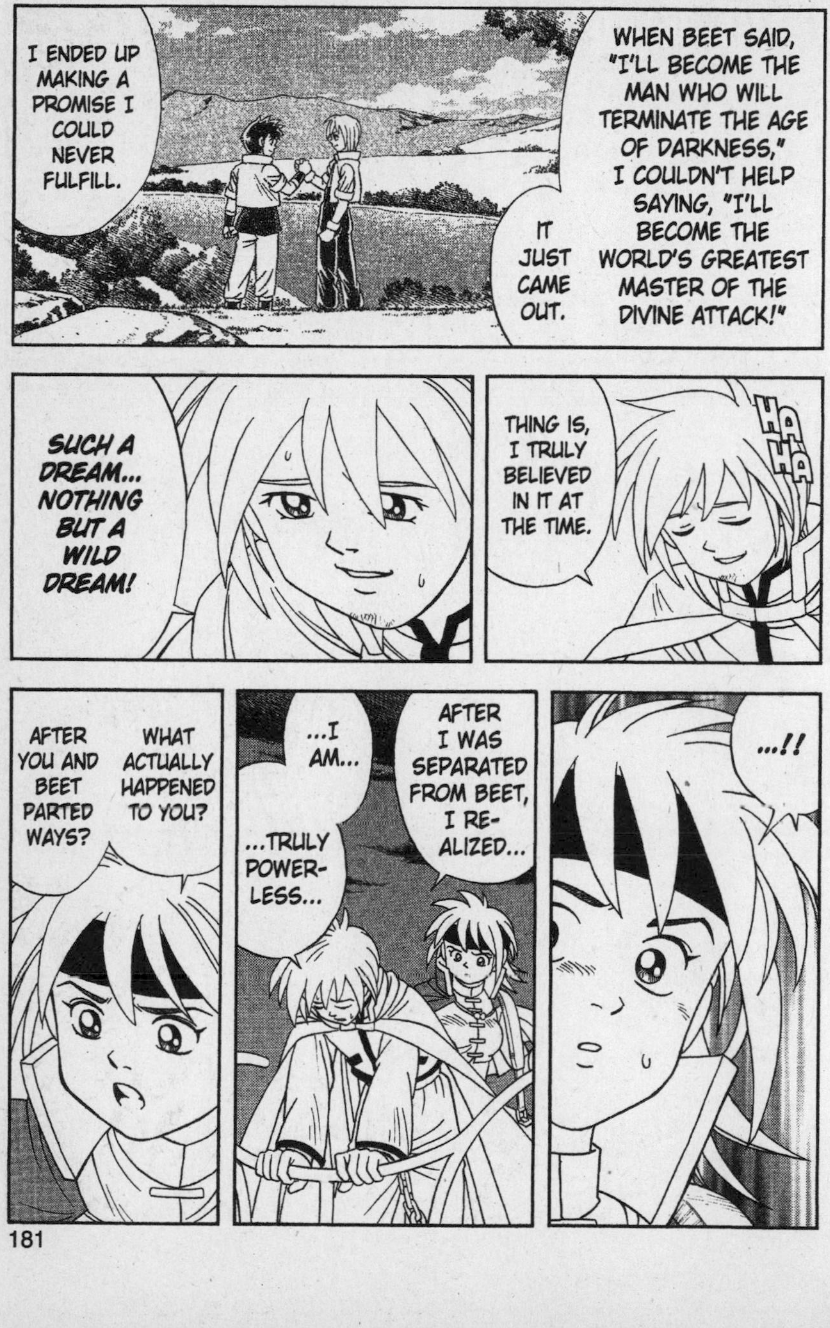
WHEN BEET SAID, "I'LL BECOME THE MAN WHO WILL TERMINATE THE AGE OF DARKNESS," I COULDN'T HELP SAYING, "I'LL BECOME THE WORLD'S GREATEST MASTER OF THE DIVINE ATTACK!"
IT JUST CAME OUT.
I ENDED UP MAKING A PROMISE I COULD NEVER FULFILL.
THING IS, I TRULY BELIEVED IN IT AT THE TIME.
HA HA
SUCH A DREAM... NOTHING BUT A WILD DREAM!
...!!
AFTER I WAS SEPARATED FROM BEET, I RE-ALIZED...
...I AM...
...TRULY POWER-LESS...
WHAT ACTUALLY HAPPENED TO YOU?
AFTER YOU AND BEET PARTED WAYS?

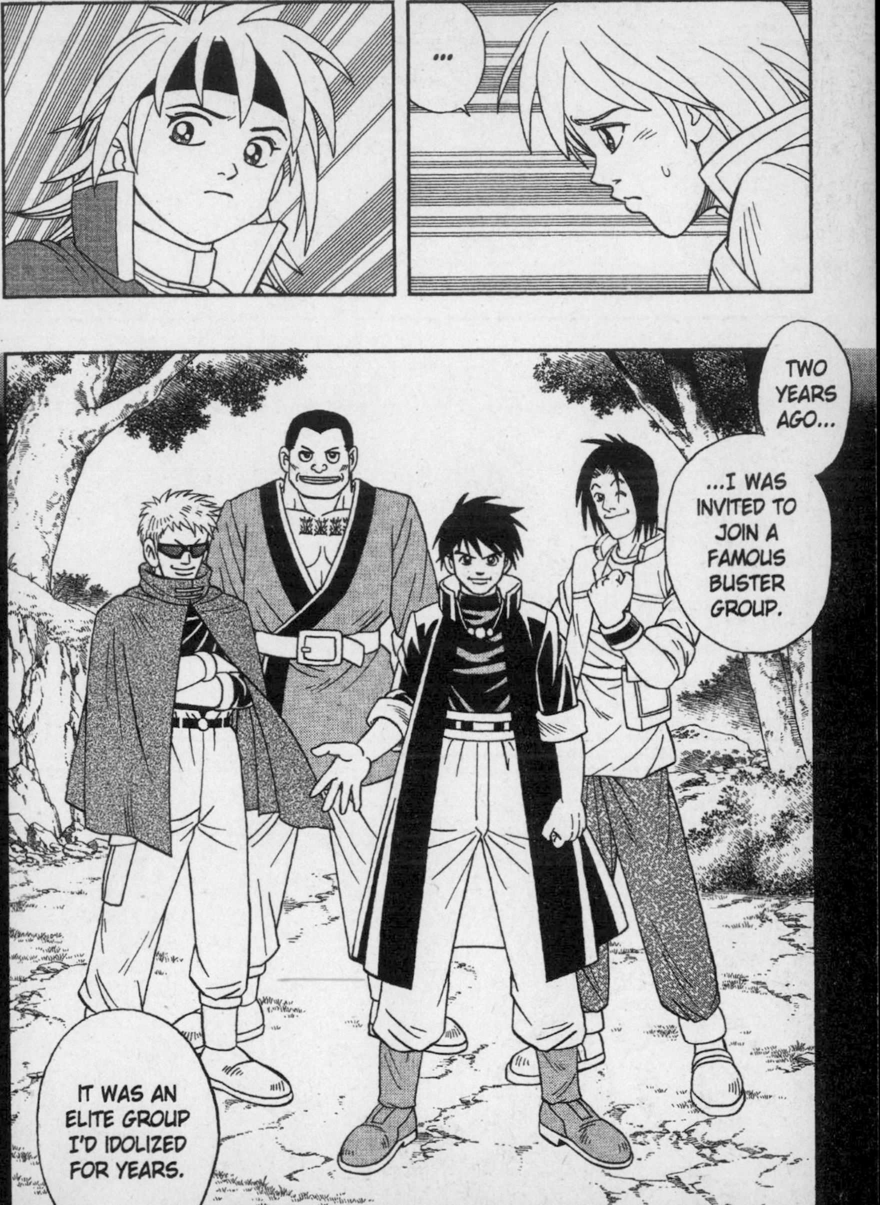
...
TWO YEARS AGO...
...I WAS INVITED TO JOIN A FAMOUS BUSTER GROUP.
IT WAS AN ELITE GROUP I'D IDOLIZED FOR YEARS.

READ THIS WAY

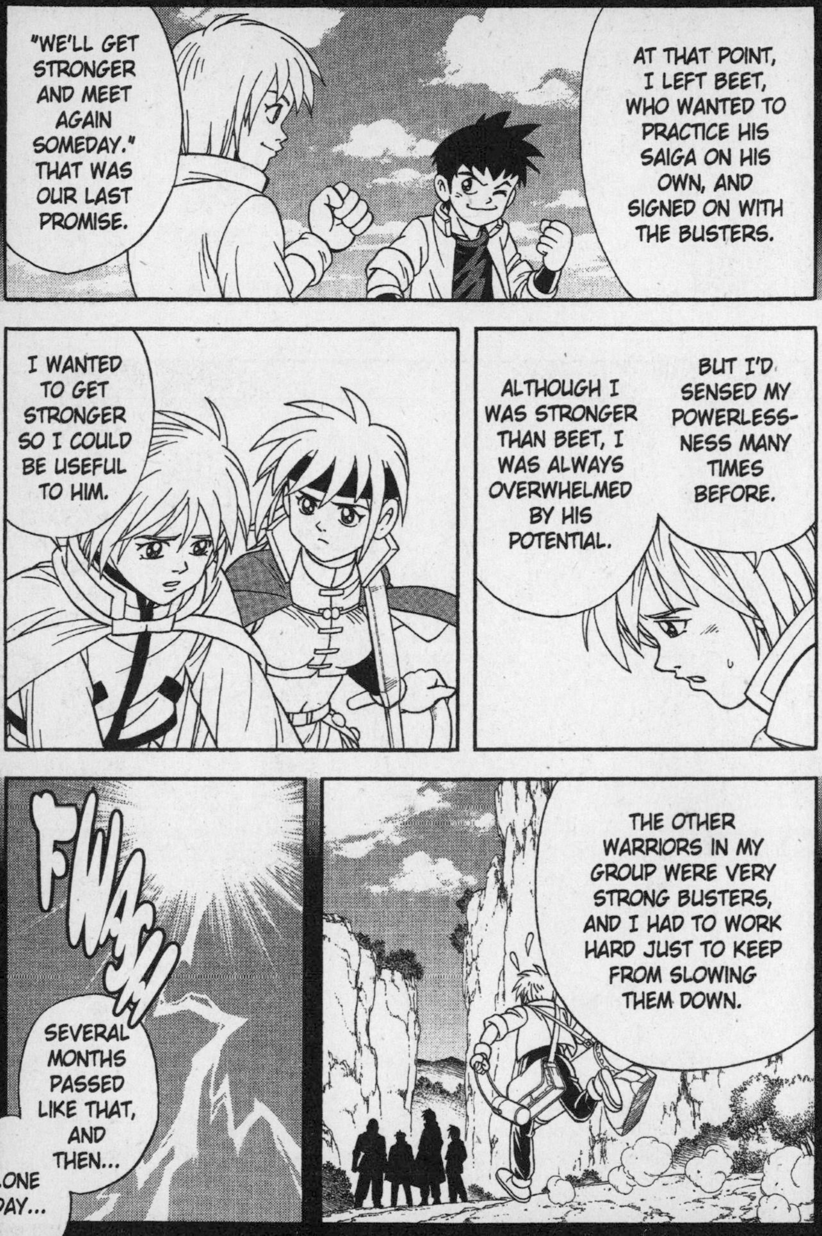
AT THAT POINT, I LEFT BEET, WHO WANTED TO PRACTICE HIS SAIGA ON HIS OWN, AND SIGNED ON WITH THE BUSTERS.
"WE'LL GET STRONGER AND MEET AGAIN SOMEDAY." THAT WAS OUR LAST PROMISE.
ALTHOUGH I WAS STRONGER THAN BEET, I WAS ALWAYS OVERWHELMED BY HIS POTENTIAL.
BUT I'D SENSED MY POWERLESS-NESS MANY TIMES BEFORE.
I WANTED TO GET STRONGER SO I COULD BE USEFUL TO HIM.
THE OTHER WARRIORS IN MY GROUP WERE VERY STRONG BUSTERS, AND I HAD TO WORK HARD JUST TO KEEP FROM SLOWING THEM DOWN.
FWASH
SEVERAL MONTHS PASSED LIKE THAT, AND THEN...
...ONE DAY...

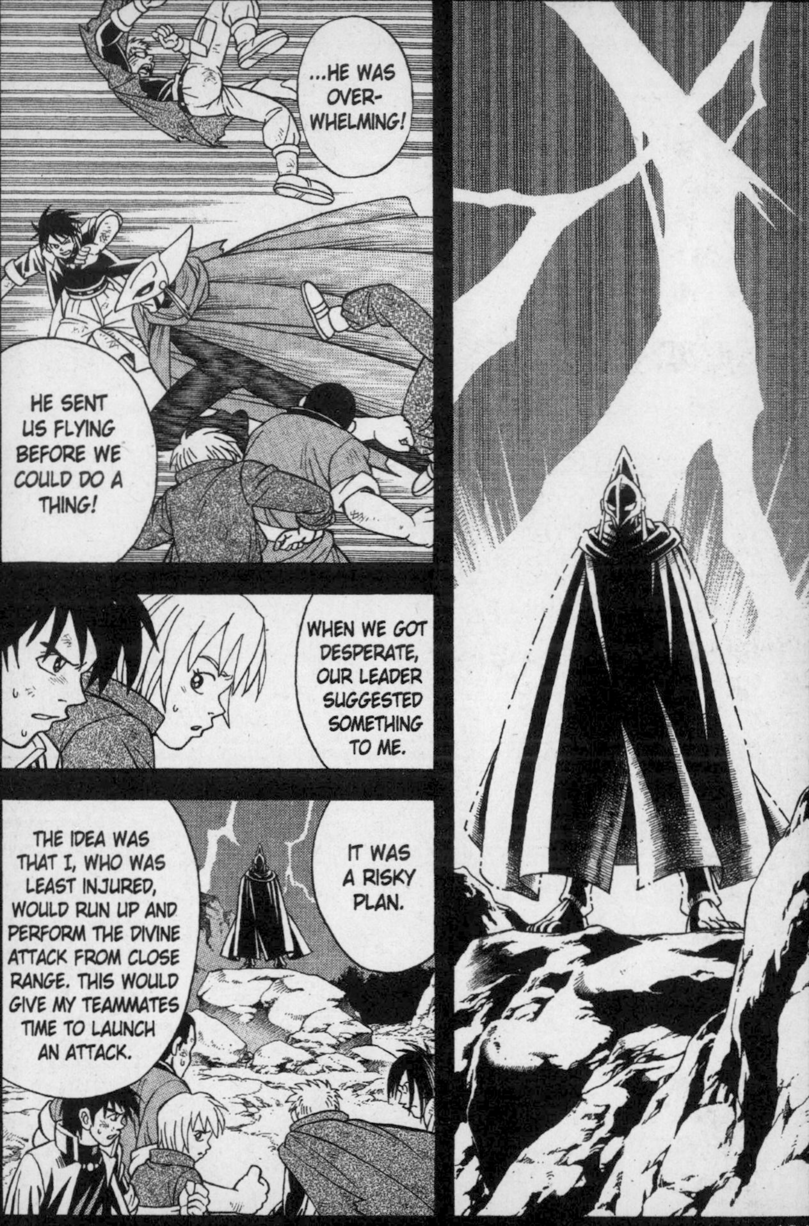
...HE WAS OVER-WHELMING!
HE SENT US FLYING BEFORE WE COULD DO A THING!
WHEN WE GOT DESPERATE, OUR LEADER SUGGESTED SOMETHING TO ME.
IT WAS A RISKY PLAN.
THE IDEA WAS THAT I, WHO WAS LEAST INJURED, WOULD RUN UP AND PERFORM THE DIVINE ATTACK FROM CLOSE RANGE. THIS WOULD GIVE MY TEAMMATES TIME TO LAUNCH AN ATTACK.

READ THIS WAY

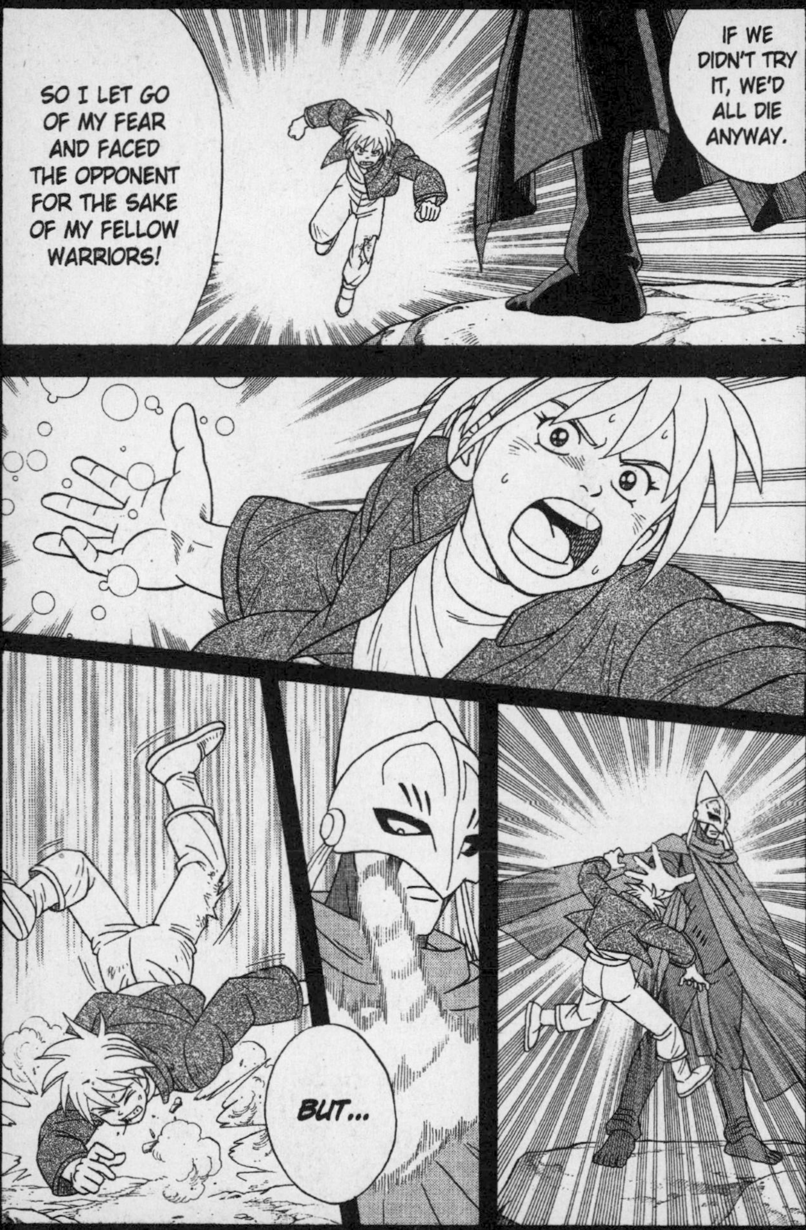

IF WE DIDN'T TRY IT, WE'D ALL DIE ANYWAY.
SO I LET GO OF MY FEAR AND FACED THE OPPONENT FOR THE SAKE OF MY FELLOW WARRIORS!
BUT...

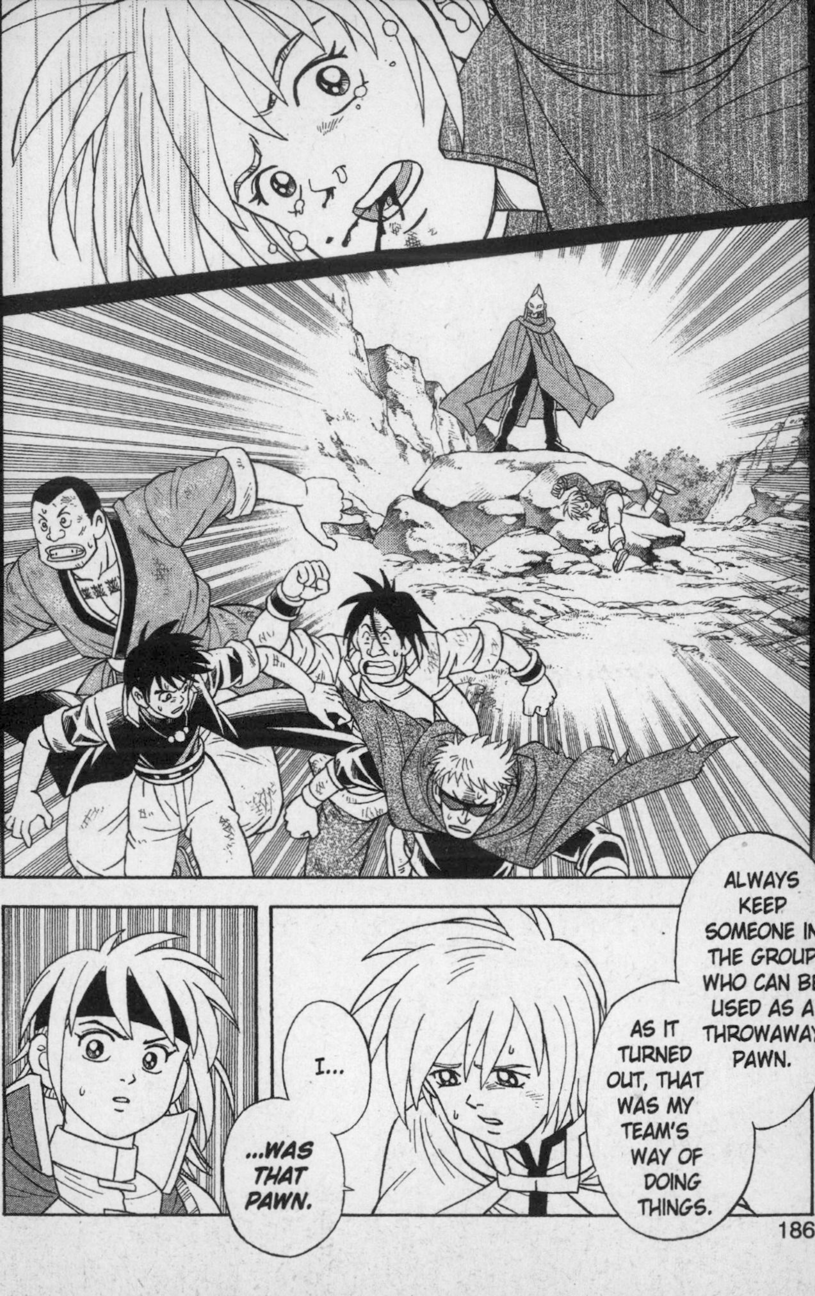
ALWAYS KEEP SOMEONE IN THE GROUP WHO CAN BE USED AS A THROWAWAY PAWN.
AS IT TURNED OUT, THAT WAS MY TEAM'S WAY OF DOING THINGS.
I...
...WAS THAT PAWN.

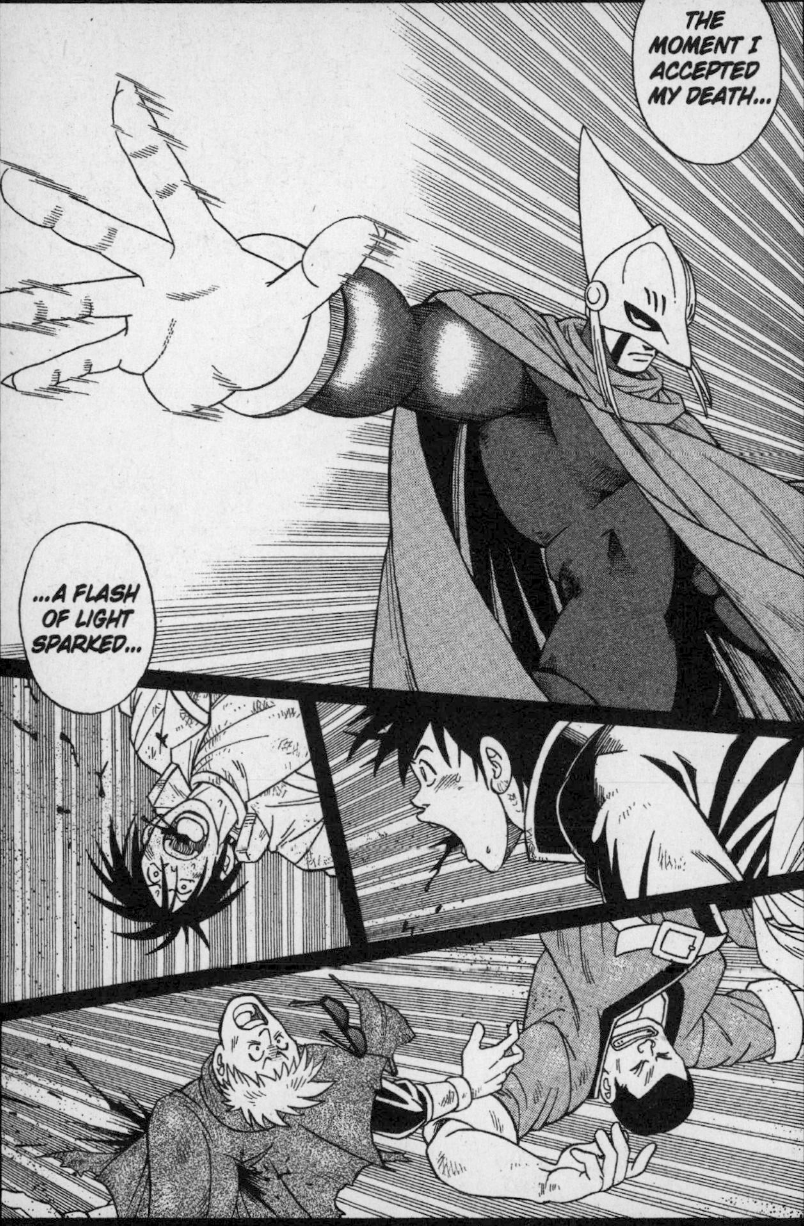
THE MOMENT I ACCEPTED MY DEATH...
...A FLASH OF LIGHT SPARKED...

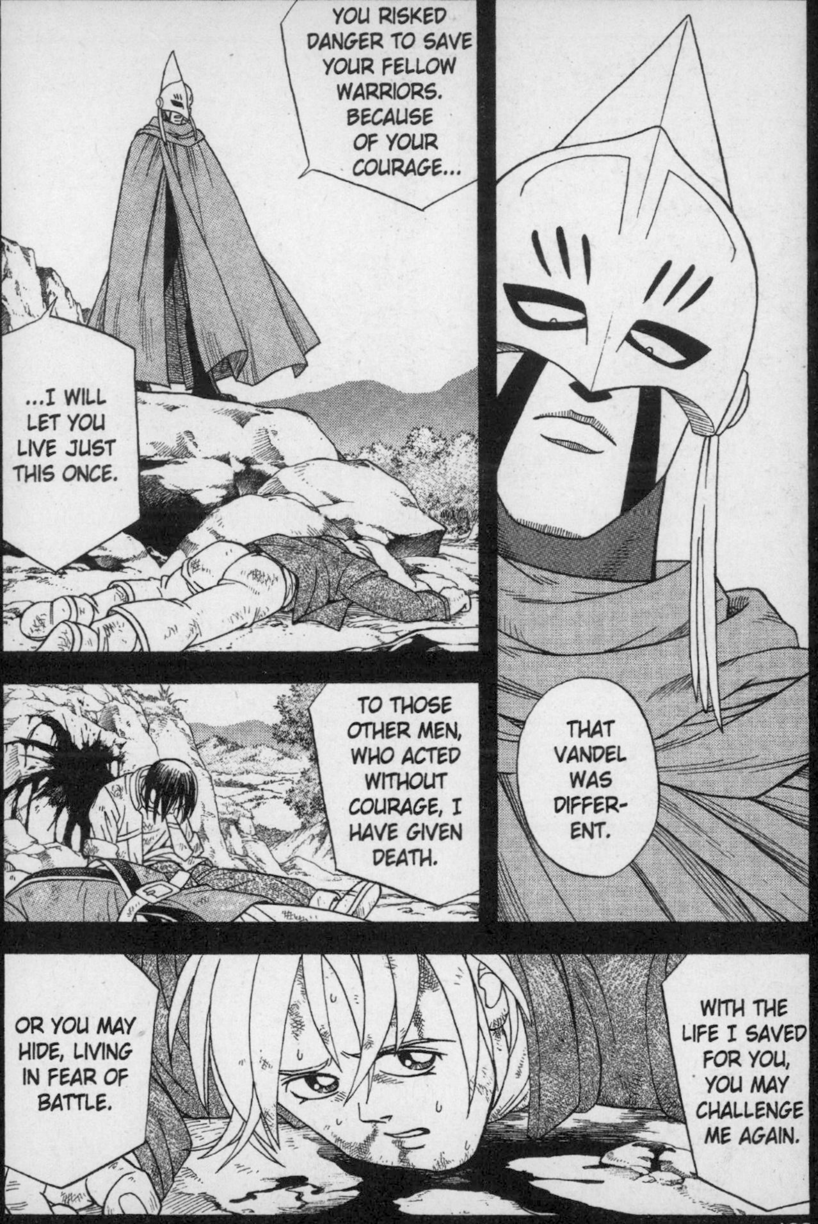
THAT VANDEL WAS DIFFER-ENT.
YOU RISKED DANGER TO SAVE YOUR FELLOW WARRIORS. BECAUSE OF YOUR COURAGE...
...I WILL LET YOU LIVE JUST THIS ONCE.
TO THOSE OTHER MEN, WHO ACTED WITHOUT COURAGE, I HAVE GIVEN DEATH.
WITH THE LIFE I SAVED FOR YOU, YOU MAY CHALLENGE ME AGAIN.
OR YOU MAY HIDE, LIVING IN FEAR OF BATTLE.

READ THIS WAY

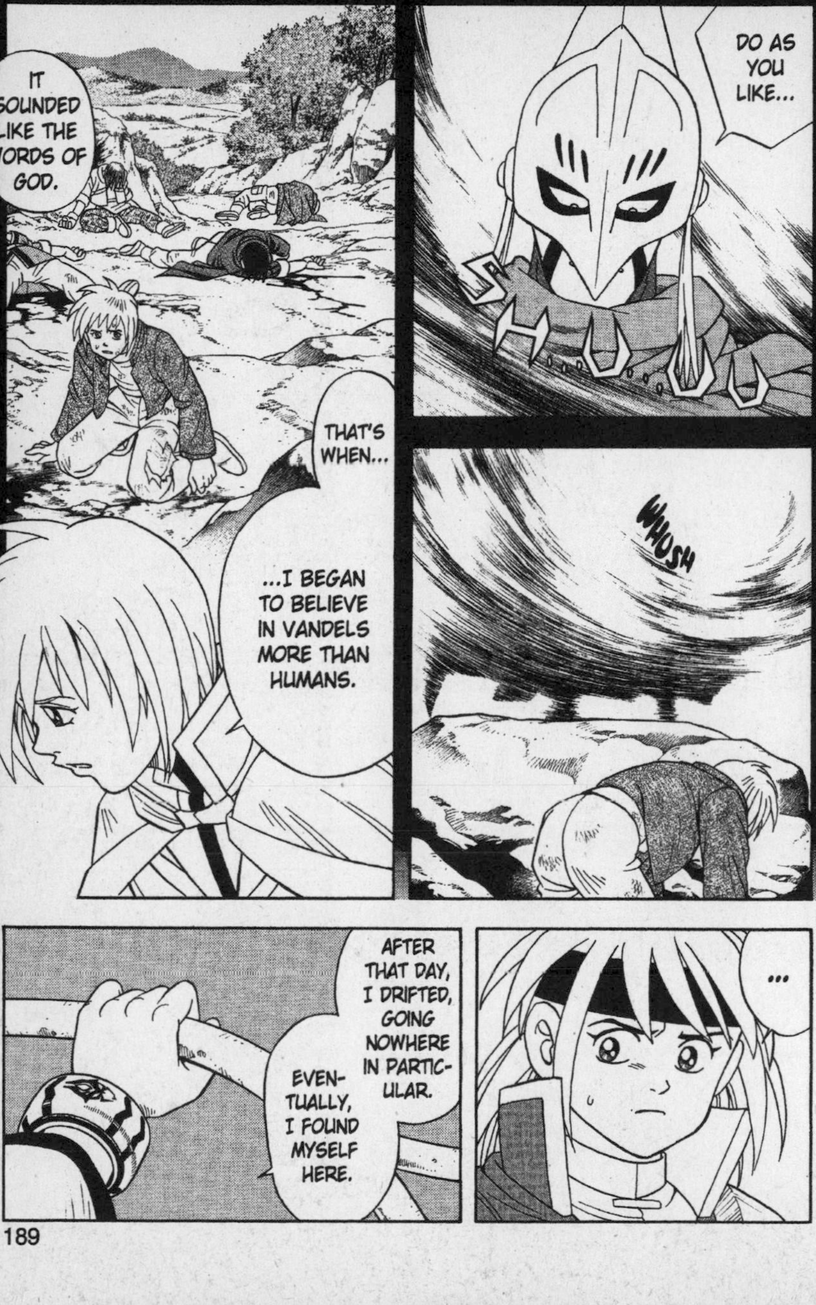

DO AS YOU LIKE...
WHOSH
IT SOUNDED LIKE THE WORDS OF GOD.
THAT'S WHEN...
...I BEGAN TO BELIEVE IN VANDELS MORE THAN HUMANS.
...
AFTER THAT DAY, I DRIFTED, GOING NOWHERE IN PARTIC- ULAR.
EVEN- TUALLY, I FOUND MYSELF HERE.

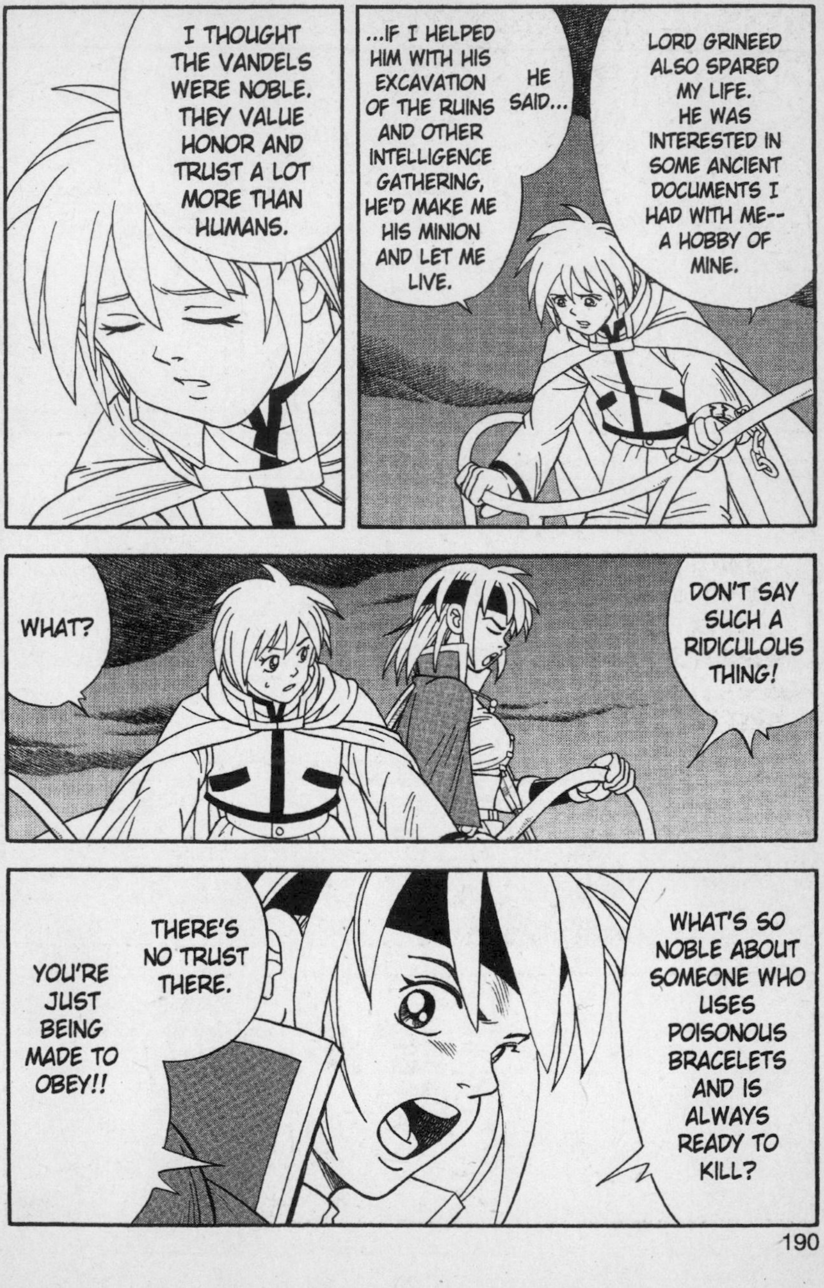

LORD GRINEED ALSO SPARED MY LIFE. HE WAS INTERESTED IN SOME ANCIENT DOCUMENTS I HAD WITH ME-- A HOBBY OF MINE.
HE SAID...
...IF I HELPED HIM WITH HIS EXCAVATION OF THE RUINS AND OTHER INTELLIGENCE GATHERING, HE'D MAKE ME HIS MINION AND LET ME LIVE.
I THOUGHT THE VANDELS WERE NOBLE. THEY VALUE HONOR AND TRUST A LOT MORE THAN HUMANS.
DON'T SAY SUCH A RIDICULOUS THING!
WHAT?
WHAT'S SO NOBLE ABOUT SOMEONE WHO USES POISONOUS BRACELETS AND IS ALWAYS READY TO KILL?
THERE'S NO TRUST THERE.
YOU'RE JUST BEING MADE TO OBEY!!

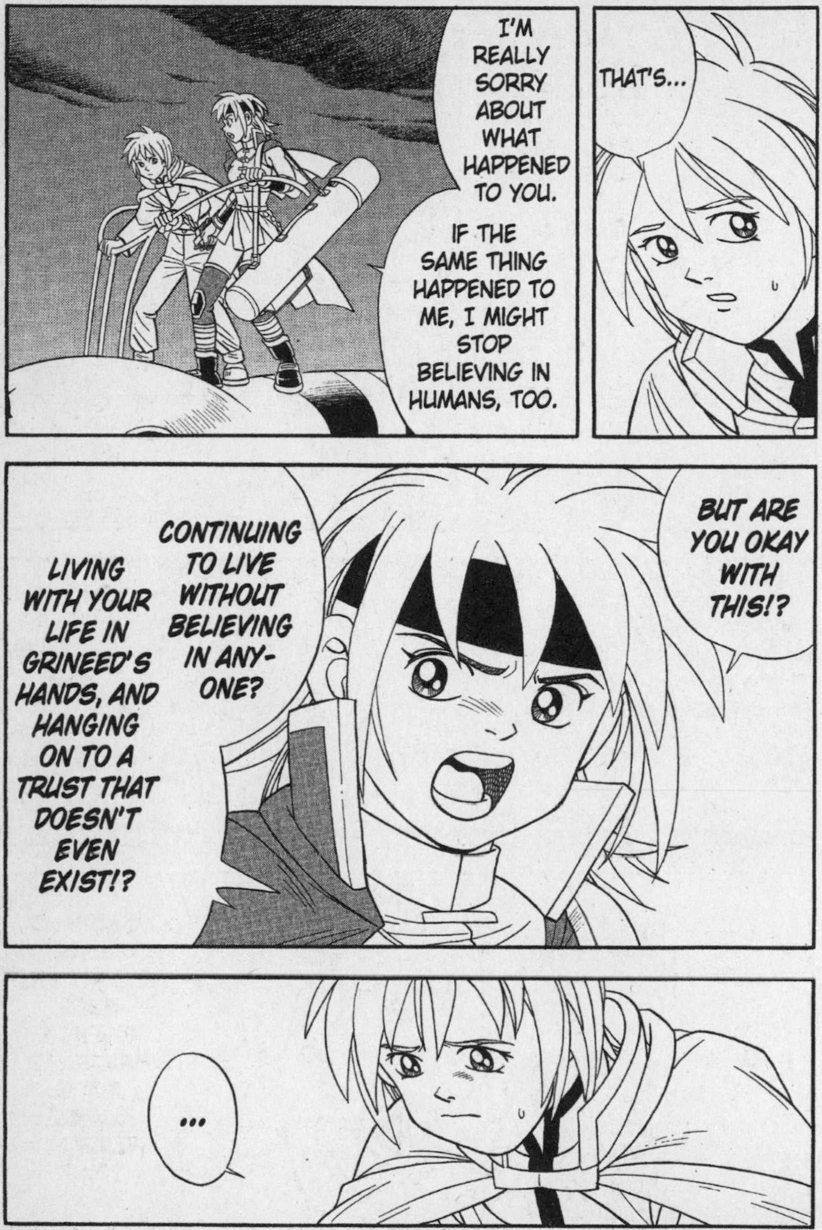
THAT'S...
I'M REALLY SORRY ABOUT WHAT HAPPENED TO YOU.
IF THE SAME THING HAPPENED TO ME, I MIGHT STOP BELIEVING IN HUMANS, TOO.
BUT ARE YOU OKAY WITH THIS!?
CONTINUING TO LIVE WITHOUT BELIEVING IN ANY-ONE?
LIVING WITH YOUR LIFE IN GRINEED'S HANDS, AND HANGING ON TO A TRUST THAT DOESN'T EVEN EXIST!?
...

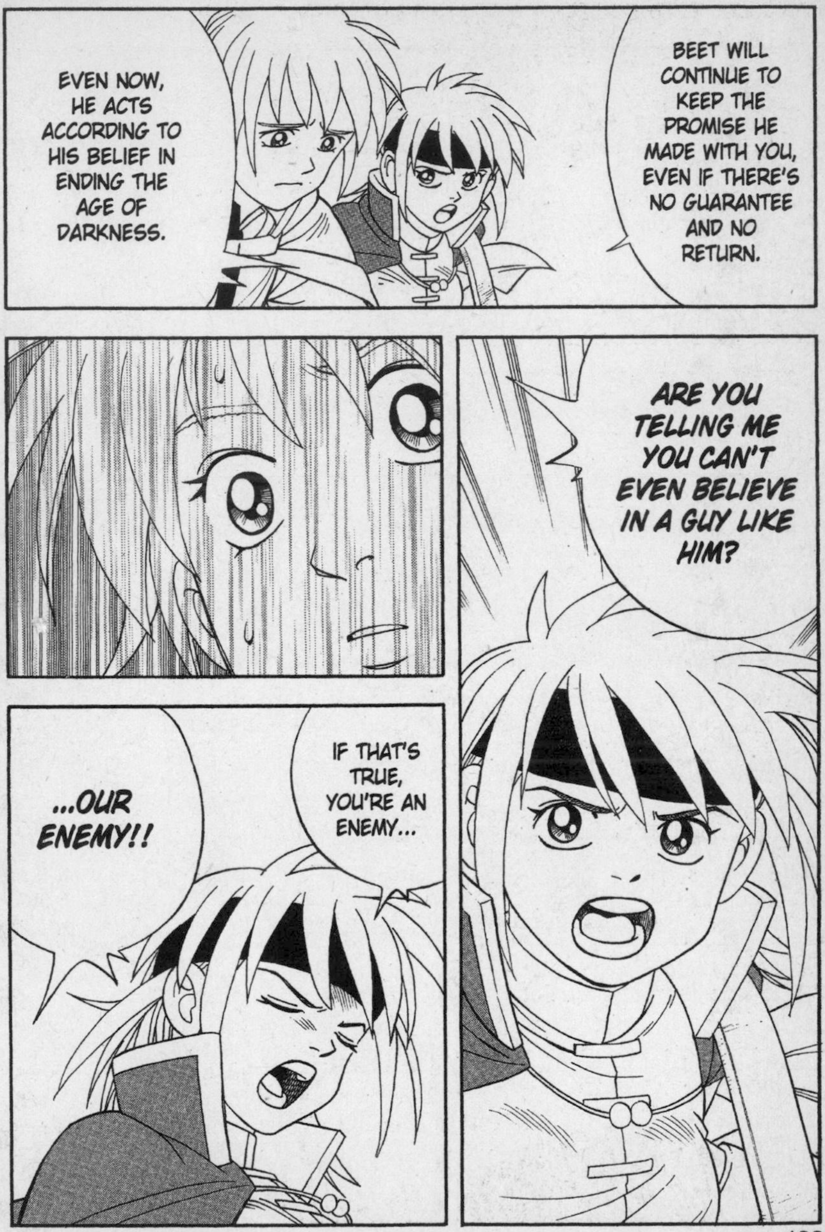
BEET WILL CONTINUE TO KEEP THE PROMISE HE MADE WITH YOU, EVEN IF THERE'S NO GUARANTEE AND NO RETURN.
EVEN NOW, HE ACTS ACCORDING TO HIS BELIEF IN ENDING THE AGE OF DARKNESS.
ARE YOU TELLING ME YOU CAN'T EVEN BELIEVE IN A GUY LIKE HIM?
IF THAT'S TRUE, YOU'RE AN ENEMY...
...OUR ENEMY!!

READ THIS WAY

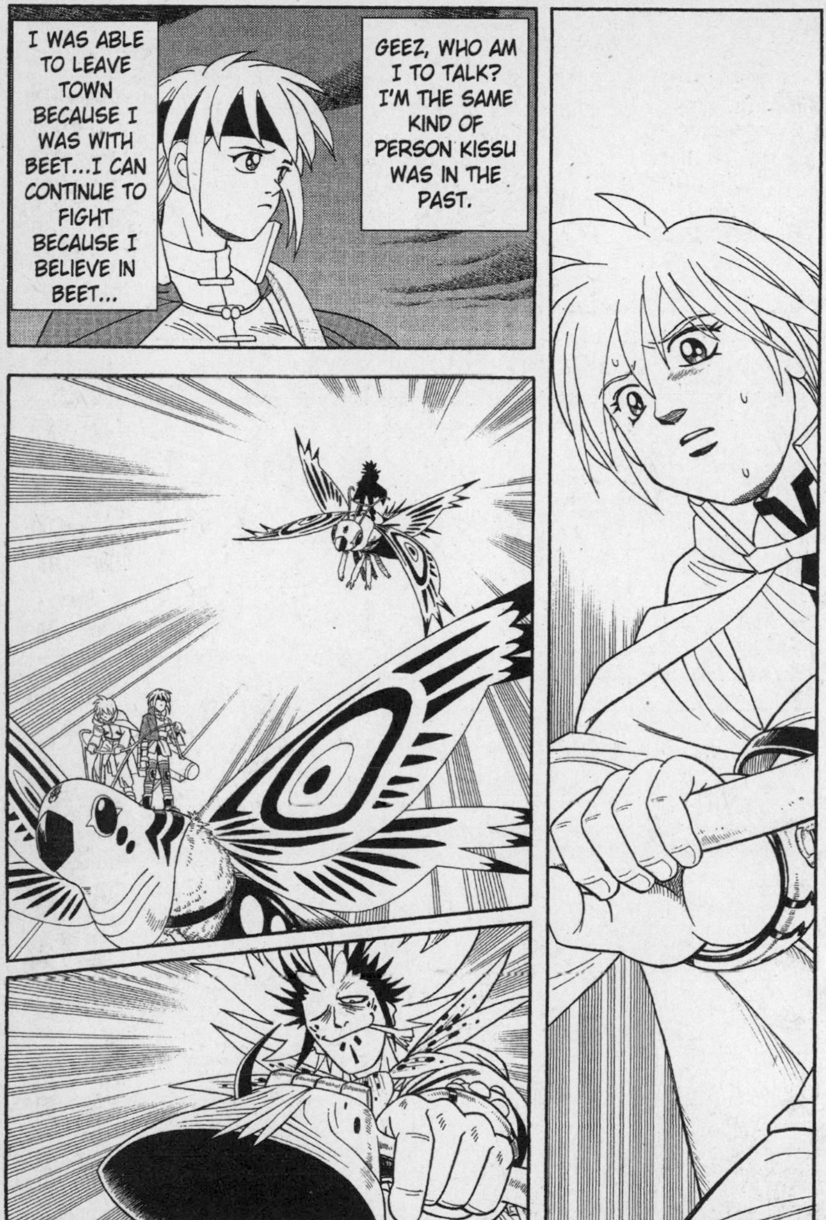
GEEZ, WHO AM I TO TALK? I'M THE SAME KIND OF PERSON KISSU WAS IN THE PAST.
I WAS ABLE TO LEAVE TOWN BECAUSE I WAS WITH BEET...I CAN CONTINUE TO FIGHT BECAUSE I BELIEVE IN BEET...

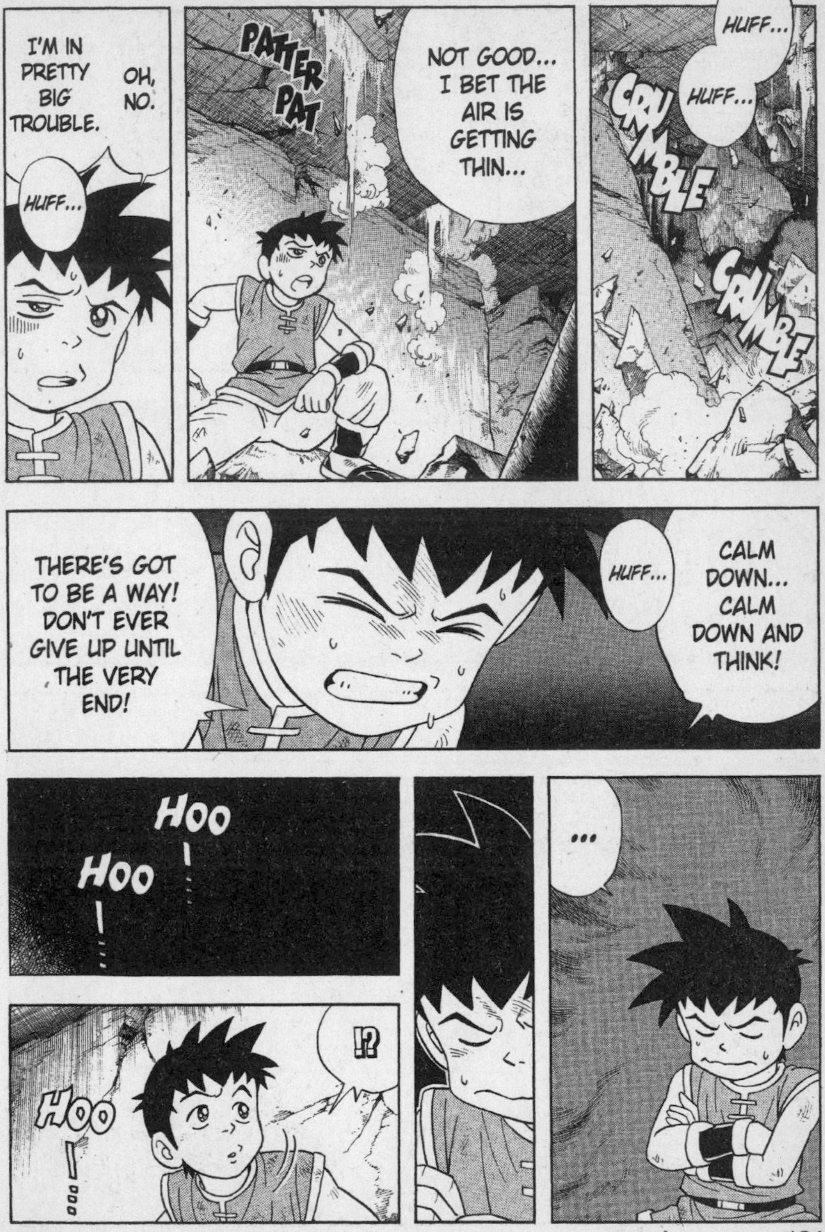
HUFF...
HUFF...
CRUMBLE
CRUMBLE
NOT GOOD... I BET THE AIR IS GETTING THIN...
PATTER PAT
OH, NO.
I'M IN PRETTY BIG TROUBLE.
HUFF...
CALM DOWN... CALM DOWN AND THINK!
HUFF...
THERE'S GOT TO BE A WAY! DON'T EVER GIVE UP UNTIL THE VERY END!
...
HOO!...
HOO!...
!?
HOO!...

READ THIS WAY

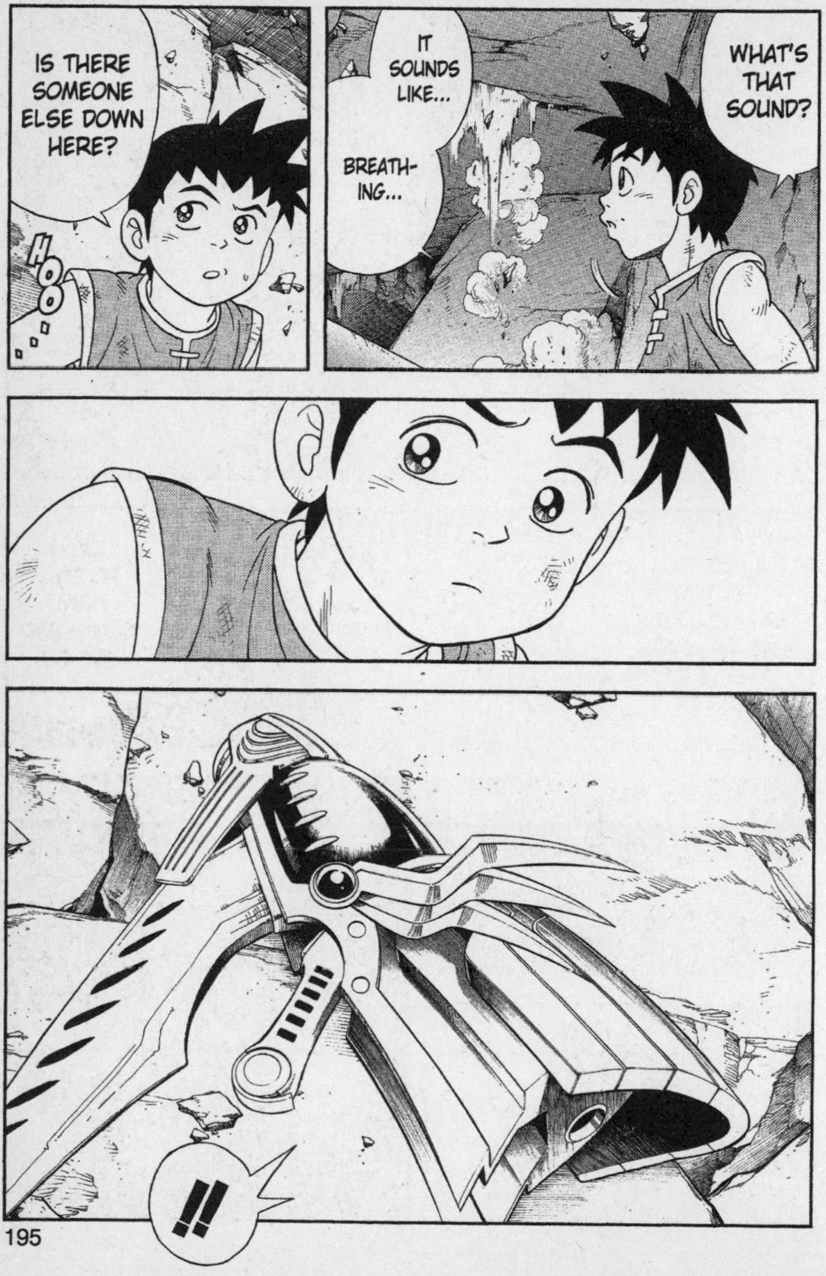
WHAT'S THAT SOUND?
IT SOUNDS LIKE...
BREATHING...
IS THERE SOMEONE ELSE DOWN HERE?
HOO
!!

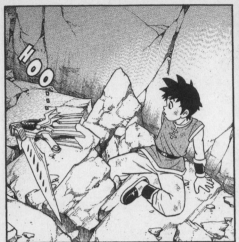

HOO...
HOO...
IT'S COMING FROM HERE!
THE CYCLONE GUNNER'S BREATHING!!
HOO...
THAT MEANS...
...MAYBE...

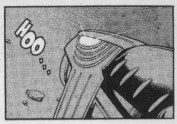

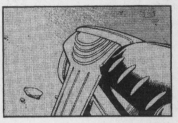

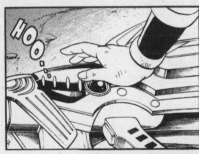

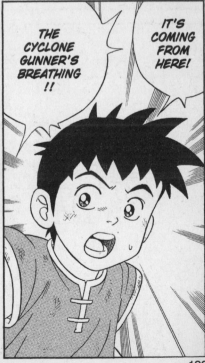

READ THIS WAY

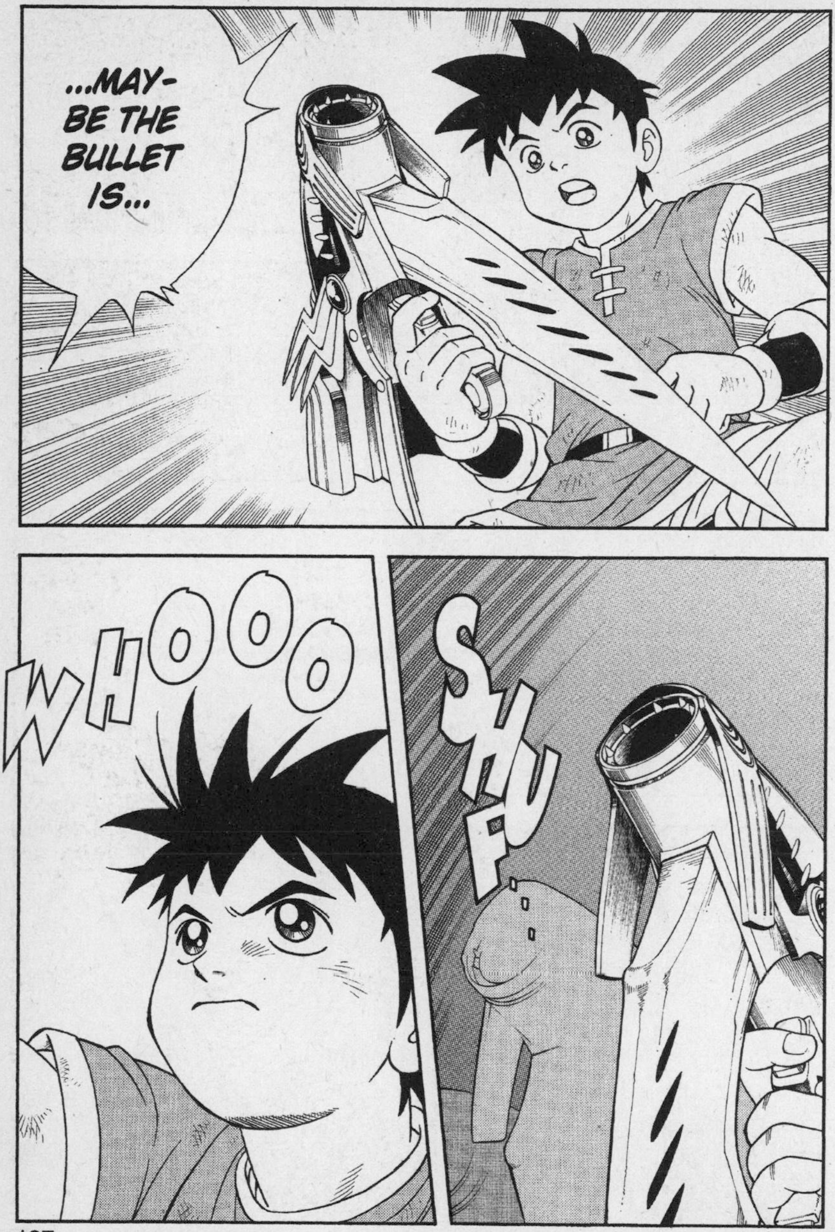
...MAY-BE THE BULLET IS...
SHUF
WHOOO

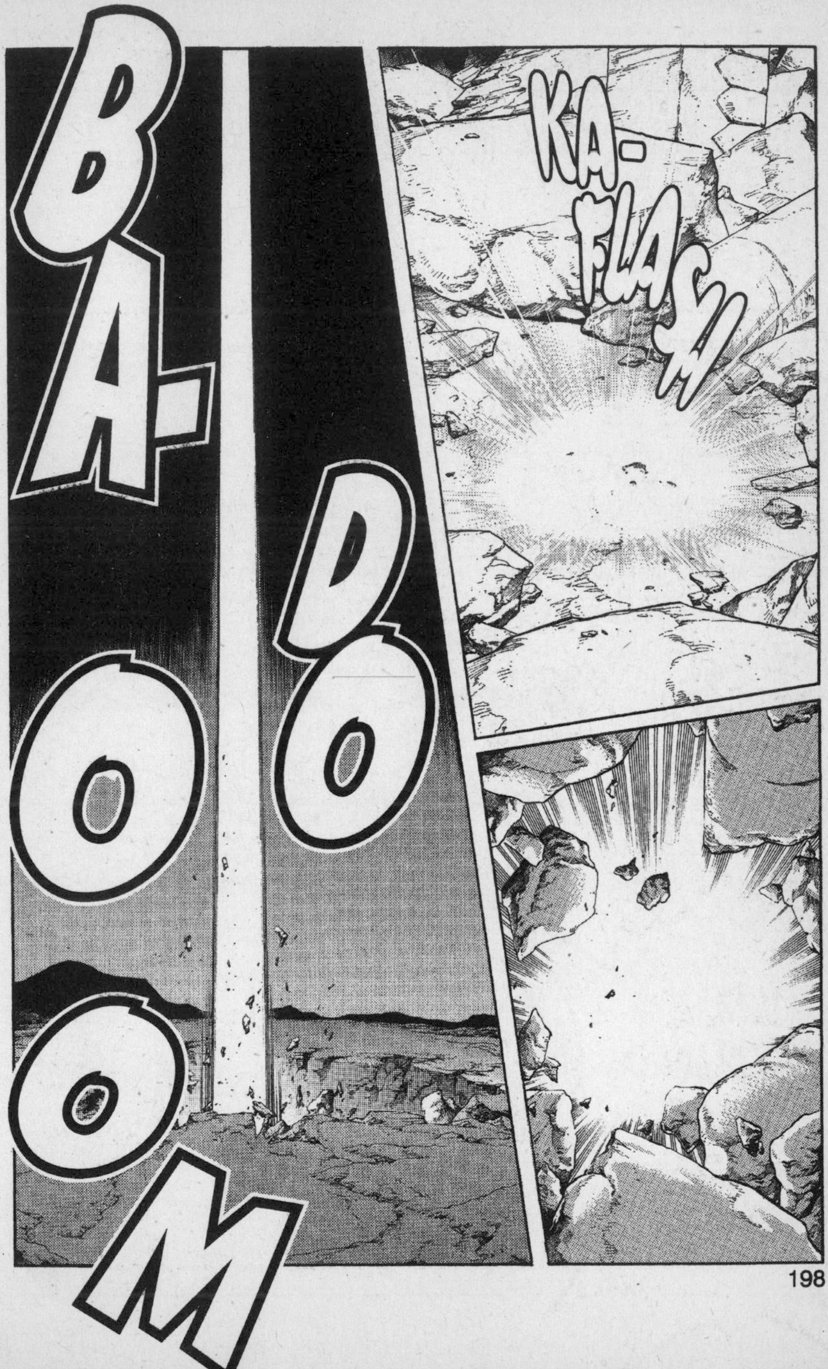
KA-
FLASH
BA-DOOOM

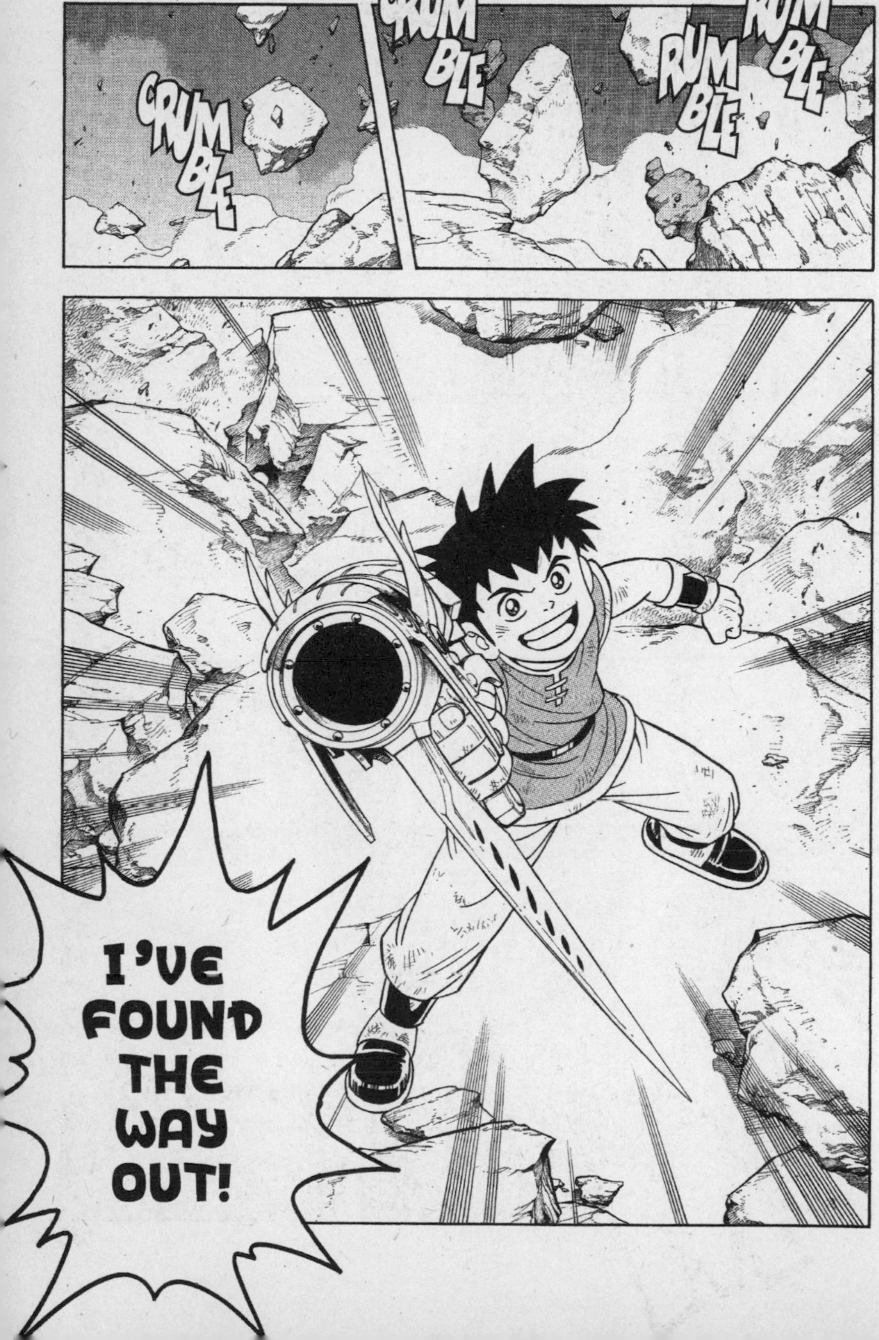
RUMBLE
RUMBLE
CRUMBLE
CRUMBLE
I'VE FOUND THE WAY OUT!

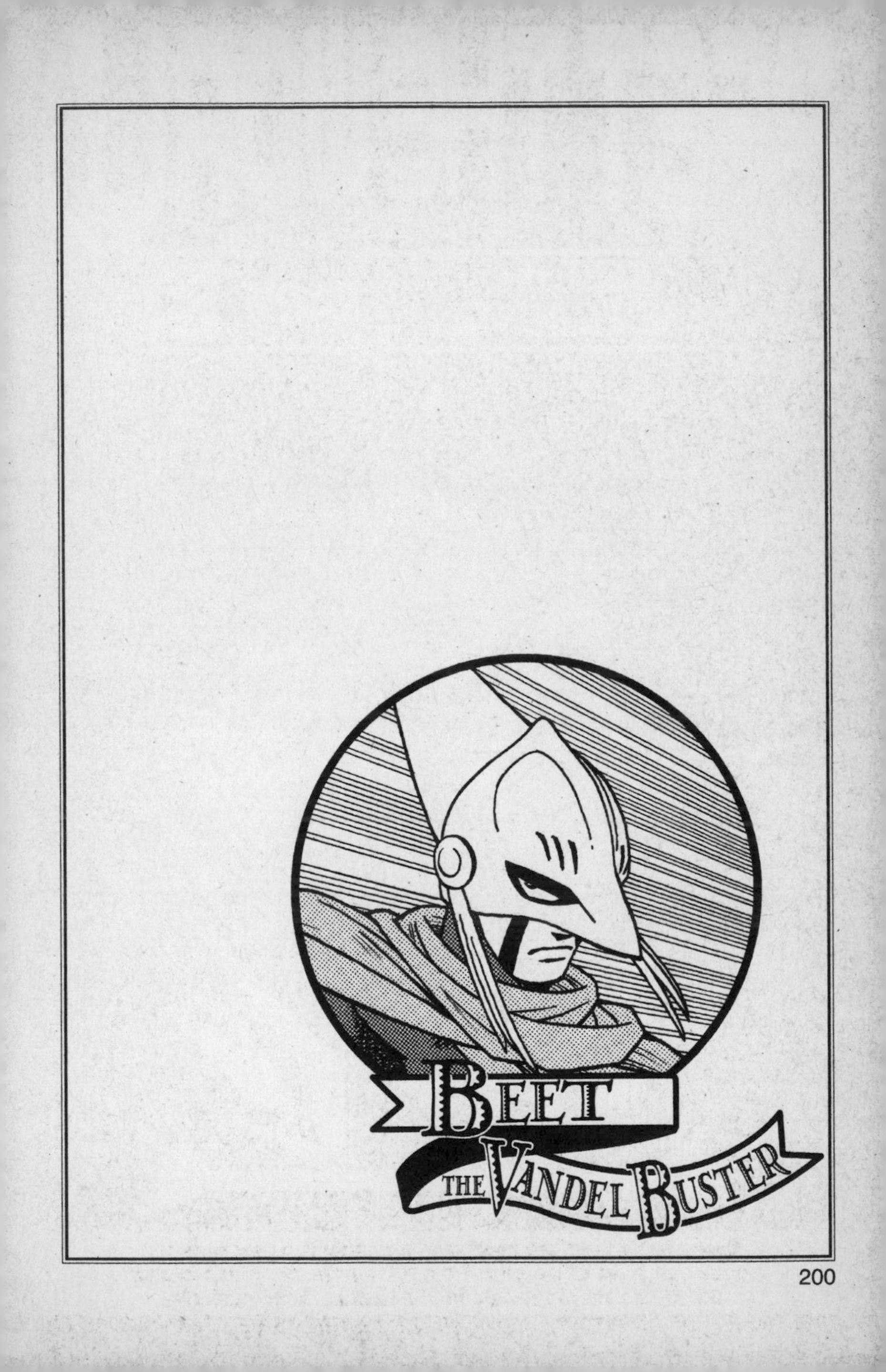
BEET
THE VANDEL BUSTER

BEET THE WORLD

THE WORLD OF

BEET the VANDEL BUSTER · PART 3

Beet and his team are heating up for battle in a new territory!
Here's part three of our end-of-the-volume special, which focuses
on the secrets of their world of adventure! Read carefully!!

GATE

A GATE IS A STRONG "LIVING WALL" OF IRON THAT PROTECTS HUMANS FROM THE MONSTERS OF THE DARK AGE.

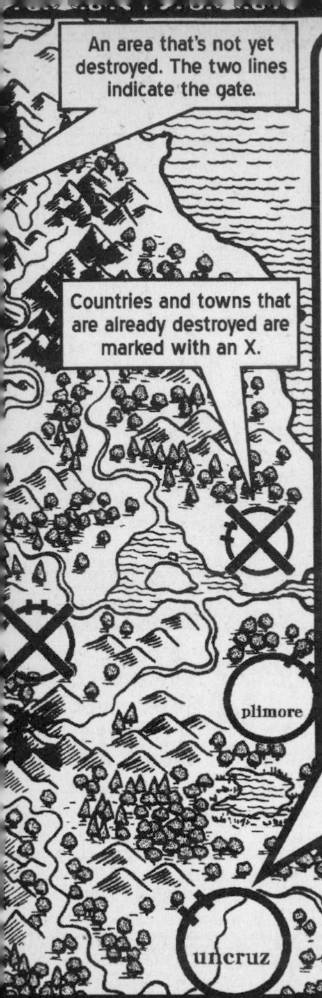

An area that's not yet destroyed. The two lines indicate the gate.
Countries and towns that are already destroyed are marked with an X.
plimore
uncruz

UNCRUZ

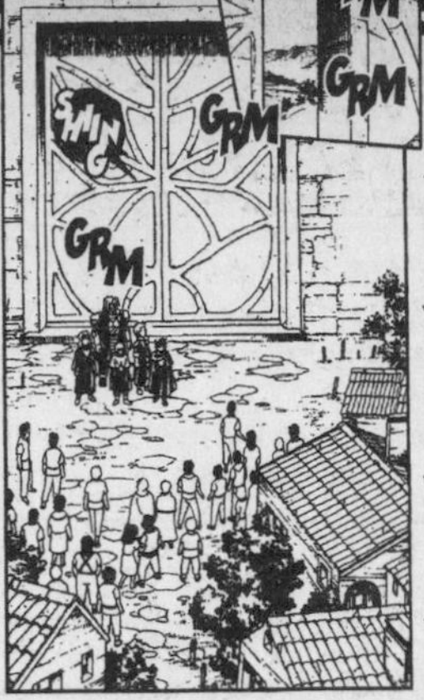

GRM
GRM
SHING
GRM
GRM

▼ This is a gate with average defensive power.

Hometown of Beet and Poala. Low-level monsters multiplied inside the gate, causing trouble.

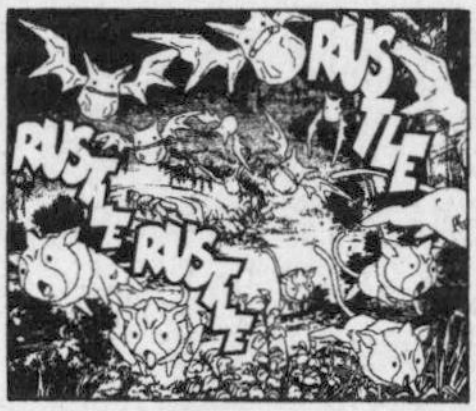

RUSTLE
RUSTLE
RUSTLE

▼ Monsters are in the ponds!

The "gate" is a defensive wall that protects countries, towns and villages around the world from the Vandels. At this point, it is not an exaggeration to say that there is no country in existence that does not have a Gate to protect its citizens. The Gate itself has a will of its own--it can think and make conversation. Using the eyes that are attached to either side of its doors, the gate can confirm the state of the enemy. The sky above the wall is sealed by a holy shield, so that airborne monsters cannot easily penetrate it. However, once monsters enter through the gate, they will not be affected by the shield--so it's important to be careful. Just like the Appraisers' Houses, the Gates are controlled and managed by the Association of Busters.

MAP OF THE WORLD OF BEET

This is the map Beet gets at Ledeux. It may be part of an extensive world map.

BEYOND THE BIG RIVER OVER HERE...
...IS THE STRONGEST COUNTRY IN THESE PARTS...
...TRO-WANA!

▶ The manager of the Appraiser's House at Ledeux made an exception and gave it to him.

trowana

deuola

ledeux

▶ The pride of Trowana, this gigantic gate has superior strength. It's probably impossible to break through from the outside.

TROWANA

A strong country that somehow manages to withstand Grineed's invasions. In addition to soldiers, Trowana hires many Busters who are stationed there. Trowana successfully produces enough food to be self-sufficient.

FWASH

◀ The gate's sky shield is also extremely powerful. It can evaporate monsters in an instant!

LEDEUX

A port city for crossing the big river. Since it is a relatively safe area, it is full of refugees.

▶ It is an unusual town with two gates, one facing the land and another facing the big river.

CHAK
YOU MEAN TO GO ACROSS THE BIG RIVER?

◀ The water gate protects the town from water monsters. Its calm manner of speech is impressive.

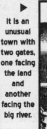

BLACK HORIZON

A LAND OF DESPAIR COVERED BY DARK CLOUDS. IT IS AN AREA WITHIN THE CONTROL OF GRINEED AND HIS MINIONS.

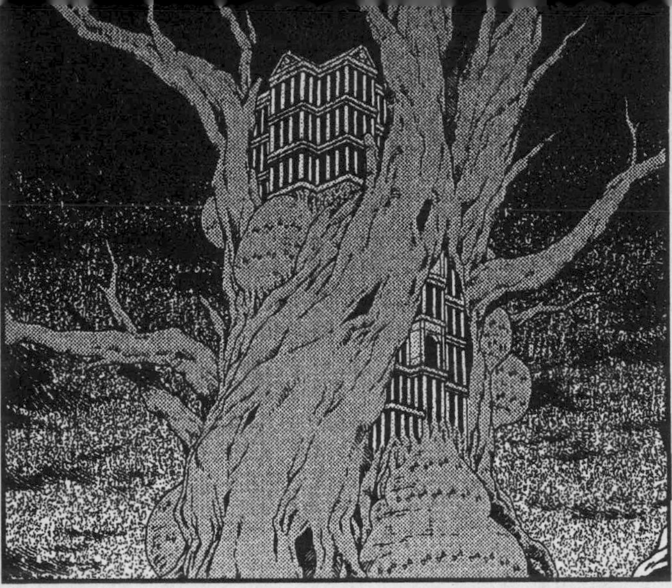

The area controlled by the Vandel Grineed, known as the "Clever Honcho of Deep Green," has been transformed into a hellish place due to the influence of swarms of monsters. People call it the Black Horizon. The insect-type monsters released by Grineed have distorted the ecological structure of nature. Now the sky is always covered by dark clouds, and the land is withered black. People who live there have not seen direct sunlight for over twenty years. It can certainly be called a land of despair. Grineed prefers to use insect-type and plant-type monsters, primarily because they multiply so quickly. His motto is to invade efficiently.

▶ Every forest is filled with monsters like Black Smoky Cicadas and Mega Dragonflies.

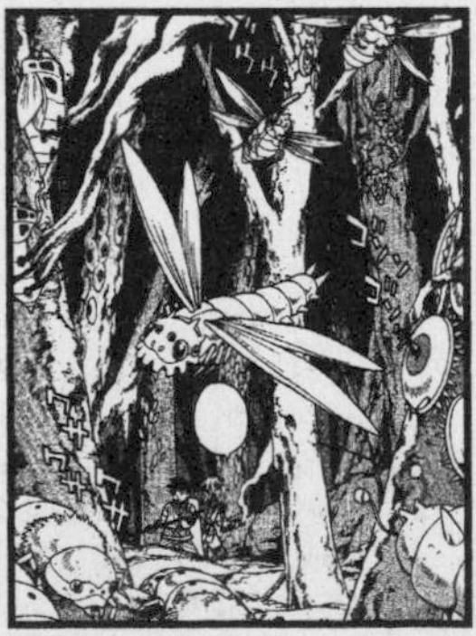

Most of the countries and towns beside Trowana have already been annihilated by Grineed. Grineed's headquarters are located in the northwest of the Black Horizon. His home is literally a nest of monsters, which continue to multiply daily. Unless it is destroyed, the sun will not shine over the Black Horizon again!

Grineed's Minions: Three Vandels

Even other Vandels submit to Grineed and serve him.

THE FLASHY SCARLET BULLET FRAUSKY ★★★★★

This assassin is the strongest of Grineed's minions. He is an extremely difficult Vandel to defeat. He has numerous biological firearms hidden all over his body and uses them to cruelly kill his targets.

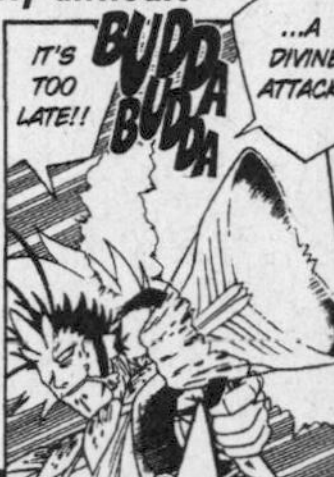
...A DIVINE ATTACK?
IT'S TOO LATE!!
BUDDA BUDDA BUDDA

▶ His right arm, when pulled off, becomes a handgun.

THE BLACK SPIDER VENTURA ★★★

He's a coward with over-sized ambitions. He has spider-like abilities, and his duties for Grineed mainly consist of scouting and gathering intelligence.

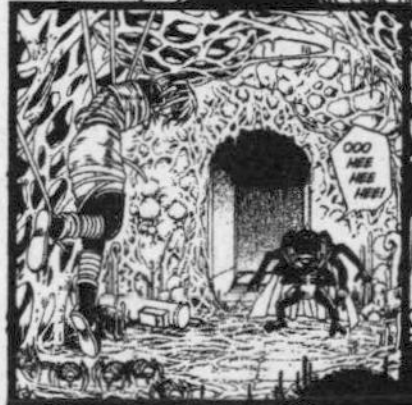
OOO HEE HEE HEE!

▶ From his eight arms and legs, he shoots viscous fibers that he uses to capture his enemies.

THE DARK STRATEGIST ROZZGOAT ★★★★★

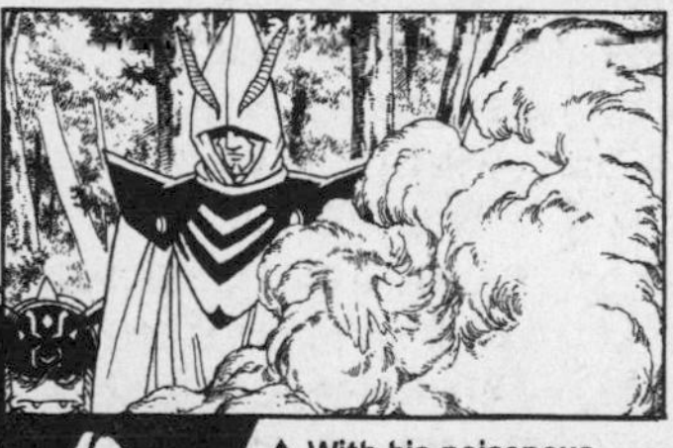

▲ With his poisonous powder, he can throw his enemies into confusion and vanish. He's an elusive being.

As Grineed's faithful right-hand man, he has the authority to command in place of Grineed. Always self-possessed and calm, he appears to be a brainy type. His abilities are still unknown, but from the way his antennae are formed, he could have moth-like powers.

Coming Next Volume...

There are good Vandel Busters and lousy Vandel Busters, but who knew there were crooked ones? Milfa, that's who. She's a Broad Buster—part of a police force that watches out for Busters and makes sure none go over to the dark side. She's very interested in Beet, though not professionally...Milfa thinks Beet is cute, much to Poala's dismay. But is there time for romance when Vandels like Frausky and Rozzgoat are after you? And what about Kissu and his past loyalty to Grineed? Should Beet rat out Kissu to Milfa?

Available in June 2005!

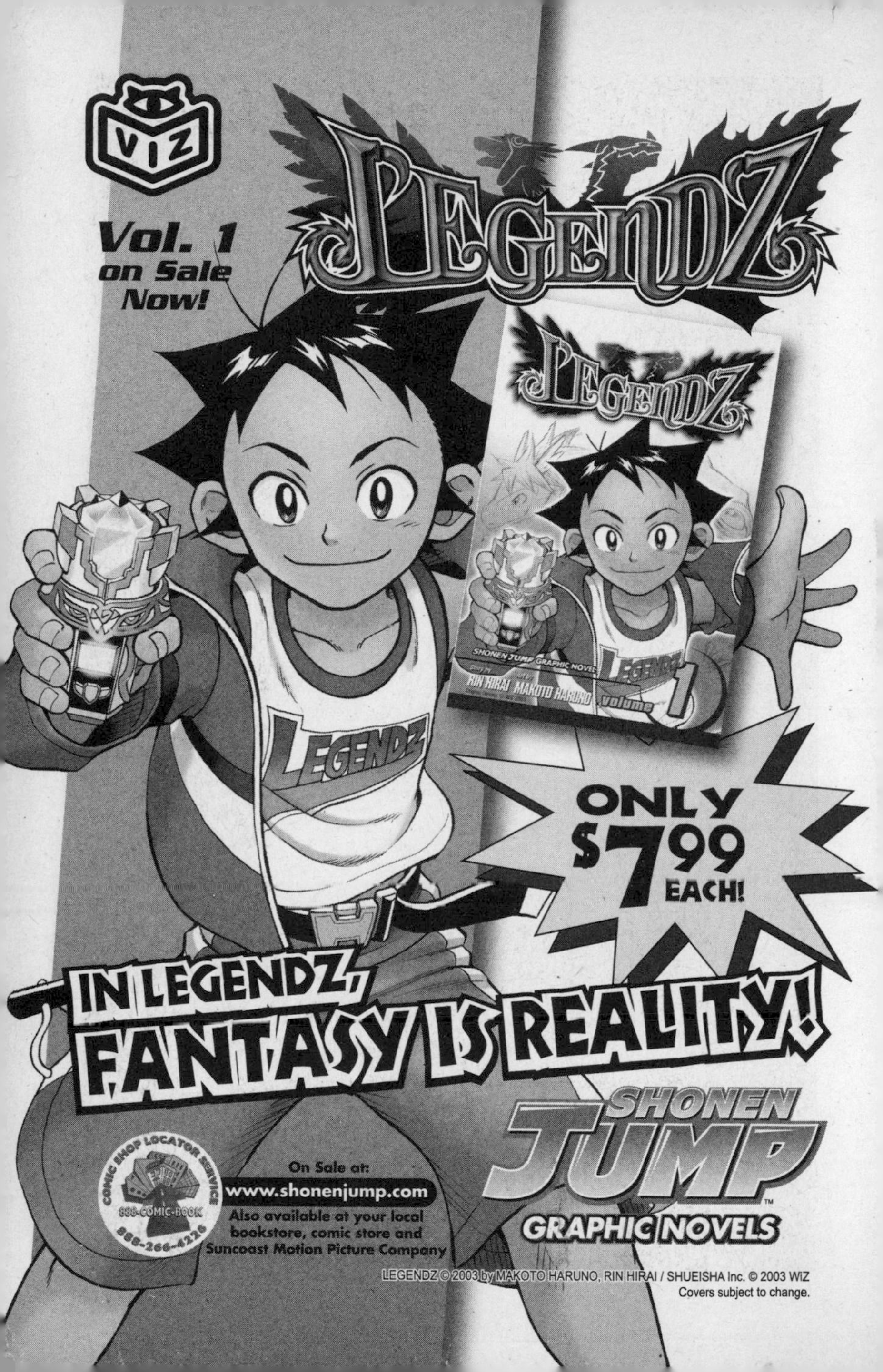
VIZ
LEGENDZ
Vol. 1 on Sale Now!
SHONEN JUMP GRAPHIC NOVEL
RIN HIRAI MAKOTO HARUNO
LEGENDZ volume 1
ONLY $7.99 EACH!
IN LEGENDZ, FANTASY IS REALITY!
SHONEN JUMP GRAPHIC NOVELS
COMIC SHOP LOCATOR SERVICE 888-COMIC-BOOK 888-266-4226
On Sale at:
www.shonenjump.com
Also available at your local bookstore, comic store and Suncoast Motion Picture Company
LEGENDZ © 2003 by MAKOTO HARUNO, RIN HIRAI / SHUEISHA Inc. © 2003 VIZ
Covers subject to change.

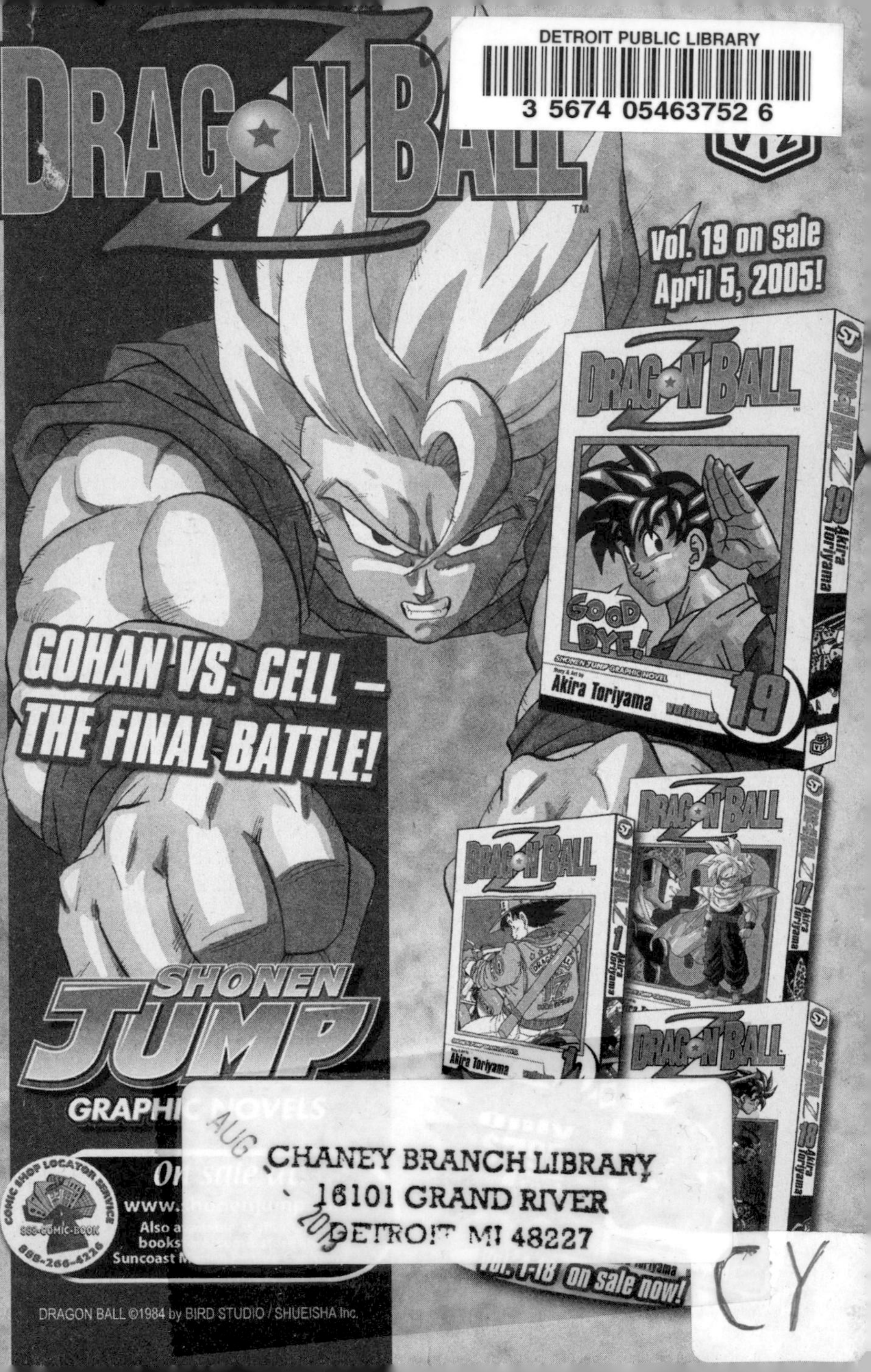
DRAGON BALL Z
Vol. 19 on sale April 5, 2005!
DRAGON BALL Z
19 Akira Toriyama
GOOD BYE!
SHONEN JUMP GRAPHIC NOVEL
Akira Toriyama
volume 19
GOHAN VS. CELL – THE FINAL BATTLE!
DRAGON BALL Z
17 Akira Toriyama
DRAGON BALL Z
1 Akira Toriyama
Akira Toriyama
DRAGON BALL Z
18 Akira Toriyama
Vol. 1-18 on sale now!
SHONEN JUMP
GRAPHIC NOVELS
COMIC SHOP LOCATOR SERVICE
888-COMIC-BOOK
888-266-4226
DRAGON BALL ©1984 by BIRD STUDIO / SHUEISHA Inc.